T0369292

Blood and the Covenant

The Historical Consequences Of The Contract With God

Pierre Parisien

Order this book online at www.trafford.com
or email orders@trafford.com

Most Trafford titles are also available at major online book retailers.

pparisien@videotron.ca

Printed in the United States of America.

ISBN: 978-1-4269-4209-9 (sc)
ISBN: 978-1-4269-4210-5 (hc)
ISBN: 978-1-4269-4211-2 (e)

Library of Congress Control Number: 2010913509

Trafford rev. 11/08/2010

www.trafford.com

North America & international
toll-free: 1 888 232 4444 (USA & Canada)
phone: 250 383 6864 • fax: 812 355 4082

To my children:
Michelle, Suzanne, Régine, Erik.

Special thanks to:
Yves Parisien and Nadine Chamorel for their support and Typo hunting.
Aurèle Parisien and Jennifer Roberts for editorial guidance and computer advice;
Alan Smith, my typist, for his patience.

Contents

Chapter I – From the Horse's Mouth

1) – Biblical Readings That Don't Make It To The Pulpit

A

And the Lord said to Moses, "Fear him not: for I have delivered him into your hand, and all his people and his land; and you shall do to him as you did to Sihon, king of the Amorites, which dwelt at Heshbon. So they smote him, and his sons, and all his people, until there was none left alive: and they possessed his land. (Numbers 21: 34-35)

B

And Israel stayed in Shittim, and the people began to commit whoredom with the daughters of Moab who invited the people to take part in the sacrifices of their gods; and the people ate and bowed down to their gods. And Israel associated with Baal-peor; and the anger of the Lord was kindled against Israel. And the Lord said to Moses, "Take all the heads [leaders] and hang them up against the sun, that the fierce anger of the Lord may be turned away from Israel." And Moses said to the Judges of Israel, "Slay everyone of your men that were joined unto Baal-peor." (Numbers 25: 1-5).

C

And they warred against the Mediamites, as the Lord had commanded Moses, and they slew all the males and they slew the kings of Midian: namely Evi and Rakem, and Zur, and Hur, and Reba, five kings of Median;

they also slew Balaam, son of Beor, with the sword. And the children of Israel took all the women of Midian captives, and their little ones and took the spoil of all their cattle, and all their flocks, and all their goods. And they burned all their cities where they dwelt, and all their goodly castles, with fire. And they took all the spoil and all the prey, both of men and of beasts. And they brought the captives, and the prey, and the spoil to Moses and Eleazar the priest, and to the congregation of the children of Israel, at the camp at the plains of Moab, which are by the Jordan near Jericho.

And Moses, and Eleazar the priest, and all the princes of the congregation, went forth to meet them outside the camp. And Moses was angry with the officers of the army, with the captains over thousands and the captains over hundreds, which came from the battle. And Moses said to them, "Have you saved all the women alive? Behold, it was these that caused the children of Israel, through the counsel of Balaam, to commit trespass against the Lord in the matter of Peor, and there was a plague among the congregation of the Lord. Now therefore kill every male among the little ones, and kill every woman that has known a man by lying with him. But all the women children that have not known a man by lying with him, keep alive for yourselves." (Numbers 31, 7-18)

D

[Context: Moses had remained secluded on Mount Sinai for forty days and forty nights, to receive from Yahweh various instructions and the two stone tables of the law. The Hebrews had grown restless and worried. Aaron, egged on by the people, had made them a god -- a golden calf -- to lead them. Moses was enraged.]

... then Moses stood in the gate of the camp, and said, "Who is on the Lord's side? Let him come unto me." And all the sons of Levi gathered themselves together unto him. And he said to them, "Thus said the Lord God of Israel, 'Put every man his sword by his side and go in and out from gate to gate throughout the camp, and slay every man his brother, and every man his companion, and every man his neighbor'." And the children of Levi did according to the word of Moses; and there fell of the people that day about three thousand men. (Exodus 32: 26-28)

E

Then Sihon came out against us, he and all his people, to fight at Jahaz. And the Lord our God delivered him to us; and we defeated him, and his sons, and all his people. And we took all his cities at that time, and utterly destroyed the men and the women, and the little ones, of every city, we left none alive. (Deuteronomy 2: 32-34)

F

So the Lord our God delivered into our hands Og also, the king of Bashan, and all his people and we smote him until none was left to him alive. And we took all his cities at that time, there was not a city which we took not from them, sixty cities, all the region of Argob, the kingdom of Og in Bashan. All these cities were fenced with high walls, gates, and bars; beside a great many unwalled towns. And we utterly destroyed them, as we did to Sihon king of Heshbon, utterly destroying the men, women, and children, of every city. But all the cattle, and the spoil of the cities, we took for a prey to ourselves. (Deuteronomy 3: 3-7)

G

And it shall be, when the Lord your God shall have brought you into the land that he swore to your fathers, to Abraham, to Isaac, and to Jacob, to give you great and goodly cities, which you did not build, and houses full of all good things, which you did not fill; and wells which you did not dig; vineyards and olive-trees, which you did not plant; when you shall have eaten and be full; then beware lest you forget the Lord, which brought you forth out of the land of Egypt, from the house of bondage. (Deuteronomy 6: 10-12)

H

When the Lord your God shall bring you into the land you are going to enter and possess, and He has cast out many nations before you: the Hittites, and the Girgashites, and the Amorites, and the Canaanites, and the Perizzites, and the Hivites, and the Jebusites, seven nations greater and mightier than you; and when the Lord your God shall deliver them and utterly destroy them; you shall smite them, and utterly destroy them; and you shall make no covenant with them, nor show mercy for them; neither shall you make marriages with them; you shall not give your daughter to his son, nor take his daughter for your son. For they will turn away your son from following me, that they may serve other gods; so will the anger of the Lord be kindled against you, and destroy your suddenly. But thus shall you deal with them; you shall destroy their altars, and break down their images, and cut down their groves, and burn their graven images with fire. For you are a holy people to the Lord your God: the Lord your God has chosen you to be a special people unto himself, above all people that are upon the face of the earth. (Deuteronomy 7: 1-6)

I

And you shall consume [exterminate] all the people which the Lord your God shall deliver to you; your eye shall have no pity for them: neither shall you serve their gods; for that would be a snare for you. (Deuteronomy 7: 16-17)

J

If your brother, the son of your mother, or your son, or your daughter, or the wife of your bosom, or your very best friend, entices you secretly, saying, "Let us go and serve other gods, which you have not known, nor your fathers; namely, of the gods of the people which are round about you, or far away from one end of the earth to the other end; you shall not consent nor listen to him; nor shall you pity him, nor spare him, nor conceal him: but you shall surely kill him; your hand shall be first upon him to put him to death, and afterwards the hand of all the people. And you shall stone him with stones, that he die; because he has sought to thrust you away from the Lord your God,...." (Deuteronomy 13: 6-10)

K

If you hear it said of one of the towns that the Lord your God is giving you to dwell in, that certain men, the children of wickedness ... have seduced the inhabitants of their city, saying, "Let us go and serve other gods, which you have not known"; then shall you inquire, and make search, and ask diligently; and, behold, if it be truth, and the thing certain, that such abomination exist among you; you shall surely smite the inhabitants of that city with the edge of the sword, destroying it utterly, and all that is therein, and the cattle thereof, with the edge of the sword. (Deuteronomy 13: 12-15)

L

When thou approach a city to fight against it, then proclaim peace unto it. And if it make you an answer of peace, and open [its gates] to you then it shall be that all the people found therein shall be tributaries unto you, and they shall serve you. And if it will make no peace with you, but will make war against you, then you shall besiege it; and when the Lord thy God has delivered it into your hands, you shall smite every male thereof with the edge of the sword; but the women, and the little ones, and the cattle, and all that is in the city, even all the spoil thereof, you shall take for yourself; and you shall eat the spoil of your enemies, which the Lord your God has given you. Thus shall you do to all the cities which are very far off from you, which are not of the cities of these nations. But of the cities of these people, which the Lord your God gives you for an inheritance, you shall leave alive nothing that breathes; but you shall utterly destroy them; namely, the Hittites, and the Amorites, the Canaanites, and the Perizzites, the Hivites, and the Jebusites; as the Lord your God has commanded; that they teach you not to do after all their abominations, which they have done unto their gods and make your sin against the Lord your God. (Deuteronomy 20; 10-18)

M

[Regarding the famous battle of Jericho] So the people shouted when the priests blew with the trumpets: and it came to pass, when the people heard the sound of the trumpet, and the people shouted with a great shout, that the wall fell down flat, so that the people went up into the city, every man straight before him, and they took the city. And they utterly destroyed all that was in the city, both man and woman, young and old, and ox, and sheep, and ass, with the edge of the sword. (Joshua 6: 20-21)

N

And it came to pass, as they [the Amorites] fled from before Israel, and were running downhill to Beth-horon, that the Lord cast down great stones from heaven upon them all the way to Azekah, and they died: more died from the hailstones than from the swords of the Israelites. (Joshua 10: 11)

O

So Joshua conquered all the country of the hills, and of the south, and of the vale, and of the springs, and all their kings: he left none remaining, but utterly destroyed all that breathed, as the Lord God of Israel commanded. (Joshua 10: 40)

P

[Context: The tribe of Dan was looking for land to settle in] ... and came to Laish, unto a people that were at quiet and secure; and they smote them with the edge of the sword, and burned the city with fire. And there was no deliverer, because it was far from Zidon, and they had no business with any man; and it was in the valley near Beth-rehob. And they built a city, and dwelt there, and they called the name of the city Dan. (Judges 18: 27-29)

Q

[Context: A man travelling with his concubine spends the night in the home of a citizen of the Benjamite town of Gilbea. A depraved group of men gather in front of the house and pound on the door.] Now as they were making their hearts merry, behold, the men of the city, children of wickedness, surrounded the house and beat at the door, and spoke to the master of the house, the old man, saying, "Bring forth the man that came into your house, that we may know him." And the man, the master of the house, went out and said to them, "Nay, my brethren, nay, I pray you, act not so wickedly; seeing that this man has come into my house, do not do this. Behold, here is my daughter a maiden [virgin], and his concubine: them I will bring out now, and you may humble them, and do as you want; but to this man do not do so vile a thing." But the men would not listen to him: so the man took his concubine, and pushed her unto them; and they raped her, and abused her all night until the morning: and at daybreak they let her go. Then the woman came at dawn and fell down at the door of the man's house where her master was, till it was light. And her master rose up in the morning, and opened the doors of the house, and went out to go his way: and behold, the woman his concubine was fallen down [dead] at the door of the house, and her hands were on the threshold. (Judges 19: 22-27)

R

[The prophet Samuel speaking to King Saul:] Thus said the Lord of Hosts, "I remember what Amalek did to Israel, how he ambushed them as they came up from Egypt. Now go and smite Amalek, and utterly destroy all that they have, and spare them not; but slay both man and woman, infant and suckling, ox and sheep, camel and ass.
(I Samuel 15: 2-3)

S

[Context: David, fleeing Saul, took refuge with a Philistine king, Achish, who granted him the town of Ziklag for his family and his six hundred men. From there David made his living by raiding towns (including Hebrew towns) for booty]

And David and his men went up, and invaded the Geshurites, and the Gezrites, and the Amalekites: for those nations were of old the inhabitants of the land that extends to Shur, even to Egypt. And David raided the land, and left neither man nor woman alive, and took away the sheep, and the oxen, and the camels, and the clothing. Upon returning he would come to Achish and Achish would say, "Where have you raided today?" And David would say, "Against the south of Judah," or "Against the south of the Jerahmeelites," or "Against the south of the Kenites." And David left neither man nor woman alive, to bring evidence to Gath, saying, "David did this and this will be his manner as long as he lives in the country of the Philistines. (I Samuel 27: 8-11)

T

And after it came to pass that David attacked the Philistines and subdued them; and David took Metheg-ammah out of the hands of the Philistines. And he defeated the Moabites, and used a length of rope to measure [those who would live and those who would die], casting them down on the ground; and measuring two lengths for those to be put to death, and with one length to keep alive. And so the Moabites became David's servants, and brought gifts. (II Samuel 8: 1-2)

U

[Context: "At the turn of the year, the season when kings go out to battle" [just for the hell of it, it seems], Joab, David's general, went forth and devastated the land of Ammon. He took the town of Rabbah and left it in ruins. David joined him:] And he brought out the people that lived there, and cut them with saws, and with harrows of iron, and with axes. Thus did David deal with all the cities of the children of Ammon. (I Chronicles 20: 3)

V

And Elijah [the prophet] said to them, "Take the prophets of Baal [450 of them]; let not one of them escape. And they took them: and Elijah brought them down to the brook Kishon, and slew them there. (I Kings 18: 40)

W

... And as he was going up the road, there came forth little children out of the city, and they mocked him, and said unto him, "Go away, you bald head; go away, you bald head." And he turned back, and looked on them, and cursed them in the name of the Lord. And there came forth two she bears out of the wood, and tore up forty and two children of them. (II Kings 2: 23-24)

X

Then Menahem attacked Tiphsah, and all that were therein, and ... because they did not open their gate to him, punished it; and all the women therein that were with child he ripped up. (II Kings 15: 16)

Y

And Amaziah strengthened himself, and led forth his troops, and went to the valley of salt, and slew ten thousand of the children of Sei. And another ten thousand left alive were taken away captive by the children of Judah, who brought them to the top of the rock, and who cast them down from the top of the rock, and they were all broken in pieces. (II Chronicles 25: 11-12)

Z

O daughter of Babylon, who art to be destroyed; happy shall he be, that rewards you
As you have served us.
Happy shall he be, that takes
and dashes your babies against the stones. (Psalm 137; 8-9)

2) – Biblical Body Count

One hundred and twenty-six battles are mentioned in the Old Testament. The number of enemy casualties are given in forty-seven of them. Since Chronicles I and II are a rehashing of parts of the Torah (Pentateuch) care must be taken not to count the same engagement twice. In the great majority of these clashes, the killing was directly ordained or indirectly sanctioned by Yahweh. In nine instances the fighting was between Hebrew tribes, but even in these cases the killing was done at the behest of Yahweh as collective punishment for sin. In the following table, body counts resulting from internecine battles between Hebrew tribes or factions are underlined. With one exception, the numbers given refer to the losing side.

Levites vs. other Hebrews (Exodus 32)	3,000
Joshua vs. City of Ai (Joshua 8)	12,000
Joshua vs. 29 other cites (Joshua 8) estimate	300,000
Judah vs. Canaanites and Perizites (Judges 1)	10,000
Ehad vs. Moabites (Judges 3)	10,000
Gideon vs. Midian fighters (Judges 8)	120,000
Jephta vs. Ephraimites (Judges 12)	42,000
Israelites vs. Benjamites (Judges 20)	
Israelite casualties	40,000
Benjamite casualties	25,000
Hebrews vs. Philistines (I Samuel 4)	43,000
David vs. Arameans (II Samuel 8)	20,000
David vs. Edomites (II Samuel 8)	18,000
David vs. Arameans, again (II Samuel 8)	41,000
David vs. Israelites (II Samuel 18)	20,000
Ahab vs. Arameans (1 Kings 20)	100,000
plus victims of falling wall of Aphek	27,000
Abijah (Judah) vs. Israelites (II Chronicles 13)	500,000
Amazia vs. Arameans (II Chronicles 25)	20,000
Pikah (Israel) vs. Judah (II Chronicles 28)	120,000
Total number of bodies	**1,371,000**
Number of Hebrew bodies	750,000
Number of other bodies	621,000

It is interesting to note that Hebrew casualties account for more than half of the total. However, with the exception of the clash between the Hebrews and the Philistines at I Samuel 4, these were the result of internecine conflicts.

The numbers, or course, refer to fighters. As in most conflicts, it's safer to be a combatant than an innocent civilian. The numbers given in the Old

Testament may be exaggerated. Certainly, the half million count for the conflict between Judah, under Amazia, and Israel is very suspect: a half million corpses is a lot of infectious waste to dispose of. In gauging the significance of these numbers, we must keep in mind that the population of the planet at that time was much smaller than that of today, and that all this occurred in a very small corner of the Earth. 1,371,000 is probably comparable to the 6,000,000 of the Holocaust. And that number may be small compared to the toll taken of ordinary people as city after city was proscribed (all killed). For example, Moses and Joshua killed all of King Og of Bashan's soldiers, then captured all sixty of his towns, dooming all cities (see F in part I of this chapter). No number is given but certainly the casualties must have been in the hundreds of thousands.

I have counted 20 clashes where there are no estimates of casualties, not counting the large number of engagements that must have occurred during the final phases of the Chaldean and Assyian conquests of Israel and Judah. Two or three events are duplications of events in the first list, since that one does not include civilian casualties.

Hebrews vs. Amorites (Numbers 21)
Hebrews vs. Midianites (Numbers 31)
Hebrews vs. the king of Sihon (Deuteronomy 2)
Hebrews vs. Og of Bashan – 60 towns (Deuteronomy 3)
The Conquest of Jericho (Joshua 6)
The Conquest of Jerusalem (Judges 1)
The Tribe of Judah vs. hill country and Canaanites (Judges 1)
Gideon vs. Mediamites at Penuel (Judges 8)
Judah vs. Towns of Benjamin (Judges 20)
Hebrews vs. Philistines at Mizpah (1 Samuel 7)
Saul vs. Ahimelech and the Priests (1 Samuel 22)
Saul vs. Amelekites (1 Samuel 15)
David's Raids from Ziklog (1 Samuel 27)
David's vs. Philistines (II Samuel 8)
David vs. Moabites (II Samuel 8)
David vs. Town of Rabbah (II Samuel 12)
David Massacres Towns of Ammon (I Chroniclers 20)
John kills all Bael worshippers (II Kings 10
Menahem Massacres Tipshah (II Kings 15)
Jehoshaphat vs. Amman, Moab and Seir (II Chronicles 20)

Yahweh and angels also engaged in warfare. There are many cases of Yahweh sending plagues to enemy forces or inducing discord, confusion, even insanity in their ranks. Considering the state of medical science and the living conditions existing at that time, it is no surprise that plagues were common. How does one differentiate been a plague sent by a god or one brought on by natural causes? Was it a deity that sent unfavorable winds and disease to the Spanish Armada? Was it God who afflicted the French army with yellow fever in Haiti? But Yahweh interfered in more direct and obvious ways. In Exodus 12, the Lord killed all first-born Egyptians; in Exodus 14, he drowned the Egyptian army in the Red sea, in Joshua 10, he threw stones at the retreating Amorites, killing more of them than the Hebrews had; in II Kings 19, an angel of the Lord killed 185,000 Assyrians.

Chapter II – Reader's Guide

Sorry for the shock treatment! It was necessary. We are taught from infancy that the Bible is the word of God and that religion is a special realm of human activity that is beyond the reach of the critical faculties. Hence we call the book the "Holy Bible," its holiness being a consequence of its godliness. So awed are we by its sacredness that we approach it with a mind addled and diminished. Even hard-headed scholars of an agnostic or atheistic point of view often fail to keep in mind that an ancient myth is still only a myth; that a superbly written Santa Claus story is still only a Santa Claus story; and that a fairytale passed down from generation to generation is still only a fairytale.

It is to counter this awe that I begin this book with a Chapter consisting almost entirely of excerpts that illustrate the barbarous violence and the moral depravity that infests much of the Old Testament. [Those who feel that I am "cherry picking" exceptional and untypical excerpts in order to make my point need only read the "historical" segment of the Holy Scriptures, from Exodus to II Kings – to convince themselves that the book is one long unremitting bloodbath. But, you must be read with both eyes open! Actually, just choosing pages at random and skimming them would be sufficient to gather enough evidence.]

But isn't the Old Testament a Jewish document, and am I not therefore open to the charge of anti-Semitism? – Not at all! The people of the Old Treatment were Hebrews, a rather primitive Semetic group of tribes, whose culture and religion were drastically different from those of the people we know as Jews. It is impossible to determine just when Hebrews 'morphed' into Jews, but the contemporaries of Jesus could certainly be called Jews, although modern Jews are, again, markedly different from *that* prior group.

Anthropologists and demographers can find no criteria for classifying Jews as a distinct race: African Jews look African, European Jews look European (except in Nordic countries, where there *is* a difference) and, when there was a Jewish community in China, they looked Chinese.

Jesus was a Jew – and self-consciously so – and stated that his ministry was directed at Jews. The Apostles were Jewish. Even Paul, who was the first missionary to the gentiles, was a Pharisee. Until the destruction of the second temple in 70 CE (*common era*, which has replaced AD, *anno domini*) the followers of Jesus prayed at the same house of worship as did all the Jewish sects that had sprouted during the intertestamentary period.

Deprived of the Temple, the Jesus followers established their churches and the other Jewish sects started meeting in the houses of religious leaders. These houses eventually became synagogues and the leaders became known as *rabbis* (although the related term *rabbin* had been in use in Palestine before the common era). Over the next few centuries a new religion was born which we call *Rabbinical Judaism.* This religion is as different and distinct from the Yahwism of the ancient Hebrews as is the Christianity of the Jesus faith. Although the Jews draw their liturgy – the calendar, festivals and rituals – from the Torah (the first five books of the Old Testament, the Pentateuch) they established the authority of the rabbis over the dictates and the laws of Moses. All deference and honor went to Moses and the Prophets, but the normative function of the religion was in the hands of the *rabbis* who, for most of their history, were not strict constructionists. From a religion based on animal sacrifice performed at one central place of worship, the rabbis molded a religion with no sacrifice and with a multitude of venues. In some ways the Christians remained closer to the Yahwist tradition: the sacrifice of the Mass is a blood and flesh ritual culminating in the ingestion of the flesh of Christ. (It is an article of faith in the Catholic Church that the wine and wafer of bread are really changed into the actual blood and flesh of Christ by the act of consecration. Most Protestant sects, however, abandoned the idea of sacrifice and their services became somewhat similar to Reform Jewish services). Another vestige of the Old Testament in Catholic and Orthodox Churches is the use of consecrated oil in certain rituals: the anointing of Kings, the ordination of priests and in the sacraments of Confirmation and Extreme Unction. Unction was important in the Old Treatment but is not practiced in Judaism.

Christians and Jews have equal claims to being children of the Old Testament. There is nothing particularly anti-Semitic about criticizing and even castigating the document.

The case of Islam is different. To the casual observer, life in some Muslim societies seems little different from life in the Old-Testament days. There are many points of similarity: in dress, in diet, in marital laws, in having one central house of worship (the Ka'ba at Mecca) and so on. The Arabs, where it all started, are, after all, Semites – which modern Jews are not – speaking a Semitic language – which Jews do not (except in Israel where the Hebrew language has been established by fiat). Although the Old Testament is not a canonical (official) document of Islam, its influence is evidenced by dozens of references in the Koran. We can conclude that the Old Testament has spawned three distinct religions: Christianity, Rabbinical Judaism and Islam.

[The New Testament was also a strong influence on Islam. There are many references to Jesus, Mary and John the Baptist, but the main borrowing from Christian scriptures is the concept of reward or retribution in the afterlife, a notion almost nonexistent in the religion of the Hebrews.]

Now that I have disposed of the putative charge of anti-Semitism, let me make clear my position in matters religious and spiritual:

I am an atheist, but not an adeist. An atheist does not believe in a personal, involved God, whereas an adeist (don't look for it in the dictionary but look for *theism* and *deism*) denies the existence of anything that is not part of the phenomenal world, and therefore outright rejects such notions as *world soul*, *cosmic intelligence*, *the God of philosophers*, *Supreme being*, as well as all forms of spirituality. I make no pronouncements regarding such notions, but I refuse to accept that the phenomenal world, reductively interpreted, is the totality of what exits. This caveat notwithstanding, I do not believe in the God of the Jews, Christians and Moslems, because I accept the logic of the *argument from evil*, that an entity that is both all-powerful and all-good can be neither the creator nor the administrator of the world we live in.

Why then, you may ask, do I spend as much time as I do reading scriptures and studying religions? There are two reasons:

1. One should not reject a body of belief that has long been accepted by his society nor assault the belief system of other people without careful examination and rigorous thinking.

2. Religion is one of the main elements of most cultures. To understand a people, one must understand its religion or religions.

Underpinning my atheistic belief system is the identification of two questions – or rather, two non-questions – that can be formulated, but never asked in anticipation of an answer (because there *is* no answer within the understanding of humans):

1. Why is there something?
2. Since there is something, why is it *this* something, and not some other something?

[Note that if there were nothing, even *nothing* would not exist, since *nothing* is a concept, and therefore, *is* something.]

One could propose that an all-powerful god could divulge the answers to these questions to a prophet who could then divulge them to humanity. But that god would first have to give that prophet senses, faculties and powers of understanding that we do not posses, so that this prophet would then not be a human being anymore.

Is there ever an obligation to believe? – Yes, there is. If you know that *A* is greater than *B* and that *B* is greater than *C*, you have a logical mandate to believe that *A* is greater than *C*. There is, however, no ethical mandate to believe that, nor any other proposition. The punishment for refusing to believe, in the above example, that *A* is greater than *C* should be no greater than being laughed at (or, perhaps, failing Logic 101). This is an important point: only the existence of a moral mandate to believe could possibly justify the Inquisition, its tortures and its killings. There is also, within the natural limitations of our senses, an evidentiary mandate to believe our perceptions. This mandate, however, is not as strong as a logical mandate. The phrase, "within a reasonable doubt," is an acknowledgement of this caveat.

There is yet another mandate pertaining to beliefs: although there is no moral mandate to believe, there *is* a moral mandate to act in accordance with our beliefs. (We will delve more deeply into this when we take up the great faith-versus-works debate.)

About Sources

Originally, I started using the Tanakh (the Jewish Old Testament) as translated from the original Hebrew by the Jewish Publication Service. Despite a few cases of "creative translation" (all Bibles have some) this is a competent and official translation into modern American English and I found it quite useful. Unfortunately, translations are covered by copyright, so I found it more practical to use the good old King James version, solidly ensconced in the public domain, as the source of my numerous quotations from the Holy Scriptures. I took the liberty of changing many archaic words and expressions into modern English. Thus, *thou* was replaced by you; *cometh* by come; etc.

A writer without competence in the original language of his sources should refer, if possible, to more than one translation as a precaution against translators' glitches. I have compared the following versions: the King James (English and Protestant); Louis Segard's translation (French and Protestant); *La Bible, Nouvelle Traductions* (French and Catholic); and, for the Old Testament, the Tanakh of the JPS.

Fortunately, the separation into chapters and verses, and the numbering of these, are with very few exceptions, the same in the commonly used Bibles. Anyone can use the family Bible to check the accuracy and appropriateness of my quotations.

But if the books that are common to the Jewish, Catholic and Protestant Bible have the same names and inner organization, the order of the books is different and some books are not common to all bibles. (For example, only the Catholic versions have the Book of the Maccabees.) None-the-less, all the excerpts used in this book can easily be found in all standard versions.

It is important to keep in mind that bibles and scriptures are not as much written as rewritten and re-rewritten. No one knows who the writers, editors, writer/editors and compilers were, nor how many there were. None of the original documents exist, in part because they may well have been intentionally destroyed so as to hide forever how much was reported and how much was invented. Even the Dead Sea Scrolls were a rewritten version of other documents which might themselves have been the progeny of even earlier sources.

These caveats are especially relevant in dealing with the Old Testament, because it is the most chronologically remote of scriptures. To compound the problem there are two Torahs: the written and the oral Torah and rabbis give equal authority to both. This gives the authors/editors more license to invent, since no one can check the historicity of their writing. [To those unfamiliar with Hebrew terms: Torah can mean "the book of Moses," that is, the first five books of the Tanakh (the Pentateuch, in the Christian Bible) or, in a more general sense, it can mean *the law*.]

In his excellent book, *Surpassing Wonder* (McGill-Queens Press) Donald Akenson has surmised that writers/editors of scriptures use a "grammar of invention," the most important rule of which is that no credit must be taken for originality or creativity. "The rule of this form of religious invention is that the more inventive it is – the more creatively it rearranges the past -- the more it has to be seen as reportorial." (p. 51).

This applies not only to the Old but also to the New Testament. This "grammar of invention" is probably followed by writer/editors of all faiths.

Establishing chronology is particularly tricky. The congruity between the historical sequence of events and the order of biblical books is a matter of much controversy. To compound the problem, it is widely held that though book A may be, on the whole, prior to book B, some of book B may be prior to some of the book A. For example, careful reading and common sense suffice to conclude that the first pages of Genesis were written much later than most of the Torah. The language is wholly different and this difference is obvious even in translation. The name *God* is used (sometimes *the Lord God)* whereas in the rest of the Torah the expressions *El Shaddai, Elohim, Yahweh, Adonai, and the Lord* are used.

Think of every book of the Bible as a deck of cards on which data is written: not only can words be erased and replaced on the cards, but any card can be taken out of the pack and inserted at a different place in that pack or it can be inserted in a different pack. Serious exegesis is not for the faint of heart!

The older the evidence, of course, the less solid it is. The portraits of both people and event can be blurred by the fog of time. What looks like one person might really be an unclear melding of two or more. For example, there might have been two or more leaders of the Hebrews during the Exodus, but a write/editor could have taken the salient points of each and invented a single leader called Moses. A man might have been famous for his strength and valor at one time and, years after his passing, he might have been inflated into Samson, a fighter, a leader and a judge – in the biblical sense. Such evidence I call *anecdotal evidence.* It is hardly more reliable than pure invention for establishing historicity. (It must be kept in mind that being historical in style and presentation is very different from being truly historical, that is, having a higher degree of historicity.)

The reader will find few references to archeological findings. Since I cannot read Hebrew, Aramean or Greek, my sources regarding the Bible will be secondary or tertiary. This is no problem: For my purpose, the scriptures themselves will suffice. Since I have already put in question the historical rigor (the historicity) of the bible, this choice may seem paradoxical. But think: what is it that moves the Christian faithful, the historical Christ or the biblical Christ? (Many scholars opine that there may be little congruity between the two.) And what is it that rabbis refer to, the real history of the Hebrews, or the version presented in the Tanakh? Both Christianity and Rabbinical Judaism are built upon the foundations of the Old Testament, as compiled, molded, emended and partially invented by its writers/editors, because that's all there is to work with.

The end of the Biblical era did not signal the end of Scriptures. I used the Mishna and the Talmud as my main sources for the formative years of Rabbinical Judaism, although I cannot claim to have read all of the latter. For Islam, I have likewise used its canonic Scriptures, the Koran, and I have referred to collections of Hadiths, without having done extensive reading on the later. Regarding Christianity I have relied on such sources as the Catholic Encyclopedia and Catholic web sites, especially those reporting on the various councils. (The fact that the Roman Church is authoritarian, hierarchical and tightly organized facilitates research – unless you're delving into Vatican secrets.)

In the case of Zionism and Israel, I have relied mostly on Zionist and Jewish sources: Rabbi Arthur Hertzberg for the precursors of Zionism; Benny Morris for the establishment of Israel; Noam Chomsky for the Israeli-American axis; and others. References to Israeli newspapers and magazines were culled mostly from the above. In all cases credit is given.

Because of the great time span covered by this book, and because I have no graduate students to help with research and neither time nor money to travel to the great libraries of the world, I have been forced to rely on these secondary sources, but I have double-checked and triple-checked references. For example writing about Middle-East affairs, I have tried to balance Israeli, Arab, UN and NGO sources to keep them all honest.

Many scholars scoff at the web as a source, and indeed, there are caveats to keep in mind when using it. But the web is, to certain extent, its own remedy. Without leaving your computer you can check any source against other web sites from competing or neutral points of view, including official sites of governmental and institutional organizations.

Chapter III – Who's Who in the Tanakh

Abraham

Abraham, ancestor of Israelites and Arabs, and spiritual father of Jesus and Mohammed, was not without serious moral flaws:

> And because of her it went well with him, he acquired sheep, oxen, asses, male and female slaves, she-asses and camels.
>
> But the Lord afflicted Pharaoh and his household with a mighty plague on account of Sarai [her original name] the wife of Abram. Pharaoh sent for Abram and said, "What have you done to me! Why did you say, 'She is my sister,' so that I took her as my wife! Now here is your wife, take her and be gone" and Pharaoh put men in charge of him and they sent him off with his wife and all that he possessed. (Genesis 12:16-21)

Since his scheme had worked rather well in Egypt (he departed with gold, silver and cattle) Abraham tried whoring his wife again. While sojourning in the city of Gerar, he again passed Sarah as his sister, and Abimeleck, king of Gerar, had her brought to him. But before he could touch her God came to Abimeleck in a dream and divulged Abraham's fraudulent scheme.

Then Abimeleck summoned Abraham and said to him, "What have you done to us? What wrong have I done that you should bring so great a guilt upon me and my kingdom? You have done me things that ought not to be done." (Genesis 20:9)

Again, Abraham profited:

> Abimeleck took sheep and oxen, and male and female salves, and gave them to Abraham; and he restored his wife Sarah to him. And Abimeleck said, “Here, my land is before you, settle wherever you please.” (Genesis 20: 14-15)

Abraham’s propensity for using people close to him for personal gain may shed light on his readiness to immolate his own son, Isaac, at the behest of a Semitic deity whom he knew as El Shaddai.

Moses

The next major figure in the Old Testament is Moses. If Abraham was the father of Israel, Moses, as Yahweh’s executive, was its dictator. (He intended to be, through his legacy, its dictator “for all times,” but was only partially successful.) He too was morally flawed, a judgment evidenced by excerpts A to L in Chapter 1 and by many other verses of the Bible.

What judgment can you come to regarding a person who orders his soldiers to kill prisoners, including women and children, but keep the virgins for themselves? (See C in Chapter 1).What judgment can you come to regarding a person who has three thousand of his own people killed because his brother made a golden statuette? (The brother, of course, escaped punishment.) (D, Chapter 1).What judgment can you come to, regarding a person who incites people to kill their own kin for having different religious beliefs or practices (B, J, K, Chapter 1).

What judgment can you come to regarding a person who has depopulated whole countrysides and dozens of cities in order to give his people houses they have not built, vineyards they have not planted, and cisterns they have not hewn? (A, C, F, G, L, Chapter 1).

A rose is a rose is a rose and a crime against humanity is a crime against humanity. And ethnic cleansing is ethnic cleansing.

And Moses was the perpetrator of many crimes against humanity and probably the inventor of ethnic cleansing. And no champion of religious freedom!Apologists will object that:

That was the way conflicts were settled in that primitive era.

He was fighting Satan hiding under the guise of evil idols and was promoting monotheism, the religion of the one true God; and this enterprise was so holy and important that any means was permissible. Every violent aggression was either explicitly commanded or condoned by God.

These arguments do not stand up to close scrutiny:

It's wrong to assume that conflicts in those days always involved the massacre of women and children and other such abominations. In spite of Hebrew provocation, the Bible relates no massacre of Hebrews during the time of Moses, Joshua and David. Later they did suffer some atrocities (not rising to the level of genocide) at the hands of Babylonians and Chaldeans, but they were never denied religious freedom until the second century BCE, under the domination of Antiochus IV Epiphanes, the Greek psychopath.

Polytheists were generally tolerant: they were always ready to include another god in their pantheon. If they saw that the devotees of a particular god were doing well they might erect an altar to that deity in hope of attracting some luck. The destructions of the Temple were military and political acts, not acts of religious persecution.When Cyrus defeated Jerusalem he was cruel to King Zedekia and his sons, because of the king's treachery, but he was quite generous with the people. He brought many notables and artisans to Babylon, where they lived relatively unfettered, were given complete freedom of religion and were allowed to participate in civic life. (In fact, the seeds of Judaism were planted here, during the exiles, by the priests.) As for the remnant that remained in Judah, they were left with sufficient workers, artisans and managers to maintain their society. There is no record of such magnanimity of the part of the Hebrews.Even if it were true that blood and gore was the universally accepted way to settle conflicts in those days, would that be a reason for endorsing a book written by the barbarians of that era, and for promoting that ethics as the foundation for the religion of our era?

The distinction between mono and polytheism is much less clear than is usually thought. For example, Haitian Voodoo is said to be a polytheistic religion because it addresses a number of deities. But these are called *Loas* in Créole, not *dieux*, and are more like saints and angels than like God. In fact, Voodooists acknowledge the existence of le *Bon Dieu*, the standard supreme being of monotheism, but consider Him to be too far above our world to be approachable (somewhat like the One of Plato or the Supreme Deity of the Gnostics). Voodoo is no more polytheistic than is Catholicism – and aren't Christian believers in the Holy Trinity (Father, Son and Holy Ghost) calling the kettle black when they accuse Voodooists of polytheism? All one needs to do, to change a pagan cult into monotheism, is choose one god; change the small g to a capital G; demote the other deities; and *voilà*, you have monotheism. The worshippers of El considered the latter to be the father of the gods. Doesn't that give him a capital G and elevate the religion to the status of monotheism?

The claim that either Abraham or Moses was the inventor of monotheism cannot be sustained. El was father of the Gods long before the epiphanies of those patriarchs. In Egypt Pharaoh Akhenaton imposed the worship of Aton, the sun-god, as the one and only God, a few centuries before the Exodus.

The Hebrews of the Tanakh never denied the existence of other deities, such as the "Hosts of Heaven" (sun-god, moon-god, etc.) and the "gods of Egypt," but they insisted that their god, Yahweh, was stronger, and didn't hesitate to confirm it by the sword. For most of their history they practiced henotheism (also called monolatry) which Webster's Third New International Dictionary defines as "the worship of one God without denying the existence of other gods." Many priests and prophets were henotheists until Antiochus Epiphanes' brutal efforts to establish Greek Mythology (including the worship of himself as an avatar of Zeus) left a bad taste in the collective palate of Israel, and turned the people toward strict monotheism.

The God of monotheism, having infinite power, cannot be held to any code of ethics, since he would then be subject to a superior power. Also, it should be evident to anyone acquainted with the world that its creator/manager is not limited by any moral code: death, suffering and injustice are everywhere. Therefore, there is no scandal in a God that is beyond morality. But this God, the object of worship of three great religions, has decreed a code of conduct for humans (although there is no unanimity on its constituent rules).

This is the most fundamental belief of these faiths: their basic theological premise is not just monotheism but rather ethical monotheism. Their God expects humans to follow this code and uses a battery of rewards and punishments to enforce it. This God, being absolute perfection, is absolutely unchanging, and therefore perfectly consistent: it is unconceivable that he would order a man to break this code. As a do-as-I-say-not-as-I-do Supreme Being, he is free of moral restraints but, by his own will, we, his intelligent creatures, are not. But the Bible is replete with instances of Yahweh permitting Moses, Joshua, David and others to break the most basic rule of this code by dispossessing legitimate owners and butchering innocent civilians. In a few cases he gave explicit orders (see N, Chapter 1; also Deuteronomy 7: 1-4) but most of the time he gave tacit approval by not reproving the conduct. We must therefore conclude that:

Yahweh was a minor deity, not God; or Moses (and other prophets) made up the stories of their epiphanies (Aaron, the brother of Moses, was the only witness – and only on a few occasions – of those purported episodes; or The writer/editors of the Bible made up those stories.

Note that no appeal can be made to the principle of necessity here. The God of the Bible, being all-powerful, can find an infinite number of alternatives that do not include breaking the moral code. This is equally true for biblical Hebrews, Islamic suicide bombers (and other terrorists), Zionist governments, and to all those who claim that their outrages are virtuous because sanctioned or requested by God.

> But Moses had his good side and seems to have had a concept of rights: You shall not subvert the rights of your needy in their disputes.
> (Exodus 23:6)

> For there will never cease to be needy ones in your land, which is why I command you: open your hand to the poor and needy kinsmen in your land. (Deuteronomy 15:11)

He anticipated modern welfare rights:

> Six years shall you sow your land and gather in its yield; but in the seventh you shall let it rest and lie fallow. Let the needy among your people eat of it, and what they leave let the wild beasts eat.
> (Deuteronomy 23:10)

He recognized the rights of strangers:

> You shall not oppress a stranger for you know the feelings of strangers having yourselves been strangers in the land of Egypt.
> (Deuteronomy 23: 9)

He understood some basic principles of jurisprudence:

> A single witness may not validate against a person any guilt or blame for any offence that may be committed; a case can be valid only on the testimony of two witnesses or more.
> (Deuteronomy 19: 15)

He was, perhaps, the first law giver to be concerned with animal rights:

> Six days shall you do your work but on the seventh day you shall cease from labor, in order that your ox and your ass may rest and that your bondman and the stranger may be refreshed.
> (Deuteronomy 23: 12)
>
> You shall not muzzle an ox while it is threshing
> (Deuteronomy 25: 4)

But in all these cases it was Yahweh speaking through Moses rather than the latter giving voice to his own feelings and principles. It's hard to reconcile the concern for strangers with his barbaric acts towards the inhabitants or Canaan and towards those Hebrews who disagreed with him. When the context makes it clear that Moses is speaking and acting spontaneously, it is his natural harshness, cruelty and ferociousness that is evident.

Aaron

While in Egypt, Aaron, Moses' older brother, was a prominent figure. Since Moses claimed to have a speech impediment, and tried to use this excuse to shun the confrontation with Pharaoh, his brother went with him to the meetings to support him. But after the flight from Egypt, Aaron lost his voice – metaphorically – and Moses seems to have found a new eloquence. A straw man dressed in priestly garments would have replaced the older brother. Moses ran everything down to the slightest detail. He designed the ephod (the priestly tunic), the Ark of the Covenant, and the altar. He specified the color of the yarns, the exact size and shapes of all the constituent parts, and what type of material to be used – which wood, which metal, which precious stones. Moses was the ultimate control freak. Whenever anyone questioned his orders he would fall flat on his face in what must have resembled a fit of apoplexy. Sometimes Yahweh would send flames or afflictions or earthquakes to punish the dissidents (Numbers 16 and others). Aaron's role was simply to be a silent, ephod-wearing witness.

Joshua

As is the case of Aaron, the character and personality of Joshua are not fleshed-out in the Bible. He is mentioned briefly in the Torah, where he is said to be Moses' assistant. The latter appointed him as his successor.

The Nevi'im, the second division of the Tanakh, opens with the Book of Joshua.

We don't know anything of Joshua's private life – his wives, children, friends. He seems to have been an able and decisive chief, but he is presented mostly as an executive in charge of mass killings. In Joshua 12, thirty-one cities are listed as having been defeated by Joshua, starting with Jericho and ending with Tierza. The usual procedure was to kill every human being – young, old, male, female – and impale the kings. (Its not specified if the poor fellows were first killed or if they were impaled alive by being stacked on a pointed stake through the anus and left there till dead.) In some cases the city was burned down and even the cattle were killed – in Jericho, Hazor, and perhaps other places – but in most cases the spoils and cattle were kept as booty.

> The Israelites kept the spoils and cattle of the rest of the cities as booty. But they cut down their populations with the sword until they exterminated them; they did not spare a soul.
> (Joshua 11:14)

And the following are the local kings whom the Israelites defeated on the west side of the Jordan – from Baal-gad in the Valley of Lebanon to Mount Halak, which ascends to Seir – which Joshua assigned as a possession to the tribal divisions of Israel in the hill country, in the lowlands, in the Arabak, in the slopes, in the wilderness, and in the Negeb [in the land of] the Hittites, the Amorites, the Canaanites, the Perizites, the Hivites, and Jebusites:

> The king of Jericho, one; the king of Ai (which is beside Beth-el), one; the king of Jerusalem, one; the king of Hebron, one; [27 kings and their cities follow, ending with;] the king of Tirza, one; all the kings thirty and one
> (Joshua 12: 7-24)

Each King headed a city or district. His defeat was a death sentence for each one of his subjects. The only numbers reported were for the city of Ai, where "the total of those who fell that day, men and women, the entire population of Ai, came to twelve thousand." (Joshua 8:25) There is no reason to think that Ai was a particularly large city compared to the others in the list. Therefore, knocking down the figure to ten thousand –

just to be safe – we can estimate that approximately 310,000 citizens were killed in that campaign.

Continuing Moses' policy of ethnic cleansing by perpetrating crimes against humanity, Joshua killed, through his soldiers, hundreds of thousands of mostly innocent humans, and did it with all the emotion of a chicken-head slicing machine in a poultry-processing plant.What judgment can you come to regarding a person who would commit such abominations? And, if you excuse him on the supposition that he did it for Yahweh, what judgment can you come to regarding such a deity?

The Judges

The period covered by the Book of Judges is best described by the last verse of the book: "In those days there was no king in Israel; everyone did as he pleased." (Judges 21:25) Yahweh decreed that the tribe of Judah would lead in the conquest of more land. They captured Jerusalem, killed its inhabitants and set the city on fire. They proscribed many towns but left others standing without dispossessing their inhabitants. However, the people they didn't kill were subjected to forced labor.Soon however, the Hebrews were seduced by the siren songs of other gods:

> And all that generation were gathered unto their fathers: and there arose another generation after them, which did not know the Lord, nor the works he had done for Israel. And the children of Israel did evil in the sight of the Lord God of their fathers, and served Baalim: and they forsook the Lord God of their fathers, which brought them out of the land of Egypt, and followed other gods, of the gods of the people that were round about them, and provoked the Lord to anger. And they forsook the Lord, and served Baal and Astaroth. And the anger of the Lord was hot against Israel, and he delivered them into the hands of spoilers who spoiled, and he sold them into the hands of their enemies round about, so that they could not any longer stand before their enemies.
> (Judges 2:10-14)

The above is an eye-opening excerpt. The Hebrews were fundamentally a polytheistic people. Only the constant efforts of the priests and the prophets kept Yahweh in a position of prominence among the hordes of Semitic and Persian deities. Even they were more henotheistic than monotheistic, as I have already written. It was not until two centuries, more or less, before Christ that the culture became truly monotheistic. Since Yahweh had promised Israel his protection, the writer/editors of the Tanakh had to find an excuse for any lapse in that protection. In dozens of instances the misfortune of the people was blamed on this dabbling with polytheism: Yahweh, a jealous god, was punishing the Hebrews for their sins. Very often foreign women were accused ofr seducing Hebrew men away from Yahweh. (There are always some men who want to blame any affront to public or private morality on those seductive females.)

Gideon

The first leader to stand out after Joshua was Gideon. An "angel of the Lord" appeared to him and announced that he had been chosen by Yahweh to deliver his people from the oppression of the Midianites.

He seems to have led in a limited number of campaigns. The main one, against the Midianites is particularly interesting. The Israelites had mustered 32,000 soldiers. The lord told Gideon that with this many soldiers, Israel might take all the glory for victory and that the number must be drastically reduced so that he, Yahweh, could claim all the credit. The army was reduced in two steps to a mere 300 men. Yahweh caused the Midianites to panic into utter confusion and kill each other. (Judges 7:2)

Yahweh was not only jealous but also vainglorious. One reason he sent so many scourges against Egypt was to manifest his overwhelming power to Pharaoh, the Egyptians and the gods of Egypt.[It is surprising that the Hebrews never proselytized except, probably, during the intertestamentary period. Since Yahweh was so eager to spread his renown, one would think that he would have demanded a missionary effort as part of the Israelite contribution to the Covenant.]

Jephta

The next important and interesting figure was Jephta. He was the son of Gilead and a prostitute. Gilead also had sons by his wife and they eventually drove Jephta out. He fled to the Tob country where he assembled a band of toughs and went out raiding with them.When the Ammonites attacked Israel, the elders of the land of Gilead asked Jephta to return and help in the defense of the place. They promised that if he were successful they would make him commander of Gilead.

He accepted and took steps to get Yahweh on his side.

> And Jeptha made a vow to the Lord and said, "If you shall without fail deliver the children of Ammon into my hands, then whatever come forth from the doors of my house to meet me, when I return in peace from the children of Ammon, shall surely be the Lord's, and I shall offer it as a burnt offering."
> (Judges 11:30)

Unfortunately, when he returned home victorious, it was his daughter, an only child, who came out to greet him. She accepted the consequences of the vow but asked to be allowed a grace period of two months to go to the hills with her friends and "bewail her maidenhood." When she returned her father immolated her. The Bible makes a point of saying that "she had never known a man."

This story proves that human sacrifice was not unknown in Israel – which explains Abraham's willing acceptance of the Lord's request for the sacrifice of his son, Isaac.

The war against the Ammonites led to a senseless confrontation between the Gileadites and fellow Hebrews from the tribe of Ephraim. Jephta won again and 42,000 Ephraimites were killed.

Samson

Everyone is familiar with the saga of Samson but many ignore that he led Israel for twenty years. His story is but a minor episode in the Old Testament but there are a few points of interest besides his prodigious feats of strength.

He seems to have been attracted to foreign women. Three are mentioned: his Philistine wife, a Gazite whore and the treacherous Philistine, Delilah. The man had to be one of the most gullible of all time. Three times Delilah asked him how he could be made helpless; each time Samson gave her a false answer; each time he was ambushed by Philistine men who used the bogus "secret"; each time he broke his bonds and defeated them; yet it seems he never suspected that his welfare was not a high priority in Delilah's mind. Finally, after much nagging and accusing he told her the secret of his strength. The story of his downfall and eventual revenge is common knowledge.The writer/editors of the Tanakh included this legend to make two points: First, no matter how badly Israel may be injured, it will always come back and impose its revenge like Samson did; and second, foreign women are not to be trusted by Hebrew men.Samson's moral sense is questionable. He once made a bet with thirty Philistine men that if they could solve a riddle he would give them each a complete set of clothing, but that, should they fail, they would give him thirty sets. The Philistines cheated and Samson went to a nearby town, slew thirty men who had no part in the cheating, and gave their clothing to the winners of the bet. He seems to have harbored a genuine hatred for the Philistines and to have terrorized them at every opportunity. When they found the secret of his strength and captured him, he committed suicide as a necessary step in the killing of thousands of them.

There is a remarkable parallel between the dynamics of Samson's mission and that of a modern suicide bomber: encouraged by his cultural and religious background, a member of an oppressed group rebels and commits acts of terrorism until, faced by a hopeless situation, and having nothing to lose, he sacrifices his life as the price to pay for killing as many oppressors as possible. A suicide bomber is Samson all over again.

Everyone Doing as He Pleases

The resettling of the twelve tribes was still not complete: the tribe of Dan still did not have a home. They scouted the countryside and found a territory populated by a peaceful people:

> ... and they came unto Laish, a people that were quiet and secure: and they smote them with the edge of the sword, and burnt the city with fire. And there were no deliverers because it was far from Zidon, and they [the people of Laish] had no business with any man ... And they rebuilt the city and dwelt there ...
> (Judges 18:27-28)

What is interesting here is the absolute lack of moral outrage that the writer/editors evince toward an act of savagery and injustice. Time and again throughout the Old Testament, such actions are described with a tone more appropriate to a trivial statement such as "John got dressed and sat down for breakfast."

The last episode of Judges, however did manage to elicit a measure of disapproval from the scribes:

A Levite was travelling in the territory of the Benjamites. He stopped in the town of Gibeah where an old man offered the hospitality of his house for the night. The men of the town came to the door and asked that the stranger be brought out of the house so that they might be intimate with him. The old man entreated them not to perpetuate such an outrage with someone to whom he had offered the protection of his home.

> Look, here is my daughter, a virgin, and his concubine; I will bring them out now, and you can humble them and do with them whatever is your pleasure, but to this man do not do so vile a thing. But the men would not listen to him, so the man [the Levite] took his concubine, and brought her forth to them; and they "knew" her until the morning; and when the day began to spring, they let her go. (Judges 19:24-25)

In the morning the concubine was found dead, her hand on the threshold of the house. The Levite took her to his home on a donkey. He cut up her body into twelve pieces and sent a piece to each of the twelve tribes, asking for revenge.

The Israelites, minus Benjamin, mustered 400,000 fighters. They took to the field against the Benjaminites. Over three days, tens of thousands of men fell on both sides. Finally the Israelites prevailed and then went to all the towns of Benjamin and slaughtered every living thing before setting fire to the houses.

Now, 600 Benjamanite soldiers had fled to the wilderness. The Israelites relented and wished to allow the tribe to reconstitute itself. However, all the women of Benjamin had been killed and the Israelites had vowed not to give any of their daughters to any of their males. But one town had not participated in the campaign. Soldiers were sent there and they killed everyone except virgin females. The latter were given to the surviving Benjamite soldiers, but their number was insufficient. A fake raid was arranged so that Benjamite men could kidnap Hebrew wives without the fathers of these brides reneging on their vows.

This story offers another example of the lack of respect and concern the ancient Hebrews had for women (although they are far from unique in this respect) and of the banality of mass murder. It also illustrates the use of military power as a punishment. This always ends up being collective punishment – the innocent suffering along with the guilty, sometimes for just living in the same city, sometimes for belonging to the same religion, ethnic group or political party. It is usually easy to find a moral (or "moral") pretext for military action. (Are we not, according to the Bible, all sinners, personally and collectively?) Nowadays this pernicious policy is more harmful than ever: rockets, airplanes and high explosives can be sent to wreck terrible havoc without the disincentive of body bags returning from the front.

The Book of Judges chronicles a period of relative unimportance in the Hebrew saga but it sets the table for the rest of the Tanakh. Some of the traits and guidelines that will be replicated in later books are:

1. A human throat is as easy to slit as a goat's.
2. Women don't count for much.
3. The Hebrew people are basically polytheistic and must constantly be pressured to return to the exclusive worship of Yahweh; hence their history follows a sine-curve pattern alternating between polytheism and mono/henotheism.
4. Yahweh never reneges on the alliance but punishes severely any relapse into polytheism by delivering the Hebrews into the hands of their enemies. (In other books he also uses plagues.)
5. No distinction is made between monotheism and henotheism: one can believe in the existence of many gods, as long as he/she worships only Yahweh and militates against other gods.
6. Being a Yahweh worshiper excuses all crimes perpetrated for the furtherance of the Yahweh-Hebrew alliance, including ethnic cleansing; this moral dispensation permits murder and such crimes against humanity as ethnic cleansing and collective punishment.
7. The covenant bestows another benefit to the Hebrews: the promised land of Palestine, the land of milk and honey, bequeathed to the Hebrews regardless of whatever claims by any other parties.

Chapter IV – The United Kingdom

Samuel

Samuel's mother, Hannah, was barren. She prayed to Yahweh and vowed that if she bore a male child, she would dedicate him to the service of the Lord. When her prayer was granted she brought the child, Samuel, to the House of the Lord at Shiloh as soon as he was weaned. There he stayed and grew up as a servant of Yahweh, under the guidance of Eli, priest of the Temple and a judge over Israel. He became a prophet and Yahweh would appear to him at Shiloh. All Israel trusted and respected him.

The great crisis of his early career was the capture of the Ark of the Covenant by the Philistines. The latter killed 4,000 men, including Eli's two sons, before making off with the Ark. Soon, however, they realized that their spoil had brought them nothing but bad luck. The idol of their god, Dagon, was broken, their land was devastated by hordes of mice and the population was struck by the only recorded epidemic of hemorrhoids in history. After months of squirming in their chairs the Philistines decided to return the cursed object to the Hebrews. Their priests and diviners insisted that the god of Israel must be paid an indemnity. They suggested five golden hemorrhoids and five golden mice. (One wonders who sat in the plaster to make molds.) And so, they sent the Ark of the Covenant and ten golden artifacts back to Israel.

When Samuel was very old, the people worried about their future leadership, since Samuel's sons were weak and corrupt. The elders asked Samuel to appoint a king over them. At first the prophet was displeased. He prayed to Yahweh who reluctantly agreed with the elders. Through some obscure process of divination Saul son of K'ish, a Benjamite, was chosen and Samuel anointed him king.

Saul

Samuel's role was to be a mentor to Saul and a conduit between the king and Yahweh. The conflict between Hebrews and Philistines continued. Saul's son, Jonathan, was one of the Hebrew champions. The Lord, through Samuel, ordered Saul to take revenge against the Amelakites who had attacked the Hebrews as they wandered during the exodus from Egypt. Yahweh's instructions were to kill men, women, children, sucklings, oxen, camels and asses. (see R, Chapter 1) But the soldiers kept the best of the cattle as spoils.

> Saul struck the Amelekites from Availa to Shar, near Egypt. And he took Agog, the king of the Amelekites alive, and utterly destroyed all the people with the edge of the sword. But Saul and the people spared Agag, and the best of the sheep, oxen, fatlings, lambs and all that was good, and would not utterly destroy them: but everything that was vile and cheap they destroyed utterly.
>
> Then came the word of the Lord to Samuel, saying, "I regret that I have set up Saul to be king, for he has turned back from following me, and has not performed my commandments. And it grieved Samuel; and he cried unto the Lord all night.
> (I Samuel 15:7-12)

When Saul returned the prophet berated him, then personally cut down King Agog of Amalek. Saul begged Samuel not to abandon him but the prophet answered, "I will not return with you: for you have rejected the word of the Lord, and the Lord has rejected you from being king over Israel." (I Samuel 15:26)

Saul was to continue as king for some time but he was a lame-duck king. Yahweh instructed Samuel to find David, the son of Jesse the Bethlehemite, and anoint him, which the prophet did. David, however, continued guarding his father's sheep.

But the spirit of the Lord departed from Saul and an evil spirit from the Lord troubled him. And Saul's servants said to him, "Look, an evil spirit from the Lord troubles you. Let the king now command your servants who are before you, to seek out a man who is a gifted player on the harp, and it shall come to pass, when the evil spirit from God is upon you that he shall play with his hand, and you shall be well. (1 Samuel 16:14-16)

By a coincidence worthy of a soap opera script, David happened to be a skilled musician, and one of the courtiers had heard of him. He was hired as Samuel's private ghost buster.

One day, while delivering food to his three older brothers who were fighting the Philistines, he wandered into the challenge which Goliath, the terrible champion of the enemy, was addressing to the Hebrews. David accepted the challenge and, as everyone knows, killed Goliath with one shot from his sling. Seeing their champion thus vanquished, the Philistines took to their heels. They were pursued and many were killed.

Saul requested a meeting with David that provides us with one of the most intriguing verses in the Bible:

> and it came to pass, when David had stopped speaking to Saul, that the soul of Jonathan [Saul's son] was knit with the soul of David, and Jonathan loved him as his own soul. (I Samuel 18:1)

This is one of the verses that have fed the speculation by some that David was bisexual.

David was put in charge of all the soldiers. When he would return from battle the women would sing:

> Saul has slain his thousands;
> David his tens of thousands!
> (1 Samuel 18:7)

This distressed Saul greatly and he began to fear and hate David. One day as the latter was playing his lyre to sooth Saul, the king threw a spear at him, trying to pin him to the wall. Saul sent David on dangerous missions, hoping that the Philistines would do his dirty work. Then he arranged to have his daughter, Michal marry David, that she might be "a snare to him." (The bride's price was one hundred Philistine foreskins).

The plot between Saul, David and the Philistines had more twists and turns than a modern soap opera: David fought and defeated the Philistines; to reward him Saul sent men to David's home to kill him, but Michal helped him escape; he escaped to the wilderness with some of his men;

Saul and his troops hunted him; David hid in caves, in the fields and in small towns. Twice David caught Saul and could have killed him, but each time he let him go, refusing to slay "the Lord's anointed." Each time Saul cried, confessed his guilt, and swore to end his pursuit. Throughout the love between David and Jonathan remained strong.

> … David arose out of a [hiding] place towards the south,
> and fell on his face to the ground, and bowed three times:
> and they kissed one another and wept one with another;
> David wept more. (I Samuel 20:41)

Out of desperation David and six hundred men took refuge in the land of the Philistines, where Saul could not pursue them. They settled in the town Ziklag under the protection of King Aschih. To make a living they raided the towns of the Geshevistes, the Gizrites and the Amelakites. David's practice was to leave no one alive so that no one could testify against him. (See S, Chapter 1)

This is very eye-opening, as the murders weren't perpetrated on orders of Yahweh, nor could they be construed as being committed to further the cause of Yahweh: David killed to eliminate potential witnesses to his crimes, just like the Mafia does.

Without David, the Hebrews did not fare well against the Philistines. To make matters worse, Samuel died and when his ghost was summoned by a sorceress, it told Saul that Yahweh had taken the kingship from him and given it to David. The ghost also told him that he and his sons would die on the morrow and that the Hebrews would suffer a defeat.

The augury came to past. David mourned Saul and Jonathan and intoned a dirge which included these words:

> I grieve for you,
> My brother Jonathan:
> Very pleasant have you been to me:
> Your love to me was wonderful,
> Better than the love of women.
> (II Samuel 1:26)

King David

David, it seems, needed no prophets, no dreams and no visions to speak to the Lord: he just talked to him person-to-person. Furthermore, as with

Moses and Joshua, Yahweh actually got involved in battles as though he were a super soldier. He told David to settle in the Judean town of Hebron. There he was anointed king of Judah.

The war between the House of Saul and the House of David raged on for some time, Hebrew killing Hebrew. It was a war of attrition, but the tribes of the kingdom of Israel (Saul's side) finally came to David and anointed him King of Israel, so that both kingdoms became united. David reigned thirty-three years over the Union.

His first campaign in his new role was against the Jebusites of Jerusalem. He captured the stronghold of Zion and renamed it the City of David. In the process he had all the blind and lame Jebusites killed – 2,500 years before Hitler.

> On that occasion David said, "Those who attack the Jebusites shall reach the water channel and strike down the lame and the blind, who are hateful to David." That is why they say: "No one who is blind or lame may enter the Houses." (II Samuel 5:8)

[To be fair, he did treat Jonathan's last surviving son, Mephiboset, who was lame in both feet, with respect and kindness; but that was only because of his love for Jonathan and a vow he had made.]

Fighting was not David's only pastime. He acquired more wives and concubines and fathered eleven children in Jerusalem.

When the Philistines heard that David now reigned over the two kingdoms they marched against him. Yahweh promised David his help and blessing and the latter defeated his foes on two occasions.

David decided it was time to bring the Ark of the Covenant from its temporary site in the House of Abinadah to the House of David in Jerusalem. At one point the oxen pulling the cart stumbled and one of Abinadah's sons touched the Ark to stabilize it. He was immediately struck dead by Yahweh "for his indiscretion." David was not only God-fearing, but actually God-dreading. (Yahweh seems to have been the only being he had any respect for.) He parked the Ark in the house of Obed-edom the Gittite. After three months David, hearing that nothing but good had happened to Obed-edom, brought the Ark to the City of David amid dancing and rejoicing. David was dancing and whirling and, since Hebrews wore no more under their robes than the Scots do under their kilts, exposing himself. His first wife, Michal, observed this and "despised him for it."

> Then David returned to bless his household and Michal the daughter of Saul came out to meet David, and said "How glorious was the King of Israel today, who uncovered himself today in the eyes of the handmaids of his servants, as one of the riffraff might do." And David said to Michal, "It was before the Lord, which chose me before your father and before all his house to appoint me ruler over the people of the Lord, over Israel: therefore will I play before the Lord and be even more vile, and will be base in my own eyes, but by the slave girls that you speak of, I will be honored." Therefore Michal the daughter of Saul had no child unto the day of her death.
> (II Samuel 6:20-23)

This incident is of little importance but is cited because of the insight it affords into David's character.

Another illuminating episode is related in II Samuel 11: David lusted after Bathsheba, the beautiful wife of Uriah the Hittite, an officer under Joab, the king's military leader. David slept with her and she got pregnant. David then arranged to have Joab place Uriah in a very dangerous position and the latter was killed in battle. David then married Bathsheba – after, of course, the proper period of mourning.

The man loved war and killing. In II Samuel 8, he captured (and probably slew) 21,700 soldiers of King Zobah, 22,000 Arameans who had come to their rescue and, in another battle, 18,000 Edomites. In the same chapter, he butchered an undetermined number of Moabite citizens by making them lie down and, using a length of rope as a measure, slaughtering two thirds and sparing a third. (See T, Chapter 1) In II Samuel 10, he killed 40,700 Arameans, which made the survivors reluctant to henceforth help the Ammonites. In I Samuel 12, he attacked Rabbah of Ammon, "and he brought forth the people that were therein, and put them under saws and under harrows of iron, and under axes of iron, and made them pass through the brick kiln. And thus did he to all the cities of children of Ammon." (12:31) In the JPS version of the Tanakh, the same verse reads, "and he led out the people who lived there and set them to work with saws, iron threshing board and iron axes, or assigned them to brick making. David did this to all the towns of Ammon." The two versions suggest very different interpretations. Fortunately, both the King

James and JPS are in agreement in I Chronicle 20, in which another writer/editor gives yet another version.

> and he brought out the people that were in it and cut them with saws, and with harrows of iron, and with axes. Even so dealt David with all the cities of the children of Ammon.
> (I Chronicles 20:3)

The last version seems much more plausible, considering what the Bible tells us about the character of David. [The Tanakh is a rather reliable rendition of the old texts (Hebrew, Greek and Aramean) but in II Samuel 12 I suspect we have a case of "creative translation."]

There is yet another body count in II Samuel. David's son, Absalon, tried to wrest the kingship of Israel from his father. Eventually it came down to a pitched battle between the Judahite followers of David and the Israelite backers of his son. The father's side won and 20,000 soldiers of the northern kingdom died, including Absalom.

The total number of David's victims accounted for in II Samuel is 121,700. This doesn't include the people killed in David's raids when he was living in Ziklag, nor the people of all the towns of Ammon, nor the victims of a few more minor battles. Unlike Moses and Joshua, David did not kill in order to establish his people in Canaan. He and his enemies fought, it seems, because they didn't know what else to do with their time. There is another difference between the prophets of the Torah and David: the former, thought savage and cruel, did not go out of their way to torture their victims as David did in killing the citizens of Ammon. The number of his victims is staggering when we consider the population of the planet at the time was but a small fraction of what it is now, and that all the action happened within an area that could be covered on foot in a few days.

What judgment can you come to regarding a person who kills innocent people to keep them from ever testifying against him?

What judgment can you come to, regarding a person who gets the wife of a loyal officer pregnant and then plots to have him killed in combat so he can marry the woman?

What judgment can you come to, regarding a person who stacks the citizens of a city like cordwood and then slaughters two thirds of them?

What judgment can you come to regarding a person who empties many cities of their citizens and then hacks them to pieces?

David was a psychopath and a sexual glutton (possibly bisexual to boot) who had no respect for human dignity and rights. The only being he had any respect for was Yahweh. Whenever he showed any concern for anyone it was because of that person's relation to the Lord. Even his loyalty to Yahweh is suspect. In many of his songs, prayers and psalms, he sang his own merits and reminded the Lord of the credits he had accumulated, and for which he expected to be recompensed, together with his descendents.

> He brought me out to freedom,
> He rescued me because he was pleased with me.
> The Lord rewarded me according to my merit,
> He requited the cleanness of my hands.
> For I have kept the ways of the Lord
> And have not been guilty before my God;
> I am mindful of all his rules and have not departed from his laws.
> I have been blameless before Him,
> And have guarded myself against sinning –
> And the Lord has requited my merit
> According to my purity in his sight.
> (II Samuel 22:20-25)

It is one of the great scandals in the Old Testament that a man of such low moral character was – and still is – touted as the perfect king. In the two Books of Kings, whenever a sovereign is criticized for doing "what was displeasing to the Lord," he is compared to David, the paragon of royal saintliness.

Personal Note

I went to school in Catholic institutions. I remember very clearly how teachers would sing the praises of David and Moses and Joshua without reservation in spite of the horrible ethical records of these prophets. It was for God! For establishing God's kingdom on Earth! The pagans had no rights! The Catholic Church has always, in theory, rejected the principle that the end justifies the means; yet isn't the Old Testament about the end (God's sovereignty) justifying the means (ethnic cleansing and other crimes against humanity)? *L'erreur n'a pas de droits* (Error has no rights), I remember reading …

Solomon

David was nearing the end of his life. His oldest surviving son, Adonija, was boasting that he would become king. But the priest Zadox, the prophet Nathan and other influential citizens preferred Solomon, the son that David had with Bathsheba, after the death of her husband, Uriah. At their suggestion she reminded David of his promise to make Solomon his successor. That very day, while Adonija was prematurely celebrating his ascension to the throne, Zadok, Nathan and some loyal soldiers took Solomon to Gibon and he was anointed king. One of his first acts as sovereign was to have his half brother killed. (This kind of scenario was to be repeated many times in the sordid story of the kings of Israel.)

David had left a large kingdom to his son, covering a big chunk of the Middle East from the Euphrates to the Egyptian border. Solomon used the human and natural resources of this land to build the temple, his palace and other palatial residences, including one for the daughter of the Pharaoh, whom he had married. It took seven years to build the Temple and thirteen for his palace. The description of the Temple and of various objets of the cult covers about six pages in I Kings.

Such a construction project required a huge workforce which could only be maintained by the use of slaves and forced labor. The Old Testament is ambiguous about Solomon's policy regarding slavery. In Chapter 5 it is stated that he imposed forced labor on all Israel, but according to Chapter 9, no Israelites were enslaved.

> King Solomon raised a levy out of all Israel and the levy was thirty thousand men. And he sent them to Lebanon, ten thousand a month: a month they were in Lebanon and two months at home: and Adoniram was in charge. And Solomon had seventy thousand porters and eight thousand stone workers in the mountains, besides the chief of Solomon's officers who supervised the work, three thousand and three hundred, who ruled over the workers.
> (I Kings 5:13-16) [in the JPS Tanakh: I Kings 5:27-30]

> And all the people that were left of the Amorites, Hittites, Perizzetes, Hivites and Jebusites, which were not of the children of Israel, their children that were left after them in the land, whom the children of Israel were not able utterly to destroy, upon those did Solomon levy a tribute

> of bondservice [slavery] unto this day. But of the children of Israel Solomon made no bondsman [slave].
> (I Kings 9:20-22)

Solomon changed the institution of slavery in Israel. Before, Hebrew and foreign slaves had been mostly household servants and laborers in family farms. They did the chores, worked in the fields and helped take care of the children. They were often considered part of the family. But under Solomon slavery was industrial. In mines, factories, and plantations slaves were treated and used much like draft animals.

[It is noteworthy that in Egypt the Hebrews slaves had owned their own houses in their own town of Goshen and raised their own cattle. They were undoubtedly subject to forced labor, but compared to Black slaves in the Americas, they were in Club Med.]

When the construction was finished, a great feast was held when the Ark of the Covenant was taken from the city of David, Zion, and brought to the temple. Solomon delivered a long supplication to Yahweh which passed in review many aspects of the relationship between Yahweh and Israel, while putting Solomon's own personal stamp on the cult.

> The Lord said that he would dwell in the thick darkness. I have surely build you a house to dwell in, a settled place before you to abide in for ever.
> (I Kings 8:12-13)

When Solomon talked about "a place where you may dwell for ever," he meant it literally. Yahweh may preside over the Host of Heaven but henceforth he would dwell in his Temple where his name abides. The party lasted fourteen days.

The supplication, for all its fervor, falls short of declaring that Yahweh is the one and only God.

> Oh Lord God of Israel, there is no God like you, in heaven above, or on the earth beneath, who keeps covenant and mercy with your servants that walk before you with all their heart.
> (I Kings 8:23)

No God like you falls short of *You are the only God*. Yahweh may be unique (among other gods) and he may be the most powerful god, but he is not yet the God of Monotheism. Also, without abandoning the claim that Yahweh is Israel's God and that Israel is God's chosen people, Solomon admits that other people may revere him and pray to him.

> Moreover concerning a stranger, that is not of your people Israel, but comes out of a far country for your name's sake; (for they shall hear about your great name, and your strong hand, and your outstretched arm;) when he shall come and pray towards this house; hear you in heaven your dwelling place, and grant all that the stranger calls for: that the people of the earth may know your name, to fear you as do your people Israel; and that they may know that this house, which I have built, is called by your name.
> (I Kings 8:41-43)

It is not surprising that Solomon believed that foreigners could have recourse to Yahweh: he was an internationalist, especially in love.

> But king Solomon found many foreign women together with the daughter of Pharaoh, women of the Moabites, Ammonites, Edonites, Zidonians, and Hittites; of the nations concerning which the Lord said to the children of Israel, "You shall not join them neither shall they join you: for surely they will turn away your heart after their gods: Solomon conjoined with these in love. And he had seven hundred princesses and three hundred concubines: and his wives turned away his heart. For it came to pass, when Solomon was old, that his wives turned away his heart after other gods and his heart was not perfect with the Lord his God, as was the heart of David his father. For Solomon went after Ashtoreth the goddess of the Zidonians, and after Milcom the abomination of the Ammonites.
> (I Kings 11:1-5)

Note that two themes are presented that are repeated many times in the Old Testament: Foreign women can seduce Hebrew males into the worship of gods other than Yahweh; and, secondly, David was the paragon of the perfect king.

Solomon was much less warlike than his predecessors. His talents and interests were more in the areas of administration and large-scale projects. His main endeavor, however, was his own quasi apotheosis – his wealth and glory.

When, in his old age, he dabbled with polytheism (Ashtoreth from Phoenicia, Chumash from Moab and Milcorn from Ammon), a prophet, Abijah of Shiloh, arranged a meeting with Jeroboam, an able man who had been put in charge of the forced labor, and told him that the Lord had chosen him to be the next king of Israel. Abijah tore his robe into twelve pieces and gave Jeroboam ten, each symbolizing one of the twelve tribes he would lead. Judah, however, was to be kept for the House of Solomon, in recognition for the faithfulness of David. Fearing Solomon, Jeroboam fled to Egypt and stayed there until the king died.

Chapter V – The Divided Kingdom

Rehoboam and Jeroboam

Solomon was suceeded by his son Rehoboam who invited Jeroboam and his retinue to a meeting. The ten northern tribes asked that the harsh yoke that Solomon had imposed on them, especially forced labor, be lightened, in return for which they would serve Rehoboam. The latter replied that his yoke would be much harsher than his father's had been. The representatives of the northern tribes returned home. When Adoram, the man in charge of forced labor, was sent north, he was pelted with stones and killed. Jeroboam was made king.

Rehoboam mustered an army from the House of Judah and the tribe of Benjamin, but a "man of God," Shemia, said that God had forbidden war between kinsmen and the army turned back. So, with a whimper rather than with a bang, the Hebrews separated into two kingdoms, Judah and Israel, never to be united again.

Both countries were off to a bad start. Jeroboam feared that his people might fall under the influence of Judaists whenever they would go to the Jerusalem Temple to offer sacrifice. He therefore had two temples built in Israel, at Bethel and Dan.

He installed a golden calf in each to receive sacrifices. During the first ceremony at Bethel, a "man of God," nameless and undocumented, predicted that someday the priests of the Israelite cult, who were not Levites, would be slaughtered and that human bones would be burned upon the altars. Later, the prophet Alija cursed Jeroboam and said that the House of Jeroboam would lose every male and that the king would have no heirs. That same day his son, who had been sick, died.

As for Rehoboam in Judah, he built many shrines, pillars and sacred posts to many gods, probably including Yahweh. The Lord used king Shishak of Egypt to punish Rehoboam. The Egyptians marched against Jerusalem and carried off all the treasures of both the Temple and the royal palace. (This pattern was to be replicated over and over during the rest of Hebrew history: Yahweh would use alien rulers as his rod to punish his people for their sins.) While all this was going on, Judah and Israel were in a constant state of war. According to II Chronicles 13 (but not mentioned in Kings), during one battle, the army of Judah killed 500.000 soldiers of Israel.

Tels Pères, Tels Fils

Both kings were succeeded by sons – Abijam in Judah and Nadab in Israel – who were as idolatrous as their fathers. The Old Testament code words to indicate this are "he did what was unpleasant to the Lord." Between the death of Solomon in 928 BCE and the end of the Judean monarchy in 587, that is, during four and a half centuries, twenty kings reigned in Judah and twenty in Israel (the Israelite monarchy ended in 722). Some of the reigns were very short: Zimri, for example, reigned only seven days in Judah. Most of these kings were polytheistic and "did what was unpleasant to the Lord," although many of these probably included Yahweh as one of their gods. Most of them rate only a passing mention – a verse or two – in the Bible. Only seven of the twenty kings of Judah were Yahwist – and most of them were weak Yahwists who couldn't eradicate polytheism in the land. As for Israel, only one king, Jehu, was a Yahwist, and even he couldn't eradicate Baal and other idols completely. It is clear that during that time the Hebrews were a polytheistic society, despite the constant efforts of priests, prophets, "men of God" and some kings to impose the straight and narrow path of henotheism or monotheism. Only a few of these kings deserve a place in our redaction, together with the prophets they interacted with.

Ahab and Jezebel

Jeroboam ruled eighteen or so years. He was followed by a list of equally polytheistic kings who usually gained control through murder and intrigue, and whose reigns were short and bloody. Nadab lasted one year, as did Elijah, and Zimri held the crown for only seven days. Prophets such as Abijah of Shiloh, Jehu son of Hanani, and various "men of God"

– unnamed ad hoc prophets – participated in the action and fulminated against foreign gods such as Ashtoreth, Chumash, Miilcom and others.

The seventh successor of Jeroboam was Ahab. He reigned for twenty years and those years were of capital importance. Ahab married Jezebel, daughter of King Ethbaal of the Phoenicians. She was an ardent devotee of the god Baal and, under her influence, Ahab also became a Baalist. He built a temple to Baal in Samaria and erected altars and sacred posts. However, he continued to also worship Yahweh. In his two battles against King Ben-hedad, the Aramean, he was helped by the Lord. This is understandable, since it seems that some Hebrews confused the two deities. Also, to add to the confusion, the plural form *Baalim* was often used and local deities were often called *Baal*, as in *Baal of Yam* and *Baal of Uggarit*. (In the time of Abraham, a similar confusion had resulted in the indiscriminate use of the singular form *El* and the plural *Elohim* for god.)

Jezebel was an aggressive and dominating woman. She spared no effort – and no crime – to establish Baal as the dominant deity. All other rivals to Yahweh, except Asheroth, faded into the background. Baal was the most formidable rival to Yahweh, ever. (Since he was a nature god – a god of fertility, of rain and wind, etc. – it is tempting to speculate that, had he won the competition, the planet might be in a better state.)

The queen had no scruples. Ahab wanted to buy a neighboring vineyard but its owner, Naboth, refused to sell his inheritance. Jezebel arranged to have false witnesses testify before a jury of elders and nobles of the town that Naboth had "reviled God and king." The poor man was forthwith stoned to death and Ahab was able to take possession of the vineyard.

> And the word of the Lord came to Elijah the Tishbite, saying, "Arise, go down to meet Ahab king of Israel, who is in Samaria: he is in the vineyard of Naboth, where he has gone to possess it. And you will speak to him, saying 'Thus said the Lord, in the place where dogs licked the blood of Naboth shall dogs lick your blood also.
> (I Kings 21:17-19)

Elijah the prophet also said that the House of Ahab would disappear and that his wife Jezebel and all his line would be devoured by dogs or by the birds of the sky. Three years later the King was killed by an arrow while fighting the Arameans. His blood ran down into his chariot. After the burial, the chariot was flushed out at the pool of Samaria and the dogs lapped up the blood. Some years later, Jezebel was defenestrated at the command of King Jehu and her body was eaten by dogs. (II Kings 7:30-37)

Elijah and Elisha

Batman and Robin

Batman ascending to heaven in the batmobile and leaving Robin to carry on the good work.

All other prophets of any importance have a book devoted to them in the Old Testament. Only Elijah and Elisha are denied that honor, yet Elijah was a central figure in the great battle between Yahweh and Baal.

We first meet him in Chapter 17 of Kings, when he tells the then King, Ahab, that "as the Lord God of Israel lives, before whom I stand, there shall not be dew nor rain these years, but according to my word." The king's reaction is not described in the Bible, but it must not have been very positive, as Elijah, on advice from the Lord, went into hiding at the Wadi Cherish, where ravens brought him meat and bread every morning and every evening.

Eventually the Wadi dried up. Yahweh then arranged for him to meet a widow:

> … he called to her, and said, "Fetch me, I pray you, a little water in a vessel, that I may drink." And as she was going to fetch it, he called to her and said, "Bring me, I pray you, a morsel of bread in your hand." And she said, "As the Lord your God lives, I have no cake, but a handful of meal in a barrel, and a little oil in a jar, and look, I am gathering two sticks that I may go in and prepare it for me and my son, that we may eat it, and die." And Elijah said to her, "Fear not; go and do as you have said: but make me a little cake first, and bring it to me, and after make some for you and for your son." For thus said the Lord God of Israel, "The barrel of meal shall not waste, neither shall the jar of oil fail, until the day that the lord sends rain upon the earth."
> (I Kings 17:10-14)

And, indeed, they ate bread for many days. One day, however, the widow's son fell gravely ill and died. The poor woman blamed Elijah for bringing Yahweh's vengeance for her sins upon her son. The prophet took the boy's body from her, brought it to his room and lay it on his bed.

> And he cried unto the Lord, and said, "O Lord my God, have you also brought evil upon the widow with whom I sojourn, by slaying her son?" And he stretched himself upon the child three times, and cried unto the Lord and said, "O Lord my God, I pray thee, let this child's soul come into him again. And the Lord heard the voice of Elijah, and the soul of the child came into him again and he revived.
> (I Kings 17:20-32)

Much later, in the third year of the drought, Yahweh told Elijah to go to King Ahab and that he, Yahweh, would then send rain upon the earth. When the King saw Elijah approaching he accused him of bringing trouble to Israel, whereupon the prophet replied that the trouble was caused by Ahab himself for disobeying the Lord and following the God Baal. Elijah then challenged the king to gather all the people, including the 450 prophets of Baal and the 400 prophets of Asherah, to stage a contest in which the lone remaining prophet of Yahweh would dress a bullock ready for sacrifice and pray Yahweh to send fire to consume the sacrifice, while the Baal prophets would do the same with another bullock, but would beseech Baal to send the fire. The Baalists went first, but nothing happened. When it came to Elijah's turn, the Lord sent fire, although the prophet had drenched the meat, the wood and the trench.

> Then the fire of the Lord fell and consumed the burnt sacrifice, and the wood, and the stones and the dust, and licked up the water that was in the trench. And when all the people saw it, they fell on their faces and they said, "The Lord, he is God; the Lord, he is God." And Elijah said to them, "Take the prophets of Baal; let not one of them escape. And they took them; and Elijah brought them down to the brook Kishon, and slew them there.
> (I Kings 18:38-41)

And then the rains came.

Jezebel was not amused by Elijah's murderous triumph. The latter thought it prudent to go into hiding in the wilderness. He was suffering from a severe case of depression. Yahweh manifested himself to Elijah in order to cheer him up and to give him a task: to return to the wilderness of Damascus and anoint Hazael, king of Aram, and Jehu, king of Israel. The Lord also announced that Elisha was to be Elijah's assistant and successor. Yahweh added that Jehu would kill whoever escaped Hazael and that Elisha would kill whoever escaped Jehu, leaving only seven thousand Hebrews in Israel, those that had not worshipped Baal.

This is baffling, as Hazael was not a Hebrew and Aram was an enemy of Israel. Also, these anointings were anticipatory, as the recipients were not to assume their functions or perform their actions till much later. Jehu, for example, would need another anointing from Elisha, after Elijah's death.

[The Books of Kings are confusing: so many kings, prophets, and gods, many of which had similar names such as Rehoboam and Jeroboam, Hezekiah and Zedekia; Jehoahaz, Jehoiakim and Jehoiachin. At one point Joram, also known as Jehoram, was king of Israel while another Joram, also known as Jehoram, was king of Judah. Also, a king may sometimes be a champion of Yahweh, and sometimes a champion of Baal.]

King Ahab was succeeded by Ahazia. The latter was injured and sent messengers to enquire of Baal-Zebub, the god of Ekron, whether he would recover. Yahweh felt slighted and, through an angel, told Elijah to intercept the messengers and to ask them if there were no god in Israel capable of answering their questions. They returned and reported this encounter to the king who sent a captain with fifty men to escort the prophet back to him. Elijah called down fire from the Lord and the men were consumed. Another captain and his fifty men were sent with the same result. A third party was sent but the captain pleaded for his life and that of his men.

> And the angel of the Lord said unto Elijah, "Go down with him [Ahazia]: be not afraid of him." And he arose and went down with him. Thus said the Lord, "Because you sent messengers to enquire of Baal-zebub, the god of Ekron, as though there was no God in Israel to answer your questions, therefore you will not come down of that bed on witch you are lying, but shall surely die
> (II Kings 1:15-16)

When it was time for Elijah to die, Yahweh took him up to heaven in a whirlwind. Elisha walked with him up to the Jordan while fifty disciples followed at a distance. Elijah took his mantle, rolled it up and struck the water which receded to the right and to the left, so that both men crossed on dry land. Elijah told Elisha that if the latter saw him as he was taken to heaven, then his spirit would pass on to Elisha. A fiery chariot pulled by horses of fire appeared and Elijah was taken to heaven. Elisha saw it.

> And he took up also the mantle of Elijah that fell from him, and walked back to the bank of Jordan and he took the mantle of Elijah that fell from him and struck the waters and said, "Where is the Lord God of Elijah?" and when he also had struck the water they parted hither and thither, and Elisha went over. And when some of the prophets from Jericho saw him they said, "The spirit of Elijah does rest on Elisha." And they came to meet him and bowed themselves to the ground before him.
> (II Kings 2:13-15)

Miracles were Elisha's forte. The second followed the first immediately: the local people complained about the quality of the water from their spring, that it shortened life and made the ground barren. Elisha asked for a dish with salt in it. He threw the salt in the spring, and said a few words from the Lord, and the water became wholesome.

His third miracle, however, wasn't so nice and helpful: some boys teased him and he cursed them in the name of the Lord, thereupon two bears came out of the woods and tore apart forty-two of the children. (See T, Chapter 1)

Many of Elisha's miracles were almost replicas of Elija's earlier feats. Like his mentor he multiplied a jug of oil to benefit a widow; where his mentor had replicated over and over a jar of flour, he dealt directly with the bread, feeding a hundred men with twenty loaves (II Kings 4:43); like Elijah, he brought a woman's son beack to life and did it using the same technique, by superposing his body over the boy's (and he needed only two repetitions wehreas Elija had needed three). (II Kings 4:32-35)

Elisha's most important mission was the anointing of Jehu as king of Israel. Elija had already anointed him, but that had been in anticipation of future events. Elisha sent a disciple to secretly anoint Jehu son of Jehoshaphat. The disciple managed to separate Jehu from his comrades, poured the oil on his head and, in Yahweh's name, proclaimed him king over Israel. He then fled while Jehu returned to his friends. When he related what had happened they sounded the horn and shouted, "Jehu is king."

It is interesting to the skeptic among us that many of the miracles of this prophetic pair seem to have been trial runs for similar miracles later ascribed to Jesus: the multiplication of bread, the replenishing of liquids (oil for the prophets, wine for Jesus) and the resuscitation of a widow's son. Elijah never cured leprosy but both Elisha and Jesus did. Even the latter's famous walk on the water had an antecedent: when a disciple dropped a borrowed axe head in the Jordan, Elisha made it float to the surface so it could be picked up.

Elisha had a long career: he prophesized, it seems, during the reigns of five kings of Israel and four of Judah, if we include his period of apprenticeship under Elijah. Even death couldn't stop his miraculous career. Some time after his demise, some Israelites were burying a body in a gravesite next to Elisha's. A group of Moabite marauders were seen approaching. In their haste the people threw the body into the prophet's grave and when it touched Elisha's bones, the dead man sprang to life and stood up. (One may wonder why the grave was open?)

Jehu

It seems that Jehu, son of Jehoshaphat never fought any major battles against any of the great enemies of Israel – Moab, Edom, Philistia, Aram – which left him free to concentrate on the slaughter of fellow Hebrews. He put together quite a record.

At the time of his anointing Joram was still king of Israel. He was in Israel recuperating from wounds he had received fighting the Arameans, and entertaining King Ahazia of Judah who had come on a visit. Jehu mounted his chariot and drove to Israel. The two kings went to meet him, each in his chariot. Jehu shot an arrow through Joram's heart, and his men mortally wounded Ahazia. Jehu continued to Jezreel where Jezebel, the widow of Ahab, still lived. He had her thrown out of a window to her death. Dogs devoured her body as had been prophesized by Elija.

Ahab had seventy descendents, all young princes living in Samaria and reared by local notables. Jehu threatened the latter and called for the heads of their charges. Next day, seventy baskets arrived in Jezreel, each with a princely head in it. The king then proceeded to kill anyone in the city who had been in any way connected to the house of Ahab. On its way to Samaria, his party crossed a group of forty-two kinsmen of Ahazia. The king had them slaughtered. (What the heck he was on a roll; why stop now?)

Jehu was a staunch Yahwist. He tricked the priests and worshippers of Baal into believing that he was a Baalist, in order to lure them up to the temple of Baal for a solemn assembly and a great sacrificial ritual. Jehu had his men encircle the temple and then rush in and kill all the worshippers. Thus did he finish the job started by Elijah and thus was Baal defeated and his followers exterminated in Israel.

It is interesting to note that all of Jehu's atrocities were sanctioned by Yahweh:

> And the Lord said to Jehu, "Because you have done well in executing that which is right in my eyes and have done to the house of Ahab according to all that was in my heart your children to the fourth generations shall sit on the throne of Israel.
> (II Kings 10:30)

Apologists say that his was merely an application of the principle of *an eye for an eye*, since Jezebel had persecuted Yawist prophets and had an undetermined number of them killed. But she only killed the prophets not the worshipers: Jehu killed all the Baalists – men, women and children. This behavior – fully condoned by Yahweh – was in direct contravention to Moses' law that "The fathers shall not be put to death for the children, neither shall the children be put to death for the fathers: every man shall be put to death for his own sin." (Deuteronomy 24:16) Also, since Ahab worshipped both Baal and Yahweh, it is doubtful that he or Jezebel would have participated in the wholesale murder of Yahwists.

Chapter VI – The Great Debacle

It was during Jehu's reign that the disintegration of Israel gained momentum.

> In those days, the Lord began to cut Israel short: and Hazael [Aramean king] harassed them in all the borders of Israel: from Jordan, eastward, all the land of Gilead, the Gadites, and the Reubenites, and the Manassites, from Arroer, which is by the river Arnon, even Gilead and Bashan. (II Kings 10:32-33)

The writer/editors of the Old Testament faced a problem: the covenant was based on a promise of Yahweh to protect his people and guide them to victory and power, and in return the Hebrews were to obey his law. But things were falling apart. The ruling elite was busy with internecine killings – and other acts of treachery – and the people were worshiping all kinds of gods. One would expect that the writer/editors, being henotheists, would have downplayed the strong polytheistic proclivity of the people and their leaders.

But Yahweh had to be exonerated and his honor had to be saved: the solution to the quandary was to blame everything on the sins of the Hebrews, chief of which, by far, was the worship of other gods. Yahweh did not break his promise; rather, Israel broke faith with its God and deserved punishment. Therefore idolatry, instead of being hidden under the rug, was made prime-time news, and what would now be considered outrageous assaults against the principles of human rights and religious liberty, were touted as examples of featly and loyalty to Yahweh, "our God." [Most religions have, at some time, practiced this ethical inversion, but the Old Testament provides many of the more egregious cases.] Even Jehu, staunch Yahwist as he was, was blamed for not destroying the golden calves at Bethel and Dan, and for not completely turning away from "the sins of Jeroboam, which made Israel to sin." (II Kings 10:31)

To give an idea of the state of governance that prevailed during that era, let me present a thumbnail sketch of some of the kings:

Ahasia: king of Judah, killed by Jehu,

Athalia: mother of Ahasia; upon hearing of his death killed the rest of the royal family, except Joash, son of Ahasia, who was hidden; reigned 12 years; killed on order of the priest Jehoiada.

Amaziah: son of Joash; assassinated by his courtiers.

Azariah: son of Amaziah; a Yahwist, but did not destroy the shrines; struck by leprosy; lived in isolation while his son Jotham ruled.

Zecharia: son of Jeroboam; king over part of Israel (Samaria) for 6 months; killed by Shallum who succeeded him.

Shallum: reigned in Samaria one month, killed by Menahem who succeeded him,

Menahem: nice man – when the city of Tipha resisted he killed all and eviscerated all pregnant women.

Pekahiah: son of Menahem; reigned over Israel in Samaria two years; killed by his aid Pekah who succeeded him.

Peka: king over Israel and Samaria for 20 years; lost part of his kingdom to King Tiglath-pileser of Assyria who deported the inhabitants to Assyria; killed by a conspirator, Hoshea son of Elah.

Ahaz: son of King Jotham of Judah; a polytheist who sacrificed his son by fire; had a replica of the heathen altar in Damascus built in Jerusalem

The kingdoms, especially Israel, were falling apart. Hoshea, the killer of Pekah, would be the last king of the northern kingdom. It is for this reason, rather than for any intrinsic merit on his part, that he rates a closer look.

Hoshea

He ruled nine years over Israel. He did "that which was evil in the sight of the Lord, but not as [much as] the kings of Israel that were before him." King Shalmaneser of Assyria marched against him and Hoshea became a vassal of the Assyrian and paid tribute. But, a few years later, Hoshea established relations with the king of Egypt and stopped paying tribute.

Shalmaneser jailed him and lay siege to Samaria which he took after three years. He carried away the Israelites to Assyria and settled them in Halah, in Habor, and in the cities of the Medes. Scholars estimate that the fall of the northern kingdom occurred in 722 BCE or thereabouts.

Chapter 17 of II Kings contains a long explanation of the guilt that Israel had incurred and for which they were now being punished.

> For as it was that the children of Israel had sinned against the Lord their God, which had brought them up out of Pharaoh king of Egypt, and feared other gods, and walked in the ways of the heathen whom the Lord cast out from before the children of Israel …
> (17:7-8)
>
> … And they left all the commandments of the Lord and made molten images, even two calves, and made a grove, and worshiped all the hosts of heaven, and served Baal. And then caused their sons and their daughters to pass through the fires, and used divination and enchantments, and sold themselves to do evil in the sight of the Lord, to provoke him to anger. Therefore the lord was very angry with Israel, and removed them from his sight: there was none left but the tribe of Judah only.
> (17:11-18)

For some mysterious reason, Shalmanezer brought men from Babylon and other Assyrian cities and placed them in the cities where the departed Hebrews had lived. But Yahweh sent lions to kill some of them. They spoke to the king, explaining that they didn't know the ways of the god of the land, which is why he sent the lions against them. Shalmanezer sent one of the Yahwist priests from among the departed Israelites to teach the people how to fear the Lord of the land. But the people didn't abandon their original gods; they just added Yahweh to their menu of deities.

This was nothing new. Polytheists were generally liberal and easily accepted other gods in their pantheon. If you noticed that a neighbor who worshiped a different god was prospering, you may built an altar to that god in the hope of sharing in his good graces. Also, in the case of mixed marriages, husbands usually respected the religious beliefs of their wives and often built altars for their gods. It was always good to have as many heavenly protectors as possible. Only the Hebrew prophets and priests violently objected to this attitude and practice. Many nations knew Yahweh and some worshipped him along with their own gods. The Yahwist clergy, however got a taste of their own medicine from Jezebel and later Antiochus IV Epiphanes. It should be noted that Jezebel was as much a heno (or mono)theist as the Yahwists, the main difference between Yahweh and Baal being the name. All this begs the question: who were the real barbarians, the many-gods worshippers or the one-god worshipers?

Hezekiah

Hezekiah, son of King Ahaz of Judah, was a staunch Yahwist and a rather successful king. The writer/editors ascribe his success to his faithfulness. He destroyed the shrines, pillars and scared posts of competing gods but, unlike other strongly Yahwist kings, he didn't kill heretical Hebrews.

King Sennacherib of Assyria attacked Judah and captured its fortified towns. Hezekia gave him all the gold and silver of the temple and Royal Palace but the Assyrian monarch sent envoys with a large force to inform Hezekia that the invaders would not withdraw. The prophet Isaiah sent a message from Yahweh to his king:

> By the way that he [Sennacherib] came, by the same shall he
> return, and shall not come into this city, said the Lord.
> For I will defend this city, to save it,
> For my own sake, and for my servant David's sake.
> (II Kings 19:33-34)

That same day an angel of the Lord came and struck down 185,000 Assyrian soldiers. Sennacherib returned home where he was assassinated by his own children.

Hezekia ruled over Judah for 29 years and was succeeded by his son Manasseh.

Manasseh

Manasseh had a long career: fifty-five years on the throne of Judah. Unlike his father, he was an enthusiastic polytheist who rebuilt the shrines, sacred posts and altars that his father had destroyed. He consulted "familiar spirits" and ghosts, practiced divination and even sacrificed his own son by fire. He also placed altars and graven images within the confines of the

House of the Lord. He had so many innocent people killed that blood ran in the streets of Jerusalem.

> And the Lord spoke through his servants the prophets, saying, "Because Manasseh king of Judah has done these abominations ... and has made Judah also to sin with his idols: therefore thus said the Lord God of Israel, "Behold, I am bringing such evil upon Jerusalem and Judah, that whoever hears of it, both his ears shall tingle." (II Kings 21:11-12)

According to II Kings, Manasseh died unrepentant, of natural causes. He was succeeded by his son Amon, who followed in the wicked ways of his father and was killed by a conspiracy of courtiers two years later.

According to II Chronicles, however, Yahweh sent officers of the Assyrian army as punishment. They took him captive and brought him to Babylon in fetters. In these dire straights he experienced a conversion and humbly prayed to the Lord, who returned him to his kingdom. He removed the foreign gods and commanded the people to worship the Lord of Israel.

Josiah

Manasseh was succeeded by his son Amon who was murdered after a reign of only two years. The people killed the murderers and made Josiah, Amon's eight-year old son, king. He reigned thirty-one years and was a constant and fervent Yahwist, like his ancestor David.

During an audit of the silver donated to the Temple by the faithful, the high priest Hilkia announced to the scribe Shaphan that he had found a book of the law in the House of the Lord. (II Kings 22:9) Shaphan read it for himself and then read it to the king who reacted as though hit by a bolt of lightening and rent his clothes (biblical kings and priests were always rending their clothes). Hilkia and a few notables were commanded to ask instruction of the Lord.

> Go inquire of the Lord for me, and for the people, and for all Judah, concerning the words of this book that is found: for great is the wrath of his Lord that is kindled against us, because our fathers have not obeyed the words of this book, to do according to all that is written concerning us. (II Kings 22:13)

The committee went to the prophetess Ulda. The news was not good.

> Thus said the Lord. "Behold, I will bring evil upon this place and upon its inhabitants according to the book which the King of Judah has read: because they have forsaken me, and have burned incense for their gods, they have provoked anger with all the idols they have made with their hands; therefore my wrath shall be kindled against the place and shall be quenched." (II Kings 22:16)

She added, however, that because Josiah had personally been blameless, the Lord would wait until after his death to put this threat to execution. The king embarked upon a manic whirl of altar, sacred post and pillar demolishing. (Whether the impetus came from the king of from Hilkia and the priests we will never know.) He assembled huge numbers of people to accompany him on those holy raids.

> And the king commanded Hilkia the high priest; and the priests of the second order, and the keepers of the door, to bring out of the temple of the Lord all the vessels that were made for Baal and for the grove [of Asherah] and for all the host of heaven and he burnt them outside Jerusalem in the fields of Kidron, and carried the ashes of them to Beth-el. And he put down [killed] the idolatrous priests, whom the kings of Judah had ordained to burn incense in the high places in the cities of Judah, and in the place round about Jerusalem, them also that burnt incense to Baal, to the sun, and to the moon, and to the planets, and to all the hosts of heaven.
> (II Kings 23:4-5)

The diatribe continues unabated for sixteen more verses. Two sentences are worth picking out of this raving discourse:

> And he broke down the houses of the sodomites [male prostitutes] that were in the house of the Lord, where the women wove hangings for the grove (23:9)

and

> And he slew all the priests of the high places [altars] that were there, and burned the men's bones upon them, and returned to Jerusalem (23:21)

Taken at face value, Chapters 22 and 23 are astounding. The Temple – the house of the Lord – had become the abode of all the gods and goddesses who were Yahweh's sworn enemies! The Temple – the house of the Lord – was now the place of business of male prostitutes! The countryside dotted with altars, sacred posts and pillars to Baal, Asherah, the host of heaven, Molech (who consumed children), Milcolm, Ashtoreth, Chemosh ... ! Hebrew fathers sacrificing their sons and daughters to Molech! The priesthood divided into loyalties to different gods!

And no prophets! No prophets to steer the Hebrew people back to Yahweh! No prophets to cast the light of truth through the fog of ignorance!

Yet the Ark of the Covenant was still in the Holy of Holies, the ten commandments of Moses still inscribed on the tablets. Didn't Hilkia, the high priest, enter the Holy of Holies once a year, on the day of atonement? How could he have been ignorant of the "God of your fathers" until he chanced upon the long lost scroll of the Teaching?

And this scroll? How could it have been lost? It was almost as holy and important as the Ark of the Covenant. The Temple was built, not only as the home of Yahweh, but also as a safe repository of the Ark, the Scroll of the Law, and perhaps other such documents. It seems inconceivable that this scroll could have been lost without anyone noticing its absence!

It is hard to understand why Josiah would feel so deeply his own guilt and the guilt of his people, and why Yahweh would be so enraged at his chosen people for their ignorance of the law – so enraged that he decided to abandon them. More: that he decided to send heathen enemies to destroy Jerusalem and his own dwelling (the Temple) and his own people.

It wasn't their fault: they didn't know! They had no idea! It was as though the religion had never existed – as though Yahweh was just another deity in the Semitic pantheon!

[We will examine this possibility when we consider the historicity and factuality of the Old Testament]

The End of Judah

After the pious, back-to-the-roots zeal of Jehu in Israel and Hezekia in Judah, the successors of those kings failed to maintain the fideistic ardor, and the people again fell prey to their long-established proclivity for polytheism. After Josiah's death at the hands of the Egyptian king Neco, the Hebrew people settled back in their old idolatrous habits. Josiah was succeeded by his son Jehoahaz who, in his short tenure of three months, managed to do "that which was evil in the sight of the Lord." For reasons unexplained in the Bible, Pharaoh Neco arrested him and brought him back to Egypt, where he died. Neco appointed Eliakim, another son of Josiah, king of Judah, changing his name to Jehoiakim. The pharaoh imposed a tribute on the king and the people. Jehoiakim reigned eleven years doing "that which was evil in the sight of the Lord."

The military power in the region passed from Neco to King Nebuchadnezzar of Babylon. Jehoiakim became his vassal for three years. When he rebelled, Yahweh used that circumstance as an opportunity to heap more punishment on the Hebrews. They fell victim to raids by Chaldeans, Arameans, Moabites and Amonites.

Jeoiakim was succeeded by his son Jehoiachin who followed in the idolatrous ways of his father. Three months after his coronation, Nebuchadnezzar attacked Jerusalem. Jehoiachin and his retinue surrendered. They were exiled to Babylon along with 10,000 warriors, craftsmen and smiths. All the treasures of the Temple and of the royal palace were plundered, but enough people were left in Jerusalem to maintain a viable society.

The king of Babylon made Mattania, Jehoiachin's uncle, king of Judah, changing his name to Zedekia. He reigned eleven years and did "that which was evil in the sight of the Lord." But in the ninth year of his reign he rebelled against Babylon. Nebuchadnezzar attacked Jerusalem and, after a siege of two years, captured it.

Zedekia was put on trial, his sons were slaughtered in his sight and then his eyes were put out. The king was put in fetters and brought to Babylon. The House of the Lord, the royal palace and the houses of all the notables were burned. The wall that protected the city was also breached in many places. For the second time the citizens were exiled to Babylon, but again enough peasants were left to tend to the vineyards and the fields.

Nebuchadnezzar placed Gedaliah in charge of this remnant. He reassured the people that the Chaldeans would not harm them as long as they stayed in the land and served the king of Babylon. However, some time later a party of Hebrews killed Gedaliah. The people then fled to Egypt to escape the Chaldeans' revenge. Thus, in 587 BCE, or thereabout, did the kingdom of Judah come to an end.

In Babylon, Nebuchadnezzar was succeeded by King Evil-meradah, who took Jehoiachin out of his fetters and gave him lodging and sustenance for the rest of his life.

Chapter VII – Born Again

The Hebrew Diaspora started more than a century before the two deportations to Babylon. The Assyrian king, Shalmanezer, conquered Samaria and deported the Samarian Hebrews to Assyria, being careful to settle them in towns. Later he replaced them, in Samaria, with Assyrians. He went so far as to send to the latter a Yahwist priest to teach them the "ways of the god of the land." Of course these new Yahwists also kept worshipping their old gods, so that polytheism and syncretism remained the main characteristics of the religions of Mesopotamia.

The exile to Babylon was a different story. King Nebuchadnezzar of Babylon, a Chaldean, captured Jerusalem and took its king, Jehoiachin, along with about 7,000 able men back to Babylon as captives, appointing Zedekia as king over the remnant. Ten years later (c. 587), after Zedekia had rebelled, Nebuchadnezzar destroyed the traitors' family, deported most of the remaining Judeans to Babylon, burned the Temple, the royal palace and all the houses of the notables. Enough Judeans were left, however, to tend the fields and vineyards.

In spite of the cruelty directed at the king and his sons, the Chaldeans were rather generous and enlightened toward the vanquished Hebrews. In Babylon, the exiles were allowed to participate in civil activities while given cultural and religious freedom. Some fifty years later, when the Persians had replaced the Chaldeans as the superpower, Cyrus, king of Persia, who seems to have adopted the gods of all his subject people, issued the following proclamation:

> Thus says Cyrus king of Persia: "the Lord God of Heaven has given me all the kingdoms of the earth; and he has

> charged me to build him a house at Jerusalem, which is in Judah. Who is there among you of all his people? His God be with him , and let him go up to Jerusalem, which is in Judah, and build a house of the Lord God of Israel (he is the God) which is in Jerusalem. And whoever remains in any place where he lives, let the men of his place help him with silver and with gold, and with goods: and with beasts, besides the freewill offering, for the house of God that is in Jerusalem"
> (Ezra 1:2-4)

According to Ezra 2:64-5; 42,360 Judeans plus 7,337 male and female servants made the trip back to Judea, each person going to his original town.

These same numbers are given in the Book of Nehemia, but the chronology is completely different. In Ezra the people settled under Sheshbazzar, governor of Judah during Darius' reign, but in Nehemia the exact same number returned under Zerubbabel in the twentieth year of King Artaxerxes – therefore more than twenty years later.

The return to Jerusalem and Judah and the rebuilding of the Temple is covered in the two books, *Ezra* and *Nehemia* but, as we have just seen, the two are far from concordant. It is as though two books were sliced, and then the slices were shuffled like a deck of cards, and then separated again into two books, the one ascribed to Ezzra being placed first. Ezzra is mentioned in Nehemia, but the latter is never mentioned in the first book. Neither book tells us anything about the history and state of the Hebrews in Babylon. Nehemia, however, points a grim picture of those that were living at that time in Judah and Jerusalem. (These would be the remnant that were never exiled and those that had previously returned.)

Reconstructing intuitively the content of both books, we can come to a synthesis that makes some sense and is probably fairly close to fact:

In the first year of King Cyrus, the latter issued a proclamation that permitted any Hebrew exile so willing to return to Jerusalem and help rebuild the House of the Lord God of Israel. He invited all exiles to help with donations of gold, silver and livestock and released all the vessels and implements that Nebuchadnezzar had taken as bounty.

A large group accepted the invitation and returned under the leadership of Joshua and Zerrubbabel. Work was started on the Temple. The local residents, Assyrians and Chaldeans, settled there to replace the exiled Hebrews, and who worshipped Yahweh (probably along with their old gods) asked to assist in the work. Their offer was refused. [Considering the munificence of Cyrus, this was a mean-spirited decision: these people were probably no more polytheistic than many Hebrews and were, it seems, sincere Yahweh worshippers.]

The locals engaged in political action against the rebuilding and it was stopped. After Darius found a scroll that proved that Cyrus had given his blessing to the enterprise, he sent a strong letter to the governor of the province of Beyond the River (which included Judah) and reconstruction of the Temple was completed. However work on the Wall of Jerusalem and its gates had not begun.

During the reign of King Artaxerxes, Nehemia, the royal cup bearer, upon hearing the plight of the Hebrews in Jerusalem, obtained a charter to rebuild the city's fortifications. He left Babylon with a military escort. Again, the Ammonites, Ashodites and Arabs tried to stop the work by politics, death and violence but the Hebrews managed to finish the job.

In the seventh month, a great assembly was held in the square before the Water Gate. This occasioned the first mention of Ezra, priest and scribe, in the Book of Nehemia. He was the featured preacher. He brought a scroll of the teaching of Moses and read from it. (It was probably the scroll that Hilkia "found" in the temple during Josiah's reign.)

On the second day, Ezra found the writings about the festival of booths which was supposed to be held during the seventh month. The whole community gathered branches, made booths, and dwelt in them. This had not been done since the days of Joshua. On the twenty-fourth day of the month there was another assembly. This time:

> … the seed of Israel separated themselves from all strangers, and confessed their sins and the iniquities of their fathers.
> (Nehemia 9:2)

The Levites delivered a complete synopsis of the glory days of Israel ending with a new emendation of the commandments. The first of these was, "We will not give our daughters to the people of the land nor take their daughters for our sons (9:30)

The book of Ezra also attaches much importance to social purity:

> Now when these things were done, the princes came to me saying, "The people of Israel, and the priests, and the Levites have not separated themselves form the people of

> the lands, who do according to their abominations like the Canaanites, the Hittites, the Perizites, the Jebusites, the Ammonites, the Moabites, the Egyptians and the Amorites. For they have mingled themselves with the people of those lands: yea, the hand of the princes and rulers have been chief in the trespass."
> (Ezzra 9:1-2)

Ezra rent his garments and tore hair out of his head and beard. A crowd gathered around him and one Shecaniah, son of Jehiel said:

> ... We have trespassed against our God, and have taken strange wives of the people of the land: yet now there is hope in Israel concerning this thing. Now therefore let us make a covenant with our God to put away all the wives and such as are born of them according to the counsel of my lord, and of these that tremble at the commandments of our God; and let it be done according to the law."
> (Ezra 10:2-3)

Ezra made the Israelites take an oath to do so, but at the next assembly they decided that the separation should be planned and that, this being the rainy season, it was not right to send people out in the open.

The Book of Nehemia ends on the same topic:

> In those days also I saw Jews that had married wives of Ashdod, Ammon and Moab; and their children spoke half in the speech of Ashdod and could not speak in the Jew's language, but according to the language of each people. And I contended with them and cursed them, and hit some of them, and tore off their hair, and made them swear by God, saying, "You shall not give your daughters to their sons nor take their daughters for your sons, or for yourselves."
> (Nehemia 13:23-25)

What is striking about both books is the blatantly explicit racism, which is hard to explain, considering the rather lenient treatment the Hebrews had received in Babylon and the generous cooperation offered by the Persian kings. Ezra and Nehemia refer to the passage from Deuteronomy in which Moses said:

> You shall not make marriages with them; your daughter you shall not given to his son, nor his daughter shall you take for your son. For they will turn away your son from following me, that they may serve other gods: so will the anger of the Lord be kindled against you and destroy you suddenly.
> (Deuteronomy 7:3-4)

But Moses also said, later:

> When you go forth to war against your enemies, and the Lord your God has delivered them into your hands, and you have taken them captive, and you see among the captives a beautiful woman and you have a desire for her and you would have her be your wife; then you shall bring her home to your house; and she shall shave her head and pare her nails; and she shall take off he raiment of her captivity, and shall remain in your house and bewail her father and her mother a full month: and after that you shall go unto her [make love to her] and be her husband and she shall be your wife.
> (Deuteronomy 21:10-15)

There are even stronger declarations of universal brotherly love. Yahweh, quoted by Moses, said:

> And if a stranger sojourns with you in your land, you shall not wrong him. But the stranger who dwells with you shall be to you as one born among you, and you shall love him as yourself; for you were strangers in the land of Egypt: I am the Lord your God.
> (Leviticus 19:23-24)

The phrase, "for you were strangers in the land of Egypt" is repeated many times in the Old Testament, with the implication that the golden rule should apply to all. (To be fair, the phrase, "you shall not give your daughter to his son, nor take his daughter for your son" is also repeated a few times.)

Moses himself was married to a Cushite woman, for which he was reproached by his siblings. (Yahweh punished his sister, Miriam, with a skin condition that lasted seven days.) Moses had no compunction about killing those who disagreed with him – including other Hebrews – and he didn't hesitate to order the massacre of whole populations; he saw nothing wrong with using houses that others had built or drinking the wine of vines others had planted; but his motivation does not seem to have been racist – at least not in the same sense that Ezra's and Nehemia's was. One reason for his ambivalent attitude toward miscegenation was his distrust of women: he saw them as seductive temptresses who could lead men away from Yahweh and toward the gods of other people.

[The ideal of racial purity is as fictitious in the case of Hebrews as in the case of any other group. The Hebrews, especially in the time of Moses and Joshua, were constantly bringing female slaves form their campaigns (the males they preferred to kill). It doesn't require a Ph.D. in human sexuality to figure that this implied a lot of gene mixing.]

The bigotry of Ezra and Nehemia is hard to understand, and even harder to condone. The Babylonians – both Chaldean and Persians – had been rather kind and respectful in their dealings with them after the wars. It was Cyrus who took the initiative in suggesting and facilitating the return; and Darius and Ataxerxes were nothing if not helpful. The people that had been settled in Judah to replace the exiles had become semi-Yahwists (and the prefix *semi* would apply to many Hebrews also). It seems the Hebrews missed a golden opportunity. Their neighbors were already half converted. A little effort and sympathy would have turned most of them into full Yahwists. Should not such missionary work have been considered part of the convenantal duties, since Yahweh seemed to crave fame and glory?

Perhaps Ezra and Nehemia considered the Hebrews a very special elite (think of the words *so that the holy seed have mingled themselves with the people of those lands* – a pregnant phrase indeed) and were therefore disinclined to increase the membership. An elite that accepts too many recruits risks losing or, at least, diluting and degrading its status. Perhaps this explains why Jews have shunned proselytizing, except during a few exceptional periods.

Chapter VIII – Historicity and Factuality

Historicity

So far we have taken the Old Testament at face value, confident that the Bible can fall on its own two feet and convinced that the Word – as printed, read and preached – is what really matters. But now we must go a little further and ponder the question of the historicity of the document: Does the part of the Holy Scriptures that is written in a historical style tell us the real story, or is it just made-up stuff presented as though it were history? Or is it something in between?

If the latter is the answer, we have an unsettling pair of problems: how to discriminate between the real stuff and the made-up stuff; and what attitude to adopt about a book that is supposed to be the unerring word of God, but that is only partly true. Either it is the word of God or it isn't; but if it is, should it not be all-true?

In court, it is not always necessary to prove or disprove every statement of a witness. Often, it is sufficient for the prosecutor or defense attorney to destroy the credibility of the witness, even if the evidence so used is not directly connected to the case. If we can find one episode of substantial importance in the Old Testament and convincingly show it to be of very dubious historicity, we will have impugned the credibility of the whole document

Chapters 7 to 14 of Exodus provide us with such an episode. It is the story of the battle of wills between Moses (as Yahweh's agent) and Pharaoh, King of Egypt. Certainly, the flight from Egypt is the seminal event in the biblical narrative and one that is most frequently referred to in the rest of the document. Genesis is a patched-together introduction (most of it of later provenance) but Exodus is really "Chapter One." If it can be shown to be of dubious veracity, the claim to historicity of what follows will be seriously impugned.

Prima facie, even for someone who stands in credulous awe before miracles, the story seems "over the top" – all that water turning into blood; frogs invading homes; lice, followed by insects, followed by locusts; pestilence killing the cattle; boils and inflammation; hail killing the cattle already dead of pestilence; the first-born killed by an avenging angel; and finally, the parting of the Red Sea. Many internal inconsistencies have been pointed out by Robert Ingersol (*Some Mistakes of Moses*) and other freethinkers. How could Egyptian magicians duplicate the transformation of water into blood if all water had already been so converted? The miracle of the frogs was also duplicated by the Egyptians; but, since no modern magicians would claim that the creation of living beings is within the purview of his craft, how could such a miracle be accomplished without the assistance of Yahweh? Did other gods help? Why bring swarms of locusts (8th plague) to devastate a land already ruined by the insects of the 4th plague? Did more than one year lapse between the two events? The 5th plague, a severe pestilence, resulted in the death of all farm animals belonging to Egyptians (none of the curses affected the Hebrews), so why did Yahweh send hail (7th plague) to rekill them? Could it be that years elapsed between the two events?

Only seven days separated the first two plagues, the blood and the frogs. No other chronology is given, but the narrative implies a fairly rapid succession of disastrous events. Yet, for this chain of happenings to make sense – even miraculous sense – many years would be required for the whole episode.

But to really put the whole story to rest, we need the input of generations of historians and archeologists – or rather, the lack of input. It is generally agreed that Egyptians had been using papyrus – a kind of writing surface made from reeds, and more durable than paper – since approximately 3000 BCE, which is about 1000 years before the exodus. Commemorative inscriptions on tombs and temple walls can be even older. Steles, slabs or pillars of stone also used for commemorative inscriptions, likewise predate papyrus. There is historical and archeological proof that Egypt had, for that time, a sophisticated civil service that kept business, legal and other records. The Bible itself bears witness to this: didn't Joseph, who had been sold into slavery by his jealous brothers, end up being the pharaoh's right-hand man, ably administrating the whole country?

And yet, in spite of the tradition of record keeping and in spite of the existence of a civil service, not a word about the plagues!

The Nile turns to blood, but no scribe takes notice!

Frogs, lice, locusts, and other insects cover the land in succession, but the bureaucrats make no records!

All the cattle die of pestilence, but no one misses the milk or the steaks|

All Egyptians (no Hebrews) suffer from inflammation and boils but the medical profession produces no dossiers!

All first born of man (except Hebrews) or beast are killed in one night, but no stele or temple wall bears witness; no grieving parent expresses his or her pain on papyrus!

The pharaoh's army is swallowed up by the Red Sea but no officer writes a report and no scribe scratches a piece of papyrus.

It is inconceivable that such momentous and bizarre events could have happened in a relatively sophisticated society without leaving the slightest trace in that country's records. By way of comparison: some five hundred years earlier, a people, the Hyksos, had been driven out of Egypt; that exodus did not escape the scrutiny of historians. Of course, the Hyksos were a much more numerous and powerful group than were the Hebrews – but then, their departure was not accompanied by large-scale and grotesque events that directly affected the life of very Egyptian citizen.

There are other incentives to skepticism. For example, the fact that the name of the king of Egypt is never given: he is referred to only as "Pharaoh." Names were extremely important to the Hebrews – and to other peoples. The Tanakh is replete with names such as "Johaziel, son of Zacharia, son of Benaiah, son of Jeiel, son of Mattaniah the Levite." Certainly, after all his dealings with the monarch, Moses must have known his name. Could it be that it was the writer/editor of the story that didn't know? (Most scholars think the pharaoh's name was Ramses II, a name familiar to modern users of condoms).

We can come to only one logical conclusion: the plagues of Egypt never happened! The biblical story of the flight from Egypt is a pure fabrication. At best, a small group of disaffected Semites managed to escape from a country where they were oppressed and subjected to forced labor. Historians who do not have a particular interest in the Bible have taken no interest in this minor chain of events. In the long run, the exodus – or, rather, the *story* of the exodus – was a seminal event, but at that time, it resulted in no important change in the political situation in that part of the world and no one took notice except, centuries later, the writer/editors of the Torah (Pentateuch). To readers of the Bible however, the fraudulent nature of the text ought to result in a sea change: the writers have lost credibility; the claim of being "the word of God" has evaporated. The very existence of Moses becomes uncertain and the belief that he was the original writer of Deuteronomy becomes untenable. His contemporaries, knowing that the many references to the plagues were bogus, would have ridiculed him, and Moses was not a man who would endure ridicule.

And the cancer has spread in both directions, infecting what was written before and what was written after, weakening even the claims of the New Testament and the Koran.

The Historicity of Genesis

There are other parts of the Old Testament that are of very dubious historicity, such as the Book of Genesis – especially the first segments – and the story of the discovery of the "Book of the Teaching of the Lord" by the priest Hilkia.

Since I can't read Hebrew nor Aramean, I will, in examining these, rely mostly on the biblical text itself, which contains the seed of its own vitiation.

It is surprising how differences in style and in the evolutionary state of language survive translation. (It is also interesting to compare different translations.) Much could be written just on the translations of the different Hebrew names of God (or god) especially his usual proper name, Yahweh (written as YHWH in Hebrews texts since the name of the deity was not supposed to be pronounced).

Let me make a point here that I have already alluded to, and to which we will return with greater detail later:

Taking the Bible literally, and reading it carefully, it is clear that the Hebrews were not, during most of the historical period covered by the Old Testament, a monotheistic people. At times they seem to be enthusiastically polytheistic. The priests and prophets, however, were fierce defenders of Yahweh as the sole object of Hebrew worship: from their point of view, no punishment was too great for whoever breached that rule. But they did not deny the existence of other gods until just a few centuries before the birth of Christ.

"*God* with a capital *G*" is a very different word than "*god* with a lower case *g*." Capital-G-God, without any qualifier, refers to a unique spiritual entity whose unity has always been and will always be, and who has no equal and no challenger. There is, however, a little wiggle-room here: God can be personal (therefore somewhat anthropomorphic) or impersonal;

It can be transcendental or immanent; It can be ethical (in the sense of imposing a code on humans) or amoral.

Lower-case-gods are another kettle of fish. Most monotheistic religions have a pantheon of gods, but they call them *angels*, *djins*, *spirits*, *saints*, etc. Many supposedly polytheistic religions are no more so than many of the "great religions." (The dogma of the Trinity is another reason to question the monotheism of most Christian churches.)

God, unqualified, pure-and-simple is a late arrival in the history of Hebrews. All expressions such as "your God," "my God," "our God," "the Lord," "the lord God," "the Lord of Israel," "the God of your fathers," usually do not refer to the unique God of monotheism. Hence when the Book of Genesis opens with, "In the beginning God created the heaven and the earth" we are perplexed. After reflection we suspect that those words were written much later than the corpus of the text it introduces. "In the beginning" was written near the end. But just a page later, in Chapter 2, the word *God* is used twice, and is then replaced by *the Lord God*, which is used eleven times. This suggests that Chapter 2 was the work of a different writer and was written at a different time than Chapter 1. In Chapters 6 to 9, the story of Noah and the Flood, *God* takes precedence over *the Lord*. In Chapter 17, *the Lord* appears to Abram (renamed Abraham) and introduces himself saying, "I am El Shaddai." (*El* means *God*, or *the god*, therefore *El Shaddai* should probably be translated as *the god Shaddai*.)

[The sentence, *I am El Shaddai*, comes from the 1986 translation of the Tanakh by the Jewish Publication Society. The King James version has *I am the Almighty God*, an example of creative translation. Some French translations have *l'Éternel*, (the Eternal) for almost all mentions of *God*, *the Lord, Yahweh,* etc. – another case of creative translation, since it covers up the confused mixing of the meanings of *god* and *God* so often found in the Old Testament. Just arbitrarily using lowercase *g*'s and capital *G*'s to suit the translator's bias is one way of appreciably altering the meaning of a text.] Later, in Chapter 17, El Shaddai says:

> And I will establish my covenant between me and you and your seed [descendents] after you in their generations for an everlasting covenant, to be a God to you, and to your seed after you. And I will give you, and to your seed after you, a land wherein you are a stranger, all the land of Canaan, for an everlasting possession; and I will be their God. (Genesis 17:7-8)

Note that the use of the indefinite article in *To be a God:* even El Shaddai seems to believe that he is only one of a number of gods. Also, the use of the possessive adjective in *their God* implies that there are other Gods who could make covenants with other people.

The story of Joseph (Genesis: 37-50) is another instance of anachronism. Joseph is the first Jew in the Bible: there is nothing Hebrew about his character and personality. He shunned violence; he didn't take revenge on his brothers who sold him into slavery; he didn't evince any religious or ethnic bigotry, yet remained true to his roots. He was a great example of a person in ethical balance. His duty to his kin, to human beings in general, and to his employer, the Pharaoh, did not crowd out his duty to himself; nor was the latter exercised at the expense of the former. The recognition of the self as ethical object is one of the basic elements of Rabbinical Judaism. The story of Joseph is a product of Jewish culture, not Hebrew culture, and had to be written toward the end of the Old Testament era.

There are other reasons to deny the historicity of Genesis. *Prima facia*, it piles on miracle over miracle over miracle as though God were guilty of overacting. Also, it is in direct contradiction to well-established scientific facts and principles. It is likewise in contradiction with itself, presenting, for example, two different accounts of creation. These flaws, and others, have been pointed out and dealt with competently years ago by such writers as Robert Ingersol (see *Some Mistakes of Moses*, reprinted by Prometheus Books) and Joseph McCabe (see *The Forgery of the Old Testament*, also reprinted by Prometheus). I will defer to these modern classics and not delve further into what has already been well covered.

We can come to the conclusion that the Book of Genesis is a hodgepodge of inventions by an undetermined number of writers working at different times and put together by an unknown writer/editor toward the end of the Old Testament period. Think: why should anyone feel compelled to believe in the story of Abraham, a figure barely discernable – even as a mythical personage – through the fog of time, considering that there were no witnesses to the revelations that gave him and his descendants a special status among the peoples of the planet and promised them the bequest of a land already occupied. Never has so much been claimed on the basis of mere hearsay.

Historicity of the Oral Torah

There is a difficult problem in any analysis and evaluation of the historicity of the Tanakh: the role of the Oral Torah. The relative importance of the written word and of the oral tradition is the subject of much controversy among historians and religious scholars. One problem is that oral traditions are eventually written down and/or written about. Are they then still part of the oral tradition or have they become part of written documentation? Some rabbis have opined that the oral tradition should remain so and that the tendency to commit it to writing should be resisted. This would, of course, give rabbis greater leeway in the exercise of religious creativity in the steering of the religious movement to which they subscribe. (There is good and bad here and we will return to this topic anon.)

With the exception of the Ten Commandments, God did not present prophets with written documents – neither e-mail nor faxes existed in biblical times. The same is true of all religious traditions. Therefore virtually all scriptures start as 'oral' (or 'telepathic') communications. In some cases they may be quickly committed to writing, in other cases they may be transmitted form mouth to mouth or from generation to generation by trained professional memorizers. This can give oral communications a reliability approaching that of the written word. Prayers, songs, poems and other formalizations can also approach that degree of trustworthiness. However, most of the oral tradition is floating somewhere in the collective consciousness as legends, stories, sayings, rumors, and old wives' tales. To test the reliably of these I suggest a simple experiment: assemble a group of, say, ten to twenty persons; write down a story; read it in privacy to the first person you pick at random; have that person repeat it from memory to the next person, and so on down the line; ask the last person to write down the story he has heard; compare this to the original text. Your faith in the oral tradition will be seriously put to the test.

Case in point: the story of Hilkia and Josiah (II Kings 22 and 23):

As related in Chapter 6, the high priest Hilkia found a "scroll of the Teaching" in the temple .He had a scribe read it to King Josiah (who reigned from 639 to 609). The king, a pious man, tore his clothing in anguish because, being completely ignorant of the law, he had not obeyed it. He sent a delegation to the prophetess Huldah who predicted that Yahweh would bring disaster to Judah and Jerusalem because the people had not followed the Law. (How could they, since they knew nothing of it?) Josiah convoked all the people to a meeting at the House of the Lord. The scroll was read and then all the objects in the Temple that were not devoted to Yahweh were taken outside and destroyed. What was in the House of the Lord is indicative of the state of the religion in Judah (and remember that Judah was always more purely Yahwist than Israeli). There were "vessels that were made for Baal, Asherah and all the hosts of heaven." The king also had the houses of the sodomites (male cult prostitutes) that were in the Temple destroyed. Outside the Temple, he broke down altars that had been built for Ashoreth, Milcolm and Chemosh. He had their priests killed even though they had been ordained by previous kings of Judah.

If there is any truth to the Moses story, the situation facing Josiah and Hilkia was the result of the complete breakdown of the Oral tradition and a proof of the unreliability of the Oral Torah. If however, the story is not true, then the Scroll of the Law "found" in the temple was an artifact of Hilkia, or some other priests, and the first stage in the invention of the Old Testament – to be continued in Babylon during the exile and finished in Jerusalem after the return.

Factuality

Few scholars have doubted the historicity of Jesus. This historicity is necessary but not sufficient to establish Christianity as the one true faith. There are other facts in this universe besides historical facts, such as the facts of science and mathematics. For Christianity to be the one true faith a number of facts are essential:

- There must be a God that exists in the same sense that I exist; that the Rock of Gibraltar exits; that the proposition "2+2=4" exists independently of mathematicians and mathematical theories.
- This God must be both transcendental (distinct from the world) and immanent (involved with the world).
- This God must be a moral being in the sense that he has created a moral code and expects humans to follow it.
- This God, though simple and indivisible, must have three aspects: the Father, the Son, and the Holy Ghost.
- Jesus must be the incarnation of the Son.

If any one of these conditions is not factual, Christianity fails the test of factuality.

Webster's *Third International Dictionary* defines *factuality* as "the quality or state of being a fact or factual." The expression *naked fact* is a redundancy: facts are always naked. You can dress them up with higher meanings, nobility, spirituality, metaphoric implications, beauty even ugliness: it doesn't change their status as facts. A rose is a rose is a rose … or isn't.

Objects are not facts. The Rock of Gibraltar is not a fact, but the proposition *the Rock of Gibraltar exits* is a fact. Anything that can be the subject of a proposition establishing or implying existence has factuality.

To have factuality an entity must exit independently of the mind thinking about it. God has factuality only if it would exist even if there were no thinking minds in the universe (besides, perhaps, God's mind). Pantheism, the doctrine that the cosmos as a whole is God (which reduces the question of God's existence to a mere tautology) does not belong to the category of things about which a factuality judgment can be made. Anyone is free to adopt such an attitude – and that's what it is, a matter of attitude – and facts are irrelevant. Similarly, any doctrine that views God as a symbol for all the mysteries that we can't fathom are outside the purview of factuality judgments. Strangely, the proposition "2+2=5" does fall within the purview, precisely because we can assert that it is *not a fact*.

[Now, the above should not be interpreted as denying that such teachings may have spiritual value. We can meditate about them, as long as we realize that we are not dealing with positive or negative factuality.]

A fact is or isn't: there is no such thing as partial factuality because, strictly speaking, there is no such ting as a semi fact: but one can assign degrees of probability to a thing, event, state or situation having factuality; one can construct a factuality index from, say, nil, to low, to median, to high, to absolute.

To assign a factuality index to any entity is to make a value judgment: it is intuitive and personal rather than scientific. Myself, I would assign a factuality index of nil to the biblical story of creation, to the legend of Noah and the Flood, to the gods of Mesopotamia (including Old Yahweh), to the plagues of Egypt, to the splitting of the Red Sea. To the figure of Abraham I would assign a low rating, but to Moses, a medium rating. David and the kings of I Kings and II Kings get a high rating; Cyrus, Darius and Philo all get a score incrementally close to absolute.

We must, always, keep in mind the distinction between entities that have intrinsic existence and those that have merely extrinsic existence, that is, those that depend on the human mind for the foundation of their being. Suppose that Harry believes in the real existence of the great god Booblah. His belief is a fact. The engrams in his brain that cause this belief are also facts. What is not a fact is the intrinsic existence of the great god Booblah. Its factuality index is incrementally close to Zero!

The Fallout

The extremely dubious historicity of many parts of the Old Testament casts the shadow of doubt regarding the divinity of Jesus and the factuality of the Angel Jibril, Allah's envoy to Muhammad.

Jesus accepted both the historicity and factuality of the entire Tanakh, including many items that even basically fideistic publications, such as Edward Blair's *Abingdon Bible Handbook*, find difficult to accept as historical documents (or as based on historical documents). Limiting our search to the Gospel According to Matthew, references are made to the following highly questionable items:

- Abel (23:35)
- Noah and the Ark (34:38)
- Sodom and Gomorrah (10:15)
- Jonah and the Whale (12:40)
- Daniel and the Abomination of Desolation (24:15)
- (Most of these are also found in other Gospels)

The latter merits critical scrutiny. The story of Daniel and his friends in the furnace is well -known, as well as the story of the "writing on the wall" and other visions of Daniel. The first part of the book (verses 1-7) about the furnace episode and other adventures, was written in the third person by an unknown writer at an unknown time (probably a few centuries after the supposed events). Among other inaccuracies the author makes a gross mistake in the sequence of Babylonian kings. Also, Blair suggests that the personage of Daniel may be partially a tracing of an ancient legendary figure, a Daniel who was a Cannanite king and the hero of many stories.

Should not Jesus, if he was the Second Person of God, know what's believable and what's not in the Tanakh? It seems that he accepted everything in the book as true. This delivers a serious blow against the position that he was God.

As for the Angel Jibril, there is overwhelming evidence in the Koran that, as the mouthpiece of Allah, he assumed that the Old Testament was the word of God. He made no distinction between the conceivable and the egregiously implausible. The general index of Marmaduke Pickthall's *The Meaning of the Glorious Koran* (Dorset Press) contains:

- 6 references to Adam
- 1 to Cain and Abel
- 6 to Noah, 10 to the Ark and 2 to the Deluge
- 8 to the Days of Creation
- 3 to the Garden of Eden
- 5 to Jonah and the Whale

Jibril scores no higher on the factuality index than do the above personages or events.

Retrothinking

The great enemy of factuality is retrothinking: starting with a desired conclusion and working backward until you can find or invent the premises you need to sustain that conclusion. (Sometimes, you don't even need the "premises": just repeating that conclusion and quoting well-known persons who, themselves, keep repeating that conclusion can create the illusion that said conclusion is well established as fact. Also, if you are the infallible leader of a strong organization, premises are not necessary, save to keep up appearances.)

Retrothinking is one of the main tools of exegesis and the *modus operandi* of religious, political, and even scientific apologists.

The Invention of Mariology

Mariology, the "science" of Mary, has its roots in early Christianity but is basically an invention of the Catholic Church. When Catholics recite the prayers of the rosary they address Mary 50 times, God the father 5 times and the Three Persons of the Trinity 5 times. Yet, Mary is a very minor player in the Gospels. There are only about 10 references to her in the 4 books. Outside of supplying the womb for the gestation of Jesus she has little importance and receives little respect. When she made a comment to Jesus about the absence of wine at a wedding, he answered, "Woman what have I to do with you?" (John 2:4) Mary Magdalene gets more notice and is much more fleshed out as a person: Mary is almost invisible even when present.

So, how did she end up being "Queen of the World" and "Queen of Heaven"? The answer is a case in point of retrothinking. It started as a grassroots movement sometime in the first or second century. At first it was strongest in the Eastern churches, but by the middle of the fifth century the special status of Mary was widely accepted by lay and clergy throughout Christianity.

The virgin birth of Christ had Biblical force from Mathew 1:5, where it is written that Joseph "knew her [Mary] not till she had brought forth her first born." And, of course, there is the story of the Annunciation which St. Luke, "having had perfect understanding of all things from the very first," assures his friend, Theopilus, in Chapter 1, that the angel Gabriel appeared to Mary and told her that she would bear a son through the workings of the Holy Ghost (Luke 1:26-31). It seems that most Christians accepted the Virgin birth from the first centuries of the Common Era.

The dogma of the Perpetual Virginity of Mary (that she remained a virgin to her last day) took longer to establish itself. It also took more invention and arm twisting. Not only is it not supported by anything in the Bible, but the latter is quite clear that Jesus was part of a large family: He had four brothers and an unknown number of sisters. In Mathew 13:56, his bothers are named: James, Joseph, Simon and Judas. There are other references to one or more of them in other parts of the New Testament. Also, doesn't the statement that Joseph didn't "know Mary" until she had given birth to Jesus (Mathew 1:25, as cited above) strongly suggest that he "knew her" after that birth? But many influential clerics thought that the vessel that had carried the Christ, the Second Person of the Trinity just *had* to be virgin forever – another instance of the early Christian view of sex as dirty and disgusting. In 649, at the Lateran council Pope Martin I declared that anyone who didn't believe that Mary's virginity remained "equally inviolate after birth" must be condemned. A proposition that was contrary to the word of the Bible became official dogma!

The dogma of the Assumption of Mary is the claim that Mary was raised to heaven by the power of God – not by personal power as in the case of Jesus. (Whether she died first or was assumed while alive is not decided.) There is no serious biblical basis of this belief. None was necessary. There was a ground swell of veneration for Mary, who had become a star in the same sense that Elizabeth Taylor, Babe Ruth and John F. Kennedy were stars – out starring, at times, even her son. By the end of the fist millennium the feast of the Assumption was celebrated early on August 15. After the promulgation of the dogma of Perpetual Virginity, the Vatican started receiving millions of signatures on petitions asking that the Assumption be made a dogma. Scholars looked for arguments and Biblical support. They argued that since Mary, as the vessel for the divine fetus, had been declared a perpetual virgin: it made sense that her body would be spared physical corruption and decay. All they found in the Bible, however, was St. John's description of a part of the vision of Revelation in which a pregnant woman "clothed with the sun, and the moon under her feet, and upon her head a crown of twelve stars." (Revelation 12:1) The exegesists figured that a crown of twelve stars implied that the woman presumed to be the Virgin Mary, *had* been assumed to heaven. On November 1, 1950, on the basis of such meager retrothinking, Pope Pius XII, proclaimed the dogma of the Assumption of Mary.

The factuality index of Mary, simply as the mother of Jesus of Nazareth, is as high as the latter's, but the Virgin Mary, Queen of the World and Queen of Heaven, is an invention of the Christian religion, especially the Vatican.

Retrothinking in Science

Many of the books that purport to criticize, abrogate or rewrite the Bible use the same exegetical thinking that religious apologists use. (Repeating from Chapter XI: "The interpretation of nonsense [such as the Revelation of St. John] is nonsense. By the same token, the interpretation of speculation is speculation.") A perfect example of retrothinking is found in Chapter 4 of Richard Dawkins' book, *The God Delusion.* Dawkins, an atheist, is an evolutionary biologist who has found his prophet, Charles Darwin, and who repeatedly invokes the latter's favorite mantra *natural selection.* (There's something almost biblical about it.)

Now, natural selection is a great idea. It's unimpeachably logical: only a mutation that strengthens and improves an organism in the context of its environment will advance its evolutionary 'career'. Dawkins firmly believes that astronomical numbers will eventually trump microscopic probabilities and that this is the motor that drives evolution. No matter how infinitesimal the chance of a particular mutation happening, with enough organisms and enough time, it *will* happen.

But we are dealing with change here, and change happens to a pre-existing entity, situation or process. Therefore, mutations and natural selection cannot provide an answer to the existential equation – why is there something? – and cannot absolutely eliminate the possibility that a creator god may be involved.

But the conflict between huge numbers and minute possibilities exists not only in the biological sphere but also in the astronomical one. Life-as-we-know-it can only exist within special, restricted conditions which only hold on planets, and then only on a few planets – perhaps only one. The believers in intelligent design claim this as proof that God loves the Earth and its inhabitants and planned everything to make our eventual appearance on the planet a certainty. Dawkins retorts that since there are many millions of planets in the universe, pure luck can account for the emergence of life on one of them.

On the cosmological scale we find a similar problem. Carbon-based life can only emerge within a narrow band of quite exact values for certain constants, such as the electromagnetic force, the strong force, the electron mass, the proton mass, etc. The fact that our universe is fine-tuned for life is taken as another proof of intelligent design, but Dawkins retorts that if we just postulate that there are a very great number of other universes within a huge multiverse, and that each may have its own set of constants and physical laws – a speculation previously advanced by a few thinkers – then, again, big numbers can trump tiny probabilities. This is a case of scientific *chutzpah* of biblical proportion: there is not a scintilla of evidence for this theory. Deistic agnosticism has not been refuted!

Note how Dawkins retrothinks: He starts with a cherished conclusion, the truth of which he is incapable of doubting – that natural selection explains the existence and evolution of the world – and he retrothinks, looking for probative premises. He ends up accepting as true a pure unsubstantiated speculation. Why is the multiverse conjecture accepted as truth? – Because it justifies the conclusion. The conclusion proves the premises and the premises prove the conclusion.

Chapter IX – The Major Prophets

Prophets were not soothsayers – although they often made predictions. They were not priests – but a few of these doubled as prophets. They were not shamans or miracle workers – although some of them are credited with miracles. They did not prophesy through dreams (visions are not dreams) – but a few of them interpreted dreams.

So what were prophets? – Prophets were like those individuals in business and politics that have no discernable talent but have great connections. Prophets however needed only one connection – Yahweh.

Prophets spoke to God and God spoke to prophets. (The conversation, of course, might take place in the seer's mind, outside the awareness of bystanders). There were no objective criteria to identify prophets: anyone who claimed to be one and found acceptance by kings, priests, and/or the people was one. Sometimes a *coup-de-théâtre*, such as speaking in tongues and dancing in ecstasy, helped gain acceptance. Moses was primarily a dictatorial leader, but he was also a prophet, since he had conversations with Yahweh. So were Joshua and David. Some non-Hebrews were prophets of the Old Testament: Ballam son of Beor, Melchizedek, king and priest of Salem, and the Persian king, Darius. The case can be made for other non-Hebrews. The Bible makes references to many prophets to whom no book is dedicated, for example: Nathan, who prophesized to David regarding the king's adultery and treachery toward his paramour's husband (II Samuel 12) and the prophetess Hulda who passed judgment on the lost scroll during Josiah's reign. (II Kings 22) Many very minor prophets are not even named. These were ad hoc seers who were given their fifteen minutes of fame to deliver a divine message to a King or official and were referred to as "a man of God." (Why they were believed is never explained.)

Other gods also had their prophets. Baal had a whole regiment of some 450 prophets who were killed on Elijah's orders (I Kings 18). Israel also had hordes of seers: the king of Israel summoned 400 of them for consultations during a meeting with King Jehoshaphat of Judah. (I Kings 22)

We have already dealt with the prophets of the books from Genesis to Kings, especially those known as the Elder (or Former) Prophets: Samuel, Elijah and Elisha. These were not only seers but were also king makers who had considerable political power. The prophets we will now be concerned with – the Later Prophets – were more like critics, muckrakers' and whistle blowers than king makers. [Rabbi Joseph Telushkin, in his book *Biblical Literacy*, has quite rightly remarked that Judaism is the only religion that has accepted within its canon writings by authors who, in other religions, would be considered heretics and enemies of the faith.] Nevertheless, many of them have had considerable influence in the religious development of Judaism, Christianity and Islam. Three of them, the *Major Prophets*, are particularly important: Isaiah, Jeremiah and Ezekiel. The others are known as the *Minor Prophets*, twelve in number (thirteen in the Christian Bible, with the addition of Daniel).

The Former and Later prophets lived in different social and political contexts. The first functioned in an Israel that was militarily powerful and at times dominant. The latter worked in a society that was besieged by Chaldean and Assyrian enemies and was either falling apart or straining to pull itself together.

Ezekiel

In order of appearance, Ezekiel is the last of the three major prophets, but we will start with him because, in spite of his strangeness and his weird visions, he establishes a standard profile by which we can measure other seers. Isaiah might have played that role, but he is a melding-into-one of two – probably three – different prophets. As for Jeremiah, he was too irascible and fractious to be a template.

Ezekiel was among the Hebrews exiled during the first deportation to Babylon in 597 BCE. His career started when he received his first vision from Yahweh. He saw four very strange winged creatures, each with four faces, front, back, left and right. Fire danced between them. Other strange objects moving in strange ways filled the vision until the prophet noticed the "semblance of a throne" on which he discerned "the appearance of the likeness of the glory of the Lord." The latter told him to eat a scroll which a hand brought to him and then to go prophesy to the House of Israel (which did not exist at that time except in a dream world).

There followed a series of visions with dreams within them, and dreams with visions within them. The message was one of unspeakable horror to befall the Hebrews as punishment for all their sins, especially their worship of other gods.

An example:

> Moreover the word of the Lord came to me, saying "Also, son of man," thus said the Lord God unto the land of Israel: "An end, the end is coming upon the four corners of the land. Now is your doom coming upon you, and I will send my anger upon you, and will judge you according to what you have done and I will make you pay for all your abominations and I shall not spare you, neither will I have pity: but I will punish you for your ways and for the abominations in your midst; and you shall know I am the Lord. (Ezekiel 7:1-4)

Punishment will be horrible:

> Therefore the fathers shall eat their sons in your midst, and the sons shall eat their fathers; and I will execute judgment against you, and the whole remnant of you will I scatter unto all the winds. 'Wherefore as I live,' said the Lord God, 'Surely because you have defiled my sanctuary with all your detestable things, and with all your abominations, therefore will I also diminish you; neither shall I spare, neither will I have any pity. A third part of you shall die of pestilence, and with famine shall they be consumed; and a third part shall fall by the sword; and I will scatter a third part into all the winds, and I will draw out a sword after them.'
> (Ezekiel 5:10-12)

Ezekiel was transported in a vision to Jerusalem (much like Mohamed was, centuries later) and Yahweh showed him all the abominations displayed in the city and in the Temple: Icons of other gods, Hebrews burning incense to these, men bowing to the sun rising in the east, women bewailing Tammuz, a Babylonian god. As in the rest of the book, the only abominations that concern Ezekiel are those directed at his god, Yahweh, involving other gods, icons, images and, of course, the wicked people of Jerusalem and Judah. Compared to these, murder, rape, fraud, theft, torture, persecution are mere peccadilloes. In fact the perpetrators of these crimes are often doing the Lord's work by punishing the disloyal Hebrews, and are therefore to be commended. That Yahweh was, himself, regarded as merely a local deity can be inferred by his own words in Chapter 11, when the Lord quotes the remaining inhabitants of Jerusalem addressing the scattered diaspora of the House of Israel:

> Keep far from the Lord; the land has been given in heritage to us.
> (Ezekiel 11:15)

The implication seems to be that away from Jerusalem and the surrounding region Yahweh is not God any more. If he were the unique, all-powerful God, would anyone have the audacity to tell people – especially people of Hebrew lineage – to stay away from him? Not only is Ezekiel's god a local deity, but he is a particularly nasty one. In the above visions, he orders a "man clothed in linen" to go throughout the city and mark the foreheads of all the men who denounce the abominations. Other selected men are given a more bloody task:

> Go after him [the "man clothed in linen"] through the city, and smite: spare no one and have no pity: slay utterly old and young, both maids, and little children, and women: but come not near any man upon whom is the mark; and begin at my sanctuary...
> (Ezekiel 9:5-6)

Another indication of the limitation of Ezekiel's god is this sentence, to be found also in other books of the Bible:

> They shall be my people and I will be their God. (Ezekiel 11:20)

In Chapter 20 Yahweh again seems to acknowledge his finiteness, but here he sounds less violent and more conciliatory.

> As for you, O House of Israel, thus says the Lord God: go, everyone of you, and serve your idols, and, if you will not obey me, at least do not pollute my holy name with

> your gifts and your idols. For in my holy mountain, in the highest mountain of Israel, said the Lord God, there shall all of Israel, all of them in the land, serve me …
> (Ezekiel 20:39-40)

The prophet, as Yahweh's mouthpiece, continues to berate the Hebrews (especially other prophets – "false prophets," of course) until Chapter 25, where his ire is shifted to other nations and city-states. These are accused of past misdeeds and retribution is predicted against them: Ammon, Moab, Edom, Philistia, Tyre, Gidon, Egypt. There had always been bad blood between Ammonites, Moabites and Hebrews: no side lacked legitimate claims against the others. But Ezekiel gives strange reasons for prophesizing doom. Because the Ammonites said "Aha" when Yahweh's sanctuary was profaned, and because the Moabites said that the House of Israel was no better than other nations, great desolation is predicted. (Ezekiel 25)

Egypt is fated to endure 40 years of devastation:

> And I will make the land of Egypt desolate in the midst of countries that are desolate and her cities among the cities that are laid waste shall be desolate forty years: and I will scatter the Egyptians among the nations and I will dispense them through the countries.
> (Ezekiel 29:12)

At the end of that period, Yahweh will cause them to return to Egypt where they will be a nation of mediocre importance and power.

None of this ever happened: it was a false prophesy!

About Tyre, Ezekiel was half right. He predicted that Nebuchadnezzar would attack it but would gain no booty and no profit for himself and his soldiers. The prophet then predicted that Yahweh would deliver Egypt to Nebuchadnezzar as payment for his efforts. (The king was doing God's work.)

This is what really happened. Nebuchadnezzar laid siege to Tyre for thirteen years, from 587 to 573, when he finally captured it. He did not destroy it. Later he mounted a campaign against Egypt, but nothing much came of it.

The prophesy was basically false. The only part that was true was the siege of Tyre, but since this lasted from 587 to 573 and Ezekiel's prophetic career was from 593 to 570, the seer was merely predicting the past. His ministry ended two years before the fall of the city, therefore that event is not registered in the book.

It is interesting to note that Ezekiel never vituperated against the Chaldeans, Assyrians and Babylonians, the people who were really beating up on the Hebrews at that time and on whose good will his safety depended, since he was living in Babylonia.

In Chapters 33 to 48 the focus shifts back to the Hebrews (although the poor Edomites still get hammered – Ezekiel just couldn't leave a dead horse alone). Now, however, the prophet looks to the future, predicting a miraculous return of the scattered remnants of the Israelite and Judean diaspora. Yahweh, addressing the mountains of Israel, says:

> ... and I will multiply men upon you, all the house of Israel, all of it; and the cities shall be inhabited, and the wastes shall be rebuilt: and I will multiply upon you man and beast; and they shall increase and bring fruit; and I will settle you as you were before, and you will do better than ever: and you will know that I am the Lord.
> (Ezekiel 36:10-11)

And, speaking now to Israel, the Lord continued:

> For I will take you from among the heathen, and gather you out of all countries and bring you unto your own land.
> (Ezekiel 36:24)

Another vision came to the prophet. He was transported by the hand of God to a valley full of dry bones. Yahweh commanded Ezekiel to order the bones to come to life. And they did.

> And he said to me, O mortal, these bones are the whole House of Israel. [...] Prophesy, therefore, and say to them: Thus said the Lord God: I am going to open your graves, O my people, and bring you to the land of Israel.
> (Ezekiel 37:11-12)

Yahweh further promised that Judah and Israel would be reunited as one nation with one King, which is identified as David – probably meaning a descendant of David, or a king *like* David.

> Thus they shall remain in the land which I gave to my servant Jacob and in which your father dwelt; they and their children and their children's children shall dwell there forever, my servant David as their prince for all time. (Ezekiel 37:25)

The book of Ezekiel ends with a detailed blueprint for the new Israel: the plan and dimensions of the second Temple, the role of the Levites and priests, the liturgy and rituals, and the new allotment of the land to the twelve tribes.

Most of the prophesies dealing with the return of the Hebrews and the future glory of reconstituted Israel were never realized. Of course, many Hebrews did return, but considering that many had been left behind when the elite was exiled and that the latter were given very liberal treatment in Babylon, this return was to be expected. Ezekia's words could be construed as an exhortation more than a prediction. Most of the diaspora from the northern kingdom of Israel did not return; the unification of Judeans and Israelites into one people, under one king, occupying one land never happened; the second Temple was not built according to Ezekiel's plan; and the enduring ("for all time") golden age under one king never became history.

We must keep in mind that all prophetic books were last handled by writers and editors, often years after the lifetime of the prophets, that what is ascribed to one author may be a compilation of the work of a small number of authors writing at different times, and that the writer/editors had the opportunity to delete, change and invent text. What seems like prophecy may just be an instance of foretelling the past. However, when a prognostication deals with time beyond the career of the editor, we have a different situation – and a different rating on the factuality index. Predicting the past is a lot safer than predicting the future, which accounts for the frequent recourse to retrogressive prophesy in religion.

Despite his weirdness, Ezekiel can help us define what we may call the standard model of Old Testament prophecy: first the Hebrews are berated for their disloyalty to Yahweh and their worship of other gods; then their enemies are cursed although their role as the agents of Yahweh's revenge is acknowledged; and finally a "day of the Lord" is prophesized when Yahweh will destroy the enemies and re-establish the "remnant" of Israel safely in the promised land, where they will live happily ever after in complete harmony with their god.

[Note that *Israel* has two meanings: 1) The northern kingdom which ended in 722, and 2) the Hebrew nation as a whole. This second meaning remained in common usage even after the demise of the northern kingdom.]

Surprisingly, it is the weird and magical side of Ezekiel that has been influential. Writers of apocalyptic literature and of fantastic fiction owe him a debt of gratitude.

Isaiah

There is no Isaiah: there are *three* Isaiahs – well, almost certainly two, and very probably three. No one knows the names of the second and third, so scholars call them Second Isaiah and Third Isaiah. To add to the confusion, it is strongly suspected that inventions by unknown writer/editors are present in all three sections. First Isaiah refers to chapters 1 to 39; Second Isaiah to chapters 40-55, and Third Isaiah to chapters 56-66.

First Isaiah

First Isaiah prophesized during the reign of Jotham, Ahaz and Hezekia of Judah, approximately from 740 to 700. Like Ezekiel his first words are reproaches directed at the Hebrews, but unlike the former he is more interested in social justice and honesty than in proper liturgy.

> To what purpose is the multitude of your sacrifices unto me? Said the Lord:
> I am full of the burnt offerings of rams, and the fat of fed beasts;
> And I delight not in the blood of bullocks, or lambs, or she-goats.
> (Isaiah 1:11)

> Cease to do evil; learn to do well
> Seek justice, relieve the oppressed,
> Protect the fatherless, plead for the widow.
> (Isaiah 1:16-17)

Isaiah is incensed at the corruption of the elites:

> The Lord will enter judgment with the ancients of his people and the princes thereof:

For you have eaten all the vineyard;
The spoil of the poor is in your houses
What right have you to beat my people to pieces
And grind the faces of the poor? (Isaiah 3:15)

Yahweh may be angry but he will not abandon Israel:

In that day shall the branch of the Lord be beautiful and glorious,
And the fruit of the earth shall be excellent and comely
For the survivors of Israel
And it shall come to pass, that he that is left in Zion
And he that remains in Jerusalem
Shall be called holy …
(Isaiah 4:3)

Isaiah is very aware of the double-edged sword of Yahweh: he will use the Assyrians to punish the Hebrews but, that done, he will punish the King of Assyria for his pride and arrogance. (Isaiah 10).

The Lord shall not only redeem the remnant of Judah, but will extend his benevolence and protection to other Hebrews, such as parts of the diaspora of the northern kingdom that are dispersed in Assyria, Egypt, Pathos, Nubia, Elam, Shinar, Hamath, and the coastlands. (Isaiah 11)

He shall set up a sign of the nations
And shall assemble the outcasts of Israel
And gather together the dispersed of Judah
From the four corners of the earth.
(Isaiah 11:12)

In the end Israel will be secure and triumphant:

Behold, God is my salvation;
I will trust and not be afraid;
For the Lord Yahweh is my strength and my song;
He also has become my salvation.
(Isaiah 12:2)

Isaiah has a meandering and obscure thought pattern. He jumped from one topic to another with little respect for logic or concern for chronology. For all his esotericism, Ezekiel is easier to follow and understand. After announcing the final victory and permanent security of Israel, Isaiah follows with a series of oracles against old adversaries: Noab, Damascus, Egypt, Tyre, among others. To some, doom is predicated, and to others, hard times followed by redemption. Some of the predictions were obviously false prophesies.

Babylon

The oracle:

> Every one that is found shall be thrust through;
> And everyone that is related to them shall fall by the sword.
> Their children also shall be dashed to pieces before their eyes;
> Their houses shall be soiled and their wives ravished.
> (Isaiah 13:15-16)

The reality:

Cyrus took Babylon without bloodshed. The city was never destroyed, but was gradually abandoned as people moved to other towns, some of which had been built for the soldiers of Alexander the Great.

Egypt

The oracle:

> In that day, Israel shall be the third party with Egypt and with Assyria
> Even a blessing in the midst of the land:
> Whom the Lord of Hosts shall bless, saying
> Blessed be Egypt my people
> And Assyria the work of my hands
> And Israel my inheritance
> (Isaiah 19:20-25)

The reality:

Never happened. Egypt and Assyria never converted to Yahwism. Israel, Egypt and Assyria never formed an axis of virtue.

Tyre

The oracle:

> And it shall come to pass after the end of seventy years
> That the Lord will visit Tyre,
> And she shall return to her business,
> And shall commit prostitution with all the kingdoms of the world
> Upon the face of the earth
> And her merchandise and in her business shall be holiness to the Lord:
> It shall not be hoarded nor laid up;
> For her merchandise shall be for them that dwell before the Lord,
> To eat sufficiently, and for durable clothing.
> (Isaiah 23:17-18)

The reality:

The seaport of Tyre had a long history of being a political concubine to a series of foreign kings and nations, but throughout it kept doing business. During First Isaiah's probable time of prophetic activity, it was besieged by Shalmanezer V and captured by Sargon II (sometime in the last quarter of the 8th century). In 669 BCE, about halfway between the careers of First and Second Isaiah, it capitulated in good terms to Ashurbanipal. This was followed by a century of commercial prosperity. Could there have been 70 years of business recession during all these perturbations? – Possible. Around 325 the city fell to Alexander the Great and thousands of citizens were killed or sold into slavery. Tyre never fully recovered but kept doing business until destroyed by the Muslims in 1291 CE. Could a four-year recession have followed Alexander's victory? – Possible. Could a writer/ editor, decades or a century later have "predicted" such a situation? – Even more possible!

As for the prediction that Tyre, after its economic resurgence, would devote all its profits to the economic welfare of Yahweh's followers: it shows egregious misunderstanding of the nature of the business world! Besides, Tyre had never been controlled by Israel and had never converted to Yahwism.

Chapters 24 to 35 are incoherent and rambling. One moment Isaiah seems to say that Yahweh is for all people, another moment the Lord is only concerned with saving *his* people. Isaiah seems to imply a second coming of Yahweh (on the "day of the Lord") and a revival of faith for Israel, but other nations are sometimes seen as enemies and sometimes as children of the Lord. Something holy and wonderful will happen, but nothing is clear, nothing is really said.

In Chapter 36, poetry changes to prose; the rhapsodic and quasi apocalyptic becomes historical – at least in style. From metaphors and symbols, the focus changes to real people: King Hezekia, King Sennacherib, the Pharaoh. But on reading we get a feeling of *déjà vu*. No wonder! Chapters 36 to 39 are a word-for-word repetition of a part of II Kings starting at Chapter 13, Verse 13 and ending at Chapter 20, Verse 19. Since Isaiah is referred to in the third person, these four chapters are the work of another – perhaps the writer/editor responsible for II Kings. Such is the inglorious ending of First Isaiah.

Second Isaiah

Second Isaiah, the Isaiah of the Babylonian exile, prophesied to promote the idea of a truly monotheistic God and to save for Israel a privileged relationship to that God, and a holy destiny as the future lone superpower.

The chapters are replete with pithy statements in which Yahweh himself tells us he is the only God:

> I the Lord, the first
> And with the last; I am he.
> (Isaiah 41:4)
>
> Before me there was no God formed,
> Neither shall there be after me.
> I, only I am the lord
> And beside me there is no savior (43:10-11)
> There is no God beside me (45:5)
> I have made the earth
> and created man upon it (45:12)
> The creator of heaven who alone is God (45:18)

But Israel remains the chosen people:

Fear not, you worm Jacob and you men of Israel
I will help you said the Lord,
And [be] your redeemer, the Holy One of Israel (41:14)
… I give waters in the wilderness […]
To give drink to my people, my chosen.
This people have I formed for myself;
They shall proclaim my praise (44:20-21)
And I said unto Zion, "You are my people" (51:16)
The Holy One of Israel will redeem you –
He is called God of all the Earth. (54:5)

Israel, prophesied Second Isaiah, will teach all nations the truth of Yahweh the only God:

Behold my servant [Israel] whom I uphold;
My elect in whom my soul delights;
I have put my spirit upon him;
He shall bring forth judgment to the Gentiles […]
He shall bring forth judgement unto truth. (42:1-3)
I will also use you as a light to the Gentiles
That you may bring my salvation to the ends of the Earth
(49:6)

But the Hebrews will exact a price for performing this service:

Thus said the Lord God,
Behold, I will lift up my hand to the Gentiles
And set up my standard to the people:
And they shall bring thy sons in their arms
And your daughters shall be carried on their shoulders
And kings shall tend to your children
And queens shall be your nursemaids:
They shall bow down to you with faces toward the earth,
And lick up the dust of your feet …
(Isaiah 49:22, 23)

But old habits die hard. Yahweh may be the New Yahweh, the creator of everything, the manager of everything, the God of everyone, the author and enforcer of the Law – the universal moral code for everyone and for all times – but the Old Yahweh is still lurking in the shadowy part of the collective Hebrew mind: the old lover of Israel; the old sworn enemy of Baal, Asherah, Milcom, Molech; the grantor of national salvation and of title to land; the old magician. Second Isaiah has not killed this Yahweh. Old habits of mind and old habits of tongue keep inflecting his discourse:

> I your Redeemer, the holy one of Israel (Isaiah 41:14)
> I the God of Israel will not forsake them (41:17)
> The Holy One of Israel, your Savior (43:3)
> I give men in exchange for you
> And peoples in your stead (43:4)
> [I] give drink to my people, my chosen.
> This people have I formed for myself; (43:20-21)
> For I will place salvation in Zion, for Israel, my glory (46:13)

This superposing of New Yahweh and Old Yahweh, first encountered in Second Isaiah has survived the prophet.

Second Isaiah has proclaimed his share of false predictions:

> Put on your beautiful garments, O Jerusalem, the holy city:
> For henceforth there shall no more come into you the uncircumcised and unclean.
> (Isaiah 52:1)

The Persians, Greeks and Roman soldiers, administrators and civilians who passed through Jerusalem or lived there long after the prediction was made were not circumcised. Every year, during the Holy Week, hundreds of Christian pilgrims throng to Jerusalem: most of the males therein are not circumcised.

> Behold, I have created the smith
> That fans the coals in the fire,
> And that produces an instrument for his work;
> And I have created the waster to destroy.
> No weapon that is formed against you shall prosper [succeed];
> [Isaiah 54:16-17]

Only Superman is immune to human weapons, but it seems that Second Isaiah was prophesying that Hebrews would henceforth be invulnerable. No need to disturb the dust of archives to refute this!

Two chapters deserve special mention.

1. In Chapter 45, Yahweh speaks directly to Cyrus, king of Persia, designated as his anointed. This would give Cyrus a quasi-prophetic status, although in Verses 4-5 Yahweh says, "I have called you by your name though you have not known me. I am the lord and there is none else." Yahweh tells the king to rebuild Jerusalem and "let my people go without price and without payment." (45:13) This may seem to be a prediction but, since Cyrus' accession to the throne coincided with the very beginning of Second Isaiah's fifteen year prophetic career, it is likely another prediction of the past.
2. In Chapter 53, a mysterious servant of the Lord is described. The description would seem to be an augury of the coming Messiah (Christ?). The parallel is stunning: like Jesus the servant bears and expiates the guilt of mankind.
   Whereas he bore the guilt of the many
   And made intercession for sinners (53:12)

But the servant is described as appallingly ugly, "beyond human semblance". There is no mention of Jesus being ugly in the Gospels.

The idea that the gods of other peoples have no reality besides the idols of wood, stone or metal that represent them is expressed many times in the Old Testament. This is unfair: many among the heathens were certainly intelligent enough to understand that an icon is merely an arbitrarily designed representation of a spiritual entity (whether it really exists or not) for the purpose of helping the devoted attain a meditative state. If a statue of Baal were the same thing as the god Baal, then each statue would be a different Baal. Certainly, pagans had enough sense to realize that this is crazy.

Third Isaiah

The contrast in style and content between Second and Third Isaiah is not as obvious as that between First and Second Isaiah. The vast majority of scholars agree that First and Second Isaiah represent different prophets – or groups of prophets – but the verdict regarding Second and Third is not so one-sided.

The difference is more one of emphasis than of content: Third Isaiah is less insistent on the uniqueness of God but stresses the universality of his governance. However, he agrees with Second Isaiah that Israel is special in the eyes of Yahweh and is due preferential treatment.

His section of the book, Chapters 56 to 66, starts and ends with the idea that Yahweh is for all peoples and nations.

> Do not let the son of the stranger that has joined himself to the Lord speak, saying,
> "The Lord has utterly separated me from his people."
> [...]
> Their [non Hebrew worshippers] burned offerings and sacrifices
> shall be accepted on my altar
> For my house shall be called a house of prayer for all people.
> (Isaiah 56:3-7)

> It shall come that I will gather all nations and tongues:
> And they shall come and see my glory;
> [...]
> And will send those that escape of them [missionaries?] to all the nations
> [...]
> That have not heard my fame, neither have seen my glory;
> And they shall declare my glory among the Gentiles
> [...]
> And I will also take of them for priests and for Levites, said the Lord.
> (Isaiah 66:18-21)

In between, Third Isaiah can't make up his mind: one moment he militates for the universality of the Yahweh faith, and the next he makes it clear that Israel is the chosen one, special unto the Lord and destined to be the lone superpower, with all the concomitant advantages.

> But the Lord shall arise upon you,
> And his glory shall be seen upon you,
> And the Gentiles shall come to your light,

And kings to the brightness of your rising
[…]
Your sons shall come from afar
And your daughter shall be nursed at your side,
[…]
The abundance of the sea shall come unto you.
(Isaiah 60:4-5)

The prophet has other areas of interest. He rails against Hebrew idolaters but doesn't neglect sins of injustice and oppression:

Is this not the fact that I have chosen
To loosen the fetters of wickedness,
To undo the heavy burdens
And to let the oppressed go free,
And that you break every yoke?
As it is not to share your bread with the hungry,
And bring the poor that are cast out to your house?
When you see the naked that you cover him,
And that you not hide from your own kin.
(Isaiah 58:6-7)

He also faults Israel because "truth is fallen in the street and equity cannot enter."

Third Isaiah gives no credit to the Hebrews for their redemption. As Moses had made clear, Yahweh had chosen the Hebrews of Abraham's time arbitrarily, since they had no particular merit. By the same token the Lord would now redeem them for his own reasons.

And the Lord saw it [injustice] and it displeased Him
That there was no judgement
And he saw that there was no man,
And wondered that there was no intercessor:
Therefore His arm brought salvation unto Him.
(Isaiah 59:15-16)

The role of Yahweh as puppet master is also strongly suggested by these words that the prophet put in the mouth of some non-Hebrew believers:

> You, O Lord, are our father, our redeemer;
> Your name is everlasting.
> O Lord, why have you made us err from your ways?
> (Isaiah 64:16-17)

It seems that God is being blamed for our sins, as though human will were not really free. [Muhammed has the same difficulty: in the Koran it is Allah that decides who is good and who is bad, therefore who will be saved and who will be dammed.]

Third Isaiah had his share of false predictions:

> For the nation or the kingdom that does not serve you [Israel] shall perish;
> Yea, those nations shall be utterly wasted.
> (Isaiah 60:12)

Certainly, Egypt and Rome survived. Also:

> Your sun shall no more go down;
> Neither shall your moon withdraw itself;
> For the Lord shall be your everlasting light,
> And the days of your mourning shall be ended.
> Your people also shall be all righteous:
> They shall inherit the land for ever.
> (Isaiah 60:20-21)

A return to the Garden of Eden, no less! With a guarantee not provided in the original! Without the treacherous apple! Has that second earth paradise manifested itself? Is there a glow on the historical horizon auguring its eventual existence? Are there any facts to ground all this prophetic ebullience? Have Isaiah and Hezekiel any connection to factuality?

Jeremiah

Jeremiah had a long prophetic career: from about 627, through the second deportation to Babylon in 587, and on to an undetermined date after his forcible extradition to Egypt; serving under the reigns of Josiah, Jeoahaz, Jehoiakim, Jehoiachin and Zedekia in Judah, and Pharaoh Neco in Egypt.

The prophet had a profoundly paranoid personality: he railed against everyone and everything, especially his own country and people. For this he was called a traitor and was beaten, empoisoned and half starved.

> His paranoia affected all his actions and statements:
> Oh that I might leave my people and go from them!
> For they are all adulterous, an assembly of treacherous men.
> [...]
> Take heed everyone of his neighbor
>
> And trust not in any brother
> For every brother will utterly betray
> And every neighbor will slander.
> (Jeremiah 9:2-4) (In the Tanakh, 1-4)

Against his Hebrew enemies:

> Therefore deliver up their children to famine and pour out their blood by the force of the sword; and let their wives be bereaved of their children, and be widows; and let their men be put to death; let their young men be slain by the sword in battle. (Jeremiah 18:21)

He was prone to episodes of extreme self pity:

> Accursed be the day when I was born
> Let not the day when my mother bore me be blessed.
> Cursed be the man who brought tidings to my father, saying,
> "A male child is born to you;"
> (Jeremiah 20:14-15)

Jeremiah even felt rejected by Yahweh:

> Will you be toward me as a liar, and as a well that fails?
> (Jeremiah 15:18)

The main sin of the Hebrews, of course, was the worship of other gods – and Yahweh was, indeed, a jealous god. Jeremiah, being paranoid, easily understood Yahweh's resentment, rage, and vengefulness. One may wonder: Is it the Lord's rage or the prophet's rage that is being expressed in the following verses ... or both?

> The children gather wood, the fathers kindle the fire, and the mothers knead the dough to make cakes for the Queen of Heaven [the goddess Astarte] and pour out drink offerings to other gods, that they may provoke me to anger. [...] Behold, my anger and my fury shall be poured out upon the place, upon man, and upon the beasts, and upon the trees of the field, and upon the fruit of the field, and upon the fruit of the ground; and it shall burn, and shall not be quenched.
> (Jeremiah 7:18-20)

But Jeremiah didn't completely neglect sins against man:

> Thus said the Lord: execute judgment and righteousness, and deliver the victim out of the hands of the oppressor; and do no wrong, do no violence to the stranger, the fatherless, the widow, neither shed innocent blood in this place.
> (Jeremiah 22:3)

Like the great majority of prophets; Jeremiah believed that Yahweh would use the devotees of other gods to punish Israel, but that after this punishment had been inflicted, the Lord would then punish the punisher.

> "So, I will bring a nation against you from afar, O house of Israel," said the Lord "it is a mighty nation, it is an ancient nation [...] They are all mighty men and they shall eat up your harvest, and your bread, which your sons and your daughters should eat. [...] They will attack your fenced cities, where you feel secure, with the sword. But nevertheless in those days," said the Lord, "I will not make a final end of you."
> (Jeremiah 5:15-1)

The last sentence is interesting: it reiterates a prophecy in Third Isaiah that Israel, though severely punished, will not be annihilated. After the punishment has been inflicted, the Lord will punish the punisher:

> For lo, I began to bring evil on the city which is called by my name, and should you be unpunished? You shall not be unpunished: for I will call for a sword upon all the inhabitants of the earth, said the Lord of hosts. (Jeremiah 28:29)

There are two points of interest in this thought:

1. Yahweh is punishing people for something that is really *his* doing. ("I began to bring evil on the city…"). [The tension between the infinite power of God and human free will is problematic in all Scriptures, and is most noticeable in the Koran.]
2. The punishment will be meted out to "all the inhabitants of the earth," a collective punishment not unlike, except in scope and provenance, some of the raids of the Israeli military and some of the bombings by American forces. Collective punishment is one of the basic themes of the Old Testament. Even Yahweh, according to Moses (Deuteronomy 5:9) visits "the iniquity of the father upon the children unto the third and fourth generations." But then, had not the Lord already visited the guilt of Adam and Eve's great sin upon every human child of every generation? Note that Moses, in Deuteronomy 24, decreed that "a person shall be put to death only for his own sin." No monotheistic religion has ever settled that question.

Jeremiah often seems to be prophesying for Nebuchadnezzar. For this reason he was considered a traitor by many Judeans and was cruelly persecuted. At one point he was lowered into a pit inside a prison and would have starved to death had not an Ethiopian eunuch from the king's palace interceded for him.

> And to the people you will say, "Thus said the Lord: 'Behold, I set before you the way of life and the way of death. He that remains in this city shall die by the sword, and by the famine, and by the pestilence: but he that goes

> out and surrenders to the Chaldeans that besiege you, he shall live'"
> (Jeremiah 21:8-9)

Small wonder the Judeans didn't consider him a great patriot! He seems to have thought of Nebuchadnezzar as a kind of prophet of Yahweh whose mission was to mete out to Judah its necessary retributions.

> And now I have given all these lands into the hand of Nebuchadnezzar, the king of Babylon, my servant; and the beasts of the field have I given him also to serve him. And all nations shall serve him, and his son, and his son's son until the very time of his land comes, when many nations and great kings will defeat him. And it shall come to pass that the nation and kingdom which will not serve the same Nebuchadnezzar the King of Babylon, and that will not put their neck under the yoke of the King of Babylon, that nation will I punish, said the Lord, with the sword, and with the famine, and with the pestilence, until I have consumed them by his hand. (Jeremiah 27: 6-9)

But Jeremiah still managed – barely – to fit within the pattern best exemplified by Ezekiel. Despite his natural affinity for doom and gloom, he did force himself to write some two thousand words about the day of the Lord, which would bring redemption, peace and security to Israel.

> Thus spoke the Lord God of Israel, saying, "Write down these words that I have spoken to you in a book. For lo, the days come," said the Lord, "that I will bring back from captivity my people Israel and Judah," said the Lord: "and I will cause them to return to the land that I gave to their fathers, and they shall possess it."
> (Jeremiah 30:2-3)

Even good news cannot but be expressed in the habitual vocabulary of the great doomsayer:

> For I am with you, said the Lord, to save you:
> Though I extinguish all nations where I have scattered you,
> Yet will I not extinguish you
> But I will chastise you in measure,

> And I will not leave you altogether unpunished.
> (Jeremiah 30-11)

Despite his dourness the prophet found an utopian corner in his heart:

> I will put my law in their innermost being
> And write it in their hearts;
> And I will be their God
> And they shall be my people.
> (Jeremiah 31:34)

And in Verse 36, Yahweh promised that this blessedness would last as long as the laws of physics stand.

After this uncharacteristic attack of good cheer Jeremiah returned to his comfort zone of doom and gloom. He returned to pouring bile over the Hebrews for their neglect of Yahweh and their dabbling with other deities, giving a double dose to Hebrews who, against his advice, had emigrated to Egypt. He then systematically passed judgment and pronounced dire fate on Egypt, Babylon (and the Chaldeans), Ammon, Philistia, Moab, the Ammonites, Edom, and a number of other cities and nations. In view of his obsequious admiration of Nebuchadnezzar, it is surprising how much wrath he directed at Babylon.

His frustration is understandable: for the time being, at least, Babylon was the clear winner. The Book of Jeremiah acknowledges that by ending with a copy of the tragic conclusion of II Kings: Jeremiah 52:1-27 is identical with II Kings 24: 18 to 25:21. (Note that First Isaiah also ends with a long quotation from II Kings.)

Like many prophets and priests of that time, Jeremiah can't seem to decide whether he's a henotheist or a monotheist.

Sometimes he seems to be a believer in a unique, all-powerful God:

> … Gentiles shall come to you [God] from the ends of the earth, and shall say, "Surely our fathers have inherited lies, vanity, and things wherein there is no profit. Shall a man make gods unto himself, and they are no-gods? Therefore behold, I will this once cause them to know my hand and my might; and they shall know that my name is the Lord.

(Jeremiah 16:19-21)

More often he sounds like a henotheist who has not quite made the leap of faith to true monotheism, as when he uses the phrase, "I will be your god and you will be my people" – which is often repeated in the book. The God of Rabbinical Judaism, Christianity and Islam is by definition, everybody's God: he would never say, "I will be *your* God." Jeremiah was a henotheist or, at best, a monotheist unsure of himself; and when Yahweh speaks through the prophet he sounds unsure:

> Because your fathers deserted me – declares the Lord – and followed other gods and served them and worshiped them; they deserted me and did not keep my instructions. [...] Therefore I will hurl you out of this land to a land that neither you nor your fathers have known and there you will serve other gods, day and night; for I will show you no mercy.
>
> (Jeremiah 16:11-13)

Yahweh himself appears to acknowledge the reality of other gods, although he seems confident that he is the strongest deity:

> The Lord of hosts, the God of Israel, says;
> Behold, I will punish the multitude of No [a local god]
> And Pharaoh, and Egypt, with their gods and their kings;
> (Jeremiah 45:25)

Also, the gods Chemosh and Malcolm, together with the priests and attendants will be sent into exile by Yahweh. In Chapter 50, the latter says:

> Babylon is taken. Bel (god of Babylon) is confounded, Merodack is broken in pieces
>
> Her idols are confounded, her images are broken in pieces.
> (Jeremiah 50:2)

Note that a distinction is made between a god and representations in figures and images of that god!

Free Will

It is curious that the most accusatory of prophets would also be the most deterministic:

> Oh Lord, I know that the way of men is not in himself
> That when he walks it is not he who directs his steps.
> (Jeremiah 10:23)

Also:

> In those days, and in that time, says the Lord
> The iniquity of Israel shall be sought for, and there shall be none
> And the sins of Judah, they shall not be found
> For I will pardon those whom I allow to survive.
> (Jeremiah 50:20)

Yahweh runs the show! It is he who directs the least step we make when we walk. When we sin, it is God's will, and when we practice virtue, it is in accordance with his will. In other words: it is God who sins when we sin and God who is virtuous when we are virtuous. So why does Jeremiah direct so much ire and wrath against us when the moral onus for our sanctions rests with God. There is nothing new here: in Exodus, it is Yahweh who hardens Pharaoh's heart and makes him refuse freedom to the Hebrews (just so Yahweh may flex his muscles and show those Egyptians who's boss). In the previous chapters we have seen how the problem of free will dogs both Third Isaiah and the prophet Muhammad. Later we will realize that Christianity does not escape that trap.

Predictions

There is more to being a prophet than making predictions. Some seers made few. But prediction is the litmus test of prophecy. However, few bother to check the color of the litmus paper. Predictions prove the validity and genuineness of a prophet, and a prophet, being holy, wouldn't lie, would he? And God, being all-good, wouldn't lie to his prophet, would he? So almost every believer accepts that a prediction is a test, and then assumes that the prediction is true. To a critical thinker, however, every unrealized prophecy lowers the factuality index of a prophet's message.

Like Isaiah, Jeremiah made many prognostications that never materialized. A few examples follow.

The prophecy:

> For thus says the Lord: "There will always be a man from David's line to set upon the throne of Israel. And there shall always be someone of the line of Levitical priests before me to offer burnt offerings and to kindle most offerings, and to sacrifice continually.
> (Jeremiah 33:17-18)

The reality:

> The line of David stopped occupying the throne millenniums ago. After the destruction of the second Temple in 70 CE, sacrifice ceased to be part of Jewish worship, and the Levites lost their priestly function and their collective identity.

The prophecy:

> Behold, the days come, says the Lord,
> That the city [Jerusalem] shall be built to the Lord
> From the tower of Hennaed to the gate of the corner
> [...]
> It shall be holy to the Lord:
> It shall not be plucked up nor thrown down any more for ever.
> (Jeremiah 31:38-40)

The reality:

> Jerusalem and the Temple were destroyed by the Romans in 70 CE.

Some forecasts did come true. For example:

> … and I [the Lord] will give all Judah into the hands of the king of Babylon and he shall carry them captive into Babylon and shall slay them with the sword.
> (Jeremiah 20:4)

But the forecasted events occurred in 597 for the first deportation and in 587 for the second, while Jeremiah's career ended in Egypt some years after the second deportation. The seer had an opportunity to foretell the past, and so did the writer/editor who eventually gave the text its final form and included it in the Scriptures. Prophecies that were fulfilled were predictions of the past – a rather safe exercise, but useless as a litmus test for establishing prophetic legitimacy. But taking the above prophecy at face value, there is still a problem with it: the Chaldeans did not "slay with the sword" neither the deportees nor the Hebrews left in Judah. Their domination was relatively progressive.

Christianity has added a twist to past-event predictions: since the Gospels and other early scriptures were not put to paper till years after the death of Christ, writer/editors had the opportunity to make the story of Jesus fit certain Old Testament prognostications that seem to anticipate a Messiah. Back to the future?

As for prognostications into the real future, beyond the manipulations of the prophets themselves, or of the writer/editors that had the final word, that is another story. The three Major Prophets and most of the Minor Prophets predicted a glorious and peaceful future for Israel and for Jerusalem – after the ordeal of retribution – a future in which they would be dominant in the world, under the special protection of Yahweh. Nothing of the sort happened! As predictors of the real future, the prophets were a dismal failure and the factuality index of their prognostications is close to nil.

Chapter X –
The Minor Prophets – Plus Two

Some minor prophets were, indeed, minor; others were quite important. There are twelve of them in the Tanakh, but many Christian writer/editors opine that Daniel belonged to that group, which would give us thirteen.

Abstracting Daniel, the order of the prophets is the same in Christian Bibles and the Tanakh. (We will deal with Daniel separately). The seers are not presented in strictly chronological order: Amos was most probably the earliest, but is placed after Hosea and Joel. Some of the prophets are impossible to date with any accuracy. (For establishing probable and appropriate dates, I have deferred to the judgment of Edward P. Blair in the *Abingdon Bible Handbook*, an honest if somewhat fideistic guidebook.) More important than exact dates and chronological order is the temporal relation between a prophet's active career and the Babylonian exile. Among the Major Prophets, First Isaiah (740-700) was pre-exilic; Second Isaiah (550 6o 535) and Ezekiel (590 to 570) prophesized during the exile; while Third Isaiah (520 to 450) was post-exilic; Jeremia, who just wouldn't quit, spanned the whole Babylonian adventure.

Most of the twelve minor prophets were pre-exilic: Amos, Hosea, Joel, Obadiah, Micah, Nahum, Habakkuk and Zephaniah. Haggai, Zechariah and Malachi were post-exilic. Jonah – he of the big fish – is undatable.

About half of them follow the Ezekiel model: accusations against the Hebrews, followed by a diatribe against Gentile nations (while recognizing their role as the "rod of Yahweh") followed by a prediction of the return to Jerusalem and Judah, and ending with a glowing prophecy of an earthly paradise centered in Jerusalem. Sometimes the order of the first two elements is reversed. The degree of emphasis and the relative importance given to each part of the model varies. Amos, Hosea, Joel, Micah, Zephaniah and Zachariah are fairly close to the Ezekiel model; Nahum and Habakkuk have some points of similarity; but Jonah, Hagai and Malachi fall outside the mold.

Besides the three basic divisions of the model, there are two secondary criteria that can help differentiate the seers.

1. The relative importance of religious formalism versus civic/humanistic values, and
2. The role assigned to other nations in the wonderful post-return world

Let us take a closer look at the more important and interesting of these prophets:

Amos

Amos was an ordinary working man who felt the call to prophesy. He was equally acerbic in his denunciation of Damascus, Gaza, Tyre, Edom, Ammon, Moab, Judah and Israel. He predicted calamity for the Hebrews but didn't mention any exile. Through him Yahweh declared the end of Israel, but added:

> But I will not utterly destroy the house of Jacob
> [...]
> In that day I will raise up the tabernacle of David that is fallen
> And close up the breaches thereof;
> And I will raise up his ruins
> And I will build it as in the days of old.
> (Amos 9:8-11)

The book ends with the hopeful promise:

> And I will plant them upon their land,
> And they shall no more be pulled up out of their land which I have given them,
> Said the Lord thy God.
> (Amos 9:15)

Unless Yahweh meant the nation-state of Israel in modern times (which has still not found peace and stability) this was obviously a false prophesy.

Amos has to be considered one of the great prophets because he was the first to downplay formal religiosity in favor of what we would call today *left-wing values*. Through him Yahweh said, talking of Israel,

> … I will not turn away the punishment thereof;
> Because they sold the righteous for silver;
> And the poor for a pair of shoes;
> They trample into the dust of the earth the head of the poor
> And turn aside the ways of the meek …
> (Amos 2: 6-7)

Yahweh, in his anger will spur their offerings:

> I hate, I despise your feast days,
> And I will not smell in your solemn assemblies
> Through you offer me burnt offerings and your meat offerings, I will not accept them:
> Neither will I regard the peace offerings of your fat beasts.
> Take away from me the noise of your songs
> For I will not hear the melody of your viols.
> (Amos 5:21-23)

First Isaiah (who post-dated Amos) would expand on that theme with even greater poetry, but Amos was the pioneer!

Hosea

Hosea, like Amos, prized virtues and values over mere rituals:

> For I desired mercy, and not sacrifice;
> And the knowledge of God more than burnt offerings.
> (Hosea 6:6)

He was a strange prophet, using his person and life as metaphor. He was ordered by the Lord to marry a prostitute since Israel had prostituted itself with respect to its divine lover, Yahweh:

> And the Lord said to Hosea, "Go, take unto you a wife of whoredoms and children of whoredoms; for the land has committed great whoredom, departing from the Lord." (Hosea 1: 2)

Hosea married Gomer, a prostitute, and she bore him two sons and a daughter.

He seems to have been a henotheist rather than a monotheist. Through him Yahweh said, in a moment of anger, "for you are not my people and I will not be your God" (1:8)

Later, Yahweh will say:

> And I will say to them which were not my people, "You are my people"
> And they shall say, "You are my God."
> (Hosea 2:23)

The concept of a truly universal unique God, creator and lord of all peoples seems foreign to Hosea. He keeps using phrases such as, "for you have gone a-whoring from your God." and, "my God rejects them" and, "you must return to your God" and, "I am the Lord your God from the land of Egypt, and you shall know no god but me."

The prophet never strays from his paradigm: his troubled marriage with a prostitute is a metaphor of the relationship of Israel and its god and, just like the lovers of the faithless wife were real people, the other gods that keep reducing the Hebrews are also real.

But Hosea will take back Gomer and Yahweh will redeem Israel.

Zechariah

Zechariah was at least two prophets – and probably more. Chapters 1-8 were likely the work of one man – let's call him First Zechariah – but, as with all prophets, the text was worked over by later writer/editors. For the sake of convenience, we may call the author(s) of Chapters 9 to 14 Second Zechariah, but this part of the book is likely a mish-mash of two or more writers collated by later editors.

First Zechariah's main concerns were with the completion of the Second Temple and with the promotion of its chief builders Zerubbabel, as a messianic king who would lead Judea to a new age of peace, prosperity and hegemony. This part of the message was received in light visions, all in one night. In one of these, two crowns are made. Zechariah is instructed to place one on the head of Josiah, high priest of Judah, who is told that a branch of the house of David would build the Temple, then sit on the throne and rule. Most scholars think that the second crown and the throne were meant for Zerubbabel, but that since the latter disappeared from history after the rebuilding, editors subsequently erased him out of the vision. As predicting prophecies, the eight visions are a failure, but they have value as reinforcement of two aspects of the book of Isaiah: the universal reach of Yahweh and the generous acceptance of all righteous people into the holy family.

> And many nations shall be joined to the Lord that day,
> And shall be my people.
> (Zechariah 2:11 [2:15 in the Tanakh]

Second Zechariah is inconsistent and often irrational (not surprising, since it is probably a conflation of a number of prophets and writer/editors). In 9:7, the book accepts the remnant of Philistia – a classic enemy of the Hebrews – as a new clan in Judah and as Yahweh worshippers – but in Chapter 11, it rails against Lebanon and Bashan.

In Chapter 14, ten very specific predictive prophecies are put forth: none of them materialized and some were downright preposterous.

1. The capture and ravaging of Jerusalem, the exile, and the survival of a remnant – all of which happened at least 50 years before the start of Zechariah's career – would happen again, as though history would repeat itself;
2. On the day of the Lord, the topography of the land round Jerusalem will be altered. The Mount of Olives will split into an Eastern and a Western part and the "Valley in the Hills" will be stopped up.
3. The day of the Lord shall have no diurnal or nocturnal parts, but would be a twenty-four period of something in-between.
4. From that day fresh water shall flow from Jerusalem to the Eastern Sea and the Western Sea through summer and winter.
5. The Lord shall reign supreme over the whole earth.
6. Jerusalem shall never be destroyed again.
7. A plague will affect all the people that warred against Jerusalem:

> Their flesh shall rot away while they stand on their feet,

> And their eyes shall fall out of their holes,
> and their tongues shall rot in their mouths.
> (Zechariah 14:12)

8. On that day Judah will join in the fighting in Jerusalem, and take vast quantities of gold, silver and clothing from other nations.
9. The same plague that struck the enemies of Judah will also affect their horses, mules, camels and asses.
10. All the surviving enemies of Jerusalem shall make a yearly pilgrimage to the city to observe the Feast of Booths, and any country that neglected this would receive no rain.

Whoever was responsible for allowing this into the canon of the religion was having a bad day at the office. None of it ever came true! *Prima facie*, it sounds crazy, and in retrospect it has proven to be so. Prediction of the results of probative experiments is the classic means of establishing factuality in science. It has been the road linking theory and fact, and it has been a good road. It doesn't work in religion: predictive prophecy has been a dismal failure.

Zephaniah

Zephaniah starts with a Big Bang in reverse:

> I will utterly consume all things from the land, said the Lord.
> I will consume man and beast;
> I will consume the fowls of heaven, and the fishes of the sea
> And the stumbling blocks with the wicked;
> And I will cut off man from the land, said the Lord.
> I will also stretch out mine hand upon Judah,
> And upon all the inhabitants of Jerusalem;
> And I will cut off the remnant of Baal from this place.
> (Zephaniah 1:2-4)

Since Zephaniah was a contemporary of King Josiah, it is hardly surprising that he would take on Baal, who had idols of himself within the very walls of the temple. On "the day of the Lord" – a favorite expression of most Late Prophets – Judah itself shall be devastated, but a "remnant"

– another favorite term – will survive as a holy people who "shall do no wrong." In 3:80-, Yahweh also seems to accept remnants of all nations.

> For them I will give to the people a pure language
> That they may all call upon the name of the Lord,
> To serve him with one consent.
> From beyond the river of Ethiopia
> My suppliants, even the daughters of my dispersed, shall bring my offering
> (Zephaniah 3:9-10)

It is unclear if the people referred to are only the remnant of the Hebrews displaced when the Northern kingdom of Israel was destroyed in 722, or if the remnants of all nations (after the world-wide devastation) are included.

Zephaniah, like the majority of the Later Prophets was an eschatologist, that is, he was concerned with the end of things, of man, and of institutions. But none of the Twelve was an apocalyptist. The difference between an eschatology and an apocalypse is akin to the difference between a black-and-white movie and a Technicolor movie with crazy special effects. Another point of difference is that, whereas eschatologists deal with the future, including death, apocalypses deal with eternity, including resurrection and the afterlife. Hebrews did not believe in resurrection. At death, they held, the soul goes to a dark, gloomy underworld and just stays there in a semi comatose state. Salvation meant salvation of the people, of their culture and religion and of the land – especially Jerusalem. This explains why Gentiles were not usually included in the eschatological model and why apocalypses appeared only at the very end of pre-Christian times. Even at the time of Christ, only the Pharisees believed in the afterlife; the Sadducees, the priests of temple worship, did not. Even today, although Jews believe in life after death, it is seldom mentioned and almost never used as an incentive for being virtuous.

By starting badly with Yahweh's pledge of the total destruction of everything, the book of Zephaniah is almost an apocalypse – but not quite. Daniel would be the pioneer in that domain.

Daniel

The Christian Bibles place the Book of Daniel among the prophetic books, between the three Major Prophets and the twelve Minor Prophets of the

Tanakh. The latter places it among the Writings (*Kethuvim*) considering it *hagadah*, edifying fiction. The Jews have it right: Daniel was not a prophet because Daniel did not exist.

The story is placed in sixth century Babylon during the reigns of Nebuchadnezzar, Belshazzar, Cyrus and Darius, but the writer/editor has Darius succeeding Belshazzar, although historically, it should have been Cyrus. No contemporary would have made that mistake. There are other historical inconsistencies as well as stylistic clues that strongly suggest that the story was written in the second century.

The first seven chapters were written in the third person. They relate the saga of Daniel and three friends who were chosen to be deported to Babylon, where they would be taught the Chaldean language, and exposed to Chaldean culture for three years, so that they may then enter the king's service. Daniel proved to be an able interpreter of dreams, much to Nebuchadnezzar's pleasure. He and his friends were elevated to high positions, but incurred the jealousy of local Chaldean courtiers. When they refused to worship a golden statue, the king, at the instigation of his courtiers, had Daniel's friends – the famous Shadrack, Meshack and Abed – Nego of the well-known Negro spiritual – thrown into a superheated furnace. When the three came out unscathed, the king was impressed with the power of their God and promoted them.

Nebuchadnezzar was succeeded by his son Belshazzar, but Daniel maintained his position and renown. When a ghostly hand wrote three words on the wall of a banquet hall while the king and his courtiers were drinking wine out of the gold and silver cups that had been stolen from the Jerusalem Temple, the king's seers were unable to decipher them but Daniel gave an interpretation that was accepted. Strangely, although the interpretation predicted doom for the monarch, the later "clothed Daniel with scarlet, and put a chain of gold about his neck and made a proclamation concerning him that he should be the third ruler in the kingdom." (Daniel 5:29) – A rare case of a bringer of bad news being exalted.

That night Belshazzar was killed and Darius the Persian took over. (This is a gross error: Cyrus succeeded Belshazzar.) Again, the courtiers conspired against Daniel and convinced the new king to have him thrown into the lion's den. When, the next morning, Darius found Daniel alive and well, he ordered all his subjects to "tremble in fear before the God of Daniel." (In fact, both Cyrus and Darious were very liberal in religious matters, seeming to adopt the gods and practices of whoever in their kingdom they happened to be dealing with.)

The above stories were invented four centuries after the events they purport to relate. They are full of historical mistakes. There is no reason for any critical and rational person to believe them.

Chapters 8 to 12 are written in the first person. They narrate their visions of Daniel. The first describes a battle between a ram with one horn higher than the other, and a one-horned goat. The goat battered the ram, breaking its two horns, but then the goat grew very large and its big horn was broken, being replaced by four horns which sprouted in four directions. One of these horns sprouted a small horn which then grew simultaneously…

> … towards the south, towards the east, and towards the pleasant land. And it waxed great, even to the host of heaven; and it cast down some of the hosts and of the stars to the ground, and stamped upon them. Yea, he magnified himself even to the prince of the host, and by him the daily sacrifice was taken away and the place of sanctuary was cast down and a host was given him against the daily sacrifice by reason of transgression, and it cast down the truth to the ground; and it practiced and prospered. (Daniel 8:9-12)

There is little here that conveys any meaning if we limit the intention of the word *meaning* to its *ratiocinative signification*. The vision is purely visual. Paintings and moving pictures, like music, *do* have meaning, but it is an inner meaning that cannot be verbalized. Verbal description of these artifacts must necessarily convey less meaning than the original object; hence, any interpretation of a dream or vision is suspect.

However, in the vision, Gabriel, described as having a human form and a human voice, offers a vague and partial interpretation. (Most Christians and Muslims probably identify this figure with the Angel Gabriel, although the word *angel* is not used by Daniel.) Since this partial interpretation is part of the vision, it must be given more weight than an interpretation proposed by someone who is not a party in any way to the event.

Interpretations furnished by the dreamer or visionary should also be given this extra weight. The visual and auditory parts of a dream are not the whole dream. Every dream exists in its own dream world and the dreamer knows that world. For example, Figure *x*, in a dream, may be, say, a murderer and the dreamer may know this although there is nothing in the dream to indicate this. Hence, the dreamer is in a better position to interpret his vision than anyone else. (We will return to this point when dealing with the Apocalypse of John.)

The last vision, in Chapters 11 and 12, is more concrete than any other of Daniel. It has *some* meaning and interpretation is therefore more likely to have some significance. It is possible to see it as a prediction by Yahweh of the political and military events linking the Persians, the Greeks and the Israelites. Greece, Moab, Edom, Egypt, Libya are identified by name. Adumbrations of Alexander the Great and Antiochus Epiphanes can be discerned. The sequence of events is plausible. But believers should not exult: working in the second century BCE, the anonymous writer of the Book of Daniel was merely predicting the past.

Although the story of Daniel is nothing but a pious tale with a false prophecy, it has points of interest. For the first time in the Old Testament, the resurrection of the dead, rather than mere maintenance in an eternal coma, is proposed. However, only *some* of the dead will arise:

> And many of them that sleep in the dust of the earth shall awake, some to everlasting life and some to shame and everlasting contempt.
> (Daniel 12:2)

[Of course the prophet Elijah was taken to heaven by a chariot of fire, but he did not die first. This is the only mention, in my recollection, of heaven – in the sense of *paradise* – in the Old Testament.]

It is this reference to resurrection that establishes the Book of Daniel as the first true apocalypse.

The book introduces two figures that would become important to Christians and Moslems: Gabriel and Michael. Although Daniel never uses the word *angel*, there is little doubt that the angels known by those names are the identities referred to.

Although the book is written from a genuinely monotheistic point of view, the hold of ancient polytheistic and henotheistic modes of thinking is not completely broken:

> But in his estate shall he honor the God of Forces: and a god whom his fathers knew not shall he honor with gold and silver and with precious stones, and pleasant things. Thus he will subdue fortifications with the help of

> a strange god, whom he shall acknowledge and increase with glory.
> (Daniel 11: 38-39)

Other apocalypses by other writers followed. For two hundred years or so, the genre was quite popular and was taken seriously. However, the book of Daniel is the only apocalypse included in the Tanakh. The New Testament, of course, accepted one more, the *Revelation of John*, also known as the *Apocalypse*, which was the Christian culmination of a Jewish tradition.

The Revelation of John

It is doubtful that the John of the Revelation was the author of the Gospel of John. Scholars are not sure of his identity.

The book starts with seven short letters dictated to John by an angel and to be delivered to seven angels representing the seven churches of Asia. These are followed by an uninterrupted series of visions requiring some colorful, cascading prose, and one poem. In contrast to the apocalypse of Daniel, here there is no merciful angelic guide to help with inspiration; and here the author doesn't furnish any assistance for the understanding of his artifact.

> By way of example let me quote a few verses from the first vision:
> And immediately I was in the spirit and behold, a throne was set in heaven, and someone sat on the throne. And he that sat had the appearance of a jasper and sardine stone: and there was a rainbow round about the throne, that looked like an emerald. And round about the throne were four and twenty seats: and upon the seats I saw four and twenty elders sitting, clothed in white raiments; and they had on their heads crowns of gold. And out of the throne proceeded lightening and thundering and voices: and there were seven lamps of fire burning before the throne which are the seven spirits of God. And before the throne there was a sea of glass like crystal: and in the midst of the throne, and round about the throne, were four beasts full of eyes before and behind. And the first

> beast was like a lion, and the second beast was like a calf,
> and the third beast was like a flying eagle.
> (Revelation 4:2-7)

What is the meaning of this? Imagine that someone gives you a recording of the background music of a movie about which you know absolutely nothing, and asks you to come up with the script of the film, using no other clue but the music. Impossible, you would say; but the task would be only a little bit more difficult than coming up with an interpretation of the above text that would make sense and impose itself as a plausible and correct interpretation.

From a ratiocinative point of view, *the interpretation of nonsense is nonsense*. [By the same token, *the interpretation of speculation is speculation*.]

Chapter XI – Y H W H

What's in a Name

The god of Israel had many names. It is doubtful that they all referred to the same spiritual entity. According to the *Dictionnaire des noms propres de la Bible* (Éditions du Cerf, Paris, 1999) *Yahweh*, usually spelled YHWH in Hebrew texts, is mentioned 6,800 times in the Old Testament, while *Elohim* is mentioned 2,550 times. *Shaddai*, the name by which the god of the Hebrews first identified itself to Abraham is found 40 times. *Elyôn*, sometimes translated as *the most high*, is used 27 times. *El* is sometimes used as the name of the main god, but sometimes it is a prefix meaning *the god*. Thus, *El-Shaddai* (used 8 times) means *the god Shaddai. El-Roi, El-Alam, El-Betuel, El-Berit and El-Eyon* are all mentioned at least once. It seems that the Hebrews were desperately looking for a special god just for them, but had a difficult time finding, picking and inventing one. To add to the confusion, *Elohim*, used 2,500 times, is a plural form of *El*, which suggests that *the gods* could be a plausible translation.

Most translations of ancient texts conceal this significant confusion by rendering all those proper names for *god*, or *gods*, by *the Lord*, or *God*. Just capitalizing *god* to *God* can change the meaning of a sentence. The worst offenders are those French translations that use the expression *l'Eternel* (the Eternal) to translate *Yahweh, Elohim, a*nd other proper names of the Hebrew deity (or deities). Note that by using the definite article *l'* (the), the suggestion is made that there is only one such deity, and that if there were other pretenders, they would not be eternal. The honor of French translators is saved by *La Bible, Nouvelle Traduction*, published by *Editions du Cerf*. Here *Yahweh* is not translated, and, to boot, the vowels are dropped as they are in the Hebrew text, giving YHWH. No other translation, to my knowledge, has been as honest in treating the proper name of the Hebrew deity (or deities).

It is intriguing that the Book of Genesis starts by using the word *God* eighteen times in the rendition of the creation story. Only in the second – and quite different – account of creation starting, curiously, in the middle of Verse 4 of Chapter 2, is another expression read, *YHWH God*, and only in Verse 4 of Chapter 4 is YHWH used alone.

This suggests strongly that this part of Genesis was written much later than most of the Pentateuch, and written by a number of different writer/editors.

Most scholars – believers and unbelievers alike – maintain that the Hebrews were not originally monotheists. That the populace had a strong propensity for polytheism is made abundantly clear by the Old Testament itself. As we have seen, the writer/editors could not deny it, since spiritual harlotry (going after other gods) was the justification for Yahweh not living up to the promises of the covenant.

One and All

The covenant is the central theme of the Old Testament and the essential part of the heritage it bequested to the New Testament and the Koran. But a covenant is only as good as the characters of its participants and it is therefore necessary to get to know Yahweh as much as the text of the Scriptures will permit. We have already done some of this work but, at the risk of being redundant, I must delve again into the biblical text.

Yahweh's name is used in Genesis before the saga of Abraham. It is found in the story of Noah, yet many generations must have passed before the revelation to Abraham. But, as I have stated, the first pages of Genesis were written centuries later, when the need for an introduction was felt.

Joshua, shortly before his death, assembled all the people and delivered an oration that began with these words:

> Thus said the Lord, the God of Israel, your fathers dwelt on the other side of the flood [beyond the Euphrates] in old time, even Terah, the father of Abraham, and the father of Nachor, and they served other gods.
> (Joshua 24:2)

Note that Joshua did not say "false gods" but rather "other gods;" and that he made no claim that Yahweh was a universal god but rather that the was "the god of Israel." (In all the translations I have read, *god*, is capitalized when referring to Israel's deity, but not when denoting other deities. But that is the work of the translators – an instance of creative translation.) That other gods remained real in the mind of Hebrews is attested by this vow of Jacob – renamed Israel – two generations after Abraham:

> If God will be with me, and will keep me safe on this journey, and will give me bread to eat, and clothes to put on, so that I return to my father' s house in peace, then shall the Lord [Yahweh] be my God. (Genesis 28:20-21)

Hardly the words of a true monotheist! Obviously Jacob thought that there were other gods and that he was free to choose which one would be *his* god. The use of the definite article and of a limiting qualifier such as *of Israel* does not suggest universality:

> "Moreover," he said, "I am the God of your father, the God of Abraham, the God of Isaac, and the God of Jacob."
> (Exodus3:6)

At no point in the Torah does Yahweh claim to be the unique, universal God of all creation and of all peoples. In fact, through the mouth of Moses he does the opposite:

> … against all the gods of Egypt I will execute judgment,
> of the Lord.
> (Exodus 12:12)

Would Yahweh execute judgment against something that doesn't exist? In Deuteronomy, preaching the law to the assembled nation, Moses said:

> … and when you see the sun, and the moon, and the stars, even all the host of heaven, do not be tempted to worship them, for the Lord your God has divided them unto other nations under the whole heaven.
> (Deuteronomy 4:29)

Here Moses seems to be proposing that Yahweh is the strongest god, probably the leader of all the gods, and that he has allotted other gods to other nations, saving the Hebrews for himself.

In his last homily the prophet reminisces about Yahweh's guidance of his people through the desert:

> So the Lord alone did lead him [Israel] and there was no strange god with him. (Deuteronomy 32:12)

To be fair, there are a few verses that deliver a more monotheistic message, such as Deuteronomy 4:34-35: "To you it was demonstrated that you might know that the Lord he is God: there is none else beside him."

Considering the context of other statements of Moses about Yahweh, this seems a tad too forthright an affirmation of monotheism: I suspect a ham-fisted intrusion by a later editor. For more than a millennium the Hebrew people kept flirting with monotheism without really practicing it. As for the priests and prophets: most of them were henotheists who worshipped only Yahweh, but didn't deny the existence of other gods. By the same token, some foreigners also believed in the existence of Yahweh and sometimes worshipped him along with their own gods.

Almost 400 years after Moses, King David, reputed through the ages as the most loyal and steadfast Yawist of all the kings, seems to have accepted the existence of other gods. Hectoring the Philistines he said, "All the earth shall know that there is a god in Israel" (I Samuel 17:46) implying that other gods existed and had elected domicile in other places.

Talking to Saul about the latter's attempts to have him killed, he complained bitterly:

> … for they [Saul's men] have driven me out this day from sharing in the inheritance of the Lord saying, "Go serve other gods."
> (I Samuel 26:19)

Since the days of Moses, household idols were considered an abomination, and their worship was punishable by death. Yet, there was at least one such idol in David's household, and his wife, Saul's daughter Micha, used it to save his life. Saul had sent some men to David' s home to kill him. Micha, who was aware of the plot, let her husband out a window, placed a household idol in his bed, covered it with a blanket, and put a net of goats hair on its head. (I Samuel 19:13)

At times it seems that Yahweh was perceived as a particularly powerful god, or as the chief god, or as the father of the other gods, as instanced in Psalms 82:

> God stands in the congregation of the mighty;
> He judges among the gods.

And later, in the same psalm:

> I have said, "You are gods
> And all of you are children of the most High,
> But you shall die like men,
> And fall like one of the Princes.

The most thoroughgoing monotheist of all the prophets was Second Isaiah, yet even he often blundered into locutions reminiscent of the old polytheism, as we have seen in Chapter VIII. Sometimes he contradicts himself in a single sentence:

> For your redeemer [is] the Holy One of Israel;
> The God of the whole earth shall he be called.
> (Isaiah 54:5

Certainly, Second Isaiah, though truly monotheistic, wasn't ready to abandon the privileged position of Israel as God's preferred child.

A Biblical Profile of Yahweh

Since Yahweh was a strongly anthropomorphic god, he must have had a personal character. What kind of god was he?

From the ethical point of view he was off to a bad start from the very first line of the Bible. When Adam ate of the forbidden fruit, God visited his guilt upon all his descendants, for all time – hardly fair toward all of us. Later, in Deuteronomy, he relented a little, limiting the duration of his other maledictions to four generations:

> … for I the Lord your God am a jealous God, visiting the iniquity of the fathers upon the children into the third and fourth generations …
> (Deuteronomy 5:9)

Later still, in the New Testament, the Christ, through his blood sacrifice, redeemed mankind further – but it was only a partial redemption: man was still denied the blessings and advantages of the Garden of Eden.

[To be fair: Moses did say that parents shall not be put to death for the sins of their children, nor children for the sins of their parents (Deuteronomy 24:16) – a principle sometimes observed in the breach.]

Before the Babylonian Exile, Yahweh was thought to be the source of both good and evil. He had a satanic side, which explains why Satan is not mentioned until after the return.

There are many references to Yahweh's unholy side. He was often cruel, vengeful and violent (see Chapters 1 and 3). He ordered Moses, Joshua and others to kill thousands and at times specified that women and children were not to be spared. For instance: Because the Amelikites had harassed the Hebrews during their exodus from Egypt, some generations ago, Yahweh ordered Saul to attack Amelek and kill all that breathes. Saul spared Agar, the king, and took the best sheep and oxen as spoils. (See, Chapter 1) For this Yahweh rejected Saul as king and chose David to replace him.

Unlike later conceptions of God, Yahweh was not infallible. In Samuel 15, Verses 10-11, he tells Samuel, "I regret that I have set up Saul to be king: for he has turned back from following me and has not performed my commandments." There are other occasions when he expressed self-doubt and regrets. Also, when he replaced the stone tablets of the commandments, which Moses had shattered, he couldn't remember what had been written on the original pair and came up with a different set of laws. (Compare Exodus 20 with Exodus 34)

The Lord was represented as extremely vainglorious. He multiplied the plagues of Egypt, it seems, just as much to show off his power as to free his people. His own words are witness to this divine vanity:

> For I will at this time send all my plagues upon your beasts, and upon your servants and upon your people; that you may know that there is none like me in all the earth … And I have spared you [from annihilation] to show through you my power; and that my name may be declared throughout all the earth.
> (Exodus 9:14-16)

Also:

> Then I will stiffen Pharaoh's heart and he will pursue them [the Hebrews] that I may gain glory through Pharaoh and all his hosts: and the Egyptians shall know that I am the Lord. (Exodus 14:4)

The ancient Hebrews did not paint a flattering picture of their god: he was unfair, mean, violent and vindictive. He assigned guilt by association and practiced collective punishment. For a god, he made too many mistakes. He was inconsistent, ordering his devotees to break the sacred, eternal code that he had imposed upon them. He seems to have been insecure, requiring, as he did, the obedience and adoration of a primitive people to ensure his psychological well-being, and needing to show-off his power to bolster his self-esteem. He was not always honest and truthful, as when he sent a "lying sprit" to entice king Ahab of Israel into a deadly trap. (I Kings 22:22-23)

Oneness

By the time Jesus Christ had come on the scene, Yahweh had 'morphed' into a very different entity than the one just sketched. The transformation was gradual: it is impossible to determine with any accuracy when the Hebrew people, who worshipped a particular deity to the exclusion of other equally real gods, became Jews who worshipped the one-and-only God of Rabbinic Judaism, Christianity and Islam. Much of the transformational process took place during the intertestimentary period, a poorly documented span of some 400 years between the books of Ezra and Nehemiah, and the earliest New Testament documents.

Plato

Priests, political leaders, military heroes, all played their part in the evolution of the polity and religion but, with the possible exception of Daniel – if he exited at all – there were no prophets during that period. One man, though, stepped into the breach. He was not Jewish, nor a resident of Palestine; and he never suspected that he would play a major role in the development of three religions – a role at least as important as that of Ezekiel, Isaiah or Jeremiah.

Plato was one of the great God inventors. I am not using the word *inventor* to belittle the philosopher: since his concept was of an ineffable, unknowable entity, the only way to approach that entity was to invent it.

(Some inventions are better than others; some models are closer to their object than others). Plato's invention has had a long and fruitful career. He named it the *One*: a pure spirit without qualities, faculties or any predicate that could in any way be abstracted from the one, simple, homogeneous, integral being. The One can have no passion; no likes or dislikes. It is mind, but has no distinct ideas that can be abstracted form its activity. In fact, since activity can be analyzed into separate incidents, the One cannot perform any activity.

Plato was born in 428 and died in 348 BCE. In 387 he founded a school, The Academy, which accepted students of all philosophical orientations, and remained active until at least 128 BCE. During that time Alexander the Great conquered most of the known world. After his death his generals divided his empire. Most of the world became, to some extent, Hellenized. Jews of the diaspora as well as Judeans were in constant contact with Greek culture. It's reasonable to assume that they were exposed to Platonic theology and that the concept of the One may have been a strong influence on their journey to true monotheism.

Antiochus IV Epiphanes

Another Hellenistic influence was more negative: Antiochus IV Epiphanes, who ruled over Palestine in the first half of the second century considered himself an avatar of Zeus and tried to impose the cult of his person, going so far as to install a statue of himself in the Temple. He oppressed cruelly those who objected to this, which soured the Jews against any form of idolatry, and was the main incentive for the Machabean revolt.

Philo of Alexandria

Alexandria was the home to one of the largest Jewish communities of the diaspora. Most of those Jews spoke no Hebrew, but expressed themselves in Greek and Aramean. Philo, the father of Hebrew theology and the first Jewish philosopher, was one of those Hellenized Jews. He was strongly influenced by Plato, the Stoics and Aristotle. His primary mentor was Plato, as can be evidenced by this statement of his God concept: "the pure and unsullied Mind of the universe, transcending virtue, transcending knowledge, transcending the good itself" (quoted in *The Encyclopedia of Philosophy*, published by McMillan).

But Philo was also a devout Yahwist who believed that Moses wrote the entire Torah (Pentateuch) under the direct inspiration of Yahweh. His attempt to prove that everything Plato wrote had been adumbrated, or at least strongly hinted, by Moses required considerable parsing and recourse to imaginative allegories. It was an impossible task. Philo was not a great philosopher, but he was one of the most influential. His melding of Platonic theology with the earthy and anthropomorphic Hebrew conception of the divine created the basic God concept of three major religions: Rabbinical Judaism, Christianity and Islam.

Old Yahweh, New Yahweh

The god of the ancient Hebrews – let's call him *Old Yahweh* – was an incorporeal superman who had entered into a special and exclusive partnership with a people, and who actually lived in a Temple this people had built for him. He was not a particularly admirable superman. As we have seen, he was jealous, vindictive and savagely cruel; he was deceptive; he was vainglorious, he was far from infallible; and he was arbitrary and capricious. From the point of view of the ancient Hebrews, however, he was a quite competent deity. They were not a philosophically sophisticated lot; they had never racked their brains over such abstract concepts as transcendence, immanence, infinity, contingency and necessity.

Philo's God – New Yahweh – was a completely different kind of entity. He was both transcendent and immanent: he was an entity absolutely distinct from the world, yet he managed the world down to the smallest details. Through his providence he sustained his creation and kept it from returning to chaos or nothingness by maintaining the sovereignty of the natural laws he had drafted. Yet he could – and sometimes did – override these laws by performing miracles. He had revealed himself to humanity and had imposed a strict moral code. This was the God of Philo; this is the God that the three monotheistic faiths still worship today. The only significant addition has been the dogma of creation *ex nihilo*: the Greeks and most Jews believed that matter had always exited in a chaotic state, until God imposed order upon it; St. Augustine (354-430) held that the cosmos was created from nothing and this view has been accepted by most theists.

One Name, Two Gods

The main intellectual flaw in the Old Testament is this: it starts with one concept of god and ends up with a completely different one, but because it keeps the same name, Yahweh, for both gods the fundamental transformation is never noticed, and therefore never acknowledged. This error is passed on like the baton in a relay race to the three monotheistic faiths.

It is a case of what logicians call a *category mistake*: applying to entities of category *A*, say, predicates that are applicable to entities of category *B*, but that are meaningless in category *A*. One example would be a statement such as, *the oyster is impeachable*: oysters do not belong to the category of things that can be impeached. The statement is neither true nor false; it is nonsense. Old Yahweh was just another Mesopotamian god, like Baal, Marduk, Ashoreth, El, Dagon, Molech, Milcom, etc. It belongs to the same category as those other gods. No one believes anymore in the real existence of these gods: their factuality index is nil. There is no reason why the one called Yahweh should be an exception. But the incredibility of Old Yahweh does not necessarily carry over to New Yahweh, the God of the three monotheistic religions. Existential judgments regarding the factuality of New Yahweh and those regarding Old Yahweh are independent of each other.

The Covenant

This ontological independence has great implications, especially in regard to the meaning and validity of the covenant.

As used in the Bible, the word *covenant* has many definitions: it can mean a promise, an understanding, or a more or less formal contract. The first covenant, between Yahweh and Adam and Eve, was a simple understanding: "Enjoy the Garden of Eden, but don't eat the forbidden fruit." No penalty was stipulated, but the first human couple found out soon enough that disobedience had dire consequences. The second covenant – announced to Noah after the Flood – was a mere promise made by Yahweh, not to a person, a people, or a species, but to "all flesh," that is, to all living things, that doom and annihilation would never be visited upon earth again.

With Abraham we have something approaching a formal contract between two parties. Abraham will worship Yahweh exclusively and seal the deal by circumcising himself and all his people, in return for which he and his descendants will inherit a promised land: the land of milk and honey, the land of the Canaanites.

Moses was the only human to enter into a detailed and partly written contract with Yahweh. Of course he entered it as the leader and representative of the Hebrews: the covenant was always understood as a contract between Yahweh and the Hebrew (later, Jewish) people. It couldn't be between Yahweh and the individual Hebrew, since Hebrews of that time did not believe in the resurrection of the dead, hence, salvation could only be promised to the collectivity, not to the individual.

The Decalogue (the Ten Commandments) is a summary of the essential elements of the Hebrews' obligations according to the agreement. The original Decalogue was inscribed on two stone tablets which were given to Moses during the forty days and nights that he spent with Yahweh on Mount Sinai (Exodus 20). These were the tablets that Moses angrily shattered when he saw the golden calf that Aaron had made.

In forty days Yahweh had time to give instructions much more detailed and extensive than the Decalogue. Chapters 21, 22 and 23 of Exodus is a code of civil, criminal and religious laws that have some analogue to the Babylonian Code of Hammurabi, which preceded the Mosaic code by some six hundred years.

In Chapter 34 of Exodus, Yahweh summons Moses to return to Mount Sinai to receive a copy of the original tablets:

> And the Lord said to Moses, "Hew two tables of stone like the first: and I will write upon these tablets the words that were in the first tables that you broke."
> (Exodus 34:1)

Yahweh's memory, however, failed him as the second version is quite different. For one thing, it contains eleven, not ten commandments. Only three from the original list are included. Two laws in the second version establish procedures and dates for religious feasts; nothing of this was in the original. Two more laws were about bringing offerings to the temple (which would benefit the priests) but no mention of this is found in the first version.

Chapter 19 of Leviticus has another Decalogue-like list of laws, but this time there are nineteen items, including dietary rules not previously included.

In Chapter 5 of Deuteronomy, we find another restatement, but this time it's an almost exact replica of the original.

The idea of the covenant, in all its versions, aspects and entailments, is especially dominant in Exodus, Leviticus and Deuteronomy. Its prominence continues through the subsequent books of the Old Testament. It is constantly referred to; kings, high priests and prophets reaffirm it and rededicate the people of Israel to it repeatedly. The most noteworthy ceremony was David's rededication during the enthronement of the Ark of the Covenant in Jerusalem.

None of these restatements add anything: Abraham and Moses cover the concept quite adequately. The former, for all his terseness, establishes the Yahweh side of the exchange of obligations: in return for worship, sacrificial rituals and the ablation of the foreskin, Yahweh will protect, assist in warfare, give territorial rights to land occupied and tilled by other peoples and, in the struggle to seize that land, give dispensation regarding the most grievous crimes and moral outrages. This has all the characteristics of a contract and is signed (in both senses of the word) by the ablation of the foreskins.

The actions of Moses show him to be very aware of the Abrahamic rights and dispensations, but his rhetoric is focused on the obligations imposed on the Hebrews by the covenant.

That word is used so often that it loses much of its force. Any statement that implies the existence of a personal God that has some relationship with some humans falls under the rubric of *covenant.*

There are two Yahwehs in the Old Testament. Which deity is the god of the covenant? Certainly, the god of Abraham was Old Yahweh, the Semitic deity who shared that status with El, Baal, Molech, Milcolm, Ashtoreth, etc. Although Moses is accredited in the Scriptures with a few statements that seem to lean toward monotheism, other statements of his imply henotheism. Certainly, the Hebrew people, as evinced by the Golden Calf incident, were polytheists, and even the prophet's brother, Aaron, was complicit in that incident.

Our examination of convenental history has furnished another argument for the view that Old Yahweh was not the classical God of the 3Rs (the three monotheistic religions). Would an infinitely wise and all-knowing God have forgotten the ten commandments of his original Decalogue and come up with an almost completely different "duplicate"?

It is important to my argument here to ponder again the ontological status of Old Yahweh (ontology is the study of the meaning of *to be*). He was, as I previously argued, an incorporeal superman. The priests and prophets tried to give him a special spiritual character by proscribing any iconic representation of him. But icons, as long as they are construed as a non-representational symbol and as a mere aid to meditation, do not cheapen the spiritual conception of a deity; but anthropomorphism (ascribing human qualities to non-human things) does just that. Old

Yahweh is as anthropomorphic a conception of the divine as are the gods of the Semitic, Babylonian, Greek and Roman pantheons. All such gods are creatures of the magical imagination. Before they acquire spiritual and religious dimension they are magical objects. The only real thing about them is their name, which acts as a hook on which can be hung legends, powers, images, and whatever predicates the imagination is capable of inventing. In our comparatively and partially enlightened age, no sensible person believes that such entities have a real existence in any realm except the human mind. In this respect they are on par with Superman. There is no reason to make an exception of Old Yahweh.

The One of Plato, on the other hand, is a fundamentally different concept. We can't prove its existence, but we can't disprove it either. Even New Yahweh, the God of Philo, despite the problematic melding of transcendence and immanence, is a nobler concept than Old Yahweh.

What kind of covenant can one make with something that doesn't exist? – A covenant that is just as real as the entity that supports it. If that entity is an invention, then the covenant is an invention! If that entity is a mental object, then the covenant is a mental object and no more. The covenant with Yahweh has no factuality and no validity: there is no logical mandate to believe in it. The same can be asserted of its main corollary: there is no reason to grant any validity to the notion of the promised land.

[Personal Note: In my youth I went under the knife twice (in those days the knife was held by a surgeon, not a street-gang member), once for an infection around the nails of two fingers and once for an appendectomy. Both operations were performed by an old college buddy of my father, Dr. Larocque. Sometime later my father and I made a social call on the doctor. He took us down to the basement of his house to show us his hobby.

Amazing! The whole basement, except for the area reserved for the furnace and the water heater, was taken up by a huge model train set – in fact it could, without much exaggeration, be called a train world. Trains crisscrossed highways and tracks, crossed rivers, climbed mountains, passed towns and stations, and skirted obstacles such as the furnace and the water heater.

I wondered: what if Dr. Larocque fell asleep? What would happen to his train world? – It seemed to me that it would just keep running according to the program invented and imposed by the doctor.

What if there was a glitch in the program and two trains were headed for a collision or a short circuit set one of the villages on fire? What would the doctor do? – Nothing as long as he was sleeping – although he could later repair the damage. But if he woke up in time to realize what was happening, he could turn off the current, or lift one of the locomotives off the track, or spray some fire extinguisher on the burning village, and the little people of the train world would shout, "It's a miracle, It's a miracle."

And, or course, Dr. Larocque could always, at his leisure, arbitrarily change the design of his creation: move a village, reroute tracks, and so on.

It wasn't till decades later that I realized that Dr. Larocque just might be an avatar of the God of Philo. Small wonder that the surgeries went well!]

Powers of One

Many religionists of a mystical bend subscribe to various systems of computation wherefrom Biblical words and phrases are assigned numbers that can then be used to devise secret codes to enter into the mysteries of interpretation.

It's not necessary to delve into the occult for our perusal of the role of numbers in religion: we will deal with just one number, the number *one*. *Prima facie*, it has special properties such as being the only number that's a factor of any other number. Even in grammar, *one* is special. All other numbers have the same rules, the grammar of plurality, but *one* has a set of rules just for itself, the grammar of singularity.

These peculiarities, however, do not interfere with the lives of individuals or the functioning of collectivities and institutions, but into the mathematical and philosophical realm of singularity-plurality religion has brought war.

This war was started by the singularity side: the monotheists and henotheists, but only those whose God is partly transcendental and partly immanent, that is, the God of Philo (from which we get the adjective *Philonian* and the nouns *Philonist* and *Philonism*). The One of Plato and the Prime Mover of Aristotle, not being involved with the working of the material world cannot be a cause of war. (But once the religionists got involved they managed to invent the theology of emanations and other concepts to drag the deity down to our level.) The conflict was between the Philonists of the three convenantal religions and various devotees of Middle-Eastern, Indu and Amerindian gods. It was – and is – an unfair battle: most polytheists respect and accept other peoples' gods and rituals, while Philonian monotheists are generally quick to defame, oppress and even kill those evil heathens (pagans, idolaters).

Why? Why should those who believe in one god beat up on those who believe in two or more? If I believe in two gods, does that justify you – who believe in one – aggressing me? And if, instead, I believe in no god, am I hurting you? Am I hurting your god? And just because, say, I have physical representations (icons, statues) of my gods, do I deserve to die?

The only rationale for Philonians oppressing pagans would be that:

> their god's factuality is absolutely established,
> this god is cruel, unjust and vainglorious, and
> he commands that his devotees fight his battles here on earth.

Is it any wonder that the Philonists have repeatedly perpetrated crimes against humanity?

What makes all of this difficult to comprehend is that the various positions are far from being clearly defined and distinct. What the Christians call angels and saints, many pagan religions call gods. Most polytheistic religions have a hierarchy of gods with, at their head, a supreme sovereign, such as Zeus for the Greeks and Jupiter for the Romans. Couldn't both the Greek and Roman religions be considered monotheistic? The most fundamentally monotheistic of the Philonian religions is Islam; yet even Muslims have angels and dijins as minor gods (in the sense that pagan religions use the term). The Koran says that Allah doesn't need helpers, but aren't Jibril and Mohammed themselves helpers of Allah?

The later is as vainglorious as Yahweh:

> The worst of the major sins for Allah on judgment day will be: polytheism, the murder of an innocent believer, desertion on the day of fighting for the cause of Allah, and disobedience's to parents.
> (Abbas Ahmad al-Bostani, *Recueil de Hadiths du Prophète*, Publication de la Cité du Savoir, my translation of the French translation – sorry about that.)

Note that Allah, according to the Hadith, considers worship of, and belief in other gods to be a worst sin than murder. (Note also that murder of non-believers is not even mentioned.)

Of course polytheists have also committed their share of atrocities, including human sacrifices, but there is no historical record of large-scale crimes against humanity on their part. What they are guilty of is childishness, which explains why very few logically thinking moderns take them seriously. All these products of the magical imagination, filling the mind like children with indulgent parents fill their toy boxes: the gods of the Greeks, Romans, Aztecs, Africans; the Elephant god and the Monkey god of the Hindus – the list is almost interminable. Even children have no need for these, having access to *Pokeman*, *Dragon Ball*, *Injyasha*, and other cartoons that have replaced the humor of *Bugs Bunny*, *Daffy Duck* and *Dudley Do-Right* with magic and "mysterious" powers. Polytheism has burdened us with excess baggage we don't need, but the harm it may have done pales alongside that done by the three monotheistic religions in their quest for the rewards of the covenant. Where the former has been childish, the latter have been downright murderous, killing, in periodic fits of barbaric rage, millions of innocents. (This will be covered in later chapters)

Apologists will point to the millions of innocent victims of Nazism, Soviet communism and Chinese communism as if these outrages exculpated the great religions. Hitler, responsible for about 6 million snuffed lives, was not a particularly religious man, but he did write in *Mein Kampf* that he believed that by attacking the Jews he was "doing Gods work." Certainly, only centuries of Christian anti-Semitism could have created a social and political situation in which a mass killing of the magnitude of the Holocaust could have been possible. (Note that Hitler remained a Catholic all his life and was never threatened with excommunication or other sanctions.)

As for Communist outrages they were more the results of stupid and heartless programs than of targeted killings, although this in no way exculpates the communists. What they illustrate is the inclination of all obsessional ideologies to slide into episodes of murderous extremes. The plurality of their objects of worship prevents polytheists from descending into such monomania.

Nice God, Mean God

Old Yahweh was a mean God, dispensing plagues, droughts and disasters of all kinds, commanding his devotees to kill man, woman and child, burn cities and appropriate houses and fields. He not only punished his enemies cruelly, but also his own devotees when they didn't live up to his expectations.

Jesus preached a nice God, a god of love. But this Christian God (also, later, the Muslim God, Allah) merely replaced terror in this world by terror in the world-to-come. The Hebrews simply didn't believe in the afterlife. Later Jews did, but generally limited the stay in the abode of punishment, Geheenon, to 12 years. Geheenon was more like the Christian purgatory than like Hell. The Christians and Muslims made eternal punishment one of the core elements of their theology. Catholicism invented the Sacrament of Penitence (confession) to give itself the keys to both Heaven and Hell. The phrase "Outside the Church, there is no salvation," though not interpreted literally by all clerics, has been used till recently as a very successful instrument of mind control. Excommunication was even more terrifying and was more effective against emperors and top leaders. Muslims were not spared the terror. Referring usually to those who did not accept the Koran, Mohammed repeatedly used the phrase. "A painful doom awaits them."

Why would the priestly cast paint such a negative portrayal of God, depicting him more as an ogre or demon than as a noble champion of justice? – The reason is that clerics and prophets have collectively assumed the role of mediator and intercessor between God and humanity and that portraying God as a terrifying and menacing deity enhances their importance in the minds of individuals and their authority in society.

Who needs intercessors if God is a kind and friendly being?

Chapter XII – The New Covenants

In the Christian Bible, the term *New Covenant* refers to the new relationship between God and man as testified to by Jesus Christ, not only in words, but in blood – the blood of Jesus on the cross, and the blood of the Eucharist. For many authors, the terms *New Covenant* and *New Testament* are interchangeable.

But before the new Christian covenant there was a new Jewish covenant – in fact, two new Jewish covenants. The first is the one that Yahweh promised to write in the hearts of the people of Israel and Judea:

> Behold the days come, said the Lord,
> That I will make a new covenant
> With the house of Israel and with the house of Judah:
> Not according to the covenant that I made with their fathers
> [...]

But this shall be the covenant that I shall make with the house of Israel;

> After those days, said the Lord
> I will put my law in their inward parts,
> And write it in their hearts
> And I will be their God
> And they shall be my people.
> (Jeremiah 31:31-33)

Other prophets have expressed similar thoughts, but not as clearly and passionately as Jeremiah. These seers had one thing in common: they thought that the Yahwist religion was too formalistic and ritualistic and they militated for a more personal, honest, and committed kind of worship. What Jeremiah called a "new covenant" was really a new attitude towards the old covenant, but the change was important: it adumbrated the Protestant attitude towards the covenant by individualizing what had been a collective alliance. (It didn't, however, go all the way: there was no hint of personal salvation in the Christian sense.)

There was another new Jewish covenant. It was more profound and transformative than Jeremiah's, yet it is never alluded to in the Old Testament. Its existence is due to a simple logical entailment: as Old Yahweh 'morphed' into New Yahweh, the very sense of any covenant between the deity and the Hebrew people had to change. A man cannot enter into the same compact with his dog and his wife: "I feed you and you guard my property and help me hunt game" cannot be the basis of a good marriage.

In fact, it is difficult to think of a covenant one can make with Plato's One – or even with Philo's syncretic God. A deal between an underemployed local deity and a small wandering group of tribes makes some kind of sense: "I will deliver unto you a promised land, and you will worship me exclusively and fight other gods, my adversaries." But once the Hebrews, influenced by Greek philosophy, attained the conception of a truly unique – though personal – all-powerful God, the covenant becomes difficult to formulate. The only deal one can make with an all-powerful being is a variant of the deal one can make with a hold-up man: "I give you my money and you don't shoot me."

The problem is that it's difficult to find a currency of exchange with an infinite being. The Christians did find a way to compensate God for his gift of salvation by their missionary work, but Jews, downplaying individual salvation, and concerned with the prospect of losing their privileged position as the chosen people, have generally not proselytized.

"I will be your God and you will be my people" is the most often repeated mantra of the Old Testament. In a polytheistic context there is nothing particularly racist about that statement: one of many gods makes a deal with one of many peoples, leaving other gods and other peoples free to make deals. But in a strongly monotheistic context, the implication is unavoidable that one people is privileged by the God of the universe and is therefore superior to other groups. The chosen people can have special rights, special moral dispensations and special title to land. Unless one can conclusively claim that there *really* is such a God, and that he has *really* chosen a particular people for special consideration, basing any claim on the mantra leaves the claimant open to the charge of racism. In other words, only the iron-clad factuality of the Hebrew/Jewish covenant can save the latter from a racist bias. (Remember that Moses, Joshua and others have made clear – if we are to believe the scriptures – that Yahweh's choice of the Hebrews was not based on any merit of theirs, but was arbitrary.)

The covenant proposed by Jacob in Genesis 28, which may be paraphrased as, "If I do well, you (Yahweh) shall be my God" is the converse of the classic mantra, since it is the human party that initiates the proposition and there is no guarantee of reciprocity from the Lord. This covenant is free of racist bias.

In the last analysis, unless one resorts to esoteric and overly imaginative exegesis, there are only two interpretations of *I will be your God, and you will be my people:*

1. There are a number of gods and one of them has initiated a covenant with a particular people.
2. There is only one God and he has chosen one people to be holy, special and privileged.

To be fair, as the Jews became more and more monotheistic, repetition of the mantra became less and less frequent. The idea of the covenant lived in a state of suspended animation until Jesus, Paul, and other apostles and Church fathers resurrected it.

The Second (Christian) Covenant

The Gospels make no mention of the covenant or testament until the Last Supper when, according to Matthew, Mark and Luke (but not John), Jesus instituted the Eucharist:

> And as they were eating, Jesus took the bread and blessed it, and gave it to the disciples, and said, "Take, eat; this is my body." And he took the cup, and gave thanks and gave it to them, saying, "Drink all of it; for this is my blood of the New Testament [covenant], which is shed for many for the remission of sins.
> (Matthew 26:26-28)

Like the old covenant the new one is to be sealed in blood, but not in the blood of sacrificial beasts, but in the blood of Christ himself. The imagery and the words are striking, but we are left with the same old covenant – in fact, as we shall see, we are left with a lesser pact, a vague, indefinable one.

The apostles wasted no time establishing their right of succession to the new covenant:

> You are the children of the prophets, and of the covenant which God made with our fathers, saying to Abraham, "And in our seed shall all the people of the earth be blessed." (Acts 3:25)

Also:

> And if you are Christ's then you are Abraham's seed, and heir to the promise.
> (Galatians 3:28)

Furthermore, the new alliance is superior to the old:

> [God] also has made us able ministers of the New Testament [covenant]; not of the letter but of the spirit: for the letter kills, but the spirit gives life.
> (II Corinthians 3:6)

and

> In that he said "a new covenant," he has made the first old. Now that which decays and becomes old is ready to vanish away.
> (Hebrews 8:13)

The historical evidence makes it clear that Christians believed that in passing from the Jews to themselves the covenant abandoned the former. Had the Christian Church considered the Jews as fellow covenanters, would it have been complicit in the instigation of anti-Semitism? Would the Jews of Germany and Central Europe have been the first victims of the crusades?

The Logic of the Covenant

The word *covenant* is used so often and so loosely in the Bible as to leave the reader in a state of confusion and uncertainty. Every time the word is used it seems to refer to a somewhat different concept. It's between a god and a people, or between God-with-a-capital-G and all of humanity, or between God and a particular religion, or between God and the individual believer? Is it a contract or a mere promise? Are humans to satisfy their end of the contract by works, or merely by faith?

Any belief system that postulates the existence of an incorporeal entity that is in some way involved with our world and that has a special relationship with humans which can be communicated through individuals or institutions implies the possibility – if the not the necessity – of a covenant.

Since there are many covenants in the Bible, it would be helpful to attempt a logical analysis of the basic concept:

Let us limit ourselves to covenants between two parties. We must therefore include in our analysis three entities: covenanter A (the deity), covenanter B (the human side), and the contract, written or not.

Covenanter A may be:

1. **An individual personal deity**. In the Torah this individual entity is Yahweh, but there is no logical reason why a covenant could not exist between, say, Baal and a human person (such as Jezebel) or a collectivity. Note that the term *individual deity* implies the existence of a plurality of such beings.
2. **A personal universal deity**. This would be the God of Philo and of the three major monotheistic religions. Any god that enters into any covenant is, *ipso facto*, a personal god.
3. **An impersonal deity**. This would be the God of Plato – the One – but also of other philosophers and mystics, such as Spinoza and the Buddha. Logically, no covenant is possible with such a God.

Covenanter B may be:

1. **A collectivity**, such as a family, tribe, nation, etc. Often such a collectivity (and the associated deity) are identified with a particular locality. For example, Marduk was the local god of Babylon and Babylonia. Of course, all collectivities are collections

of individuals, but there are instances when the individual aspect is particularly dominant. There is no logical interdiction against the case of God – or *a* god – communicating exclusively with just one human. Various scriptures teach us that divine communication is nearly always transmitted through one individual mediator such as Abraham, Moses, or Muhammad. (Christ, being regarded as both God and man, is a special case.) Among Christians, especially Protestants, the personal and individual aspects of the covenant and of salvation are dominant.

2. **An institution.** Whenever a group of clerics constitute themselves into an official body (Sanhedrin, Vatican, Islamic Court, etc.) it is hard to resist seeing themselves, collectively, as partners in a special covenant with the Lord – a covenant that may guarantee infallibility.
3. **Humanity as a whole**. This is the view adopted by all religions that proselytize. Now, there need be no incompatibly between the individual personal approach and this global humanist one: collectivities are collections of individuals.

The compact may be:

1. **A covenant of works** in which human beings gain their benefits by performing works. These can be tangible acts that any humanist would applaud, such as dealing honestly, practicing justice, showing compassion, sharing resources. They can also be acts and rituals that seem meaningless to anyone who doesn't share the religious culture at issue: wearing special clothing, cutting (or not cutting) hair, wearing a veil, forsaking the foreskin, attending special rituals at appointed times, making prescribed signs and gestures, repeating a mantra *x* times, avoiding certain foods, carrying a dagger, etc., etc. Note that *not* doing something counts as *works*. Unfortunately, so do violence, plundering, torture, abduction, and other forms of oppression, depending, of course, on the situation and state of mind.
2. **A covenant of faith**. Why bother with this pesky and onerous requirement of works if you can achieve salvation my merely believing, especially if you make a public proclamation of faith?
3. **A promissory covenant**. God promises protection or salvation without asking anything in return. An example of this is the Noah

covenant. (Strictly speaking, this is too one-sided to be called a covenant.)

4. **A covenant of guarantee.** God guarantees the efficacy of rituals and sacraments and ensures the infallibility of certain clerics or institutions.

Salvation

The word *salvation* is overused egregiously, not only because it is used too often but, more importantly, because it is often used without any inkling of real meaning beyond the vague notion that it is a good thing that gets individuals, collectivities or the whole species out of equally vague, wretched conditions. A simple attempt at establishing its meaning might define it as the reward – whatever it is – for fulfilling the requirements of the covenant.

The ancient Hebrews believed that upon death the souls of all humans, good or bad, were warehoused for an indeterminate time in a cold and dark abode called *Sheol*, never to be reunited with a resurrected body. Therefore, salvation of the individual, in the sense understood by Christians and Moslems, was meaningless. In its stead was the survival of a nation, Israel, and, for some prophets, the eventual hegemony of this nation.

At that time the covenant was with one particular deity chosen out of a number of Semitic and Mesopotamian gods. Since no one believes in the factuality of that pantheon, that covenant, from a philosophical point of view, is meaningless.

But eventually, Hebrews (at that point we should probably call them Jews) became truly monotheistic. Their covenantal relationship changed. They now dealt with a unique, universal – but still personal – God. However, the meaning of salvation was still unclear: at the time of Christ, some Jews, the Pharisees, believed in the afterlife, together with its rewards and punishments, while others, the Sadducees – the group from which sacrificers and temple officials came – did not. Today, most Jews believe in life-after-death, but seldom talk about it, or use it as an incentive to promote proper conduct. Judaism remains a religion primary ensconced in *this* world. (Interestingly – and tragically – the ancient idea that salvation is collective, rather than personal, has returned as a basic doctrine of Zionism.)

For Christians and Moslems, the main reward of this covenant is the salvation of the individual in a blissful, eternal abode. The main punishment for breaking faith with the covenant is damnation: eternal exile to an abode of torture. Christians also diverge from the Hebrew model in attaching more importance to faith and less to works. But faith is often manifested in works, and works are often a sign of faith: it's a matter of emphasis.

Faith vs. Works

Jesus, though often asking for faith – as all prophets must – considered works to be predominant.

> Think not that I have come to destroy the law, or the prophets: I have not come to destroy but to fulfill. For verily I say to you, "Till heaven and earth pass, not one jot or one iota shall in no wise pass from the law, till all is fulfilled. Whoever therefore shall break one of the least commandments, and shall teach men to do so, he shall be called the least in the kingdom of heaven: but whosoever shall do and teach them, he shall be called great in the kingdom of heaven."
> (Matthew 5:17-19)

This is an extremely conservative – even fundamentalist – position, much more so than that of Hillel, the most influential rabbi of the Sanhedrin. Compare this to Paul's words:

> For as many as are the words of the law are under the curse: for it is written, "Cursed is everyone that does not follow all things that are written in the book of the law to be done." But that no man is justified by the law in the sight of God is evident: for the just shall live by faith. But the law is not about faith but [says that] the man who practices its rules shall live through them. Christ has redeemed us from the curse of the law …
> (Gallatians 3:10-13)

Also

> … for the letter [works] kills but the spirit [faith] gives life.
> (II Corinthians 3:6)

And

> But they [Paul and Silas] said, "Believe in the Lord Jesus Christ and you shall be saved, you and your family
> (Acts 16:31)

And

> I had not known sin, but by the law: for I had not known lust, except the law had said, "Thou shall not covet." But sin, taking occasion by the commandment, wrought in me all manner of concupiscence. For without the law sin is dead.
> (Romans 7-9)

"For without the law sin is dead." Someone ought to tell our political leaders about this foolproof plan for eliminating crime: eliminate the law! St. Paul is implying that were there no laws against bank robbery, it would never come to anyone's mind to rob a bank.

So radical is the chasm between Jesus and Paul that we could, without doing violence to the meaning of words, call Paul the first antichrist. Of course, he was not the agent of Satan, and he was, no doubt, a loyal and selfless servant and apostle of Christ. Yet, in personality, temperament, culture, philosophy and theology, the two were at antipodes. Jesus was every inch a Jew who believed that it was only through the Jews that mankind could be saved. Paul, though ethnically a Jew (he was a Pharisee) was Roman by citizenship and Greek by culture. Had their roles in the genesis of Christianity been reversed, the religion would be very different. Since Paul had the last word, perhaps the religion should be called *Paulism.*

> [To be fair, in I Corinthians Paul does put charity ahead of faith:
> And now have faith, hope, and charity, all three; but the greatest of these is charity.
> (I Corinthians 13:13)]

It makes sense that St. Paul would stress faith. He was one of the greatest super salesmen of all time (which does not preclude his being sincere and committed). The primary aim of a good salesman is to get the signature on the dotted line – literally or metaphorically. Paul probably figured it would be easier to get people to sign (metaphorically) a pledge to believe x, y, z than a pledge to give up favorite habits a, b, c and adopt limiting rules d, e, f.

Among the apostles, James was the foremost defender of works:

> Be doers of the word, and not hearers only, deceiving your own selves.
> (James 1:22)

Also,

> Even so faith, if it has not works, is dead, being alone. Yea, a man may say, "You have faith and I have works: show me your faith without your works and I will show you my faith by my works."
> (James 2:17-18)

This dichotomy has never been resolved. Jews have tamed Moses with amendments and emendations, with subtraction and additions, but have never abandoned the idea of works. Christians have focused on faith, some almost to the exclusion of works. There are Christian sects which teach that faith is sufficient for salvation regardless of behavior, and that living a saintly life will not keep you from hell if you do not hold the right beliefs. Catholics were closer to a balanced position until Pope Paul II publicly agreed with the protestant position that faith is primordial.

One of the most radical faithaholics (faith addicts) was Martin Luther, the original prophet of Protestantism. In a letter to his friend, Philip Melanchthon, dated August 1, 1521, he asserted that faith in Jesus was sufficient to assure salvation, "even if thousands, thousands of times in one day we should fornicate or murder." Note that Luther eliminates works completely from his one-way conception of the covenant.

Faith and Science

I could never understand the fixation on "right" beliefs, to the exclusion of works, and with a complete rejection of the notion of evidence. There is no a priori moral mandate to believe! (see Chapter II). Consider this parable:

Tonight the Albert Einstein College of Modern Physics is having a commencement exercise. Twenty students will receive a doctorate in Physics. Since Albert Einstein College is a faith-based institution, the students have had very little lab time and have not been asked to perform any arduous mathematical calculations. Each student will testify to all present that he believes that Albert Einstein is the greatest physicist past, present and future; that he is the true inheritor and guardian of the legacy of Galileo, Newton and Maxwell; and that those quantum mechanicists who reject some part of Einstein's physics are heretics that must be shown the path to professional salvation. Each student will be granted a diploma attesting that he is a Doctor of Philosophy in Modern Physics.

Would anyone in his right mind hire such a person as a physicist?

The Covenant of Guarantee

The covenant of guarantee applies particularly to the Roman Catholic Church and, to a lesser extent, to the Anglican and Orthodox faiths.

Institutions that consider themselves to be special and exclusive conduits of God's grace must assume that God guarantees the efficacy of their rituals and sacraments. It is an article of faith of the Catholic Church that when one of its priests consecrates the host and the wine, the substances change into the actual flesh and blood of Christ. This is only possible if God performs the miracle on call. This is a double miracle: the actual transformation, and the trick of fooling the faithful as well as the scientific community into continuing to see, taste and analyze the body of Christ as bread and wine. Other sacraments that result in a change of state, such as confession, ordination and baptism, also depend on God's guarantee. (The Catholic Church does accept that, in the case of baptism, other Christian Churches are also beneficiaries of this guarantee.) The most striking instance of guarantee is the claim that the pope is infallible in matters of faith and morals. It's a basic, but unstated, tenet of the Roman Catholic Church that God is Catholic.

The Covenant and Demigods

In Greek mythology, Hercules, being the son of Zeus, chief god of Olympus, and Alcmene, a human maiden, was honored as a demigod. Could the human party in a covenant with God achieve the status of demigod?

In Hebrew 22:12, God said to Balaam, "You will not go with them [the Moabites]; you shall not curse the people [the Hebrews] for they are blessed." The Hebrews are called a "Holy people" a number of times in the Tanakh, but it is Second Isaiah who comes closest to making a claim for the status of demigod for them:

Thus said the Lord God,

> "Behold, I will lift up my hand to the Gentiles
> And set up my standard to the people:
> And they shall carry your sons in their arms
> And your daughters shall be carried upon their shoulders.
> And kings shall be your nursing fathers
> And their queens your nursing mothers:
> And they shall bow down to you with their faces toward the earth
> And lick up the dust of your feet; … "
> (Isaiah 49:22-23)

The name *Israel* has three different yet curiously intertwined meanings:

1. The northern Kingdom of the Hebrew people, destroyed as a political body by the Assyrians in 722 BCE.
2. The mystical body of the Hebrew/Jewish people, that is, of all Hebrews and Jews, past, present and future.
3. The modern country founded by Zionist Jews with the help of the English, French and American governments in 1948.

It is the second meaning that establishes the quasi divinity of the Jewish people in the minds of most Jews and many non-Jews. Yahweh, of course, is still God, but it's the demigod Israel that is foremost in the hearts and minds. Israel, the country, is sanctified by being the avatar and spiritual reconstruction of the Temple, destroyed in 70 CE, and by being the long-term object of the ancient prophecies.

[In *Surpassing Wonder*, Donald H. Ackenson has opined that although the Hebrews steadfastly refused to accept any iconography for Yahweh, they substituted the Temple as chief (and only) idol of the cult. In the Old Testament, Yahweh frequently interferes physically on the side of Hebrews in their conflicts with their enemies, as when he threw boulders at the Amorites fighters in Joshua 10. Could American bombs be the modern analogue of these boulders? Could the United States be the modern avatar of Israel's Yahweh?]

Not only nations, but also institutions can be defined by a covenant. The best example, by far, is the Roman Catholic Church. Regarding its mission as a direct extension of Christ's mission, the Church has always considered itself infallible. The dogma of papal infallibility, established at the First Vatican Council in 1869-70, was really a corollary and a personification of this institutional infallibility which confers the status of demigod to both the Church and its pontiff.

As previously pointed out, Protestants have always stressed the one-to-one covenantal relation between the individual faithful and his god. Does this mean that the individual believer is a demigod? – It's all in the eye of the beholder. As long as every single human being is respected as a potential covenanter, whether the individual believer is considered a demigod or not is of minor practical importance. The same can't be said of the deification of particular collectivities such as tribes, nations and institutions. A collective demigod is a dangerous thing because, as a beneficiary of divine dispensation, it may feel free to engage in war, oppression, colonialism, etc.

With or Without God

It isn't necessary to postulate God or gods to support the concept of covenant. Jean-Jacques Rousseau popularized the expression Social Contract in his *Du Contrat Social* (1992) but the notion had been around since the days of Cicero and of the system of Roman Law and was given different interpretations by such philosophers as Hobbes, Locke, Spinoza and Hume. It is as loosely conceived an idea as that of the covenant in the Bible. According to the *Encyclopedia of Philosophy* (McMillan, 1967) "it has as its center an extremely simple conceptual model, in this case that the collectivity is an agreement between the individuals that make it up." Some have postulated an actual contract in prehistoric time between a sovereign and the populace – a prehistoric Magna Carta – but this is probably not the case, and this lacuna in no way invalidates the concept. It is perhaps best conceived as grounded in the labyrinthine recesses of the minds of individual members of a social species. (It's not crazy to imagine a protocontract between a wolf and its pack, or a lion and its pride.) It's based on the awareness of the individual that he is answerable to something, although he may not know precisely what that *something* is. It may be a compact between a person and his God (or gods), or his society, or an institution, or his fellow humans (as individuals), or a philosophy, or a code of conduct. It reduces to a compact between one's consciousness and that little voice deep inside his being. All these cases fall under the rubric of *covenant.* Anyone who is unable to feel or to respond to this call of the covenant is a psychopath.

Chapter XIII – Islam

Part of Deuteronomy was, it seems, invented by the priest Hilkia, sometime in the late 7th century BCE. Some of the Old Testament was put together from unnamed sources during the seventy years of the Babylonian exile. Most of the rest of that document was semi-invented, using equally obscure sources by unknown writer/editors after the return to Judah.

A few letters of St. Paul are the only Christian documents that can reliably be dated prior to the destruction of the Temple in 70 CE, that is, some forty years after the crucifixion. The real identity of the writer/editors of the four canonic Gospels is uncertain. There is no evidence that Jesus actually said the words ascribed to him in the Bible. The New Testament is but a small selection from a welter of apocryphal material, some of which was probably as worthy of inclusion as the documents that were declared canonical.

Compared to the above, the Koran can claim a remarkable documentary reliability. (This cannot be said of the Sunna – the Tradition – the books of the word and deeds of the prophet and his contemporary disciples.) All the Surahs (chapters) of the Koran had been consigned to writing during Muhammad's lifetime and this was backed up by many disciples who had committed the whole document to memory. Before the various copies could be dispersed and possibly adulterated, and before at the memorizers passed away, the Caliph Othman, an old an staunch friend of Muhammad, had a definite version produced and consecrated as canonic. The Koran has not changed since.

One would think that this would give Islam the pole position in the competition to be considered "the one true religion." But there is a fly in the ointment (or rather, huge bumblebee): there are no witnesses. All we have is the prophet's word that the angel Jibril (Gabriel) really spoke to him and conveyed messages from Allah (God). Whenever he entered into his trances and received the messages, Muhammad was alone in a cave or other isolated place. The Scriptures of the Jews and Christians – whatever their pretensions to historicity and factuality may be – claim many witnesses. Moses was alone with Yahweh for forty days on Mount Sinai, but the people were waiting for him at the foot of the mountain and Yahweh made his presence manifest to them by "a consuming fire on the top of the mountain" and other signs.

Taking the Gospels at face value, all of Jesus' miracles and all his sermons were performed in public. When, in Surah III (183-184), Muhammad was challenged to prove his holiness by repeating Elijah's miracle of heavenly fire (I Kings 18), his only reply was that other prophets before him had performed miracles and still had skeptics and deniers. On a number of occasions (Surah XVIII: 46 for one) he said that "Allah is sufficient warrantor," so that no other witnesses were required. This is a monstrously circular argument, as when fundamentalist Christians say that they know the Bible is the infallible word of God because the Bible tells them so. Now, had Allah manifested his testimony to the people at large – or at least to some citizens of established integrity – the charge of circularity would be avoided. The fact that Muhammad was widely viewed as a man of outstanding character, intelligence and ability is insufficient to cancel the liability of not having any witnesses: the factuality index of the Koran is thereby lowered.

[Personal note: This topic brings to mind a few old memories. In the seventies and early eighties, I worked as a teacher of English-as-a-Second-Language. My students were mostly immigrants or Spanish-speaking Puerto-Ricans.

One, an earnest young Haitian man, told me that one night he had received a message from God (not a vision, as I remember, just a verbal or subliminal missive) telling him to devote his life to God. Now, this man was intelligent and broad-minded: you could always argue a point with him. Being a skeptic, I didn't believe that God has really spoken to him, but I didn't – not for a second – think that he was crazy or that he was lying.

Another student, a Puerto Rican lady in her fifties told me that one night she was sitting in her bed, thinking of her deceased father, when she clearly saw his ghost. She, also, was a rational and intelligent person. (I remember having a few philosophical arguments with her). I didn't believe that a real spiritual entity, the ghost of her father, really existed; yet it never crossed my mind that she was unbalanced, or prone to hallucinations. I just assumed that the ghost was a product of her mind caused by her deep longing for her father and conditioned by two aspects of Puerto Rican culture, *spriritismo* (spiritualism) and *santeria* (a local form of Voodoo).] In Surah XXXIII there are two verses that are very ilucidating:

> And when We exacted a covenant from the Prophets, and from you [Muhammad] and from Noah and Abraham and Moses and Jesus son of Mary. We took from them a solemn covenant;
>
> That He may ask the loyal of their loyalty. And he has prepared a painful doom for the unfaithful.
> (Surah XXXIII:7-8)

The first sentence makes clear that Islam is to be considered as a legitimate claimant and heir to the mantle of convenance. Unlike the Christian Bible, the Koran does not consider its covenant to be "a new covenant better than the first." Rather it considers itself and its share of the covenant as the final fruit of monotheism; and it does not repudiate the trunk (the New Testament) nor the roots (the Tanakh) of the tree of monotheism. It is, however, a conditional acceptance: Islam considers itself as the culmination of a historical progression and holds that Muhammad is the last prophet, closing the age of prophesy and revelation:

> Muhammad is not the father of any among you, but he is the messenger of Allah and the Seal of the Prophets;
> (Surah XXXIII: 40)

The complete absence of witnesses is the main factor that, *prima facie*, lowers the factuality index of many of the claims and statements of the Koran, but there are considerations internal to the document that further lower that index.

Allah is identical to the God of Philo of Alexandria, an entity partly transcendental and partly immanent. It is the common deity of Jews, Christians and Muslims (although the later have been more rigorous in their conception of monotheism, refusing to allow any "partners" to God and considering the Trinity as a backdoor intrusion of polytheism). The problem with Allah is that no distinction is made between Old Yahweh and New Yahweh: the name *Allah* covers both. As we have seen in Chapter 11 – and elsewhere – Old Yahweh was just one of many Semitic and

Sumerian gods. Their factuality index, individually and collectively, is close to zero. The source of Muhammad's visions and trances, if it has factuality, cannot be identical to Old Yahweh; but if identical to New Yahweh – the God of Philo – how to explain his own acceptance of Old Yahweh as part of his identity?

To further fan the embers of doubt Allah seems to accept the factuality of all the incidents in the first two books of the Judeo-Christian scriptures that, outside Islam, only the self-lobotomized clarions of the Christian Right, and some Orthodox rabbis accept as factual. The very beginning of Genesis runs completely counter to well-established science and, to boot, relates two incompatible creation stories. The story of Noah and the Flood pushes credulity to the level of insanity: each miracle must be sustained by other miracles and implies further miracles, so that God not only supersedes his own natural laws, but actually suspends temporarily the very fabric of the world he has created, including its physics, biology, logic and mathematics. Another story, the plagues of Egypt (as demonstrated in Chapter III) also scores a zero on the factuality index. Yet Allah, speaking directly to Muhammad through the voice of the angel Gibril, accepts at face value all the unbelievable stories in Genesis and Exodus, as well as a few others from other books. (Surah II, VII, XIV, LXXI, and many others.) Since the God of Philo must be considered infallible, this considerably lowers the rating of the Koran on the factuality index.

If the Koran's transmittance from Prophet to future generations is very reliable, the same cannot be said of the books of the Tradition (the *Sunna*). These are collections of *hadiths*, the sayings and deeds of Muhammad and his close associates. For obscure reasons the written documentation of these were forbidden for many years, and during that time thousands of false hadiths were fabricated. It was not until the end of the ninth century—some 250 years after Muhammad's death – that the Sunna began to be compiled. Six collections of *hadiths* were eventually recognized as canonical. The most important and revered one was compiled by al Buktari, who took sixteen years to research and authenticate 7,275 traditions that he selected out of some 600,000 he had gathered. Each of these was accompanied by the chain of transmissions form person to person that justified its inclusion. In spite of the Herculean effort invested and the great integrity of the author, it is doubtful that complete faith should be given on the basis of "A has reported that B heard from C that D told E that F, a close friend of Muhammad, had heard the prophet say that ..."

What is significant is that none of the six major compilers was interested in participating in an on-going, evolutionary process to keep their faith contemporarily relevant and progressive. Rather, all of them strived to anchor their work in the past – to a particular cultural phenomenon, during a particular period, identified with a particular person, in the past. Al Bukhari and his fellow compilers were always looking behind, not ahead, and their work was not one of interpretation, but of consolidation. They were, to use an American political term, strict constructionists. This attitude is probably an important factor in the snuffing out of the amazing cultural and intellectual ebullience so characteristic of early Islam.

[Note that al Bukhari, the compiler of the second most revered canonical book of Islam, was exiled because of his belief that the Koran was created by an inspired prophet and was not a transcript of God's timeless Law – food for thought. A similar controversy exists in Jewish and Christian theology: Is the Bible the infallible word of God, or merely 'inspired' by God? And if the latter, what are the meaning and implications of *inspired by God*? Does it mean that some of the Bible can be dismissed as ancient legends, and some retained as the word of God? And, if so, how do we discriminate between the two?]

Who was Muhammad?

Although more is known about Muhammad – as the person – than about Moses and Jesus, his formative years are still largely shrouded in mystery. What brought about, as the age of forty, such a sudden change in vocation is even more mysterious.

It's difficult to come to a balanced judgment about him. Few men have been so vilified – by popes, theologians, preachers, and drunken crusaders – and few have been so eulogized and idolized by the faithful. Yet even among the Arabs and Muslims, there are some discordant voices. According to the *Encyclopedia of Religion and Ethics*, some 350 years after the Prophet's death, Muhammad Ibn Ishak wrote a biography of Muhammad, now lost, but from which many excerpts have been quoted in other books. These paint an unflattering picture of the man: he was unscrupulous in the means he took to achieve his ends, he organized assassinations and massacres, he led raids for plunder from Medina, etc. This view seems to be too much at odds with most accounts from traditional sources to command full unquestioned credibility. Perhaps sectarian conflict can account for the discordance.

Yet there are in the Koran some verses that suggest that the squeaky clean traditional portrait of the prophet may be a mite too idealized.

> O Prophet! We have made lawful to you your wives to whom you have paid their dowries, and those that your right hand possesses [slave girls] of those whom Allah has given you as spoils of war, and the daughters of your uncles on the father's side … and the daughters of your aunts on the mother's side who emigrated with you, and a believing woman if she gives herself to the Prophet and the Prophet desires her in marriage – a privilege for you only, not for the rest of the believers – We are aware of that which We decreed upon them concerning their wives and those whom their right hands possess [slaves] – that you may be free from blame for Allah is forgiving, merciful. [Surah XXXIII: 50]

The believers were limited to a maximum of *four* wives (plus slave girls and captives) but Muhammad was given a dispensation from that law by Allah. ("How convenient" would say the "church lady" in the T.V. comedy, *Saturday Night Live*.) It's easy to see how the sexually puritanical Catholic Church would find Verse 50 egregious. There is no reason why a strongly sexual person could not also be moral and spiritual. Yet Verse 50 does raise eyebrows. More unsettling than the intimation of lustfulness is the suspicion that the prophet may have used revelations from Allah to advance his own interests.

But one thing is undeniable: Muhammad was a man of outstanding intelligence, strong character and great charisma who left a huge footprint in the sands of time.

The Military Option

Muhammad was not only a prophet: he was also a politician and military leader. By the time of his death the Arabian peninsula had been subdued and converted. It has taken the prophet 13 years to establish his authority over Medina and Mecca, but in a mere ten years he then gained control of the whole Arabian peninsula – a truly wondrous feat. The Moslem troops were much more disciplined and motivated, and better led than the motley group of tribes they fought. It seems also that conversions came easily, although there is no way of knowing how sincere most of them were. (Certainly the children or grandchildren of the proselytes became true Muslims). The "people of the book" – Christians, Jews and, later, Zoroastrians – were not converted by force although two Jewish tribes of Yathrib (renamed Medina) were expelled and dispossessed and a third had its men massacred and its women and children enslaved. Pagans, however, were given the choice of conversion, the payment of a special tribute for unbelievers, or death.

An old friend and collaborator of the Prophet was chosen to succeed him as "Commander of the Faithful," thus becoming the first Caliph. Abu Bakr was a short unprepossessing man, but strong of body and of will. A modest person, he was abstemious in dress, diet and the niceties of life. He was totally dedicated to the full flowering of Islam and indefatigable in his effort. He imparted some of his fervor to his troops. The historian, Will Durant, described the ethos of those Moslem fighters thus:

> The Arab troops were more rigorously disciplined and more ably led; they were inured to hardships and rewarded with spoils; they could fight on empty stomachs, and depended upon victory for their meals. But they were not barbarians. "Be just" ran Abu Bekr's proclamation; "be valiant, die rather than yield; be merciful; slay neither old men, nor women, nor children. Destroy no fruit trees, grain or cattle. Keep your word, even to your enemies. Molest not those who live retired from the world, but compel the rest of mankind to become Moslems or pay us tribute. If they refuse these terms, slay them."
> (Will Durant, *The Story of Civilization,* Vol.II, "The Age of Faith," p. 188)

When Abu Bakr died, another friend of Muhammad was chosen Caliph: Omar, a man even more pious, rigorous and ascetic than Bakr. One of his first acts was to demote the most capable Arab general, Khalid Ibn al-Wadi, because the latter was prone to celebrate his victories by acts of cruelty. Khalid, to his credit, remained loyal and continued to lead the troops in the field.

The Muslims extended their domination beyond Arabia, gaining control of Egypt, Syria and Lebanon. However this was not a colonial enterprise in the sense that European colonization was. The main objective was propagation of the faith by the sword, not enrichment and land grab. Civil society was not destroyed and micro management was left in the hands of the local establishment.

[We will see anon how, some centuries later, Muslims of Turkic extraction (often called Moguls) were "worthy" precursors of the Spanish conquistadors and other Christian barbarians in America.]

The Arabian campaigns set the moral tone for Holy War by putting in practice the more martial and violent injunctions of the Koran, such as:

> And fight them until persecution is ended and religion is for Allah only.
> (Surah VIII: 39)

Certainly, the persecuted have the right of self-defence, individually and collectively, but the second clause commands the prophet and his followers to fight non-believers just because they are non-believers. Notice the matter-of-fact tone of the phase: no white-horse highfalutin rhetoric here: just do it! No need to wait for a specific command from Allah, it's a standing order: just do it! The command is to fight – not necessarily to kill. Limits are not mentioned. Unfortunately other Koranic verses are more specific:

> Then, when the sacred months have passed, slay the idolaters whenever you find them, and capture them, and prepare for their ambush. But if they repent and establish worship and pay the poor-dues, then leave them be. Allah is Forgiving, Merciful.
> (Surah IX:5)

Again, belief in a divisive covenant - a covenant that selects a chosen, holy, preferred or superior people (or institution) for special treatment, to the prejudice of the rest of us – brought war, not peace.

ISLAM IN THE INDIAN SUBCONTINENT

The Arabs continued their advance into lands that were not contiguous to Arabia, both westward in Spain and eastward towards India. The further they got from home base, the more their efforts resembled classical colonialism, although their zeal for conversions – voluntary or forced –

never completely abated. Their incursions brought them in close contact with Turkic-speaking people -- a motley group of Turkmen, Mongols, Taters, etc. Some of these were converted by the sword, others willingly accepted Islam. Some Turkic chieftains actually conquered Arab-controlled lands – and ended as willing converts to Islam!

It was Arab troops that established a foothold in India. Over a period of some 70 years the Arabs had staged a number of invasions of India and had been repulsed every time. Finally, Muhammad Bin Quasim defeated and captured Indian forts including Askalanda and Multan, according to the Muslim historical annals, the *Chackanama* (from www.muktudhera.net/page13.htm)

That was in 712CE. The next invasion was led by a Turkic conqueror, Mahmud Ghaznavi. Henceforth, Muslim Turks would constitute the Islamic presence in the subcontinent. It would prove to be more bloody and savage than the Arab depredations. In *The History of Civilization*, Will Durant wrote: "*The* Mohammeddan Conquest of India is probably the bloodiest story in history." (Part I, *Our Oriental Heritage*, Simon and Schuster, p. 459). Many historians would insist that the Holocaust of Amerindians was an even more egregious crime against humanity, but comparison is difficult because part of the devastation in the Americas was due to smallpox and other European diseases.

Mahmud's secretary, Tarikh-i-Yamii of Utbi, kept a record of the campaign. After the plunder of Thanasar he wrote: "The blood of the infidels flowed so copiously that the stream was dissolved ... and people were unable to drink it."

After the battle for Mahaban, Utbi wrote:

> The Sultan returned in the rear of immense booty, and slaves were so plentiful that they became very cheap and men of respectability in their native land were degraded by becoming slaves of common shopkeepers. But this is the goodness of Allah, who bestows honor on his own religion and degrades infidelity.
> (From www.hindunet.org/hindu_history/modern moghal_astro.html) (also in www.muktadhara.net)

Obviously, God is a Muslim. And everything that is permissible to God is permissible to Muslims. This seems to go one step further rightward than moral dispensation, even though Islam very rarely refers to the covenant. But what kind of god, then, is implied? Is Allah a god that practices ethnic cleansing? (The Koran asserts that Allah is all-powerful, that any instance of sin happens because Allah allows it to happen – "Allah saves whom he wills.") Is Allah the god of slavery? Note that Allah not only grants moral dispensation, but, in his goodness, honors the deeds of his believers. (To be fair, the same rhetorical questions could also be posed about Yahweh, the God of the Old Testament.)

The next invasion was by Muhammad Ghori who, in 1186 CE captured the city of Delhi and established a dynasty, the Sultanate of Delhi, which would oppress Northern India for three centuries. Ibn Asir in his book, *Kamil-ut-Tawarikk*, reported that "The slaughter of Hindus (at Veranasi) was immense; none were spared except women and children, and the carnage of men went on until the earth was weary." (from www..hindunet.org/hindu_history). The women and children, of course, were sold as slaves throughout the Muslim world.

Ghori, however, was not selfish: he shared his glory with his top lieutenants. The exploits of one of them, Qutbuddin Aibak, were described by the historian Hassan Nizami in *Taj-ul-Ma'sin*. In one case, the defeat of the capital of Gujararet, "fifty thousand infidels were dispatched to hell by the sword," and "more than twenty thousand slaves and cattle beyond all calculation fell into the hands of the victors." (from www.hindunet.org) (also at www. Muktadara.net). Another of his conquests was the city of Kalinjar, where, according to Nizami, "The temples were converted into Mosques ... Fifty thousand men came under the collar of slavery and the plain became black as pitch with Indus."

The Sultans of Delhi were probably the all-time champions in uninterrupted oppression: mistreatment and cruelty against a huge population in one geographical area, lasting some three centuries. Will Durant gives many examples of which two follow:

1. He [Sultan Muhammad bin Tughlak] killed so many Hindus that, in the words of a Moslem historian, "there was constantly in front of his royal pavilion and his Civil Court a mound of dead bodies and a heap of corpses, while the sweepers and executioners were wearied out by their work of dragging the victims and putting them to death in crowds."
   (Will Durant, Part 1, p. 461) quoting from V.A. Smith, *the Oxford History of Civilization*, p. 245)

2. Sultan Ahamad Shak feasted for three days whenever the number of defenseless Hindus slain in territories in one day reached twenty thousand.
(Will Durant, Part 1, p. 461

Many of these sultans hired historians and scribes to document their exploits, and at least one, Firuz Shah Tughlak wrote or dictated his own record, the *Sirat-i-Firoz Shaki* (www.hindunet.org)

In his book, *A History of Civilization*, Fernand Braudel gives the following description of the colonial style of the Sultans:

> … the Muslims could only rule the country by systematic terror. Cruelty was the norm … burnings, summary executions, crucifixions or impalements, inventive tortures. Hindu temples were destroyed to make way for mosques.
> (Fernand Braudel, *A History of Civilizations*, Penguin, p. 232).

The last sentence is worth noting. There are many Muslim Mosques that, on the basis of records, inscriptions and excavations, are known or suspected to have been built on the foundations of Hindu Temples, often partly with construction material salvaged from the latter. To this day this is a sore spot in Hindu-Muslim relations.

So egregious were the exactions of the Sultans that they lost the support of both Hindu and Muslim populations. They became militarily and politically vulnerable. Eventually they would be defeated and replaced by other Muslims from the North.

The practice run was led by Timor-i-lang, known in the West as Tamerlane. In 1398, this bloody chieftain invaded Northern India, defeated Mahmud Tughlak's armies and occupied Delhi. In the process he killed a hundred thousand soldiers, including prisoners, massacred a multitude of civilians, ransacked and plundered the city and made an uncountable number of slaves. Then he returned to his home base, Samarkand, with the slaves and the wealth of generations of kings.

The Sultans climbed back onto the throne and hung on for another century. In 1526, they were finally and definitely vanquished by a Turkic descendant of Timur and Genghis Kahn: Babar (Babur), a man of heroic and legendary dimensions. He shared the ferocious qualities of the Turks in battle, but once established as ruler, he proved to be more tolerant and enlightened than any previous Muslim potentate. The dynasty he founded, the Moguls, lasted for more than two centuries, although it is hard to put a definite date for its demise since it died a very slow death.

A grandson of Babur, Jalal-ud-Din Mohammed, known universally as Akbar (the Great) was by far the best of all Muslim rulers of India and one of the greatest monarchs of all time and place. The first part of his reign was spent on conquest and consolidation of his empire in Northern India, and in this endeavor he was probably as ruthless as Turkic fighters are wont to be. But as soon as an area came under his control he established freedom of religion, equitable courts, and effective management. He eliminated the special levies on non-Muslims; he hired civil servants according to competence and without regard to religion or race; he included daughters of Indian princes in his harem; he was generous to the poor; he collected a great library (although illiterate he was not ignorant: he spent hours having books read to him). Eventually he won the respect and love of both Indus and Muslim subjects and his fame extended far beyond the borders of his realm.

He abhorred religious dogmatism and – against basic Muslims precepts -- he had an inclination for syncretism.

> ... Akbar invited the representatives of all the religions in his empire to a conference, pledged them to peace, issued edits of toleration for every cult and creed, and, as evidence of his own neutrality, married wives from the Brahman, Buddhist and Mohammedan faiths.
> (Will Durant, Part 1, p. 469)

So keen was his interest in religion and philosophy that he built a special house where Muslim (Sufi, Sunni and Chiite), Zoroastrian and Hindu scholars could discuss religion with him. Later, he and some court scholars laid the foundation of a religion which would include elements from major faiths into a kind of liberal divine monotheism. However, the religion never succeeded in implanting itself. Many Muslims believe that Akbar died an apostate.

He was followed by his son, Jahangir, who was uninterested in religion, but a keen devotee of the fine art of torture: flaying live victims, impaling on posts, crushing under elephants, and other imaginative atrocities.

When he died, his son Jahan claimed inheritance to the throne and weighted the odds in his favor by killing his brothers. Despite this bloody beginning he proved to be an able, if spendthrift, monarch whose thirty-year reign was marked by internal peace (although many citizens died in foreign wars) and by a very vigorous building program which graced India with many architectural masterpieces, including the Taj Mahal, erected to the memory of his favorite wife, Nur Jehan. Despite his extravagant spending, it was during his reign that India reached its greatest prosperity and prestige.

If he showed some of his grandfather's ability for governance, he didn't inherit any genes for tolerance. He re-established Muslim supremacy, had a great number of Hindu shrines destroyed, and persecuted Christians.

In 1657, his son, Aurangzeb, set up and led a successful insurrection. He defeated Jehan's forces, imprisoned his father (who died in jail nine years later), and mounted the throne. Despite his cruel treatment of his father, Aurangzeb was, in many ways, a saintly man. Educated by *mullahs*, he considered his religion the most important value in his life. He followed all the laws, recited all the required payers, memorized the Koran, and observed all the fasts. He was also perhaps the least cruel of the Moguls: no slaughter, no torture, no exaggerated punishments. He was hard on himself, spending no money for personal use except what he earned by the labor of his hands (sewing, copying the Koran, etc.). Benevolent as he was toward individuals, he was ruthless to all religions but his own. Thousands of Hindu temples and many Christian churches were demolished and replaced by mosques built on the original foundations; he imposed a heavy head tax on non-Muslims; he declared illegal any public expression of Hinduism.

His intolerance squandered what was left of the treasure of goodwill that Akbar had established with the Indian population. He came to this realization and died a dispirited and embittered man at the age of 89, in 1707. The Moguls hung on to the throne but their empire began to break apart. In 1739 invading Persians sacked Delhi and massacred many of its citizens. European merchants and companies – Portuguese, Dutch, and especially English – established footholds. Military personnel followed to provide protection and finally all of India became a British colony.

Ethical and Political Considerations

1. The Saga of the Moguls illustrates starkly the contrast between two views of religion:

On the one hand there was the liberal, humanistic, rational approach of Akbar.

On the other hand there was the strict, anal-retentive, inflexible, authoritarian and aggressive approach of Aurangzeb.

The first produced a society of justice, cooperation, strength, affluence, renown and happiness.

The second produced a society or repression, fragmentation, resentment and disloyalty.

The reign of Aurangzeb signaled the beginning of the end of the Mogul Sultanate.

2. The conquest of the Arabian Peninsula settles a glaring inconsistency in the Koran.
   Some verses suggest that Islam is a religion of peace and freedom, such as "Let there be no constraint in religion," (SII:256) and "Would you Mohammed, compel men until they are believers?" (SXI:100). Other verses express the command to do violence to unbelievers unless they convert, such as "I will throw fear into the hearts of those who unbelieve. Then smite them in the necks of and smite of them each finger," (SVII:12) and, "Then, when the sacred months have passed, slay the idolaters whenever you find them." (SX:5)

The conquest of Arabia was achieved under the direct leadership of Muhammad and in this campaign pagans who refused to accept Islam or pay a head tax were slain. Therefore, Islam, as conceived by Muhammad, was more a religion of war than of peace.

To be fair, the same can be said of the Yahwist religion of the Old Testament, whose scriptures, remember, are canonic to the Christian faith. The fact that there is no incitation to violence in the New Testament didn't mitigate the barbarity of Christians in their dealings with Amerindians and African Negroes

ISLAM IN THE IBERIAN PENINSULA

The Visigoths, a branch of the Goths, a Christian people that had originated in southern Scandinavia, after meandering and fighting their way south, ended upon the Iberian Peninsula (Spain and Portugal). They grew and prospered, eventually displacing the Romans as the dominant people. They suffered from internal dissention in both religion and politics. They had arrived as Arians (a heresy that denied that Christ was equal to the Father) but by the end of the seventh century they had converted to Catholicism. Their political dissensions however never got resolved.

At the beginning of the eight century, Visigoth Spain was divided into competing factions caused primarily by claims of succession to the thrones of local kingdoms. In 711, probably at the invitation of one Visigoth party, Tarki, the governor of Tangiers, crossed the Straight of Gibraltar with 7,000 soldiers, mostly Berbers. (Berbers are the Caucasoid aboriginal people of North Africa, converted to Islam.) In 712, a force of 18,000, mostly Arabs, joined them. They met little resistance and within a few years Islam was the major force in the Iberian Peninsula. However, no one really controlled the place: Visigoth Christians were still fighting Visigoth Christians, Berbers were fighting Arabs; Jews who had welcomed the Muslims as protectors still suffered the occasional massacre (as did some Christian communities); black African mercenaries (Blackamoors) and European slaves (Slovenians, who were a force to reckon with, in spite of their status) added to the confusion.

The victims of persecutions, for a change, were Christians more often than Jews. The city of Cordoba was the scene of two notable incidents. In 818 some citizens revolted against the Muslims who retaliated with a three-day massacre in which 300 Christian leaders were crucified and 20,000 families expelled.

In 850 a Christian priest purposely invited execution by insulting the prophet Muhammad and refusing to retract. He was beheaded. During the next 10years, a strange parade of voluntary martyrs marched to the chopping block after publicly blaspheming Muhammad and declaring that Islam is a false religion: 48 were beheaded. Note that a few of them who had previously been Muslims and had converted were executed for the sin of apostasy. (Kennedy B. Wolf, *Christian Martyrs in Muslim Spain*, Cambridge). The Catholic Church recognizes them as the Martyrs of Cordoba (www.newadvent.org/cathen/04389b.htm)

It wasn't until 912 that things settled down. Abd-al-Raman III managed to unite Moorish Spain and proclaimed himself Caliph of al-Andalusia (the Arab name for Spain). Under his leadership Arabs, Berbers, Christians, Jews, Blacks, Whites and in-betweeners, all participated in the areas of public administration, industry, architecture, agriculture and education to build a society that was a model for the time. The capital,

Cordoba, and the eponymous state, enjoyed international prestige. Upon his death in 961, he was succeeded by his son, al Hakam II, whose reign (961 to 976) was no less enlightened and successful.

Unfortunately, al Hakkam's son, Hisham II, was weak and Al-Mansur, a military man, became the *defacto* Caliph. He wasted no time attacking Christian towns and the Christians returned the favor. It was back to the bad old days of confusion and conflict – and massacres.

This time, the Jews were not spared. In 1066 a Jewish Vizier invited Al-Mutasim of Almeria to come to Granada and be its ruler. Other Muslims objected and defeated Al-Mutasim's force. In the best tradition of collective punishment they attacked the Jews of Granada. Many were killed and many fled to the north. The victims numbered 4,000 persons from 1,500 families.

Despite a few such anti-Jewish episodes, most historians agree that Jews were better off under the Muslim Moors than under the Christian Visigoths. One should note, however, that some Christian prelates were instrumental in disseminating translations of Moorish and Jewish philosophy and science to European scholars.

Muslims also were victims of massacres, sometimes by other Muslims (Berbers against Arabs), sometimes by Christians. Pope Alexander II sent an international force of Italians, Normans, Frenchmen and Iberians to Spain. In 1063 this army captured the Muslim city of Barbastros: 50,000 citizens were massacred or enslaved. The soldiers, of course, were doing the work of the Vicar of Christ who, certainly, was doing God's work!

There were many instances of internecine violence in the Visigoth camp. To add to the confusion kings frequently arranged to have their kingdom divided upon their death so that each son would inherit his own kingdom.

Even before the Muslim conquest of the Iberian Peninsula had been accomplished the *reconquista* (reconquest) had started. The battle of Covadonga in 722, a bare 12 years after the first landing of Muslim troops, is considered the first battle of the reconquest. The last engagement was the taking of Grenada in 1492 – 770 years later. During three quarters of a millennium there were periods of peace (and even cooperation); there were a few massacres; there were revolutions and riots in individual camps; there were local conquests and reconquests of cities and provinces.

Upon the final defeat many Moors made arrangements with some towns and agreed to convert to Catholicism and transform their mosques into churches. [These converts were known as Moriscos. Jews who converted for the same reason were called Marranos. Most of these converts remained Muslims or Jews in their hearts and followed the precepts and at least *some* rituals of their old faith in secret. They were not trusted and not completely accepted by most Catholics.]

Unconverted Muslims were expelled from Spain in 1492 and from Portugal in 1496. In 1502, under the pretext that Moors had broken the terms of their surrender and that Jews had always collaborated with them, many Moriscos and Marranos were deported. The Spanish Inquisition, authorized by the Pope in 1492, went after the Morriscos and Marranos, and finally, between the civil and religious persecutions, King Ferdinand II and Queen Isabella got what they wanted: religious homogeneity, which made the country more easily controllable and absolute power more achievable.

Many of the Jews subject to the 1492 edit of expulsion found refuge in parts of the Ottoman Empire. Sultan Beyazit II issued a decree to offer welcome and protection to the Jews. (www. science.co.il/hi/Turkish/) For the next five centuries the Empire (or parts of it) remained a comparatively safe haven for them.

Unfortunately, this rosy picture is just part of the story. There have been sporadic Ottoman massacres against Christians. The most egregious have occurred in the twentieth century: the Turkish slaughter of Christian Armenians in 1915-1917 – denied by Turkey but evidenced by many documents and visual witnesses – with 500,000 to 1,00,000 victims; and the war crimes of the Greco-Turkish war (1919 to 1922) in which both Christian Greeks and Muslim Turks were guilty of massacres of civilians.

But under all the blood and gore of the previous pages there is a seed of hopefulness. The reigns of Abd-al-Rhaman and his son al Hakam in Spain and of Ackbar in India, as well as the periods of peace and justice during the Ottoman hegemony prove that it is possible to have respect for minorities, freedom of religion and equality of opportunity under conditions of Muslim majority and/or governance. But some leaders and citizens must have the courage to look the likes of Al Qaeda and the Taliban in the eye and say; "No! There's a better way."

Chapter XIV – Medieval Christianity

Religion as "Politics by Other Means"

It should be expected that there would be interaction – conflicts and alliances – between religious and secular power centers. This is commonplace in human history. What is different and suspect in the case of Christianity is the important role of political machinations in the evolution of doctrine.

There were two interacting networks of political activity in the early church:

1. Internal chicanery between various factions within the church.
2. Recurring episodes of friction/conflict and collaboration/collusion between church and state.

It took about 400 years for Christianity to crystallize the New Testament and sift out canonic scripture from apocryphal writing and spurious inventions. The New Testament, compared to the Old and the Koran, is a rather meager document on which to base a major religion. The Synoptic Gospels are three versions of the same story, each about 18,000 words long. The Gospel according to John adds new material and a different style but is equally short. The Acts of the Apostles and the various epistles contain some verses of great importance and influence, but are mostly concerned with pastoral matters and exhortations to steadfastness and militancy. Together they are about as long as the Gospels. As for the last book, the Revelation of St. John – also known as the Apocalypse – it is a mere twelve or so pages of nonsense.

To create as imposing a religious structure as Christianity and as powerful an institution as the Catholic Church, the church fathers needed much imagination, meditation and inspiration. Unfortunately, imagination, meditation and inspiration were pre-empted by politics – often dirty, internal, brother-against-brother politics. There were so many heresies in the period from the first to the fifth century that a complete listing is impossible. Some of the major ones were Gnosticism, Marcionism, Montanism, Donatism, Pelagianism and Arianism. The issues involved were the nature of the Trinity, the relationship between God and Christ, the status of the Holy Ghost, whether the God of the Old Testament was identical to the God of Christians, whether only saintly people could be in the Church, whether people were saved by the Grace of God or by their own bootstraps, etc., etc.

Many of these heresies were initiated and promoted by duly ordained priests and duly consecrated bishops. Some came close to being a real threat to the establishment. What became Christian orthodoxy was the result of numerous political intrigues and conspiracies rather than the fruit of divine inspiration. The tactics used included exile, imprisonment, anathema and excommunication. All geographical divisions of Christianity were involved: Eastern, Western and African.

Soon, however, the antagonists started having recourse to civil authority. The involvement of Constantine, the first Roman emperor to champion Christianity (shortly after Diocletian's persecution of 303) is particularly interesting. His conversion was a gradual process, but by 313 he considered himself a chosen servant of God. However, he continued to show deference to the Sun-god and did not receive baptism until a few days before his death in 337, some twenty-four years later. (That may be because it was believed that baptism erased previous sins completely.) He seemed to have thought that his status as emperor assured him of divine guidance and he got involved in doctrinal matters about which he knew next to nothing. In 314, probably influenced by Osseous, his spiritual advisor, he summoned the bishops of the Western Roman Empire to a synod at Arles to decide a number of questions and to pass judgment on Donatism, a sect that held that only truly saintly persons should be admitted to the Church. Donatism was declared a heresy, although Donatists continued to agitate. After this, Constantine took upon himself the right and responsibility of appointing bishops, summoning councils and receiving appeals on their decisions.

But his hour of glory was yet to come:

The Eastern churches were divided by serious questions regarding the status of Christ within the Trinity. Was the Second Person of the same substance as the Father (the First Person) and therefore absolutely equal in status from all eternity? Or was Christ divine but of a lower status than the Father? Although Constantine was not yet a Christian and had little understanding of theology, he convened the first Ecumenical (general) Council of all bishops at Nice, in 325. (We can surmise that he was prompted by Ossius.) Probably under the guidance of the latter, he presided over the meeting and even presented the proposition that was voted on. Awed by the emperor, all but two of the bishops signed on to accept the Creed of Nicea and to condemn Arianism (the belief that Christ is not really divine) as a heresy, although agreement was far from enthusiastic. Arius, the founder of the faction, was exiled to Egypt until he agreed to sign on. However, Constantine mollified his position and militated for Arius' return to the Church, which happened in 335.

So, here we have a secular leader, very sympathetic to the Christian Church but not yet a Christian; having limited knowledge and understanding of theology; himself a man of doubtful moral fiber (he had one of his sons and his wife executed in 326); convening, presiding and dominating the first and arguably most important council of the Christian Church. God does, indeed, work in mysterious ways! [Final irony: Constantine was baptized on his death bed by an Arian priest.]

There have been twenty-one Ecumenical councils, the most recent being the Second Vatican Council in 1962-65. Only the first seven have been recognized by the Eastern Orthodox Churches (which separated in 1054). These were convened by the Byzantine emperors and held in or near Constantinople.

The unhealthy encroachment of secular over spiritual power continued. The first Council of Constantinople in 381, one of the most important, was summoned by Emperor Theodosius I. It gave us the Nicene Creed, an emendation of the Creed of Nicea, which is the only formula accepted, to this day, by the Roman Catholic, Eastern Orthodox, and most Protestant churches. (This bespeaks the importance of the not-quite-Christian Emperor Constantine in the evolution of Christian theology.) The council relied on Theodosius to seal and enforce its decision.

The controversy over whether Christ had two natures – divine and human – united into one person, or only one nature, continued for almost a century. Emperor Theodosius II was succeeded by his sister Pulcheria and her husband Marcian. They favored the two-nature theory and summoned the ecumenical council of Chalcedon, in 451, to settle this and other matters. As in the case of the First Council of Constantinople (and a few others) the pope did not attend which only maximized the role of the royal couple.

The eighth ecumenical council, the Fourth Ecumenical Council of Constantinople (869-70) marked the separation of Eastern and Western Christendom, although the schism didn't become official till 1054. Henceforth, the popes of the Roman Church committed themselves to a struggle for supremacy over kings and emperors. Henceforth, all councils were convoked by the popes.

The Crusades

By the time the first crusade was called the popes were the dominant political force in Europe. It wasn't an emperor or king that militated for the first crusade and organized it, but a Pope, Urban II.

But before delving into the history of the crusades, we would do well to cast a quick glance at the situation involving the Christian and Muslim worlds at that time. In 710 Muslim forces invaded Spain and eventually conquered and colonized most of the country. The reconquest of Spain by the Christians was a long and complicated affair. [The reconquest was not substantially achieved till the middle of the 13th century, almost simultaneously with the end of the crusades, which explains why Spain played almost no role in those campaigns.] In 970 the Seljuk Turk entered Persia. Gradually they converted to Islam and became Sunni Muslims. By the time of the first crusade they virtually controlled the Sunni part of the Middle East. In 1071 they captured Asia Minor from the Byzantine Christians. Meanwhile, the Shiite Muslims consolidated their domination of Egypt and surrounding areas, which gave them control of the Red Sea and the Nile Valley, an axis of great commercial importance. They were in opposition to the Sunnites and feared the Seljuk Turks.

In 1094 the Byzantine emperor sent a letter to the Pope, asking for help in his struggle against the Seljuk Turks who had taken most of Asia Minor from him. The council of Clermont was convened in 1096 to take up some theological and administrative matters. Pope Urban II used the occasion to deliver a speech of immense historical consequence, in which he urged the mobilization of the first crusade.

The acts of the Council have been lost but there are credible accounts written by a few chroniclers which have survived. The most interesting is

Gesta Frankorum Jerusalem Expugnantium by Fulcher of Chartes. According to the latter, the Pope's first sentence was, "Most beloved brethren: urged by necessity, I, Urban, by the permission of God, chief and prelate over the whole world, have come into these parts as an ambassador with a divine admonition to you, the servants of God." (www.fordham.edu/holsall/source/urban2-5vers.html)

Urban did more than advocate the first crusade. When he said, "I, Urban, by the permission of God, chief bishop and prelate over the whole world," he implied that the new covenant made the Roman hierarchy (and himself as pope) overseers of the whole world in God's name – a new and augmented interpretation of chosenness. Since he was advocating a military campaign involving many kings and countries, it is clear that he considered his authority to extend beyond the purely religious aspect. Later he did not hesitate to assert, "God commands it."

Another excerpt makes it clear that the pope thought that God speaks through his mouth as he did through the mouth of Moses:

> All who die by the way, whether by land or by sea, or in battle against the pagans, shall have immediate remission of sins. This I grant them through the power of God with which I am invested. O what a disgrace if such a despised and base race [the Turks and Arabs] which worship demons, should conquer a people which has the faith of omnipotent God and is made glorious with the name of Christ (ibid).

Note that Urban used a favorite ploy of the new covenanters, that of demonizing those individuals and collectivities that are not partners in the covenant – a particularly nasty form of racism.

Urban must have been an electrifying preacher: all present rose and cried out, "It is the will of God! It is the will of God!" The pope seized the opportunity and decreed that the phrase would be the battle cry of the crusaders. It seems that the individual Christian believed himself part of a chosen and sanctified people.

The aims of the crusaders, generally, were the recovery and defense of the Holy Sepulcher in Jerusalem, the securing of a safe route for pilgrimages to the Holy Land, and the recovery and defense of Eastern Christian lands in Asia Minor. To these must be added various projects to satisfy the opportunistic ambitions of many leaders, both religious and lay. There ware eight crusades, plus a number of ancillary expeditions, some of which were directed at Christians. The most important of these – a full-fledged crusade, really – was against a Christian Heresy, the Cathari. It was a forerunner of the Inquisition and establishes a link between the latter and the crusades. In the last analysis a crusade was a war, called or sanctioned by the papacy, against anyone perceived to be an enemy.

As a mobilization, the first crusade was a resounding success. In a way, it was mite too successful: a monk, Pierre l'Hermite, gathered a troop of common people who left before the main contingents – fighters, wives, children and all. Most of them drowned in the Mediterranean Sea or were cut down by the Muslims, but not before killing many Jews. The main forces, however, did well, capturing Edessa, Antioch, Tripoli and Jerusalem. In the latter, victory was followed by a bloody massacre of Jews and Muslims. Four Christian states were established. These formed a thin strip along the eastern coast of the Mediterranean, except for the Countship of Edessa which, though contiguous to the Principality of Antioch, was inland and surrounded by Muslim lands. The new states were isolated, distant, and dependant on Europe for their supplies – which partly explains the necessity for further crusades.

As might be expected, Edessa fell to the Turks in 1144. Pope Eugenio III called for a second crusade and the kings of France and Germany answered. This enterprise was a fiasco and the Franks lost prestige in the region.

Meanwhile the Muslims were uniting and preparing for a holy war (*Jihad*) under Nureddin, the son of the conqueror of Edessa. When he died he was succeeded by Saladin who was to become, quite deservedly, a legend in the East *and* the West. In 1187, after a number of lesser conquests, Saladin captured Jerusalem. It was obvious that the Latin states couldn't cope with their isolation. Saladin treated the conquered people kindly and both Christians and Jews accepted his rule.

Pope Gregory VIII and his successor, Clement III, militated for a new crusade, the third. The Germans, the French, and the English set out in 1189 and 1190. Many sagas have been written about Saladin and Richard the Lion Hearted, but nothing much was accomplished.

The fourth crusade was the first one that wasn't called by a pope, but when some French nobles organized it, it was immediately blessed by Pope Innocent III. The army, however, was stranded in Venice because the barons did not have the funds to pay the passage across the Mediterranean. The Venetians, to whom the money was due, agreed to postpone payment if the crusaders would help them defeat Zara, a rival city. They sailed to

Zara, conquered it, and – boys will be boys – thoroughly pillaged it, even though it was a Christian town. The army wintered in Zara. They agreed to join the Venetian force in a campaign to force Constantinople to accept a pretender, Alexius, as emperor. This was accomplished but within a year the new emperor was dethroned in defiance of the crusaders. In 1104, the latter assaulted the city, defeated it, and thoroughly sacked it. The Byzantine Empire was greatly weakened and never completely recovered. The main outcome of the fourth crusade was the end of the dream of Christian unification, so dear to a number of popes.

Since the fourth crusade had been sidetracked by the Venetians, and never came close to Palestine and Jerusalem, Popes Innocent III and his successor, Honorius III kept insisting on another crusade. Finally in 1218 an expedition set forth with the intention of capturing the Egyptian city of Damietta and then exchanging it for Jerusalem. The military leader of the army was a cleric, the papal legate, Cardinal Pelagius of Albano. Damietta was besieged for 17 months, until Sultan al-Kamiel of Egypt offered the entire kingdom of Jerusalem, west of Jordan, if the crusaders would leave Egypt. The good cardinal refused. He captured Damietta intending to continue the campaign and conquer Egypt. After almost two years of fighting his army was trapped when the Nile flooded. Pelagius was forced to give up Damietta and return to the city of Acre.

The sixth crusade was the work of Frederick II, king of Sicily. After a few years of hesitation, he set sail for the Holy Land in 1227, but turned back for health reasons, allowing the fleet to continue. He was punished with excommunication by Pope Gregory IX, but nevertheless returned to the crusade in 1228. With little fighting he managed to conclude a treaty with Sultan al-Kamiel, the same who had made a similar offer to Cardinal Pelagius during the previous crusade, and who had been rebuffed by the bellicose prelate. This deal gave the Crusaders Jerusalem, Lydda and other cities and a promise of ten years of peace. The results of Frederick's effort were not appreciated by the pope who, it appears, preferred blood and guts to diplomacy. To punish the Emperor, the pope mounted a mini crusade against his possessions in Italy. In the years following the treaty the Franks continued to squabble between factions and to pick sides in local conflicts. This led to the recapture of Jerusalem by the Turks in 1244 and to the reconquest of most Frankish lands by Sultan Alga of Egypt.

This, of couse, necessitated another crusade. The main outcome of the 7th Crusade was the capture of its leader, King Louis IX of France, and the ransom of himself and some of his men at a huge price.

But Louis was both pious and stubborn. He mounted another crusade, the 8th, but this time a plague decimated his army and Louis himself died in North Africa before he could be captured and ransomed.

The people felt that the wind had left the sails of the crusades, but the popes continued to wave the flag. A few expeditions, none of them deserving the name of *crusade*, were organized but most were directed against the growing power of the Ottoman Turks rather than toward the reconquest and control of the Holy Land, and nothing was accomplished. They were, however, not a complete waste of time: in the name of Christ the Egyptian city of Alexandria was ravaged.

If the crusaders thought that they were intellectually superior to their heathen enemies, they did nothing to substantiate that claim by their strategies, tactics or diplomacy. If they thought themselves morally superior to the "base and bastard Turks" (the words of Urban II as reported by Bolderic of Dol) they contradicted themselves in action with sackings and pogroms.

The geographical area concerned, a thin strip of land, plus an inland bubble, with the Mediterranean on one side and millions of Muslims on the other, was untenable from both the military and supply point of view. The first crusade, despite its military success, necessitated the second, and so on down the line. One of the main incentives for the whole exercise was the deliverance of the Byzantine Empire from the encroachments of the Muslims and the reunification of Christianity. The crusades failed miserably on both counts. The Byzantine empire and culture suffered a permanently damaging blow when Constantinople was sacked by the crusaders – their ostensible saviors – during the 4th Crusade and that dashed any chance for unification.

Some later Muslim intellectuals and politicians have blamed the crusades for whatever ills have subsequently befallen Islam. That seems to be a notable exaggeration. There was little in the Koran to stimulate intellectual exploration and creativity, yet the centuries following the prophet Muhammad saw a surprising and glorious flowering of philosophical, literary, mathematical and scientific activity. (It was through Arab works that Europe inherited its share of the treasures of Greek culture.) By the time the Franks attacked, the retrenchment towards fundamentalism and away from intellectual freedom that has since marked Islam had already started. Of course, the crusades didn't help, but they were not the main cause of this retrogression.

Militarily, the Arabs and Turks came out winners. Under the leadership of Nureddin and Saladin, the conflict also prompted the unification of

Islam – contentious fragmentation having been debilitating before the Crusades, and becoming a curse again, after.

Saladin was the most heroic personage of the conflict. He was not only an excellent military leader, but also an able diplomat and as humanitarian a man as circumstances permitted. Had there been someone of his stature and character in the Christian camp, some reasonable arrangement could probably have been made that would have guaranteed access to the Holy Land and some protection for Byzantium, especially after the partial success of the 1st and 6th crusades.

The combination of wrong-headedness, stupidity and savagery that characterized the Christian effort should not blind us to the fact that the Europeans had a perfect right to resist the incursions and pressure of the Seljuk and, later, the Ottoman Turks.

The most tragic outcome of the crusades was the weakening and alienation of Byzantium and the extinguishment of any hope for Christian unification. If there is one lesson to retain from the crusades, it is that there is no such thing as a holy war: whether the fighting is for land or pride or God, there is no war without sacking, rape, torture, and killing of civilians – by both sides. This is one of the reasons why war must always be the very last resort.

The longest crusade was not directed against Islam but against people who considered themselves Christians. The Cathars (also known as Albigenses) were a heretical sect that was prominent in the 12th and 13th centuries. Their theology was a radical departure from Catholic dogma. Influenced, probably, by Gnosticism, dualism was its foundation: there was a good god, the creator of the spiritual world, and an evil god, Satan, the creator of the material world. Considering everything material as evil, the Cathars rejected the eating of meat and sexual activity. (It seems that they abhorred marriage and marital sex even more than casual promiscuity.) They were a tightly organized and actively proselytizing religion, and their success and numbers greatly alarmed the Roman clergy. In Southern France (Provence) and northern Italy they had friends and protectors among the political and military elites. When it became obvious that they would not convert, Pope Innocent III called for a crusade, and in 1208, a group of barons from northern France led an army against one of the Cathar strongholds, the city of Toulouse in the south. The barons were faced with a quandary: the Cathars were a minority but were indistinguishable from Catholics. The papal legate, a priest named Araud-Amaury, solved the problem: "Kill them all," he is reported to have said, "God will recognize his own." Thousands of Catholics and a few hundred Cathars were killed – a case of poor military productivity.

There were many towns and cities with a significant Cathar population. The attacks continued for many years. In 1244, 36 years after the rape of Toulouse, Montségur, a major Cathar stronghold was destroyed and 210 Cathars were burned alive – a training exercise for the nascent Inquisition. The last important engagement of the Albigensis crusade, as it is usually called, occurred in 1255, 45 years after the Toulouse massacre. During that time the 5th and 6th crusades were being fought in the Middle East, and an even more bizarre and irrational phenomenon was taking place: the children's crusade.

Without ecclesiastical support, and almost spontaneously, two hordes of mostly six to twelve year old children, numbering in the thousands, coalesced. One group in France was led by a child named Stephen, and one in Germany was under another child, Nicholas. They set out following two different routes, expecting that when they reached the Mediterranean the waters would miraculously divide to allow them to reach the Holy Land. When that didn't happen, they found ship captains willing to transport them. Some finished at the bottom of the Mediterranean, some were sold into slavery, some were simply killed, and some were given refuge and 'adopted' by various towns along the route. Very few returned home.

This is probably the most striking incident in a centuries-long spell of collective insanity and hysteria that infected western Christianity during much of the Middle Ages. The clergy – including many popes – instead of being a calming and therapeutic influence acted more like the conductors of a crazy and cacophonic orchestra.

Another event that marked and typified that era was the fourth Lateran Council (1215) which, among other things, decreed that rulers who tolerated heresies could be deposed and lose their territories. Many innocents were executed by rulers bullied by the Church and fearful of punishment. There is no record of kings being dispossessed for failing to persecute heretics, but there are many instances of rulers being excommunicated. In those days, people really believed that the Church held the key to heaven and could doom one to damnation by withholding that key ("Outside the Church, there is no salvation"). Proud and powerful emperors donned sackcloth and crawled to Rome to beg reinstatement. This illustrates to what extent the popes had gained the political upper hand in Europe.

The Inquisition

The Albigensian crusade was the nodal point linking two related movements, the crusades and the Inquisition, the first setting up the second and the campaign against the Cathars belonging to both.

In 1231, twenty three years after the Toulouse massacre, Pope Gregory XI instituted the papal inquisition. Inquisitors were sent all over Medieval Europe – but mostly in northern Italy and southern France – to ferret out heretics. At first the latter were almost exclusively targeted, but those suspected of adultery, incest, witchcraft and devil worship were gradually added to the menu of prosecutions. Jews and Moslems who minded their business were not bothered. Many inquisitors were members of a new order, the Dominicans, who were created with that role as one of their main responsibilities.

The inquisitors determined guilt and inflicted punishment ranging from fasting, pilgrimage and flogging to confiscation of property and imprisonment. However, accused condemned to death (by fire, of course) were delivered to the civil authorities, so as not to besmirch the Church with the stench of death. (Since the civil authorities could be excommunicated for not following through, the moral responsibly really rested with the Church.) The use of torture was originally rejected but in 1252 Pope Innocent IV in the bull *Ad Extirpanda*, permitted it for drawing confessions and for obtaining the names of heretics.

In Spain, the activities of the Inquisition were at first limited because of the struggle against Muslim invaders, but once the latter had been permanently repulsed, in the late 15th century, the imposition of religious homogeneity became a major concern. Jews were the first victims, especially Jews who had converted to Christianity, but whose sincerity was questioned (the Marranos). In 1492, Jews were given the choice of exile or conversion. After that initial ethnic cleansing had run its course, the Spanish Muslims who had accepted baptism (the Moriscos) were targeted. After them the attention of the defenders of the faith turned on the relatively few Protestants. Finally the goal of both the pope and the king was achieved: religious unity. Interestingly, the Spanish Inquisition served the interests of the king even more than those of the popes, which indicates that the preponderance of power was beginning to shift back toward secular authorities.

The whole exercise was under the leadership of the Grand Inquisitor, named by the government but approved by Rome. The most famous one was Tomas de Torquemada, a Dominican who had no hesitation to use torture, confiscation and execution. It is estimated that he had thousands of Marranos, Moriscos and heretics burned at the stake.

The Spanish Inquisition was finally suppressed in 1834. It took twelve hundred years for Christianity to become a killer religion, and more than five hundred to reverse the trend.

In a sense the Inquisition is still with us. When Protestantism started making inroads in Italy, Pope Paul II, in 1542, established the Roman Inquisition. Compared to the Medieval and Spanish inquisitions, it was a moderate affair. Still, it forced Galileo to recant his theories and imprisoned, tortured and finally burned Giordano Bruno in 1600.

Gradually, the Roman Inquisition became just another branch of papal government, and it limited its sanctions to denunciations and excommunications. In 1908, its name was changed to the *Holy Office*, and in 1965 it became the *Congregation for the Doctrine of the Faith*, under which moniker it is still with us.

In the Old Testament the exclusive covenant claimed by a nation led to horrible crimes that we would now call ethnic cleansing and crimes against humanity. In more recent times the exclusive covenant claimed by an institution again led to tyranny and cruelty. All condoned by the concept of moral dispensation, and all in the name of God!

Chapter XV – Meanwhile, the Rabbis ...

The Talmud is the "New Testament" of the Jews. Biblical history, as recorded in the Bible, came to an end *circa* 430 BCE, although the writing of the Books of Ezra, Nehemiah and Chronicles took another century. Some – not all – of the Christian books continued the historical approach and chronicled the Maccabean revolt of 167 BCE. 1, 2, 3 and 4 Maccabees were written by Jews but -- probably because the Maccabees had been partial to the Sadducees and the Tanakh was edited by their rivals, the Pharisees – these books were not included in the Hebrew document. During the intertestamentary period – between the Books of Ezra and Nehemiah, and the New Testament – Jews kept writing but their work did not find acceptance in the Tanakh. (This is particularly noteworthy in the case of texts of an apocalyptic nature.)

However, the Oral Torah continued to unfold. After the destruction of the Second Temple in 70 CE, a center of Jewish learning was established at Yavneh in Palestine and after the Bar Kochba Revolt in 132, a similar center was founded at Usha in Galilee. There, sages continued to develop the Oral Torah, but this time they relied on teams of trained memorizers to achieve a reliability approaching that of written texts.

The analog of our Supreme Courts was called the Great Sanhedrin. It consisted of 71 scribes and rabbis, and was both a judicial and legislative body in matters religious, but since religion and government were intertwined to various degrees, depending on time, location and politics, the Sanhedrin had, at times, considerable power, including the imposition of the death penalty.

Hillel and Shammai

Originally the leadership of the Sanhedrin was held by pairs of sages. Each co-leader would have his "house," that is, a group of followers, and would champion a particular approach to Torah.

The most influential such pair was that of Hillel and Shammai. Hillel was the more liberal and progressive of the two. He tried to take some of the sting out of the harsh laws and punishments of Moses. In some ways he was more liberal than Jesus, who, remember, said that not one iota of the commandments of the Torah could be changed, ever. Since he lived from 70 BCE to 10 CE, he was probably an important influence on Jesus.

Shamai was the conservative one. In the many debates between them, he was, more often than not, the loser but he always accepted the majority decision of the court. Both Shamai and Hillel believed that the normative authority rested with the rabbis and sages, collectively, not with Moses (although the latter was always honored as the greatest prophet).

Shammai was not a strict constructionist, as the term is used in the United States to denote those who believe that the articles of the US constitution, being God-inspired, are to be applied to judicial and political issues exactly as written. Shammai, though a conservative, was intelligent enough to realize that laws promulgated centuries ago must be kept contemporaneous by interpretation and even modification. (American jurists and politicians should study the Talmud, paying particular attention to the role of Shammai.)

The Mishna

Around 300 CE Rabbi Judah Ha-Nasi (also known as Judah the prince) finished the written compilation of late Second-Temple Oral Torah begun by Rabbis Akiva and Meir. The document is known as the *Mishna,* a text unique in style, content and inspiration.

It is simultaneously a code of law (Halakah) and a work of astounding imagination: a code of law because it interprets the written Torah (while also adding both related and autonomous elements); and a work of imagination because it invents rules for a Temple that doesn't exist anymore (except in memory) and because many of its laws cannot be enforced, since Israel is no longer a sovereign nation and doesn't control territory. It's a complicated and complete code of laws and practices to regulate a country that doesn't exist and to honor a Temple that doesn't exist.

The style – concise yet detailed, enigmatic yet imperative, fragmented yet bountiful – is best described by example:

A. three brothers–
B. two of them married to two sisters–
C. and one of them married to an unrelated woman
D. and one of the husbands married to one of the sisters died, and the one married to an unrelated woman married his widow
E. and then the wife of the second brother died–
F. and afterwards the brother married to the unrelated woman died–
G. lo, this [surviving sister] is prohibited to him for all time,
H. since she had been prohibited to him for one moment [when her husband died she was forbidden to his brother, then married to her sister, as his wife's sister]. (Yebamoth 3:7v, Jacob Neusner, ed.)

If you think this is hard to figure out, imagine trying to do it without Neusner's bracketed explanations. Of course, most of the Misha is not as puzzling as the above excerpt, but the document does have a whimsical flavor, a little like the serious whimsy of Zen Buddhism. It is, after all, a very detailed and exhaustive description cum prescription of a sacred memory. It is as though the sages were saying: "This is how it was and how it still is in the celestial Jerusalem and the celestial Temple of our collective memory. Keep it alive in your mind and, to the extent that it's possible, live by its rules and precepts."

Upon reading the above example, one may suspect that there is an underlying form forging the content, like a sonnet in poetry, or a fugue or blues in music. The formal pattern is syntactical. The Mishna takes liberties with grammar in the interest of compactness and memorization (remember, it started as Oral Torah). There are a limited number of syntactical patterns, but this does not limit the choice of issues and normative precepts.

The Mishna differs from the Pentateuch in more ways than in style. One would think that in emending the Torah by addition it would make the yoke of the Law more onerous, but a number of factors more than mitigate this:

1. The Mishna doesn't specify any penalties, either in this world or in the next, if we except certain probably unenforceable civil penalties in Tractate Sanhedrin. (Moses was a pitbull and imparted this side

of his character to the Old Treatment: people were stoned to death or otherwise killed for working on the Sabbath; disrespecting their parents; making, keeping or worshipping an idol or familiar spirit; etc. The sages of the Mishna were more like collies, gathering and protecting the herd, than like pitbulls.)

2. Many interpretations by different sages, often contradictory, are included in many chapters, without any indication of which should be considered conclusive. To illustrate, let me distillate from Tractate Sanhedrin (9:3): *Rabbi Judah says ... and sages say … Rabbi Simon says … sages reply .. Rabbi Simon says … and sages say …* (*Sages* refer to the consensus of rabbis and scholars. Their input is not always the last one cited in an argument.) There is a lot of wiggle room there.
3. The written Torah is constantly conscious of Yahweh and constantly refers to him. Although it is unthinkable that the Mishna would exist had there never been a biblical Torah, still, it is a comparatively (and surprisingly) secular document. One can read dozens of pages without once encountering the words *God, the Lord, YHWH, Adonai, el Shadai,* or *Hashem*. There is no piety here, just law – law, it seems, for its own sake. Furthermore, none of the sages of the Mishna claims any direct revelation from God, and none makes any pretense at infallibility.

The Mishna is unapologetic. It maintains the position and attitude of Hillel, Shamai and other sages that – although Moses is to be revered as a virtual demigod – the normative function of Judaism is firmly in the hands of the rabbis. This attitude is reinforced by making few references to the Pentateuch.

Reading between the Lines

One may wonder why intelligent and committed men would bother inventing punctilious rules, many of which have no possibility of implementation, and many of which are not meant to be implemented. But the Mishna is a many-faceted crystal. The rules are not so much normative as performative and devotional. In a previous chapter, I suggested that the Temple Sacrifice could be understood as a performance for an audience of one: Yahweh. The laws of the Torah and the Mishna are also performative. The God of the Bible 'sees,' 'hears' and knows everything. What may seem like a pointless gesture, act or abstention becomes holy if done for God. The Hindu who will not eat beef because the cow is a sacred animal is doing the same thing that a Jew is doing by not eating pork because the pig, which doesn't chew the cud, is an unclean animal. Both are sacrificing for the Lord. That delicious lobster that the Jew forswears is one of millions of little sacrifices that replace the big sacrifice of temple worship. The laws are man-made, but are directed at God as proof that the covenant has not been forgotten. All these acts of compliance constitute a perpetual prayer. Just reading the Mishna and studying *halacha* are as meritious – if not more – than following the rules.

The Mishna reinforces the covenant, but what kind of covenant is it? Since the ancient Hebrews did not believe in resurrection, salvation was for the collectivity, Israel, not for the individual – although reward in this life was expected. But the Sadducees were the last Biblical Jews to deny the existence of an afterlife. Although the Mishna – as we shall see – certainly accepted and valued the collective aspect of the sacred contract, individuals now had their personal share of the covenantal benefits, not only in this world but also in the next. (Because the ancient Hebrews did not believe in Heaven and were vague about the fate of the dead in *Sheol*, Jews – to this day – though generally believing in the after-life, are reticent to talk of individual salvation and seldom use Heaven as an inducement.)

Sometimes the Mishna uses halacha to make a point rather than to add commandments or punishment. In Tractate Sanhedrin of Order Nezikim (damages) of the Talmud, there's a discussion on the different modes of execution that can be used for the crime of murder: beheading, stoning and burning. Since some of these are more painful than others, the distinctions are important. The commentary (*Gemara*) of Sanhedrin describes the various modes. In the case of burning the condemned is buried in dung up to his armpits, his mouth is forced open and a "wick" is forced down his esophagus to his stomach. The Gemara specifies that the "wick" is a bar of lead, which implies that molten lead is poured into his mouth. This is not just execution; it's torture! But be not scandalized: since the Jews did not, at that time, have sovereign authority, the sentence was probably never enforced. It's doubtful that it was intended to be enforced. I suspect that the horrible sentence was chosen simply as a way of impressing upon the reader the loathsomeness of the crime/sin being punished. It is probable that there are many other cases where the punitive is used symbolically to say something about the religious and moral domains.

Self-Imposed Apartheid

"You are a holy people" is a phrase used a number of times in the Tanakh to express the notion that the Hebrew people are a race apart – special, unique and chosen. The Mishna is even more insistent on this point. One of the main reasons for all these laws is to set Jews apart from other peoples by creating a different culture with different rules and habits, a different calendar, different foods, different places of worship, and, of course, a different God. Not only different, but better. This is accomplished not so much by extolling the virtues of the Jews but rather by drawing a most unflattering picture of the Gentiles.

A. They [the Jews] do not leave cattle on Gentiles' inns,
B. Because they are suspect in regard to bestiality
C. And a woman should not be alone with them,
D. And a man should not be alone with them
E. Because they are suspect in regard to bloodshed
(Tractate: Abodah Zarah; 5:3, Jacob Neusner, translator)

You can't trust them with your wine either – a serous problem since wine touched by Gentiles cannot be used for libations to Yahweh:

A. A gentile who with an Israelite was moving jars of wine from place to place
B. If [the wine] was assumed to be watched, it is permitted.
C. If [the Israelite] informed him that he was going away [the wine is prohibited if he was gone] for a time sufficient to bore a hole and stop it up and [for] the clay to dry.
(Tractate Abodah Zarah; 2:1, Jacob Neusner, translator)

Similar precautions must be taken with milk. If the cow was milked by a gentile, the consumption of the milk is permitted only if an Israelite was watching the activity. You just can't trust those guys.

A distinction is made between consumption and business. Some products are prohibited for personal use, but dealing in them ("deriving benefit") is permitted; others are so impure that both use and selling are forbidden. Among the later wine and wine vinegar of Gentiles, Hadrianic earthenware, and hides pierced at the heart are specifically mentioned.

(The hides so pierced are forbidden because the cut may indicate that the organ may have been taken out to be offered to a god.)

Note that the Mishna makes no mention of Christians: it's as if they do not exist. Is it because it refuses to acknowledge a rival, or because it considers Christians a wayward sect of Judaism?

The Talmud

The Talmud is the Jew's analog of the Christians' New Testament. In fact, there are two Talmud's: the Palestinian Talmud (the Yerushalmi) and the Babylonian Talmud (The Blavi). The later, which is the more extensive, was completed a century later than the Yerushalmi, in 500 CE. It has eclipsed the Yerushalmi and when one refers to the Talmud it is the Babylonian text that is meant. The Talmud has two components: the Mishna and the Gemara; the latter consisting of commentaries on the former. There are 63 tractates in the Mishna; the Blavi has commentaries on 37 of them. These commentaries are long, involved and unsystematized. They touch on many topics besides purely religious and halachic ones: history, commerce, agriculture, medicine, astronomy, magic, etc. Reading the whole Talmud is as daunting a task as reading the whole Encyclopedia Britannica. Its pages contain the laws, stories, customs and maxims of millenniums of Jewish life. In contrast to the rather secular Mishna, the Talmud is a pious document: there are many uses of God's names and many references of the Scriptures. It is also more practical than the Mishna, showing more awareness of political reality and more respect for Gentiles.

Besides the sages responsible for the Mishna, the Talmud quotes many later scribes and rabbis. The Babylonian academies, where the Mishna was studied and the Talmud written, were founded by Rabbi Rav and Mar Samuel. The former was a link between the scholars of the Mishna (the Tannin) and those of the Talmud (the Amoraim); the latter established that "The law of the state is law," thus making it a religious duty for Jews to obey the civil laws of their country of residence – a most important principle of the Talmud. This is stated in tractates *Baba Kamma* (113b), *Baba Metzia* (108a) and *Baba Batra* (55a) of *Order Nezikin*, and referred to in tractate *Gittin* of *Order Nashim*. Other important scholars were Rabbis Rava and Abbaye who were famous for their heated discussions (they seldom agreed) and Rabbi Ashi, the master editor of the Work, and his assistant, Rabbi Ravena.

Some scholars who belong to a later period and are not included in the Talmud wrote commentaries that have become intimately associated with the document. One of these sages, Maimonides (Moshe ben Maimon), was also a physician and a philosopher. Through one of his works, *The Guide to the Perplexed*, he became known and influential in the West. Note that Maimonides, who spent most of his life in Egypt, wrote mostly in Arabic. Considering his background, one would expect him to be rather liberal and progressive. Not so: his interpretations of the Tanakh and the Talmud show him to have been a reactionary and fundamentalist thinker (and one who is often quoted by fanatical Zionists). He is a classical example of a person of faith who is highly motivated by hatred for all unbelievers. In his systemization of the laws of the Torah he interpreted Deuteronomy 23:21, "Unto a foreigner you may lend at interest" as a positive commandment to charge interest:

> By this injunction we are commanded to exact interest from a heathen to whom we lend money, so as not to help him or be kind to him but rather to harm him, even in lending him money, by demanding interest which you are forbidden to do in the case of an Israelite. (Maimonides, *The Commandments*, translated b Rabbi Dr. Charles B. Chavel, Vol. I, positive commandment 198.)

The Code of Jewish Law

The first systematization of Jewish law was accomplished by Maimonides in *Mishneh Torah*, written sometime in the 12th century. The next comprehensive compilation, the *Shulkan Arukh*, was the work of Yosef Karo, a Sephardic rabbi. It has been accepted as authoritative by Orthodox Judaism. This code goes into the most intimate areas of all human activity with laser-like precision and attention to detail. In Chapter IV, dealing with the bathroom, it says:

> One should be extremely careful to wipe himself thoroughly, for should there be any excrement left, he is not permitted to say anything holy. One should not wipe himself with his right hand, for with it he puts on the *t'philin* [phylactery]. And for the like reason one is forbidden to use the middle finger of the left hand in

> wiping himself for on it he winds the strap of the *t'philin.* A left-handed person may wipe himself with his left hand which is everybody else's right.
> (Shulkan Aruckh: IV, 5)
> [Okay, I'm cherry picking here, I admit. I just couldn't resist the temptation. Let me assure the reader that this quotation is not typical – that the vast majority of the laws in the Code are not as scatological and bizarre as the above -- but it does illustrate how the Law delves in minute detail into the most personal and intimate aspects of life.]

The Torah is said to have 613 laws; the Mishnah adds more; and then so does the Talmud; finally the Shulckan Aruckh surpasses them all with about 1,500 laws! It's an awesome and intimidating corpus of regulations. How can one memorize all these rules. How can one keep from infringing by inattention? How can one relax in the performance of any activity, knowing that the Lord, who knows all, is keeping score?

But the Code is not as harsh as its sheer weight and comprehensiveness would suggest. Many of its laws are *should* laws, not *must* laws. Also, the very numerousness of the compilation tends to minimize the force of any individual law. Since following a law is meritorious and all laws seem to be given equal weight, there is a possibility of counterbalancing violations of social and humanitarian laws such as those against robbery, murder and abuse by compliance to purely religious laws such as acceptance of dogma, rules governing attire, grooming and diet, the saying of prayers and blessings, etc., etc. Also, the terror of damnation is mitigated by the fact that most rabbis teach that the stay in *Gehinnon* (Hell) is limited to 12 years – except for heretics and blasphemers, who will suffer annihilation of their souls. (Rosh Hashanah: 17a)

The Talmud vs. the Torah

In the written Torah, Law descended from Yahweh. And laws were laws: they were meant to be obeyed and, since belief in the afterlife was not yet established, punishment for serious (and not-so-serious) infractions was in the here and how. And it was often downright savage: death by stoning, strangulation or burning for such transgressions as working on the Sabbath, rebelling against one's parents, or having an idol or familiar spirit. Punishment was often collective: whole families or cities smitten for the sin of one (or a few) individuals.

In the Talmud and the Shulkan Arukh laws are human inventions: no sage claims divine revelation. The laws are directed toward God but are not from God. The strictures of the Law are mitigated by the devotional aspect: the Law becomes a form of prayer-by-action, an avenue of communication with God, and a reminder to him that Israel's covenant has not been broken.

The sages of the Mishna laid the foundation for a secular society – in which, however, religion has an important role – by basing their laws and emendations of laws on their own initiative, with no recourse to dreams, visions or miracles.

Even more important, and of more long-term consequence, was Bar Samuel's edict that in civil matters "the law of the land is the law."

The law was also a means of ingathering the Jewish diaspora – of re-assembling all those bones of Ezekiel's dream that had been scattered by the Assyrian and Babylonian deportations – and of demarking the group as a distinct and special social entity among the host of humans. [One wonders if God was, perhaps, not the primary concern of the rabbis, but rather the Great Enabler in the task of ingathering that collective demigod, Israel.]

One thing is certain: with immense dedication and effort, the rabbis succeeded brilliantly in the almost impossible mission of re-assembling the remnants (in spite of their continuing geographical scattering) and in the equally crucial endeavor of instilling in them a collective character that has endured for two millennia despite further deportations.

And all this they did without war, without ethnic cleansing, without proscribing a single city, without killing anyone.

Interpreting the Talmud

Imagine a commission of inquiry regarding an important issue. Every member of the commission stands in turn and gives his opinion or comments on a previously expressed opinion. Every word is recorded. After all have said their piece and are satisfied that they have nothing more to proffer, every person picks up his or her briefcase and heads for home. No definite conclusion has been reached, and the government, and any party that makes a request, will receive a transcript of the proceedings and nothing more.

Now imagine that instead of a commission-of-inquiry deliberation we are dealing with a conference of Talmudic rabbis and scribes. What could be the point of the exercise?

The answer is not simple. First, sometimes there is a clear preponderance of opinion, especially when a statement starts with "sages say" or is followed by "but sages permit," since we can presume that *sages* means the majority of the participants. But sometimes the sages' statement is followed by one from a well-known rabbi. Which one is more authoritative? The minority opinions are duly recorded and never condemned as heretical: they become part of the canon.

The main reason for this is to maintain the religion hospitable to adherents with vastly different beliefs, attitudes, interests, etc. This is why Judaism has been able to deal with believers, unbelievers, traditionalists, modernists, rationalists, mystics, nationalists and pietists; keeping peace in the family and obtaining cooperation from all.

[Personal note: In the Montreal Jewish Library, I got into a conversation with a middle-age woman who was very intelligent and well-read in Judaic matters. When I mentioned that I was an atheist, she remarked that it was not necessary to believe in an independently existing God: belief in God as a symbol of all that is good and noble was sufficient. I asked her to which branch of Judaism she belonged. She answered, "Orthodox." I then asked if it were possible to be both an atheist *and* an orthodox Jew. She answered yes. I said nothing but wondered (again) how one could invent his/her own God and then use it as a rationale for chosenness and moral dispensation.]

This doctrinal *laissez-faire* gives rabbis and groups of rabbis great latitude and power. The Talmud can be conceived metaphorically as a store of colors and shapes that rabbis, schools and institutions can use to build up their own image of the religion. (Of course, the situation is not quite as chaotic as in the above metaphor. Centers of consensus certainly exist and a certain uniformity of interpretation may be present in each of the three branches of Judaism. This is a contemporary aspect of the Oral Torah, of which most Gentiles and many Jews are unaware.)

Another consequence of this microstructure of the Talmud is that with enough patience and effort one can find citations to back up any criticism of the book. To quote one rabbi without reference to what other sages said in the discussion is to quote out of context. Because the Old Testament is part of the Christian canon, some critics (such as Michael A. Hoffman II in *Judaism's Strange Gods*) spare no effort in their attempt to prove that the roots of Ideological Zionism are to be found in the Talmud rather than in the Tanakh.

Because of this microstructure, comparing individual lines or statements of the Talmud and the Tanakh will get us nowhere. We must take a macro perspective and judge the documents by their effects on their adherents and by their historical consequences. The Tanakh, as demonstrated in Chapter 1, is a celebration of blood and gore – perhaps the most violent of scriptures – whereas the Talmud, except for some horrid descriptions of punishments and methods of execution, doesn't turn the stomach. The Tanakh's internal ethical system, that is, the laws and customs dealing with interpersonal and intertribal relations within the Hebrew community is horrible: person against person; tribe against tribe; Judah against Israel; king against king; Moses having hundreds of people killed because his brother fabricated a Golden Calf; the Yahweh worshipers killing the Baal followers; the list goes on and on. The Talmud has none of this: Jews respect Jews, help Jews and protect Jews, while rabbis try, with great success, to link together disparate groups of the diaspora. In fact, were it not for their failure to deal with the extreme ethnocentricity still infecting the religion, the rabbis would have created an ethos that could have been a model for the species. Therefore, the Talmud must be judged as morally superior to the Tanakh, and Rabbinical Judaism as a better religion than Yahwism.

Chapter XVI – Moral Dispensation in the New World

Unlike the crusades, colonialism was not an initiative of the Christian Church. There is no doubt, though, that the covenantal ethos, with its dismissive and racist attitudes towards non-convenanters and its moral dispensation for its adherents, was an important background element. Most of the peoples subjected to Colonialism were neither Christians, Jews, nor (initially) Muslims: therefore they did not rate a full complement of rights.

[Personal note: I remember, from my days as a student in Catholic primary and secondary schools, hearing teachers say that when Shamans performed apparently miraculous wonders, it was Satan who empowered them. Satan, after all, doesn't want his minions converted to God's religion, an idea that implies a demonization of millions. (To be fair, though, I must admit that the Church has since changed its attitudes.)]

But, if the initiative passed from church to state and from pope to king, the Christian hierarchy nonetheless remained powerful and relevant. Church approval, or toleration, was very important to secular conquerors. In an effort to maintain at least the appearance of the Church's authority in worldly affairs, the Vatican "gave" to Spain colonial rights to land west of the Azores (that is, North and South America) and to Portugal colonial rights to non-European land east of those islands.

Christopher Columbus was a ruthless conqueror more than he was an explorer. He was also a tough negotiator who drove a hard bargain. He insisted on being knighted and appointed viceroy of the territories he explored and was granted 10% of the revenues levied form them.

Columbus made four trips to America. His main interest seemed to have been gold and slaves rather than geographical exploration.

He claimed that he prepared for his first trip by studying the prophesies of Isaiah rather than maps or writings. Whenever he would encounter Indians, he would explain to them, in a language they didn't understand, how God, through the Pope, had given their land and persons to the king and queen of Spain. Later, this was formalized into a prepared text, the *requierimento*, that Spaniards were required to read out loud upon meeting a new group of Indians.

After stating that "the Lord our God" created "the Heaven and the Earth and one man and one woman" from which all nations are descended, the *requierimento* claims that God established the pope as the leader of all these nations:

> Of all these nations God our Lord gave charge to one man, called St. Peter [and his successors], that he should be Lord and Superior of all men in the world, that all should obey him, and that he should be head of the whole human race, wherever men should live, and under whatever law, sect, or belief that they should be; and he gave him the world for his kingdom and jurisdiction.
>
> One of these Pontiffs, who succeeded that St. Peter as Lord of the World, in the dignity and seat which I have before mentioned, made donation of these isles and Terra-firma to the aforesaid King and Queen [Ferdinand and Isabella] and to their successors, our lords, …

The text proceeds to claim that almost all other Indians to whom the *requerimento* had been read had agreed to become loyal vassals of the king and queen and had converted to Catholicism. The benefits of being so are then enumerated:

> If you do so, you will do well, and that which you are obliged to do to their Highnesses, and we in their name shall receive you in all love and charity, and shall leave you your wives, and your children, and your lands, free without servitude, that you may do with them and with yourselves freely that which you like and think best, and they shall not compel you to turn Christian …

Finally, the dire consequences of refusing to immediately comply with this program are made clear:

> But if you do not do this, and wickedly and intentionally delay to do so, I certify to you that with the help of God, we shall forcibly enter into your country and shall make war against you in all ways and manners that we can, and shall subject you to the yoke and obedience's of the Church and their Highnesses; we shall take you and your wives and children, and shall make slaves of them, and as such shall sell and dispose of them as their Highness may command; and shall take away your goods, and shall do all the harm and damage that we can …
> (www.healingtheland.com)

Note that the paragraph on benefits is nothing more than a monstrous lie, contrary to intent and falsified by subsequent events. (The Amerindians being sub-human pagans could not be ethical objects: to deceive them and to lie to them did not constitute sin.) Note also that the paragraph makes no sense since the previous paragraphs had impressed the necessity for all humans – and especially those being addressed – to recognize Catholicism as the only true faith and the pope and the king, through papal acquiescence, as their legitimate leaders, thus making complying Indians *de facto* Catholics. How could one say that you are free not to be a Catholic if and only if you agree that Catholicism is the only true faith?

The Christian religion had always regarded slavery as a legitimate and natural institution. It had forbidden the enslavement of fellow Christians, but some prelates had interpreted this as applying only to Christians who were born within the faith and who were not part of, and did not issue from, a pagan collectivity, thus adding race to religion as a criterion for slavery.

The last paragraph, however, is a truthful description of the consequences of being Amerindian: war without ethical limits, forced conversion, enslavement of men, women and children, loss of property, and, finally, limitless harm and damage. The only lie in that paragraph is in the first line, "But if you do not do this, and wickedly and intentionally delay to do so." There was no *if*: conversion and submission was no protection from oppression and enslavement.

Often, apologists sought support for their rationale and actions from sources even more mystical than the Roman hierarchy. Some 500 years ago a Spanish jurist, geographer and colonial functionary wrote:

> The King has every right to send his men to the Indians to demand their territory from the idolaters because he had received it from the Pope. If the Indians refuse, he may quite legally fight them, kill them and enslave them, just as Joshua enslaved the inhabitants of the country of Canaan.
> (Martin Fernàndez de Ensisco, quoted in Helen Ellerbe, *The Dark Side of Christian History*, Morning Star Books)

All the unethical and savage aspects of the Old Testament are there: chosenness, racism and moral dispensation. The White race has replaced the Jews (or Hebrews), and the promised land is now the whole planet. Note that de Ensisco was a lay person – not a cleric. Colonialism was the enterprise of kings, not popes or other princes of the Church. Despite the continued and important involvement of the Church, *colonialism represents the secularization of covenant theology.*

There is a plethora of documents, many from eyewitnesses, dating from the era, that attest to the genocidal savagery of the European Christians. One of the most significant comes from Columbus' own son, Ferdinand:

> At virtually every previous landings on this trip Columbus' troops had gone ashore and killed indiscriminately, as though for sport, whatever animals, birds and natives they encountered, "looting and destroying all they found," as the admiral's son once blithely put it.
> (Daniel E. Stannard, *American Holocaust: The Conquest of the New World*, Oxford, quoting Ferdinand Colon, *the Life of the Admiral Christopher Columbus by His Son Ferdinand*).

At some point Columbus fell ill and his men were free to roam the countryside and kill whoever they wished. Upon recovering, Columbus organized the slaughter and the depredation continued:

> In March of 1495, he massed together several hundred armored troops, cavalry, and a score or more of trained attacked dogs. They set forth across the country side, tearing into assembled masses of sick [from epidemics of European diseases] and unarmed native people, slaughtering them by the thousands. The pattern set by these raids would be the model the Spanish would follow for the next decade and beyond.
> (Stannard, p. 70)

The Amerindians had few defenders, but they had *some.* The most ardent was Bartolomé de las Casas, bishop of Chiapas, an eyewitness to some of the most horrific massacres, and the author of *History of the Indies,* and of *A Very Brief Account of the Destruction of the Indies*, and a few more books. From personal observation he wrote:

> It was the general rule among the Spaniards to be cruel; not just cruel but extraordinarily cruel so that harsh and bitter treatment would prevent Indians from daring to think of themselves as human beings or having to think at all. So they would cut off an Indian's hands and leave them dangling by a shred of skin and they would send him on saying, "Go now, spread the news to your chiefs."
> (Las Casas, *History of the Indies*, Harper and Row, p. 94, via Stannard, p. 70)

Numbers, approximately as they may be, tell the tragic story:

> By 1496, … the population of Hispaniola [Haiti and the Dominican Republic] had fallen from eight million to between four and five million. By 1508 it was down to less than a hundred thousand. By 1518 it numbered less than twenty thousand. And by 1535, say the leading scholars on this grim topic, "for all practical purposes, the native population was extinct."
> (Stannard, p. 74-75, quoting from Cook and Borak, "Aboriginal Population of Hispaniola, p. 401.)

Stannard continues with his mournful elegy:

> In less than the normal lifetime of a single human king, an entire culture of millions of people, thousands of years resident in their homeland, had been exterminated. The same fate befell the native peoples of surrounding islands in the Caribbean as well. Of all the horrific genocides that have occurred in the twentieth century against Armenians, Jews, Gypsies, Ibo, Bengalis, Timorese, Kampucheans, Ugandans, and more, none has come close to destroying this many – or this great proportion – of wholly innocent people.
> (Stannard, p 75)

It is extremely doubtful that epidemics alone could account for the complete disappearance of a people numbering in the millions. Plagues may kill the majority of a population but not all of it: there are always a number of individuals able to survive and eventually reconstitute the collectivity. Disease and a genocidal exercise worked hand in hand to do the job.

The conquistadors, having completely ravaged the people and the land of the Antilles, conquered Mexico then swept south and overran what are now Belize, El Salvador, Honduras, Nicaragua, Costa Rica, Panama and as far as Peru and even part of Chile. Their tactics had not changed, nor their ethos. Indians were murdered for any reason (including just plain fun); houses and fields were burned; livestock (mostly llamas) were killed. According to Stannard, "by 1542 Nicaragua alone had seen the export of as many as half a million of its people for slave labor (in effect, a death sentence) in distant areas whose populations had been destroyed.)" (p. 82)

Herman Cortez, one of the main leaders of the conquistadors, gives this description of a day's work in the destruction of the city of Tenochtitland:

> … I resolved to enter the next morning shortly before dawn and do all the harm we could … and we fell upon a huge number of people. As these were some of the most wretched people and had come in search of food, they were nearly all unarmed and women and children in the main. We did them so much harm through all the streets in the city that we could reach, that the dead and the prisoners numbered more than eight hundred.

> (Herman Cortez, *Letters from Mexico*, translated by A.R. Pagden, Grossman Publishers, p. 249, via Stannard, pp. 78-79)

Bernardiino de Sahagun, a sixteenth-century historian described a raid by conquistadors on Indian civilians celebrating a religious feast:

> They chopped off their hands and their heads so that they fell down dead. Then all the Spaniards began to cast off heads, arms and legs and to disembowel the Indians. Some had their heads cut off, others were cut in half and others had their bellies slit open immediately to fall dead. Others dragged their entrails along until they collapsed. (Bernadino de Sahagun, *Conquest of New Spain*, 1495, translated by Howard F. Cline, University of Utah Press, via Stannard, p. 76)

As though such blood frenzy and depraved cruelty were not enough the conquistadors also used armored dogs trained to disembowel and kill.

The era of the conquistadors was followed by that of the *encomiendas*, based on a system that gave Spanish beneficiaries title to people – tribes, bands, families, individuals – rather than title to land. This resulted in even greater cruelty. The slave owners were free to transport their human property anywhere they wished and put them to work at any task from mining to farming. Overworked and underfed, the slaves did not survive long: years were unusual, months common. Sometimes when a slave was too weak to continue working, he would be given a little food and sent back home. Since this often necessitated a trek of many kilometers, the moribund slave often died on the way. At any rate, according to Las Casas, only about ten percent of Indian slaves survived long enough to reach that pitiable emancipation.

In North and South California the *encomienda* system was applied mostly in missions – Catholic settlements headed by a padre (priest) and populated by captured slaves. At first Jesuits administered the missions. They recorded few vital statistics. They were followed by Franciscans, who *did* keep records. In mission after mission the ratio of baptisms to deaths was less than 1 to 2. How could the missions survive such a death rate? – Easy: the Spanish soldiers simply captured more Indians than were lost to disease and maltreatment. They were captured for two reasons: to forcibly convert them, and to enslave them. The padres needed slaves to work their plantations and care for their animals. Also, they derived revenue from hiring them out to military camps and installations.

European diseases and brutal oppression worked hand in hand to bring Amerindians to the brink of extinction. Weakened by smallpox, influenza, measles and a few other maladies the natives were easy prey for the Spanish and, later, English forces. Once in the missions, cramped quarters favored the spreading of disease, while malnutrition and long hours of hard labor further weekend them. [African slaves received more and better food and were much better looked after because reasonably healthy workers were more productive. In the case of Indian slaves it was more profitable to work them to death and replace the casualties by fresh captives from military raids.]

The padres added a new twist to maltreatment that even the conquistadors had not thought of:

> To be certain that the Indians were spiritually prepared to die when their appointed and rapidly approaching time came, they were required to attend mass in chapels where, according to one mission visitor, they were guarded by men "with whips and goads to enforce order and silence" and were surrounded by soldiers with fixed bayonets" who were on hand in case any unruliness broke out ... If any neophytes (as the Spanish called Indians who had been baptized) were late for mass they would have "a large leathern thong, at the end of a heavy whip-staff, applied to their naked backs."
> (Stannard, p. 139-140, quoting from James J. Rowls, *Indians of California: The Changing Image.*)

To this, add cruel punishment, wanton murder, and sadistic treatment of children and women (girls served the double duty of labor and lust) and it becomes clear that the centuries-long campaign against the Amerindians was a genocidal enterprise. If the extinction of the entire Amerindian race was not achieved, many tribes did completely disappear. Despite the capital role of epidemics in the saga of the Americas, apologists cannot hide behind the plague theory to deny genocide.

Stannard makes a good case that other Whites were no better in the treatment of Indians than were the Spaniards:

> By 1845 the Indian population of California was down to no more than a quarter of what it had been when the Franciscan missions were established in 1779. That is, it had declined by at least 75 percent during seventy years of Spanish rule. In the course of just the next twenty-five years, and under American rule, it would fall by another 80 percent. (p. 142).

At first the Americans simply continued to treat the California Indians much like the Spaniards had done: as slaves, as semi-humans not entitled to any rights, as economic assets for the chosen people. The government neither officially sanctioned their slavery nor made the slightest effort to end it. Predatory marauders combed the countryside looking for human merchandise. Young merchandise, especially female (I wonder why) brought the best prices. The parents were often killed so that the children could be sold as orphans. If any surviving parent went to the courts to seek justice it would be of no avail: by law, no Indian could testify against a White. In 1850, a law, "Act for the Government and Protection of Indians" was passed by the California legislation during the first session. It legalized the forced indenture of any Indian child if a justice of the peace was satisfied that the child had not been captured by force. The justices were easily satisfied. Ten years later the law was amended to allow for longer terms of service and to also apply to adult Indians. The enslavement of Amerindians was now official government policy.

It got worse. Because some Indians who had been driven to arid regions had, by necessity, killed some livestock, Governor Peter Burnet advocated war "until the Indians become extinct." (Albert L. Hurtado, *Indian Survival on the California Frontier*, Yale U. Press, p. 46, via Stennard, p. 144.) It is hard not to interpret this as a government-sponsored incitement to genocide and a *carte blanche* policy toward murder of Indian men, women and children.

On the Eastern Front

If the west-coast Amerindians had emigrated east to escape depredation and desolation, they would have found little relief. Although, in the beginning, the Indians and the British of Virginia and New England did engage in political and commercial activities (moistly to the advantage of the British who would not have survived their first winter or two without the help of the natives) the situation didn't last long.

Before the first successful British implantation, the Jamestown settlement in Virginia, many unsuccessful attempts were made. One of these, the "lost colony" of Roanoke, wasted no time to give an indication of what was to come:

> There, when an Indian was accused by an Englishman of stealing a cup and failing to return it, the English response was to attack the natives in force, burning the entire community and the fields of corn surrounding it. (Edmund S. Morgan, *American Slavery – American Freedom: The Ordeal of Colonial Virginia*, W.W. Norton, pp. 24-43, via Stannard, p. 105).

In New England the English settlers were Puritans. The first group, the Pilgrims of the Mayflower who founded the Plymouth colony in 1620, were particularly radical and insisted on complete separation from the Anglican Church. Later colonists were also Puritans, but not as radical nor as closely knit as the Pilgrims. There was cooperation but also distrust between the two groups.

There was less cooperation and more distrust between the British and the Indians, yet during the first decades there was trade and political interaction between the newcomers and the natives.

However, when tensions escalated to the point of violence, it was the English Christians who were treacherous and savage. When conflict arose between the Puritans and the Massachusetts tribe, Miles Standish, the military leader of the Pilgrims, lured two high-ranking warriors into a house in the settlement of Wessagussett with an invitation to share a meal (food had been very scarce for everyone). Nathaniel Pilbrick in his book, *Mayflower*, describes what ensued:

> Once they had all sat down and began to eat, the captain [Miles Standish] signaled for the door to be shut. He turned to Pecksuot and grabbed the knife from the string around the Pniese's neck. Before the Indian had a chance to respond, Standish had stabbed him with his own weapon.

> (Nathaniel Philbrick, *Mayflower: A story of Courage, Community and War*, Viking Penguin, p. 141-2).

Seven Indians were killed in that assault.

The first conflict that was serious enough to be called a war was the Pequot War in 1637. The *causus belli* was partially economic: the Puritans of Massachusetts Bay regarded the Pequot to be an economic rival. And, of course, the destruction of Indian villages resulted in a substantial land grab. As Captain John Mason, one of the English officers put it: "The Lord was pleased to smite our Enemies in the hinder Parts, and to give us their Land for an Inheritance." (John Mason, *A Brief History of the Pequot War*, Kneeland and Green, 1736, p. 21, via Stennard, p. 111).

When several ship captains were slain by unknown Indians, the Puritans used the incident as a pretext for strong military action. Philbrick describes the bloodiest encounter of the ensuing war:

> ... The Puritans fell upon a Pequot fortress on the Mystic River. After setting the Indians' wigwams ablaze, the soldiers proceeded to shoot and hack to pieces everyone who attempted to escape the inferno. By the end of the day approximately four hundred Pequot men, women and children were dead ... Bradford [governor of Plymouth] saw the devastation as the work of the Lord.
> (Philbrick, p 178)

John Mason, commander of the Connecticut troops saw the massacre from a more lofty perspective:

> And indeed such a dreadful terror did the Almighty let fall upon their Spirits, that they would fly from us and run into the very Flames, where many of them perished ... [And] God was above them, who laughed his Enemies and the Enemies of his People to Scorn, making them as a fiery Oven: Thus were the Stout Hearted spoiled, having slept their last Sleep, and none of their men could find their Hands: Thus did the Lord judge among the Heathen, filling the place with dead Bodies.
> (John Mason, *A Brief History of the Pequot War*, Kneeland and Green, 1736, p. 21)

The Pequot war officially ended with the Treaty of Hartford in 1638, but it signaled the continuation of a return to the ethos of the conquistadors. In the minds of Puritans and Pilgrims, the Amerindians – even those who had converted – had lost their souls: they could now be hunted and killed with the freedom of conscience of a hunter shooting game, or a youngster shooting a virtual target – essentially a bunch of pixels – on a television screen.

> Hunting redskins became for the time being a popular sport in New England especially since prisoners were worth good money [as slaves], and the personal danger to the hunter was now very slight.
> (Stannard, p. 116)

We live in a fast world. The 17th century was a slow world. Yet the events that constitute the early history of New England seem to us to have occurred well above the historical speed limit. In less than two decades: the Indians learned English (and a few Englishmen learned a native language); trading networks were established; the Indians divided into pro-English and anti-English tribes; the Whites learned from the Indians; and the Indians adopted some elements of European technology. Impressive, even to the speeded-up modern mind! Add to this the personal element – the loyalties, the betrayals, the quest for wealth and power, the attraction of adventure, the cultural and religious elements – and we end up with a confusing and fluid picture. Consider, also, that battles that involved only a dozen or so individuals on either side could have historically important consequences. It took twenty years before such factors engendered the Pequot war. In spite of the increased instability caused by the latter, New England soldiered on for almost four decades until the King Philip's war broke out in 1675.

According to Stannard, the war was not the inevitable result of any military or political imperative. The causes of the war were the personalities of King Philip, the sachem of the Wampanoag tribe (and leader of a loose coalition of tribes) and Josiah Winslow, governor of Plymouth; their antagonism and mutual distrust; and a smoldering and growing war hysteria and paranoia on both sides (Philip was having more and more trouble controlling his warriors).

It wasn't a simple English vs. Indian affair: some tribes sided with Plymouth and the Puritans, some with Philip and the Wampanoags, and some tried to remain neutral. Of all the conflicts in colonial America, it was the only one in which the Indians were able to inflict major damage and numerous causalities. In fact, had the colonials not enjoyed support from the mother country, the Amerindians may well have been the victors.

Indian casualties were in the vicinity of 3000; the Puritans lost about one-third of that number. Most native villages were left in ruins and likewise a dozen White towns. The economic damage was disastrous: it would be decades before the quality of life returned to the pre-war level.

But the saddest aftermath of King Philip's war was the fate of a thousand or so Indians loaded on ships and sold as slaves in the Antilles and other places.

The Wild, Wild West

The fourth of July, 1776, was not a day of deliverance for Amerindians. Many of the Founding Fathers were strongly anti-Indian:

George Washington instructed Major General John Sullivan to attack the Iroquois and lay waste all their settlements. [This after the crucial role Iroquois played on the side of the English and Americans during the French and Indian War.] (Stannard, p. 119)

Thomas Jefferson, referring to Amerindians wrote, "in War, they will kill some of us; we shall destroy all of them." (p. 120)

Andrew Jackson who, talking about his Indian-fighting days, bragged that he had preserved all the scalps of those he had killed. As ex-president he encouraged American troops to seek out and kill Indian women and children so as to exterminate the race. (p. 121)

Most federal, state, and local politicians were Indian haters and many advocated the killing of women and children, including those who were pious Christians. As Stannard put it, this was "flatly and intentionally genocidal. For no population can survive if its women and children are destroyed." (p. 119) For all practical purposes Americans were given government license to kill and expropriate all and any Indians. (An exception was Congressman David Crocket who, at the cost of his political career, opposed Jackson's policies.)

Most newspapers were a strong voice on the side of genocide. An eloquent example:

> The Whites, by law of conquest, by justice of civilization, are masters of the American continent, and the best safety of the frontier settlements will be secured by the total annihilation of the few remaining Indians.

> (L. Frank Baum, writing in the *Aberdeen Saturday Pioneer*, Dec. 20, 1891, from Stannard, p. 126)
>
> Two weeks or so later, Baum wrote, "we had better, in order to protect our civilization follow it up [The Wounded Knee Massacre] … and wipe these untamed and untamable creatures from the face of the earth." (From Stannard, p. 127)

In 1830, Congress passed the Indian Removal Act. In 1835 the Treaty of New Echota gave the government all Cherokee land east of the Mississippi in return for some land in Indian territory in distant Oklahoma and 5 million dollars (which were not really given to the tribe, but used to cover the expense of the move to Oklahoma). The Cherokees had been partly coerced and partly tricked into signing the treaty. The relocation – called the Trial of Tears by the victims – was a death march, as the Indians died by the thousands during the long and arduous trek. Other tribes, including the Choctaws, Seminoles and Creeks were subjected to similar ordeals.

Some Indians accepted relocation submissively, but others resisted. The insubordination was met with savage repression, resulting in many massacres. In only one case, the battle of Little Big Horn, did the Indians win.

One of the worst examples of racist depravity and military insanity was the Sand Creek Massacre, in Colorado, in 1864, under the command of Colonel Chivington. There were 600 Indians in the village, only some 35 of which were braves, since most men were away on a buffalo hunt. Between 400 and 500 women, children and old men were killed, scalped, cut up and dismembered; sexual parts were even cut out and paraded as trophies – a satanic massacre unmatched in savagery by Hitler's Nazis.

Congressional investigations were ordered and at one point a public meeting was held at the Denver Opera House, with the governor of Colorado and Colonel Chivington present. When the question was asked: would it be best to try to "civilize" the Indians or simply to exterminate them, the audience rose as one man and shouted, "EXTERMINATE THEM! EXTERMINATE THEM!" (David Savaldi, *Sand Creek and the Rhetoric of extermination*, University Press of America, p. 149-50, via Stannard, p. 133-4).[It's not true that the people are always good and that only evil leaders are responsible for outrages. Read *Hitler's Willing Executioners* by Daniel Jonah Goldhagen].

Colonel Chivington was never charged. He had some success as an after-dinner speaker. Years later President Theodore Roosevelt judged the massacre "as righteous and beneficial a deed as ever took place on the frontier" (Quoted in Thomas G. Dyer, *Theodore Roosevelt and the Idea of Race*, Louisiana State, p. 79, via Stannard, p. 134).

The Last major massacre occurred in South Dakota in 1890, between the toughest Sioux fighters and the 7th Cavalry. The braves were inspired by a mystical native resistance movement, the Ghost Dance. They wore a brightly colored shirt and believed that it made them impervious to bullets. The cavalry brought in four lethal Hotchkiss guns that fired explosive shells filled with grapeshot – the 19th century precursor of modern cluster bombs. They were very deadly, especially against mothers and children huddled together. The great majority of those who survived the Hotchkiss guns and the rifles were pursued and cut down by the soldiers – even young children were cut to pieces. Hundreds were killed, two thirds of them women and children.

North of the Border

In New France (later, Lower Canada and finally, Québec Province) it was government policy in the mother country *and* in the colony to interfere as little as possible with Indian life. Of course, much emphasis was put on missionary work. When the French got in trouble dealing with the natives, it was because they took sides in intertribal conflicts [Samuel de Champlain, the founder of Québec City, joined the Hurons in a raid on the Iroquois and shot one of the braves dead. The Iroquois never forgot: during the French and Indian wars they held the balance of power – on the English side.]

After the American independence, the scene moved to the plains where the aboriginals couldn't play the French against the English, nor the English against the Americans. As we have seen, the pressure against the Indians was relentless and savage. Many Indian bands, from such tribes as the Potawatomi, Blackfoot and Ojibwa found refuge in Canada where the government and the Royal Canadian Mounted Police gave some measure of protection.

Canada would look good if the story ended there. It didn't. The story started at least as far back as the 18th century in the Spanish missions of North and Southern California: an unholy alliance was formed between religious and secular authorities to control and debilitate the Indian Nation and to use and abuse its members. Americans picked up on that scheme and, in the second half of the 19th century, started experimenting with various institutional meldings of government and religious input in the education of Indian children. In 1879, the first federally sanctioned boarding school for Indian children, the Carlisle Industrial Training School, opened its doors. It soon became the model for a new educational program and within a few decades there were hundreds of such institutions.

By the mid 1880s its influence had crossed the border into Canada. The Northern model, the Canadian Residential School, would be funded (cheaply) by the federal government and administered by clergymen of the Roman Catholic, Anglican or United Church confessions. For both sides, this was a marriage made in heaven: the churches had new adherents who couldn't really say no, and the state had teachers and administrators willing to work for a pittance.

The losers, of course, were the Indian people and, especially, the children who were forcibly wrenched from their families; practically incarcerated; forbidden to express any aspect of their native culture, be it religious, linguistic or esthetic; and who were cruelly punished by the priests, masters or nuns for any infraction to the rules. The children were also used as laborers and servants for the benefit of the institution and its staff.

Moreover, as was made evident by many court cases and reports in the media, many of these children were victims of serious sexual abuse. Many experts claim that the high rate of sexual abuse – as well as suicide and alcoholism – in contemporary Indian communities can, in large part, be attributed to post-traumatic reaction to abuse suffered in childhood. Since the state paid the churches a fixed rate for each child in their care, there was a strong incentive to provide the students with the least quantity and quality of food, clothing, medical care, etc. The children were in poor physical and psychological health. Many tried to escape, and some succeeded but, having been moved a distance away from their family, they had nowhere to go and often disappeared into the wilderness.

These conditions were not limited to certain anomalous institutions, but were generalized throughout the system and throughout its history – about 130 schools from the 1840s to the 1990s. According to the Canadian Broadcasting Corporation, "In all, about 150 aboriginal, Inuit [Eskimo] and Métis children were removed from their communities and forced to attend the schools." (www.cbc.ca/news/background/aboridingals/residential schools.html)

The Assembly of First Nations reports that, "In 1991 Statistics Canada estimated that there were approximately 105,000 former residential school children survivors. By 2004, that number had dropped to 87,500."

Many Canadian institutions share the moral onus for the harm done to those children: the government of Canada, especially the Department of Indian and Northern Affairs; the RCMP (the Mounties); and the churches, especially Catholic, Anglican and United. Even two provincial governments participated: in 1929 Alberta passed the Alberta Sterilization Act, and in 1938 the British Columbia government followed suit. Among other outcomes, these laws empowered the principals of residential schools to decide if any particular female student should be sterilized, and a number of them were.

Later Developments

As I was writing these lines I learned form *CBC Newsworld* that a working group has been set up by former Indian and Northern Affairs Minister Jim Prentice to investigate the disappearance of thousands of students from residential schools, most of whom lie dead and buried in marked and unmarked graves. As in the *encomiendas* of Spanish California, many probably died from a combination of unsanitary conditions (such as overcrowded dorms), bad treatment, food deficient in quality and quantity, and disease (mostly influenza and tuberculosis). John S. Milloy, a Canadian Studies professor at Trent University, author of *A National Crime: The Canadian Government and the Residential School System, 1979 to 1986*, and a researcher for a Royal Commission on Aboriginals has referred to estimates that 24 to 42 percent of the student body of some schools died of tuberculosis. What was really scandalous is that the parents were usually not even notified, or were notified much later. (www.cbc.ca/Canada/North/story/2000/04/02/north-schools.html)

Even if it can be argued that the schools might have been helpless to prevent the deaths, what excuse can there be for not bothering to notify the parents? Bob Watts, head of a Truth and Reconciliation Commission has suggested that some deaths may have been "more criminal in nature," such as those of children who where the outcome of sexual abuse of female students.

This commission is slated to start its work in June, 2008. It has no choice but to do a thorough and honest vetting and auditing. The cat is out of the bag: the government and the churches have already paid millions in compensation to individual victims – which is tantamount to a guilty plea. On November 23, 2005, CBC News.ca reported that the Liberal government has announced that a $1.9-billion compensation package for survivors of residential schools, which includes 125 million for an aboriginal Healing Foundation and 60 million for the truth and reconciliation process.

The Canadian government may have assumed full responsibility for the residential school system in 1969, and the last school may have closed its door in 1996, but the story of the residential schools is not over!

Ethical and Political Considerations

We know from internal documents and credible historical accounts that the basic intent of the program, from its very inception, was to deprogram all traces of Indian culture in the children so as to make them assimilatable into a White and Christian society – in other words, "to kill the Indian in the man." Note that this necessitated the forcible conversion of thousands to the Catholic or Protestant faiths.

Since genocide can be cultural as well as physical, it follows that Canada participated in the genocidal assault on Amerindians.

Moral dispensation and chosenness all over again! And within the life-span of many readers of this book! Methods may have changed, but basically things have not. This late example must be seen in the historical context:

1. Whenever the polity surrenders some of its responsibilities to the clergy, harm and injustice will follow.
2. Whenever the clergy exerts undue pressure on the polity, progress will stop or slow down and harm and injustice will follow.
3. History has shown that the priestly cast (which includes rabbis, imans and voodoo priests) has no claim to moral superiority over the rest of mankind. The pretence that religion is the only force that keeps us from falling into the depths of moral turpitude is one of the great lies of history. Although, individually, clerics must be given the same respect and rights that the rest of us expect, it is a mistake to ascribe to them powers of a spiritual or magical nature beyond our reach, and to be intimidated by them.

To Be Fair

The role of the Christian clergy during the colonial period was not all negative. Influenced, perhaps, by humanism, the culture of Catholic and Protestant missionaries sent to foreign lands changed at the end of the 19th century. They were the first real globalists (since Roman times) and, discounting the good or bad of conversion to the "one true faith", there were many benefits to humanity from their work. They spread communication, education, health care, geographical knowledge (many doubled as explorers) and other good things. Sometimes these sincere endeavors ended up eroding and even suffocating native cultures but, overall, they were probably a force for good. Not to be underestimated is the tacit message that any object of proselytization must be considered a full-fledged member of the human brotherhood.

The work of the nursing orders of Catholic nuns in hospital administration, patient care and social work must not be forgotten. Unlike the teaching nuns who mixed indoctrination and education, and who often relied on intimidation and corporal punishment, the nursing orders concentrated on their core task: healing the sick, especially the sick poor.

Slavery and the Churches

Not so laudable was the role of the Churches in slavery. The Churches didn't invent slavery: it has exited since times immemorial and, sadly, has never been completely eradicated. However, with few exceptions – the Quakers, pre-eminently – religions, though debating the theological aspect of the institution, did very little on the ground until the 18th century. In medieval Europe and in the colonies clerics sometimes bought and sold slaves.

Canon III of the Christian Council of Gangra (between 325 and 365 CE) stipulates:

> If anyone, on the pretext of religion, teaches another man's slave to despise his master and to withdraw from his service, and not serve his master with good will and all respect, let him be anathema.

A thousand years later Thomas Aquinas (chief Catholic theologian) agreed with the Greek Philosopher, Aristotle, that slavery is "natural."

Independence did not bring freedom to American Negro slaves, at least not in the South. The same division into abolitionists and defenders of slavery that was to lead to the American Civil War also tended to rend apart a number of Christian Churches – and in both cases the geographical and ideological divide was the same: North against South:

> What was the final result of the Concession of 1808? The organization and development of the M.E. [Methodist Episcopalian] Church South, whose only particular and distinctive feature is that she upholds, defends and sustains her entire membership; including traveling preachers and bishops, in holding, buying, selling, and giving away slaves, as goods personal, to all intents and purposes. She defends slavery as a good, and appeals to the religion of Christ to sustain it.
> (John Dixon Long, *Pictures of Slaves in Church and State*, Philadelphia, published by the author, 1857)

Long seems to have been fair in his severe assessment: proposed Episcopal Church Resolution A124 would admit to the "complicity of the Episcopal Church in Slavery" and to the Church's "economic benefits from it."

In the 1830s a similar moral disagreement would result in a schism within the Baptist denomination. The Southern Baptists went their own way, embracing slavery, while their Northern brothers remained steadfastly abolitionists.

Very few Americans would now consider a return to slavery, yet the ethos of the contemporary religious right has some affinity to that of the Southern Baptists, Southern Methodists, and others who were the last to reject slavery.

Manifest Destiny

My old 1967 Edition of the Encyclopedia Britannica defines *Manifest Destiny*, as "a persistent and cherished tradition of U.S. history which, in its broadest conception declared that Americans are a chosen people, blessed with free institutions and ordained by God to create a model society in the wilderness." Later, in the same paragraph it adds, "In its more restricted geographical sense, the phrase refers to the desire of American expansionists in the 1840s to extend the boundaries of the United States to the Pacific Ocean."

The movement was the culmination of a well-established trend in the American ethos that started with the arrival of the "Pilgrim Fathers" in New England in 1620. The Puritans – a rigorist offshoot of the Church of England, with Calvinist-influenced ideas on church organization – considered themselves as the new chosen people, and their Church as the "New Israel." They saw themselves as the spiritual leaders of the New World. The Native Americans, the Amerindians, being pagans, had no rights, no portion of the New Jerusalem and no protection against spoliation. The religion of the Puritans was an Old-Testament kind of Christianity and their influence is still strong today. Its emphasis on the Old Testament is, in fact, the distinctive characteristic of contemporary American Protestantism – especially in the right-wing version.

Thus, the ancient ambitions of Moses and Joshua were rekindled, millenniums later, not in any European Yeshiva or Synagogue, but in Christian America!

Nor was this trend limited to the Anglo-Saxons of North America: the Portuguese and The Spanish also used the Joshua analogy to justify their even more bloody spoliation of Indian individuals, tribes and cultures. They, also, demonized them, viewing them as an accursed race under the governance of Satan. On the Internet I came across a revealing rendition of covenantal thinking by the Costa Rican biblical scholar, Elsa Tamez:

> The study of the conquest of Canaan is the most often used biblical foundation for the conquest of this continent. Juan Gines de Sepulveda [16th century philosopher] used this biblical theme to legitimate the war against its inhabitants … He justified the conquest in order to punish blasphemy, but also because the continent was a special donation by God, as the promised land. (The Pope as Christ's vicar had the authority to give lands.) God chose the Spanish to carry out this divine judgment against the infidels, and to conquer their lands. From this Sepulveda affirmed that such a war besides being licit was necessary because of the gravity of the people's concerns.
> (Elsa Tamez, "Biblia y 500 Anos" in *Revista de interpretación biblia latinoamericana*, as translated on the Internet.

Due, probably, to European influence many of the signers of the Declaration of Independence were deists rather than theists (although some of these deists remained nominally attached to one or another Protestant Church). This tendency never had an impact on the civil religion of the country: it remained covenantal and under the sway of the Old Testament.

The ethos of Manifest Destiny had always guided public policy and individual conduct but the movement didn't become institutionalized until the 1840s and didn't acquire its name until a journalist, John L. O'Sullivan, coined it in an editorial in his *United States Magazine and Democratic Review*, in 1845, in which he predicted "the fulfillment of our manifest destiny to overspread the continent allotted by Providence."

Sullivan was, perhaps, the loudest clarion for Manifest Destiny. Although American hegemony never subdued Canada, nor Mexico (South of Texas), O'Sullivan accepted no limits in the Western Hemisphere:

> Yes, more, more, more … till our national destiny is fulfilled and … the whole boundless continent is ours. (O'Sullivan, *New York Morning News*, Feb. 7, 1845, quoted in Frederick Merk, *Manifest Destiny and Mission in American History*, Harvard U. Press, 1963)

But O'Sullivan was not only a man with a mission but also a man of principle (even if the mission and the principles were incompatible):

> There are some things this nation will never do. It will never be the forcible subjugator of other countries; it will never despoil surrounding territories; it will never march through the blood of their unoffending inhabitants; it will never admit within its own Union those who do not freely desire the boon.
> (O'Sullivan, *New York Morning News*, Nov. 15, 1845, as cited in Merk)

But not all journalists and politicians were as principled as O'Sullivan. The least palatable facet of Manifest Destiny was its unmitigated racism. As Frederick Merk put it in *Manifest Destiny and Mission in American History*, "The Indian was a heathen whose land title passed, according to canon well-established, to the Christian prince and his heirs who discovered or conquered him." (p. 33) The poor Indian couldn't even ameliorate his children's status by miscegenation! On page 159, Merk, describing the ethos of the time, of course, writes: "mixed races inherit all the faults but none of the virtues of both progenitors'."

The furious debate over the possibility of forcibly annexing the whole of Mexico brought forth a number of conflicting attitudes Some wanted to annex in order to save the inferior and mongrel people of Mexico from themselves by guiding them forcibly to a more civilized state, thus making the conquest of the country a gift to humanity rather than a taking by the United States.

> The Mexicans are Indians – Aboriginal Indians as Cortez conquered three thousand [sic] years ago, only rendered a little more mischievous by a bastard civilization … The Aboriginals of this country have not attempted, and cannot attempt to exist independently alongside of us. Providence has so ordained it and it is folly not to recognize the fact. The Mexicans are *Aboriginal Indians*, and they must share the destiny of that race … we do not believe that lives the American, with a true understanding of this country's interests and duties who, *if he had the power*, would deliberately surrender Mexico to the *uncontrolled* dominion of the Mongrel barbarians, who, for a quarter of a century, have degraded and oppressed her.
> (O'Sullivan, *New York Morning News*, Dec. 24, 1847, as cited in Merk)

Others, though, were against the idea of annexation for the same reasons: the Mexican people were of inferior and degenerate quality and annexation would lead to pollution of the American race.

Some were more pragmatic and cynical. In an editorial in the *New Orleans Picayune,* Jan. 7, 1847, the writer opined that "no scrap of philosophy, nor moral essay, nor political distinction can countervail the dangerous odor of the fields in perennial blossom [Mexico] to an army of Anglo-Saxons."

Having reached the Pacific and having relinquished the idea of annexing Mexico and Canada, American expansionism set its eyes, not on vast expanses of mainland, but on islands so as to spread its influence world-wide and have military outposts for defensive purposes. Cuba and Hawaii were first coveted. Hawaii was already under heavy military influence: whalers, missionaries and sugar-plantation owners had considerable political clout. In 1893 there were signs of an uprising against the government of Queen Liliuokalani. Using the pretext of protecting Americans and their properties, marines who were already on a ship in the harbor of Honolulu went ashore and took control. The queen was deposed and a new government was organized.

On February 15, 1898, the Battleship Maine was anchored in the harbor of Havana in Cuba. The ship was blown up and 260 American sailors died. Before the cause was determined, and the perpetrators, if any, could be identified, many Americans accused Spain and militated for retaliation. In April the Spanish-American war broke out. The Americans won a number of battles, both at sea and on land. Spain conceded defeat, gave up sovereignty over Cuba and lost Puerto Rico, Guam and the Philippines to the United States. The American people, however, never felt comfortable with the idea of being an old-style colonial power, and at the end of the World War II, the Philippines became an independent country. The US abandoned its policy of insular imperialism and laid the foundation of neocolonialism by making deals with – and bullying – governments to establish military bases world-wide. (There are now more than 600 bases in about 130 countries, manned by ¼ million military personnel – the real face of American neo-colonialism.)

The attitude and doctrinal elements of Manifest Destiny have been a constant factor in American culture and politics. If at times it has not been conspicuous, it has always been ready to reassert itself.

> Our institutions will follow our flag on the wings of commerce. And American law, American order, American civilization, and the American flag will plant themselves on shores, hitherto bloody and benighted but by those agencies of God henceforth to be made beautiful and bright.
> (Claude G. Bowers: *Beveridge and the Progressive Era*, p. 67, via Merk, p. 232.

Note the claim that American law, order, civilization, and flag are "agencies of God." American will work and fight for God and in return it will be given land – grander and vaster land than the small country of Canaan. In the words of John Quincy Adams, delivered to congress in 1846, America will "subdue the earth, which we are commanded to do by the first behest of God Almighty."

As in the case of the original, this new covenant will entail a lower status – with concomitant loss of rights – for the uncovenanted, and a liberal dispensation from moral laws for the chosen.

Chapter XVII – Zionists Precursors, Propagandists and Lobbyists

Jews don't usually venture into any major endeavor without researching it, thinking about it, talking about it, and writing about it. The story of Zionism and the foundation of Israel is no exception. For two millennia, generations of sages, from the creators of the Mishna – the Tinahaim – to the rabbis of the Talmud – the Amoraim – to a long line of religious and lay scholars and leaders have slowly and patiently hewn a religion out of the ashes of the old Yahwist faith. They had two main objectives: build a religion that was both a new invention and a scion of the Torah, and gather the disparate remnants of the diaspora into a unified body. They had great success in both endeavors, but the ingathering of the fold was not geographical. The disparate remnants of the tribes were united by books, by common rituals and laws, by a network of dedicated rabbis. And it worked! Even the enlightenment (the *haskalah*) and the division of the faith into three branches (plus the Hasidim) could not prevent this.

But in the last half of the 19th century some voices were heard complaining that this was not enough, that the Jews needed a place, a home, a country. These voices got stronger, got organized and started militating. They looked for enablers within the world's countries and found some. They even found help from anti-Semites who were glad (as Jews themselves intimated) that a way had been found of getting rid of a pesky, troublesome minority.

But time moves faster nowadays than in the era of the *tanaim* and the *amorim*: the latest ingathering took less than a century.

Yehuda Alkali

Rabbi Yehuda Alkali (1796-1874) had preached the need for a third redemption, from a fideistic, orthodox, religious perspective; but perhaps because his approach was out of step with the trends of the day – Jewish emancipation and Jewish enlightenment – his efforts had accomplished little of practical importance. Still, he introduced a few important ideas that would be taken over by a number of the subsequent Zionists: the return to Palestine as the homeland and the rebirth of Hebrew as a national tongue. He also started the trend toward a reinterpretation of the notion of *Messiah.* Heretofore the Messiah had been conceived as a person sent by God – a human person or, perhaps, an angelic creature also sent by God. Alkali suggested that a proposed assembly of elders could be "what is meant by the promise of the Messiah." (Later Zionists were to come up with even more sophisticated and loose interpretations of the concept.)

Moses Hess

The next Zionist theorist of importance was Moses Hess (1812-1875) whose conception, a mere 20 years later, was much different: Hess was a secular Jew. He was the first to emphasize the nationalistic aspect of Jewish culture and to esteem it more essential than dogma or ritual.

> Judaism, like Christianity, would really have to disappear in the face of intellectual progress, if it were not more than a dogmatic religion, if it were not a national cult.
> (Moses Hess, *Rome and Jerusalem*, Lupsic, 1862, via Arthur Hertzberg, *The Zionist Idea*, Jewish Publications Service, p. 124.)

Hess was more respectful and tolerant of other religions and peoples than many later Zionists would be:

> Each nation will have to create its own historical cult; each people must become, like the Jewish people, a people of God.
> (Ibid., *via Hertzberg*, p. 125)

Again, Hess was pioneering an idea that others would develop: that Israel would be light to the world, that its redemption would show all other peoples the road to global redemption.

Another thesis of his that would be repeated by others is the prediction (which proved prophetic) that anti-Semitism would not only be a cause of Zionism but also a positive factor in its implementation.

> You think that the Christian nations will certainly not object to the restoration of the Jewish state, for they will thereby rid their respective countries of a foreign population which has already been a thorn in their sides. (Ibid., *via Hertzberg*, p. 125)

Leo Pinsker

Leo Pinsker (1821-91) was a very assimilated Russian Jew who, for the first 40 years of his life had little interest in things Jewish. Once well-established as a medical doctor he took an active interest in the practical affairs of his ethnic community while remaining a patriotic Russian, convinced as he was that the country would find the way to enlightenment and liberalism. But the Russian pogrom of 1881 shocked him enough to reverse the polarity of his mind. Henceforth he would devote most of his energy to the cause of Zionism.

Pinsker realized that legal emancipation did not entail social emancipation, so that even in democratic and liberal countries the Jews were still strangers – squatters, almost. His Zionism was practical and defensive. The main idea was to save the Jews from oppression and violence, rather than to implement some spiritual and prophetic program (although Pinsker never completely lost sight of that aspect):

> The goal of our present endeavors must be not the "Holy Land," but a land of our own...
> Thither we shall take with us the most sacred possessions which we have saved from the shipwreck of our former fatherland, the God-idea and the Bible.
> (Leo Pinsker, *Auto-Emancipation*, pamphlet, 1882, via Hertzberg, p. 194.)

Pinsker was the inventor of the expression *auto-emancipation*, which, in fact was the title of a provocative pamphlet which offended both orthodox and liberal readers. His idea that Israel must pull itself by his own bootstraps and that a new Israel must be self-created was to be taken up and expanded upon by a number of other writers and militants.

Pinsker was not only a writer: he convoked the first congress of the Hibblat Zion movement which established some colonies in Palestine.

Moshe Lilienblum

Secular Jews – some of them avowed agnostics, if not atheists – continued to dominate both the rank and file and the leadership of Zionism, but some, such as Moshe Lilienblum (1843-1910), invited the involvement and cooperation of the orthodox:

> Is not our entire community holy? Let the orthodox know that we are one with them in travail. All the plans and schemes that keep coming up for the salvation of our people originate with the Maskilim and freethinkers. (Moshe Lilienblum, *Kol Kitbec*, Vol. IV, via Hertzberg, p. 171)

For many Jews of Russia and Eastern Europe, what triggered the move to militant Zionism were the periodic pogroms, especially the Russian pogrom of 1881. It is small wonder that the situation of most Jews in most of the world – constant harassment by the political elite *and* the populace, frequent destruction of property, constant threat of deadly violence – would result in a desperate search for a solution, for salvation.

Theodor Herzl

For Theodor Herzl (1860-1904) the trigger was the Dreyfus Affair of 1894. Compared to the pogroms of Eastern Europe, this was a minor event: a Jewish military officer was unjustly accused of treason and sent to prison; he was pardoned 6 years later and completely exonerated in 1906. But France had been the first country to emancipate the Jews and had a special place in Jewish hearts. The Dreyfus affair had a political and cultural impact out of all proportion to its moral and legal dimensions. Herzl became a militant Zionist and henceforth devoted his immense energy to the cause.

His passion and unflagging zeal would lead one to suspect that he was a religious fanatic or a political extremist of some sort. Not so! He was a rational, analytical and realistic person; he became a nationalist but not a rabid one; he respected other nations and proclaimed that the Jews, once established in their own land, would be a beacon for mankind, to the benefit of all.

One must take some of his magnanimous and generous effusions with a grain of salt, however:

> It might further be said that we ought not to create new distinctions between people and we ought not to raise fresh barriers ... I say that those who think that way are amiable visionaries ... Universal brotherhood is not even a beautiful dream. Conflict is essential to man's highest efforts.
> (Theodor Herzl, *The Jewish State*, 1896, via Hertzberg, p. 223)

Herzl conveniently forgot that there were people already settled in whatever land the Jews would take over (he preferred Palestine but at some time considered Uganda and Argentina). He never mentioned the Palestinian people.

In another context he wrote, "Only desperate men make good conquerors." But if a land were empty, and permission were granted by whoever had sovereignty, there would be no necessity for "conquerors." Herzl never categorically eschewed recourse to violence, if necessary, but much favored a political and diplomatic approach:

> In solving it [the Jewish question] we are working not only for ourselves, but also for many other downtrodden and oppressed beings.
> (Ibid, via Hertzberg, p. 204)

Just two paragraphs later, he adds:

> I consider the Jewish question neither a social nor a religious one, even though it sometimes takes these and other forms. It is a national question, and, to solve it we must first of all establish it as an international political problem to be discussed by civilized nations of the world in council.

> We are a people – one people.
> (Ibid, via Hertzberg, p. 204)

Herzl was obsessed by the problem of anti-Semitism, but he saw a good side of it: anti-Semitism was the glue that held the Jews together as a nation, and it would facilitate the ingathering of the people into a land of their own, not only because Jews wanted to find refuge, but also because anti-Semites would be glad to help them leave.

> The sentiment of solidarity with which we have been reproached so frequently and so acrimoniously was in process of disintegration every time we were being attacked by anti-Semitism. And anti-Semitism seemed to strengthen it anew.
> (First Congress address, 1897, via Hertzberg, p. 227)

The First congress was called by Herzl in 1897 and held in Basel to found the World Zionist Organization. During Herzl's lifetime six more congresses were convened. By the time of his death the organizational, political and spiritual (though not religious) groundwork for the future state of Israel (48 years later) was cast. As though this work together with his "day job" as a literary editor were not enough, he found time to meet and seek the support of many powerful people, including Baron de Hirsh, the Rothschilds, the sultan of Turkey, British politicians, and even Pope Pius X. He could not have created the state of Israel without the work of many other militants but it may not be much of an exaggeration to call him the father of Israel.

Like Moses, Herzl didn't live to see the achievement of his travail. Like Joseph's remains, his bones were exhumed later and brought back to Israel.

Arthur Hertzberg ended his commentary on Herzl with these lyrical words:

> Worn out by his exertions Herzl died not far from Vienna on July 3, 1904. Forty-five years later, an airplane flying the blue-white flag of the new state of Israel brought his remains to the country of which he was the principal architect.
> (Hertzberg, p. 204)

Max Nordau

Max Nordau (1849-1928) was Herzl's most loyal and important colleague. Like his mentor, he was a completely secular Jew:

> The new Zionism, which has been called political, differs from the old, religious, messianic variety in that it disavows all mysticism, no longer identifies itself with messianism, and does not expect the return to Palestine to be brought about by a miracle, but desires to prepare the way by its own efforts.
> (Max Nordau, *Zionism*, 1902, via Hertzberg, p. 242)

Unfortunately (in my opinion) the messianic aspect of Zionism was still very much alive and would often be the justification for moral dispensation. Although Nordau was in agreement with Herzl in holding that the principle of Nationality and the escape from anti-Semitism were the main impulses of Zionism, he was overoptimistic when he wrote:

> The principle of nationality has, in its exaggerations, led to excess. It has erred into chauvinism, stooped to idiotic hatred of the foreigner and sunk to grotesque self-worship. Jewish nationalism is safe from the caricature of itself.
> (Ibid, via Hertzberg, p. 243)

Like Herzl, he was saddened and alarmed that eight to ten million Jews were experiencing serous oppression and, like his mentor, he understood that anti-Semitism would help impel the Jews to Palestine.

Ahad Ha-am

Ahmad Ha-am (real name Asher Ginsberg) and Herzl were born just four years apart and militated for the same causes, but their approaches were almost diametrically opposite. Herzl was a thoroughly secular Jew, apparently uninterested in religion, while Ha-am was an agnostic who just couldn't shake off the shackles of religion. He came from a fervently orthodox Hasidic family and became a scholar of the Talmud. But he refused to limit his reading to orthodox sources and, sometimes in his twenties, irrevocably lost his faith.

> The Hebrew word *nefesh* includes body and soul and all that belongs to them. The *nefesh*, the individual human being, lives as whole and dies as a whole; nothing survives [...] It, [early Judaism] offered eternal life here on earth. This it did by emphasizing the sense of collectivity, by teaching the individual to regard himself not as an isolated unit, with an existence bounded by his own birth and death, but as part of a large and more important whole, as a member of the social body. This conception shifts the center of personality not from the body to the sprit but from the individual to the community; concurrently the problem of life is transferred from the individual to the social plane. I live for the sake of the perpetuation and the well-being of the community to which I belong. I die to make way for others who will remold the community and save it from petrifaction and stagnation.
> (Ahad Ha-am, *Flesh and Spirit*, 1904, via Hertzberg, p. 256)

Also:

> If it is impossible to be a Jew in the religious sense without acknowledging our nationality, it is possible to be a Jew in the national sense without accepting many things in which religion requires belief ...
> (Ahad Ha-am, *On Nationalism and Religion*, 1910, via Hertzberg, p. 262)

Strange! An agnostic – perhaps an atheist – who hews to the most conservative tradition of his ex-religion: the holiness of the collectivity. But originally this collectivity was holy because it was chosen by Yahweh; Ha-am rejects that; but, as Hertzberg put it, "How could one deny God and affirm chosenness?" (p. 65) Pinsker had invented the concept of auto-emancipation; Ha-am went one step further and came up with auto-deification (although he never gave his invention a name). Jewry thus becomes its own God, eliminating the need for any external agent to support chosenness, grant moral dispensation and consign a promised land.

The Hebrews and Jews were always masters at shuttling between the individual and the collectivity, and at objectifying the latter. For example: Jacob was renamed Israel by Yahweh; the name was given to the confederation of the 12 tribes; then the name was used to denote the unified kingdom of David and Solomon; then, after the secession, the name denoted the Northern Kingdom; after the destruction of the latter, the name signified the mystical body of all Jews at all time; finally, without losing the latter meaning, it was chosen as the name of the eponymous state in Palestine. Ha-am did something similar, but simpler, with the Nietchean concept of the *superman* (also known as the *overman*): he collectivized the notion into the concept of the *super nation*.

But, logically speaking, does the conceit work? – The individual finds meaning by living for the community, but where does the community find *its* meaning, without which the individual's quest would be meaningless? According to Ha-am the community of Israel found it by becoming a "kingdom of priests and a holy nation" that was chosen at the very beginning to be an example to humanity by following the Torah.

We are back to the problems of historicity and factuality (covered in Chapter VIII). But Ha-am was an agnostic: if he could not be sure that God exists, how could he be sure that the Torah was holy – holy enough to be relevant and normative to the whole of mankind? – One partial answer is to claim intrinsic moral superiority for the Jewish people:

> He [Ha-am] appealed to common knowledge, that "it is admitted by everyone – not excluding Nietzche – that the Jewish people is unique in its genius for morality … (Hertzberg, p. 6)

From such a claim to innate moral superiority to an outright racist attitude is but a small step, and from that to self-deification, another incremental one.

Herzl laid the groundwork for the creation of the state of Israel; Ahmad He-am laid the groundwork for the Godless moral dispensation that the state of Israel so gratuitously gives itself.

Jacob Klatskin

Another Zionist writer who had little use for religion was Jacob Klatskin (1882-1948).

> … to be part of the nation one need not believe in the Jewish religion or the Jewish spiritual outlook.

(Jacob Klatskin, *Boundaries*, via Hertzberg, p. 317)

Also:

> Zionism stands opposed to all this [the content of Judaism]. Its real beginning is *the Jewish State* [by Theodor Herzl] and its basic intention, whether consciously or unconsciously, is to deny any conception of Jewish identity based on spiritual criteria.
> (Ibid, via Hertzberg, p. 319)

But after eliminating Judaism as the foundational element of the Jewish enterprise, what was left? Klatskin suggested two replacements: a land that Jews did not possess, Palestine, and a language that most did not speak, Hebrew.

> We are a nation even in the Diaspora, so long as our goal is to be redeemed from it, so long as we labor for our land and our language.
> (Ibid, via Hertzberg, p. 318)

[Personal note:
Being a Francophone Québécois (although not a *separatist*) I understand the importance of land and, especially, language in determining national identity; but even those pale in comparison to the Word of God! Do land and language bestow moral dispensation and sanction ethnic cleansing and the taking of life?]

Because the majority of Zionist intellectuals, militants and organizers were agnostics, atheists or secularists, their program left many religious Jews cold, and failed to provide either a spiritual or a national ground for moral dispensation, a necessary – as it would turn out – condition for the establishment of the Zionist state. Therefore the inclusion of a religious and pietistic minority was necessary in order to give the project a "Jewish look" and to provide an excuse for selfish and aggressive policy and activity.

It is impossible to understand the political and social dynamics of the state of Israel without taking into account the phenomenon of *piety by proxy*. Most liberal Christians consider the fundamentalist fringe of their religion to be hopelessly anachronistic and a little crazy. This is true even in the US, where the fringe has become numerically significant and politically powerful. In Islam, major factions do not hesitate to practice mutual oppression. Not so with the Jews: their concern for solidarity overrides major differences so that Orthodox, Conservative, Reform, secular and atheistic Jews can work on a common project. A Jew is a Jew is a Jew – as long as his or her mother is a Jew. Liberal and secular Jews consider that the fact that *some* Jews obey many of the punctilious and anachronistic laws of the Torah liberates them from doing so.

[Personal note:
I remember a conversation with an Orthodox Israeli woman who happened to be sitting next to me on the Amtrak train from Montreal to New York. I made the above observations and she said that, indeed, she had secular friends who had told her that "thank God, because they – the observant – do it, I don't have to."]

But there is a price to pay for their liberation: in Israel, religiously observant Jews are given many political, economic and other advantages. For example, they don't have to serve in the army, and their representation in government is out of all proportion to their ratio of the population. Piety-by-proxy is a major ingredient in what makes Israel what it is.

Yehiel Michael Pines

Rabbi Pines (1842-1912), from the Russian-held part of Poland, was one of the first to resist the "fashionable idea" of secularization:

> I have no sympathy with the currently fashionable idea, with the movement to make the Jewish people a pure secular nationality in place of the combination of religion with nationality that has enabled us to survive to this day. (Yehiel Michael Pines, *Jewish Nationalism Cannot be Secular*, 1895, via Hertzberg, p. 411)

Both pure religion with no nationalistic and ethnic content, and thorough secularism were equally anathema to him:

> The Jewish people did not, at its very beginning, come into the world as a separate entity in the ordinary way, as a result of the combined influences of race and soil, but as

> a group professing a separate faith and bound in a mutual covenant to observe that faith.
> (Pines, *On Religious Reforms*, via Hertzberg, p. 410).

Note the expression "in a mutual covenant." For Pines, the Covenant is not so much between God and the Jews, as it is between all Jews and all Jews, i.e. an act of auto-creation – or something like that.

In 1878 Pines moved to Palestine and was involved in the social affairs of the early Jewish settlers and in the promotion of the Hebrew language.

Abraham Isaac Kook

As we proceed in the sketching of the early theorists and militants of Zionism we notice a trend as many of them end up moving to Palestine and working from there. Our next figure, Rabbi Abraham Kook (1865-1935) not only emigrated to Palestine, but became its first chief rabbi.

Kook was more than a religious Zionist: he was a mystic and eschatologist who believed in the return of a real Messiah, and who expected that the "end of days" was just years away.

> But a time will come when even the lowest of the world's depths will be cleansed of its filth, even the worst of its crookedness will be set straight, and even the slightest perversion will be corrected. Then light will shine for the righteous.
> (Abraham Isaac Kook, *Orot* [Lights], compiled in 1942 from writings (1910-30), via Hertzberg, p. 425.

Strangely this effusive eschatology sounds more Christian than Jewish. It reminds one of the styles of some Jehovah's Witness tracts. In the Tanakh, the prophets sometimes considered pagan conquerors as "rods of God," punishing the Hebrews for their transgressions. Rabbi Kook considered Zionists unbelievers to be unconsciously following God's will, and therefore doing holy works, in spite of their agnosticism or atheism.

He asserted that whatever the Jews create in Israel will be "to the great benefit of the Jewish people and of the world." By definition, it seems. (Hertzberg, p. 420) He had a strong racist streak which accounts for his belief in the spiritual superiority of the Jews:

> It is a grave error ... to imagine that the Divine stuff which uniquely characterizes Israel is comparable to the spiritual content of all the other national civilizations. (Ibid, via Hertzberg, p. 425)

Samuel Hayym Landau

Samuel Hayym Landau (1892-1928) was another religious Zionist who seems to have put the nation of Israel on a higher altar than God's.

> The entire program of Zionism, therefore revolves around this idea, and all other national values are significant only to the degree that they serve as instruments of the absolute – the nation.
> (Samuel Hayyim Landau, *Toward an Explanation of Our Ideology*, via Hertzberg, p. 434)

So, who needs God? Just a few sentences later he adds, "Did not the Talmud teach that the Torah was created for the sake of Israel?" It seems that it is not the Godliness of the Torah that matters, but the Jewishness of the Torah. This is another case of auto-deification. Anything goes as long as it's in Israel's (i.e. God's) interest. (Of course, since the state of Israel did not exist at the time, Landau meant *the nation*. If an individual claimed to be God – or an avatar of God – would he not be accused of sacrilege? A sacrilege more egregious than merely using God's name in vain! Could not the same charge be directed at anyone claiming a God-like status for his nation?

Note that Landau said -- not implied, but said – that the absolute (than which noting is greater) is the nation, not God. He advances no philosophical argument to prove his point, and suggests no criteria by which to judge one nation's Godliness versus another's.

Solomon Schechter

The more we approach the time of the actual establishment of the state of Israel, 1948, the more important becomes the role of the United States and of American Jews. The foot soldiers of early Zionism – the people from whom the bulk of the immigrants came – were from Russia and Eastern Europe. But the organizational headquarters of the movement drifted: first to Western Europe, then to the United States.

Rabbi Solomon Schechter (1847-1915), born in Romania, moved in stages ever westward, first to Vienna, then to England, and finally to the US. Arthur Hertzberg called him "the greatest interpreter of Judaism to the English-speaking world." The American Zionist movement started with Schechter. Since he came to America to take over the presidency of a Conservative institution, the Jewish Theological Seminary, he gave the Conservative branch a strong momentum, which accounts for its continued preeminence in Zionism.

Like Landau, Schechter was a mystic, an eschatologist and a precursor of Jehovah's Witnesses theology. Like Landau he seems to have been either unaware or unconcerned that there were people in the Promised Land, who had acquired title to land and dwellings many years ago – perhaps centuries ago – and whose lineage was at least as connected to the land as that of any Jew.

> When Israel found itself it found its God. When Israel lost itself, or began to work at its self-effacement, it was sure to deny its God. The selection of Israel, the indestructibility of God's covenant with Israel, the immortality of Israel as a nation, and the final restoration of Israel to Palestine, where the nation will live a holy life on holy ground, with all the wide-reaching consequences of the conversion of humanity and the establishment of the Kingdom of God on earth – all these are the common ideals and the common ideas that permeate the whole of Jewish literature extending over nearly four thousand years ...
> (Solomon Schechter, *Zionism: a Statement*, 1906, via Hertzberg, p. 508)

Schechter predicts that one consequence of the restoration of Israel to Palestine will be the conversion of humanity. Elsewhere he mentions Israel's "mission to the world." What is that mission? The establishment of monotheism? "Been there done that," Christians and Muslims would retort (although Christians are somewhat compromised by their belief in the Trinity). Is the mission the establishment of justice and peace on earth? If that's the case, then Israel is hardly off to a god start! Schechter never defines this mission. Neither do the Zionists. Note also that the rabbi never mentions the role of a Messiah in the Zionist program. No need: Zionism *is* the Messiah.

Schechter was aware that Zionism was open to the charge of religious atavism, but he rejected this criticism without much factual or logical argumentation:

> The taunt of a retrogression and reaction has no terror for us. To insist on progressing when one has come to the conclusion that a step forward means ruin is sheer obstinacy.
> (Ibid, via Hertzberg, p. 511.

It never occurred to Schechter that when the current approach is not working there's another tack besides religious atavism (which, in the case of Zionism, means a 3000-year backward step): You can also develop a new approach radically different from both the ancient one *and* current one.

Judah Leon Magnes

Judah Leon Magnes (1877-1948), a Reform rabbi, was perhaps the first important American-born Zionist writer and activist. Although he qualified the Arab community of Palestine as "relatively unimportant," he – unlike many Zionists – acknowledged their existence and their rights.

Inn 1930 he courageously issued a pamphlet – *Like All the Nations* – knowing that many of his co-religionists would denounce it. The two following quotations are from Hertzberg's selected excerpts from that pamphlet:

> … it is not only the end which for Israel must be desirable, but what is of equal importance, the means must be conceived and brought forth in cleanliness. (via Hertzberg, p. 447)

and

> For the Jewish people no high end will ever justify low means. (p. 448)

Unlike Ben Gurion, Begin, Sharon, and others, Magnes eschewed the "Joshua Method," because neither the world nor "their own souls" would let the Jews become conquerors and colonizers. [Unfortunately Magnes was a better ethicist than prophet. The souls of Jews and the super-powers of the world not only allowed some of the Jews to become conquerors and colonizers, but actually helped them.]

Rabbi Mordecai Kaplan

Mordecai Kaplan (1881-1983) was a Conservative rabbi who, in many ways, was more liberal and radical then most Reform rabbis; and yet was sufficiently influenced by the Palestine-or-bust ideology to support the return to Eretz Israel for those Jews who chose that alternative.

Although his theological stance was inconsistent he seems to have rejected the orthodox view of God and to have regarded the divine in naturalistic and symbolic terms. Unlike almost all other Zionist unbelievers, however, he pushed this position to its logical conclusion, rejecting the Jewish concept of chosenness.

> Kaplan has maintained that, in all logic, the "chosen people" concept must be abandoned, for, without the orthodox God to do the choosing, even the most moral of national traditions cannot claim to be the metaphysical hub of the universe.
> (Hertzberg, p. 65n.)

But if Kaplan dismissed chosenness he nonetheless saved the notion of the promised land: he failed to see that without "the Orthodox God" the promised land is a chimera on par with chosenness, and that therefore the Palestinian Arabs individually had title to their property and that "facts on the ground" established their collective right to Palestine.

But if Kaplan was confused in his political and moral thinking regarding Zion, he was on surer ground when addressing the situation of Jews in the US and other gentile countries:

> Jews in the Diaspora will continue to owe exclusive political allegiance to the countries in which they reside.
> (Mordicai Kaplan, *The Future of the American Jew,* via Hertzberg, p. 536.)

He held that world Jewry needed both a homeland (doubling as a spiritual center) *and* a healthy Diaspora, but that each would have its own socio-political ethos.

> This means that there must henceforth be two standards of normality for Jewish life; one for Eretz Israel, where Jewish life can be lived out fully as a complete civilization … and a second standard for democratic countries like the Untied States …
> (Ibid, via Hertzberg, p. 542).

Since Kaplan, as far as I know, has never condemned, or even protested, the more egregious violations of human rights perpetrated by Israel, one may wonder if "the [standard] for Eretz Israel" includes moral dispensation. As for his principle that Jews in other countries "owe" exclusive political allegiance to those countries: it should be repeated often for the benefit of Zionist lobbyists.

Kiyus Dembitz Brandeis

Another American-born early Zionist was Louis Dembitz Brandeis (1856-1941). He received a thoroughly secular education and didn't come into more than occasional contact with the Jewish community until his fifties when he became involved with Jewish-movement workers during a strike. Shortly after that, he joined the Federation of American Zionists. During the First World War he was leader of the movement. From Washington he did important work in relation to the Balfour Declaration. In 1916 he was nominated to the Supreme Court where he served for 23 years.

Brandeis stressed that there was no inconsistency in being both a Zionist and a patriotic American. "The Jewish spirit," he writes, "the product of our religion and experience is essentially modern and essentially American." Eight sentences later he goes further: "Indeed, loyalty to America demands rather that each American Jew become a Zionist." (Brandeis, *The Jewish Problem and How to Solve It,* 1915, via Hertzberg.) The rest of the work is standard moderate Zionism with a feel good sauce: Palestine is the Homeland; Jewish culture is essentially democratic and concerned with brotherhood and social justice for individuals and nations; Zionism is non-violent and will be a boon to mankind.

Note that the equation of Zionism with "loyalty to America" is a piece of pure propaganda directed primarily at American Jews, but also at the general population and its leaders. One is reminded of the famous aphorism, "What's good for General Motors is good for America."

Martin Buber

Martin Buber was the most cosmopolitan and multidisciplinary Zionist. He was a religious existentialist philosopher, a biblical scholar, a theorist of psychotherapy, an ecumenical writer on Jewish-Christian relations, and more. He was influenced by Hasidism and by Nietzche. Hertzberg describes him as "indebted to Nietche's vision of a new society created by men of superior capacity, to his dream of a new morality and a new age. (p. 453)

As a Zionist he belongs to the religious-nationalist school with an even balance between both aspects:

> The unity of nationality and faith which constitute the uniqueness of Israel is our destiny.
> (Martin Buber, *The Jew in the World*, 1934, via Hertzberg, p. 455.).

There is something 'new age' about Buber's religiosity:

> When the prophets say that there is no security for Israel save that in God, they are not referring to something unearthly, to something "religious" in the common sense of the word; they are referring to the realization of the true communal living to which Israel was summed by the covenant with God and which it is called upon to sustain in history in the way it alone can.
> (Ibid, via Hertzberg, pp. 455-456.)

Buber's ecumenical sympathies did not weaken his conviction that Jews are a superior people:

> Israel was chosen to become a true people and that means God's people.

> (Martin Buber, *Jewish Humanism*, 1942, via Hertzberg, p. 461)

He is adamant about applying the same rules to nations as to individuals (as long as realistically possible):

> … as an individual who wishes merely to preserve himself leads and unjustified and meaningless existence, so a nation with no other aim deserves to pass.
> (Ibid, via Hertzberg, p. 459)

In an open letter to Mahatma Ghandi (1939) Buber makes it explicitly clear that the basic principles of justice are as normative for the Jewish state as for any other individual or collectivity. Regarding the intentions of Jews towards the Palestinians, he writes:

> By a genuine peace we inferred and still infer that both peoples together should develop the land without the one imposing its will on the other.
> (via Hertzberg, p. 463)

And also

> We have no desire to dispossess them [the Palestinians]. We do not want to dominate them: we want to serve with them …
> (via Hertzberg, p. 485)

Palestinians and other Arabs could relax!

Horace Mayer Kallen

Brandeis was not the only foreign-born but American-educated Zionist to have been deeply influenced by the American experience. Horace Mayer Kallen (1882-1974) even summarized Zionist ideology as a "slight modification of the Declaration of Independence":

> ... all nationalities are created equal and endowed with certain inalienable rights; among these the rights of life, liberty, and the pursuit of happiness
> (Horace Kallen, *Zionism and Liberalism*, 1919, via Hertzberg, p. 539).

This should certainly have allayed the concerns of the Palestinians! Note, again, the strong and clever propagandist aspect of Kallen's words, directed, again, at both Jewish and Gentile Americans.

Vladimir Jabotinsky

Even such a firebrand orator and impatient man-of-action as Vladimir Jabotinsky (1880-1940) made the justice-for-the-Arabs promise:

> We maintain unanimously that the economic position of the Palestinian Arabs, under Jewish colonization and owing to the Jewish colonization has become the object of envy of all surrounding Arab countries, so that the Arabs from those countries show a clear tendency to immigrate into Palestine. I have also shown to you already that, in our submission, there is no question of ousting the Arabs. On the contrary the idea is that Palestine on both sides of the Jordan should hold the Arabs, their progeny, and many millions of Jews. What I do not deny is that in that process the Arabs of Palestine will necessarily become a minority in the country of Palestine.
> (Vladimir Jabotinsky, "Evidence Submitted to the Palestine Royal Commission," 1937, via Hertzberg, p. 559.

How could such confined, cramped territory house millions of Jews without displacing the Arabs, especially since the latter have a higher birth rate, and since Jabotinsky had stipulated that the Jews *must* be a majority? Would it be necessary to sterilize a portion of the Arab women, since Jabotinsky said that "there is no question of ousting the Arabs."

As for the claim that the Arabs are lining up to reap the benefits of the Jewish presence, Jabotinsky offers no evidence and no numbers.

But when he bemoans the plight of ordinary Jews there is no question that facts and documents justify his rhetoric:

> What can be the concessions? We have got to save millions, many millions. I do not know whether it is a question of rehousing one-third of the Jewish race, half of the Jewish race, or a quarter of the Jewish race; I do no know; ... (Ibid, via Hertzberg, p. 561)

The year was 1937, four years after Kristalnacht, decades after the Russian and East European pogroms, centuries after the massacre of Jews during the Crusades and so on. Could anyone blame Jabotinsky – and the others – for decrying the plight of the Jews? The dark clouds of the Holocaust were already gathering over Germany. Something had to be done! But does this justify the deadly terrorist attack by Jabotinsky-connected organizations against the British – the Jews' best friend until then?

Another question: Was the Palestine-or-bust ideology of most Zionists the best path to salvation for the threatened Jewish masses? There was plenty of space in the US, Canada, Australia, etc. In those countries there was still prejudice, but there had never been a pogrom in any of them. There is no evidence that the Jewish lobby – and there was a lobby, and it was powerful – ever tired to gain acceptance to Jewish emigration to those lands, not even after World War II. (More on this later)

Abba Hillel Silver

Rabbi Abba Hillel Silver (1893-1963) was born in Lithuania but came to the US at the age of 9. He was ordained in 1915 and soon made a name for himself as a Zionist militant and leader. In 1943 Weizmann, as president of the World Zionist Organization, asked him to assume the leadership of the Zionist movement in America. Silver became a lobbyist for the "all of Palestine" policy both among fellow Jews and before Congress. When Congress refused to pass a declaration backing this policy he temporarily withdrew from a leadership role in the movement, but returned to his post a year later.

He was an impassioned orator, as we can judge from this excerpt from a 1943 speech to the American Jewish Conference:

> If we surrender our national claim to Palestine and rely solely on the refugee philanthropic appeal, we shall lose our case as well as do violence to the historic hope of our people. On the basis of sheer philanthropy, of satisfying

> pressing immigration needs, Palestine has already done its full share for Jewish refugees. It has taken in more than one half of the total Jewish refugees of the world, and the Palestine Arabs and their sympathizers in England and here [US] have been quick to point out that Palestine has already done all that can be expected from a small country and far more than most of the larger countries have done. It is because Palestine is the Jewish Homeland that we have the right to insist upon unrestricted immigration. It is because of the historic connection of the Jewish people with that land that the [British] Mandatory Government in the first place undertook to reconstitute it as the National Home and pledged itself to facilitate Jewish immigration …
> (Abba Hillel Silver, *Toward American Jewish Unity*, 1943, via Hertzberg,
> pp. 597-8)

Note that Silver, although a rabbi, makes no reference to God or to the Covenant, but only to ancient history (as he interprets it). Although he makes an off-hand reference to Palestinian Arabs, the thought that they too are a people with historic connection to that land doesn't seem to enter his mind. It's a case of racism by omission, a mental habit common to many Zionists.

The Question of Ethnicity

Let us, for a moment, step aside from the biographical aspect of the chapter and investigate logically who those Palestinians and who those Jews are from a genetic point of view.

The Palestinians are more truly Semitic than the Jews – no blond-haired, blue-eyed faces among them – whereas Jews share features and genetic material with the peoples in the midst of which they lived. No anthropologist consider them to be race: European Jews are white, Ethiopian Jews are black, and when there was an identifiable Jewish minority in China, they looked Chinese. What is the genetic ethnicity of the Palestinians? – Some of them are descendants of Hebrews who converted to Islam; some continue the bloodlines of the Philistines, Sumerians, Moabites, Amorites, Edomites and other Semitic peoples whose roots in Canaan may antedate

Joshua's invasion by centuries; some of them are descendants of nomadic Bedouins and Arabs who settled there centuries ago. Who can assert that they do not exist (as Golda Meir did) and have no title to the dwellings and lands that their family may have occupied for generations? Why should a Jew, on the basis that one of his ancestors may have been a soldier in Joshua's army, tell an Arab whose family has lived in his house and tilled the land around it for as long as anyone can remember that he must give up his property and leave?

Chaim Weizmann and the Balfour Declaration

Chaim Weizmann (1874-1952), like David Ben Gurion, was a militant who lived through the 1948 establishment of the State of Israel to become an important political figure in the New Country.

He was born in Russia, studied in Geneva, and emigrated to England in 1904, where he worked as a research chemist. He was an early adherent of Erzl's movement, though he often disagreed with the latter. He was the leader in negotiations which led to the Balfour Declaration. When the State of Israel was established he was asked to become its first president.

The Balfour Declaration was a letter written by Arthur James Balfour, a British foreign secretary, to Lord Rothschild, a powerful Jewish financier and philanthropist, in which he stated that "His Majesty's Government views with favor the establishment in Palestine of a national home for the Jewish people, and will use their best endeavors to facilitate the achievement of this object, it being clearly understood that nothing shall be done which may prejudice the civil and religious rights of existing non-Jewish communities in Palestine, or the rights and political status enjoyed by Jews in any other country."

Zionist leaders had hoped that the declaration would commit England, as mandatory power, to a clear policy of establishing a Jewish Commonwealth in the whole of Palestine. Lord Balfour wrote nothing of the sort. To "view with favor" is hardly a solemn promise and the caveats about non-Jewish communities in Palestine and Jews in other countries further limited the scope of the letter. Zionist haves parsed the declaration, desperately trying to impose their own interpretation upon it.

Weizmann and the Palestinians

Weizmann was one of the many Zionists who chose to ignore the very existence of the Palestinians:

> In its initial state, Zionism was conceived by its pioneers as a movement wholly depending on mechanical factors: there is a country which happens to be called Palestine, a country without a people and, on the other hand, there exists *the* Jewish people and it has no country. What else is necessary, then, than to fit the gem onto the ring, to unite this people with this country?
> (Chaim Weizmann, *Zionism Needs a Living Content*, 1914, via Hertzberg, p, 575).

However, 23 years later, he seems to have learned more about the country:

> … so must they [the Arabs] know that we have the right to build our home in Eretz Israel harming no one, helping all.
> (Report to the Palestinian Commission, 1937)

Since it would be a physical impossibility for the Jews to build their home in Palestine without displacing Arabs, it is difficult to know what he meant by "harming no one, helping all."

Weizmann was not given to sophisticated rhetoric: in the above report he wrote: "I told the Commission: 'God has promised Eretz Israel to the Jews. This is our Charter.'"

Ben Gurion

Weizmann was only president for four years – he died in 1952 – and, because of bad health and eyesight, he took little active part in politics. Ben Gurion (1886-1973) on the other hand, was prime minister and/or minister or defense from 1948 to 1953, and again from 1955 to 1963.

Born in Poland in 1886, he moved to Palestine in 1905 to work as a farm hand. He quickly got involved in local politics and soon rose to prominence. He was expelled by the Ottoman Turks in 1915 and spent three years in New York. By the end of the First World War he was back in Palestine as a soldier in the Jewish Legion of the British army. He was active in politics and was recognized as the leader of Palestinian Jews during the 40s.

As prime minister and minister of defense he was complicit in many of the outrages perpetrated by the Israeli military (more later) but as a writer and orator he preferred to ride the white horse of noble and generous sentiments. A few examples follow:

> … ours was a tiny nation possessed of a great spirit, an inspired people that believed in its pioneering mission to all men, in the mission that had been preached by the prophets of Israel. This people gave the world great and eternal moral truths and commandments. This people rose to prophetic visions of the unity of the Creator with his creation, of the dignity and infinite worth of the individual (because every man is created in the divine image), of social justice, universal peace, and love – "and thou shalt love thy neighbor as yourself." This people was the first to prophesy about the "end of days," the first to see the vision of a new human society.
> (David Ben Gurion, *The Importance of the Jewish Revolution*, 1944, via Hertzberg, p. 607)

Also:

> The difficult task we are performing on the Jewish scene is part of a tremendous movement which involves all of humanity – the world revolution, whose aims are the redemption of man from every form of enslavement, discrimination, and exploitation, no matter whether the victims are nations, races, religions, or one of the sexes.
> (Ibid, via Hertzberg, p. 616)

Compare these lofty words to the following entry in his *Independence War Diary*, for January 1, 1948, as quoted by Noam Chomsky, *the Faithful Triangle*, p. 182n:

> There is no question as to whether a reaction is necessary or not. The question is only time and place. Blowing up a house is not enough. What is necessary is cruel and strong reactions. We need precision in time, place and casualties. If we know the family – strike mercilessly, women and children included. Otherwise the reaction is inefficient. At the place of reaction there is no need to distinguish

> between guilty and innocent. Where there was no attack – we should not strike.

Will the real David Ben Gurion please stand up! That Ben Gurion didn't hesitate to resort to the principle of moral dispensation is made crystal clear by this sentence:

> The real danger that threatens is, as I have said, not entirely from the avowed "traitors of the covenant," but also form some prime movers of the Jewish revolution who do not have an uncompromising and single-minded devotion, who do not adhere without any moral, ideological, or political qualification, to the demands of the Jewish revolution.
> (Ben Gurion, *The Imperatives of the Jewish Revolution*, via Hertzberg, p. 613.)

Is this what Ahad Ha-am meant when he wrote that "the Jewish people is unique in its genius for morality"?

Chapter XVIII – The Conquest of Palestine

It's a complicated story: complicated politics and diplomacy, complicated lobbying, complicated military actions. The land had always had a special attraction for a small number of Jews, but after 1881-82 pogrom in Russia and the Dreyfuss affair in France, a group of precursors, writers and rabbis – some of which we met in the previous chapter – started militating for a Jewish homeland, or commonwealth or state. They argued that since the Jews, in spite of the emancipation, were still subject to discrimination (at best) and oppression (at worst) the establishment of a sovereign state – or something close to that – would garner respect and offer protection. In the context of the time that was a valid thesis. The first objects of the lobbying were fellow Jews. Some militants, such as Leo Pinsker, were more interested in rescuing the Jews from their dire predicament than in the politics and geography of the problem. This approach has been called *defensive Zionism* (also *practical Zionism*). Other crusaders for historical or religious reasons believed that Palestine was the only acceptable location for the new homeland, whatever the cost to Jews and non-Jews. This position we may call *ideological Zionism*, and its militants I will call the *Palestine-or-bust gang.* (From the ethical point of view, these positions are horses of totally different colors, as they are situated in different political domains and answer to different moral imperatives.)

The lobbying was very effective, especially among the Jewish Diaspora. Even Herzl, basically a defensive Zionist, ended up expressing a preference for Palestine. More Jews started buying property, especially agricultural property, in the region.

> Between 1922 and 1932 Jewish land holdings had risen from 14,500 ac. [acres] to 383,350 ac. and the Jewish population from 73,799 to 445,457 (30% of the total population). Tel Aviv had developed into an all-Jewish city of 150,000 inhabitants and £80,000,000 of Jewish capital had been introduced into the country.
> ("Palestine," *Encyclopedia Britannica*, 1987)

The Arabs were alarmed, and for good reason. Although the purchases were fair and square, and the Jews who bought land and other real estate had legitimate title to their purchases, the breakdown of the Ottoman Empire as a result of World War I, and the constitutionally vague and weak state of affairs under the British Mandate, meant that any Jew who bought land acquired *de facto* citizenship. Most of this land was purchased from Arab absentee landlords who lived outside of Palestine. The Palestinian tenant farmers who worked the land either became quasi serfs for Jewish owners or were evicted and replaced by Jewish workers. The Palestinians were being conquered through real estate transactions!

The Balfour declaration was signed in 1917. In June 1919 the covenant of the League of Nations was signed. Article 22 of the covenant granted independence to the former Ottoman Arab provinces (including Palestine) subject to supervision by a mandatory power. In 1922 the League granted mandatory power over Palestine to Britain, making reference to the Balfour declaration. Britain was put in an untenable position since the declaration and Article 22 were completely incompatible. For one thing, any logical person who understood the various official commitments would know that even a Jewish National Home that did not cover the whole of Palestine would entail the forcible dispossession and displacement of a large number of Arabs because, as the Palestine-or-bust gang insisted, Zionists were granted the right of unlimited immigration.

For some years the Arabs were rather quiet, but in 1929 there was a religious dispute at the Wailing Wall in which both sides suffered more than a hundred deaths. In 1936 the Arabs declared a general strike which lasted six months. During that time groups of Palestinians and other Arabs started an insurrection which culminated in a national revolt. By the time the insurrection petered out in 1939 Arab casualties were in the thousands and Jewish and British ones in the hundreds. The Palestinians, who had never been in a position to organize, train and arm a military sector, were further weakened by the revolt.

All this was an acute embarrassment to Britain. In 1937 a royal commission of enquiry recommended the partition of Palestine and forcible displacement of Arabs from the Jewish to the proposed Palestinian state, but in 1939 Britain issued a white paper in which it claimed that whatever pledge it had made in the Balfour declaration had already been fulfilled, and opined that unlimited Jewish immigration and forcible transfer of Arab land to Jews ran counter to the intentions of Article 22 and of the mandate. Zionists were incensed and ceased to consider Britain their best friend. After 1939 the United States progressively replaced Britain as Zionism's main ally, eventually becoming the prime broker, philanthropist, armorer, and United Nations vetoer – until it virtually replaced Yahweh as Israel's Great Enabler.

During World War II, the "fog of war" gave the Zionists opportunities for many clandestine operations targeting mostly the Arabs and the British. The Haganah became the semi-official army. It was augmented by three militias, the Palma, the Irgun and the Stern gang. Only the latter was militarily active during the early part of the war. (It was composed of rather disreputable and thuggish men and disbanded after independence (although one of its ex-members, Yitzhak Shamir, later became prime minister). The Irgun, however, had many members who took an active part in the politics of the new state and one of its leaders, Menachem Begin, became prime minister.

Thousands of Israelis joined the allied forces and acquired military training; munitions factories were established in Israel to help equip the Allies; the Zionists organized a clandestine operation to steal arms and munitions; political organizations, such as the Jewish Agency remained active. In 1944 it was estimated that Haganah could muster between 30,000 and 40,000 fighters, and its loosely affiliated militia five to ten thousand more. The end of the war found the Zionists ready and fairly well organized. Not so for the Palestinians.

All along, the Zionists were gradually reeling in the Big Fish: the United States of America. In 1942, at a Zionist conference in New York City, Ben Gurion obtained the US support for unlimited immigration of Jews to Palestine, for the formation of a Jewish army, and for the establishment of a Jewish Commonwealth in all of Palestine. More and more congressmen became pro-Zionist and President Truman applied pressure on Britain for unlimited immigration. The US was on its way to becoming Israel's protector and enabler.

The Zionists did not wait for the end of the war (1945) to go on the offensive with terrorist raids. The targets were not only Arabs, but included Britishers and others. (The Zionists insisted on *their* interpretation of the Balfour Declaration – or else!) The Irgun and the Stern gang joined forces, with the toleration and/or cooperation of the Haganah, and engaged in many raids. In November 1944, the British minister of state in Cairo was assassinated. In July 1946, a part of the King David hotel in Jerusalem that housed British officers was blown up at the cost of 91 lives. In March 1947, the Irgun killed 12 British soldiers in a grenade attack on the Officers' Club in Tel Aviv. Britishers were not the only Europeans attacked: in 1948 Count Bernadotte, a Swedish soldier and diplomat who was appointed mediator by the Untied Nations, was murdered. Without Great Britain, Israel would not have been born; but the British – unlike many other countries – tried to be fair to the Palestinians, and paid in blood for their efforts. (In June 67, during the Six Day War, the deliberate and deadly attack on the American ship US Liberty gave further proof that gratitude is not part of the Zionist ethos. But then, if you're God, what use do you have for gratitude?)

As the end of the mandate became imminent Irgun, the Stern gang and the Haganah became bolder and their operations more ambitious. Thus, in April 1948, one month before the end of the mandate, Irgun, the Stern gang and Haganah attacked the village of Deir Yassin. Israeli historian Benny Morris describes the massacre:

> Deir Yassin is remembered not as a military operation, but rather for the atrocities committed by the IZL [Irgun] and LHN [Stern gang] troops during and immediately after the drawn-out battle: Whole families were riddled with bullets and grenade fragments and buried when houses were blown up on top of them; men, women and children were mowed down as they emerged from houses; individuals were taken aside and shot. At the end of the battle, groups of old men, women and children were trucked through West Jerusalem's streets in a kind of "Victory Parade" and then dumped in [Arab] East Jerusalem.
> (Benny Morris, *Righteous Victims*, Vintage, p. 208).

In the same paragraph, Morris adds: "The adult males were taken to town in trucks and paraded in the streets, then taken back to the site and killed with rifle and machine gun fire."

In a review of the film *Munich* – a review that was really more an article – Henry Siegman makes reference to an interview in the Israeli newspaper, *Ha Aretz*, in which the interviewee, Benny Morris, states that according to recently declassified documents "in the months of April-May 1948, units of the Haganah were given operational orders that stated explicitly that they were to uproot the villagers, expel them and destroy the villages themselves." (Henry Siegman, "The Killing Equation," *The New York Review of Books*, Feb. 9, 2006). Morris adds that in many operations people were marched, put against a wall, and executed in an "orderly fashion," all this by order of the Israel Defense Force and with the knowledge of David Ben Gurion. Morris claimed that there were 24 such occasions:

> In some cases four or five people were executed, in others, the numbers were 70, 80, 100 … The worst cases were Sahila (70-80 killed). Deir Yassin (100-110), Lod (250), Dawayima (hundreds), and perhaps Abu Sasha (70). There is no unequivocal proof of a large-scale massacre at Tantura, but war crimes were perpetrated there. At Jaffa there was a massacre about which nothing had been known until now. The same of Arab al Mussawi, in the North. About half of the acts of massacre were part of Operation Hiram [in the North] in October 1948; at Safsaf, Shahilas, Jesh, Estaboun, Arab al Muwassi, Deir al Asad, Majdal, Krum, Sasa. (Ibid.)

Now, Morris is no anti-Zionist. In the same interview he said that the uprooting of the Palestinians was necessary for the establishment of Israel and that Ben Gurion should have ordered ethnic cleansing on a larger scale in order to prevent any demographic problem.

Siegman comments that "Morris seems to be arguing that when the establishment of a Jewish state hangs in the balance, there is no such category as innocent Palestinian civilians; their very existence constitutes a mortal threat to the state, and therefore to the Jewish people. That threat transforms innocent civilians into legitimate military targets." [One must not stand in the way of God, neither consciously nor innocently!]

Note that Operation Hiram took place in October 1948, 5 months after the end of the mandate. When Israel became a sovereign state, the Haganah morphed into the Israel Defense Force, and good-old-fashioned terrorism became state terrorism. In the aftermath of this terrorism hundreds of thousands of Palestinians fled to Jordan, Lebanon, and the West Bank.

On May 14, the British packed their bags and left, heaving a sigh of relief. On the same day, the Jewish National Council and the General Zionist Council proclaimed the establishment of the State of Israel, implicitly and temporarily accepting a UN partition plan, and asserted that they jointly were the provisional government. A few hours later, President Truman gave the new country *de facto* American recognition, and on the 15th the USSR went one step further, making its recognition *de jure.* On May 15 armed contingents from Trans-Jordan, Iraq, Syria and Egypt entered Palestine. Over the next months a number of military engagements occurred while Ralph Bunch, Bernadotte's successor, trudged his briefcase from capital to capital, trying to get armistices signed. The Israeli forces, better organized and much better equipped, won most battles (except a few against the Jordanian Arab Legion). Finally Bunch succeeded in getting an armistice between Israel and each of the Arab states except Iraq (which, to this day, never signed one). These armistices were nothing but glorified cease-fire agreements, yet they signaled the *de facto* end of the First Arab-Israeli War. When the dust settled Israel had considerably expanded its share of Palestine at the expense of the Arabs.

Ethical and Political Considerations

Most of the early Zionist writers and militants wrote as though Palestine was an empty land, conveniently "forgetting" to mention the Palestinian Arabs. Let me repeat, from the last chapter, part of a quotation by Chaim Weizmann: "… there is a country which happens to be called Palestine, a country without a people and, on the other hand there exists the Jewish people and it has no country. What else is necessary, then, but to fit he gem into the ring, to unite the people with this country?" A few – very few – Zionist writers and ideologues acknowledged the existence of the Palestinians – Ahad Ha'am for one – but most Jews believed the Zionist slogan, "A land without people for a people without a land." Golda Meir, Israel's first woman prime minister, put it very explicitly and bluntly:

> It was not as though there was a Palestinian people in Palestine considering itself as a Palestinian people and we came and threw them out and took their country away from them. They did not exist.
> (*London Sunday Times*, June 15, 1969, via Chomsky, p. 51)

This of course was a blatant lie; Meir knew very well that there were approximately one million Palestinian Arabs. But since they were not organized as a sovereign nation, the individual Arabs, in Meir's opinion, had no nationality and no rights. The prime minister showed a complete and willful ignorance of the Universal Declaration of Human Rights and of the 4th Geneva Convention, both of which establish the rights of individual non-combatants under conditions of warfare and occupation.

The relevant notion here is not sovereignty or nationhood, but title. Webster's Third International Dictionary lists many definitions of the word. Two are germane here:

> 2a: The union of all the elements constituting legal ownership and being divided in common law into possession, right of possession, and right of property.
> 2b: Something that constitutes a legally just cause of exclusive possession: the body of facts or events that give rise to the ownership of real or personal property.

There is no hint here that sovereignty has anything to do with it. If your family has lived in a house and tilled the land around it for many years, without anyone publicly objecting to your use of the property, you have title to that house and land regardless of your civil status. The Talmud deals at length and in detail with the notion of title, including such legalistic principles as *usufruct* and *usucapture.* In Chapter 3 of tractate *Bava Basra* in Order *(Seder) Nezikin*, the Talmud, expounding the law of *Chazakah* regarding the acquiring of land, asserts that uncontested usage of real property for three years, both day and night, is a valid basis for claiming acquisition from the prior owner. Certainly the great majority of the Palestinians chased into exile from such towns as Deir Yassin had title to their real property (as did, of course, those Jews who had bought land). To force them out – whether by terrifying them into fleeing or by herding them on buses is to rob them of their legitimate property; to do this to hundreds of thousands of victims constitutes a crime against humanity – a fortiori when the methods used include mass murder and summary execution.

It is clear that in the which-came-first game of these two peoples, it was the Zionist chicken that laid the egg of contention. As David Ben Gurion himself put it: "We came and stole their land. Why would they accept that?" The Jews, the English, the French, and the Americans have been in a position of moral deficit toward the Palestinians form the very beginning. This in no way excuses violations of universally accepted ethical principles from the Arab side; nor do these transgressions erase the moral deficit.

In the decades long tit-for-tat dynamics of the conflict, either side can always find a provocation to legitimize its own aggression, but, in the last analysis, Israel is the proactive side and the Arabs are the reactive side: the proactive side bears the preponderance of the moral onus.

To those Zionists who would point to some prior incident to justify Deir Yasin and other outrages, I would like to ask two questions:

Had count Bernadotte killed or injured any Zionist prior to his assassination?

Had the US Liberty fired at any Israeli military or civilian target prior to being attacked by Israeli planes and torpedoes?

These incidents, among others, prove that Zionists were perfectly capable of terrorist tactics in the absence of prior provocation.

Propaganda and Lobbying

At the beginning of the modern movement of Zionism, circa 1875, only about 10% of the Jews were favorable to the project. By 1948, the majority of Jews were at least sympathetic to the movement. This was the result of a massive and relentless effort of propaganda directed at fellow Jews, but also at the international community. The first arena was the nascent movement itself. Some Zionists were concerned mostly with saving Jews from egregious oppression (and, in the case of Germany in the 30s, looming genocide) and militated for a safe haven, whenever space and politics would permit. Others had a much more ideological point of view: what mattered was the fulfillment of Israel's (i.e. the Jews') holy destiny as the chosen people, the vindication of ancient, unrealized prophecies, and the exculpation of Yahweh who had not honored many of his promises. The former have been called *defensive Zionists* (also *practical Zionists*); the latter I have called *ideological Zionists*, and also informally, the *Palestine-or-bust gang*. (Henceforth, when I use the word *Zionism* without qualification, I mean *ideological Zionism*.)

Who could object to the defensive endeavor? Millions of Jews were living in intolerable conditions and, in the Germany of the 30s, were under the threat of impending doom. Something had to be done, even if corners had to be cut and if inconvenience and economic sacrifice had to be inflicted on many.

The world was neither ready nor willing to face the challenge. Even those countries that had known no pogroms were opposed to the immigration of Jewish refugees within their borders. In 1938 Roosevelt called the Avian Conference, which met in France, to discuss the refugee problem. Little was accomplished as most Western countries were unwilling to accept Jews. In 1939, the Wagner Rogers Bill proposed admitting 20,000 German refugee children to the US. The bill died in committee. (England, though, did accept 10,000 children through the *Kindertransport* program; and the Dominican Republic, alone of all Western countries, offered to accept 50 to 100,000 refugees, but only 5,000 arrived before the onset of the war.)

Perhaps the saddest story of these pre-war years is the saga of the St. Louis. On this luxury liner were 907 German Jews, upper class individuals who had been stripped of all their assets. They had entry visas to Cuba, but were turned away at the Port of Havana, because the Cuban government refused to recognize their documents. The ship then set out on a pilgrimage in search for a sanctuary. No South American country would accept them. The ship headed north, but the United States dispatched a gun ship to prevent the refugees from entering American waters. Upon hearing of this Canadian Prime Minister Mackenzie King and his immigration minister made it known that they were strongly opposed to the admission of the passengers and that, at any rate, Canada had already done too much for the Jews. The St. Louis returned to Europe.

But by the end of the war the situation had changed dramatically. Six million Jews had been murdered, often after months of incarceration under horrible conditions and of service as slave laborers. So extreme was the Nazi offence to common decency that the shackles of old fashion anti-Semitism were broken. No more did Jews have to suffer the crazy and groundless accusations of being the killers of Jesus, or the evil and cynical plotters of the forged *Protocols of the Elders of Zion*, or the cannibals who kidnapped and drank the blood of Gentile children on the feast of Passover. (Of course, there will always be little cells of pure hatred, but these are not any more in position to do serious harm to Jews.) Even the new anti-Semitism identified by Herzl was defanged.

> We now no longer discuss the irrational causes, prejudices and narrow-mindedness, but the political and economic causes. Modern anti-Semitism is not to be confused with the persecution of the Jews in former times, though it does still have a religious aspect, in some countries. The main current of Jew-hatred is today a different one. In the principal centers of Anti-Semitism, it is an outgrowth of the emancipation of the Jews.
> (Theodor Herzl, *The Jewish State*, p. 186, via Hertzberg, p. 218)

In the same paragraph he adds: "For in the ghetto we had remarkably developed into a bourgeois people and we emerged from the ghetto a prodigious rival to the middle class." This anti-Semitism of envy may have abated, but old habits die hard: in the months immediately following armistice, Western countries were still reluctant to accept Jewish refugees. A quarter of a million Jews who refused to live where they had been persecuted ended up in European refugee camps. They lived in terrible conditions, just parked there, waiting to hear what their eventual fate would be.

They were unaware that they were pawns in a political game being played by the Palestine-or-bust gang which, by then, had reduced the voice of Jewish anti-Zionists to a mere whimper. A frenzied but well-organized lobbying offensive was going on, especially in the US. Such groups as the Zionist Federation, the American Zionist Council, United Jewish Appeal, Untied Israel Appeal, B'nai B'rith, the Jewish Agency for Israel, the Jewish Agency Executive, etc. etc., spared neither time nor money to aggressively apply Zionist pressure. Every senator and congressman was courted – in some cases threatened with political reprisal.

But not one of these groups, as far as I can determine, ever lobbied to have Jewish refugees accepted in the US, Canada, Australia, Argentina, or any other place but Palestine.

Most analysts believe that the majority of these people would have chosen the US over Palestine, given the choice. So pro-Jewish were most Western leaders, and so conscious of the horrors of the Holocaust was the general population that a simple push of propaganda and lobbying would have been sufficient to bring these unfortunates to America (and/or other places) where they could have settled without dispossessing and displacing other people. As Noam Chomsky eloquently put it:

> After the war tens of thousands of Jewish displaced persons died in camps from miserable conditions and lack of care, and congressional Displaced Persons (DP) legislation gave priority not to Jews but to refugees from the Russian-occupied Baltic states, many of them Nazi sympathizers, including even SS troupers. There was little American Zionist support for legislation intended to bring DPs [Jewish Displaced Persons] to the U.S. in contrast to massive support for resolutions calling for the establishment of a Jewish State. (Chomsky, p. 93)

The main target of all that lobbying was President Truman (who, at one point, complained that he had received some 35,000 letters and propaganda leaflets from Jews). Even before becoming president, he had expressed heart-felt sympathy for the Holocaust victims. At a rally in 1944, then Senator Truman had said:

> Today, not tomorrow, we must do all that is humanly possible to provide a haven for all those who can be grasped from the hands of the Nazi butchers. Free land must be opened to these.
> (www. middleeastweb.org/us_supportforstate.htm)

Yet, Truman didn't completely trust the Jews:

> The Jews, I find are very, very selfish. They care not how many Estonians, Latvians, Finns, Poles, Yugoslavs or Greeks get murdered as DPs [displaced persons] as long as the Jews get special treatment. Yet when they have power, physical, financial or political, neither Hitler nor Stalin has anything on them for cruelty or mistreatment of the underdog. Put an underdog on top and it makes no difference whether his name is Russian, Jewish, Negro, Management, Labor, Mormon, Baptist, he goes haywire.
> (diary entry, July 21, cited in www. mideastweb.org)

Truman vacillated between backing increased immigration into Palestine or partition of the land into a Jewish and an Arab state. (The latter alternative had been consistently rejected by the Arabs.) All along, he wanted to admit more Jews into Palestine but there was opposition to the idea. The Zionists used the services of an old Jewish friend of the president, Eddie Jacobson, to arrange a meeting with Chaim Weizmann, soon-to-be president of Israel. Soon after, Truman was the first head-of-state to recognize the State of Israel.

The lobby did not consider its work done. In 1953 AIPAC, the American-Israeli Public Affairs Committee, was founded. Its purpose was to lobby the Congress of the United States and entertain a liaison with every member of that body. In short order it became the umbrella group and the coordinator for most Zionist organizations and for some non-Jewish neoconservative ones (informally and indirectly, probably).

AIPAC has been unusually effective, so effective that in 1992 AIPAC president David Steiner resigned because of a tape recording in which he bragged that he was negotiating with the new Clinton administration for the appointment of a pro-Israel Secretary of State and that AIPAC had placed a dozen people in the Clinton headquarters who were "all going to have big jobs."

(The *Washington Times*, received a copy of the tape and reported on it on Nov. 4, 1992).

As reported in Wikipedia, the on-line encyclopedia, "in August 2005, former AIPAC senior policy director Steven Rosen and AIPAC senior Iran analyst Keith Weismann were indicted for illegally conspiring to gather and disclose confidential information to Israel." The information was passed to them by Larry Franklin, a US Department of Defense employee who was sentenced to 151 months in jail on January 20, 2006. Two years after their indictments, Rosen and Weismann have still not been brought to trial.

There is no evidence that AIPAC ever spied on Israel for the benefit of the US.

Ethnic Cleansing

As we saw in the previous chapter, many of the early intellectuals of the Zionist movement waxed lyrical about how the Jewish presence in Palestine would be a boon to the Arabs and, eventually, to the whole human race; how jobs would be created; how administration and infrastructure would be improved. They were particularly insistent that the Palestinians would not be displaced, and that both ethnicities would get along just fine, to their mutual benefit.

Yet, in private moments, even those precursors showed awareness of what would ultimately be called "the demographic problem" As Benny Morris put it, "On the most basic level Jewish colonization meant expropriation and displacement." (p. 61) Arthur Ruppi, a leader of the early Jewish colonists, some twenty years before the establishment of Israel, was conscious of the problem.

> Land is the most necessary thing for establishing roots in Palestine. Since there are hardly any more arable unsettled land … we are bound in each case … to remove the peasants who cultivated the land.
> (Morris, p. 61)

There is often an extreme disconnect between the exalted humanistic rhetoric for public consumption and the actions of the Zionists on the ground. Jabotinsky wrote:

> We maintain unanimously that the economic position of the Palestinian Arabs, under Jewish colonization and owing to the Jewish colonization, has become the object of envy in all surrounding Arab countries, so that the Arabs from those Arab countries have a clear tendency to immigrate into Palestine. I have also shown to you already that in our submission there is no question of ousting the Arabs.
> (Evidence Submitted to the Palestine Commission, via Hertzberg, p. 262)

In 1932 Jabotinsky organized the illegal Haganah militia and, in the late 30s, his followers founded the Irgun terrorist group, both of which were implicated in the violent expulsion of tens of thousands of Arabs from their homes and land.

No one, however, could compete with Ben Gurion when it came to hypocrisy, as was made evident by citations in the previous chapter. With one side of his mouth he spoke of the heroic role of Israel in the "Redemption of man from every form of enslavement, discrimination and exploitation"; but with the other side he exhorted the military to "strike mercilessly, women and children included."

His duplicity was made evident in a 1937 speech in which he said:

> The acceptance of partition does not commit us to renounce Transjordan [Jordan]; one does not demand from anybody to give up his vision. We shall accept a state in the boundaries fixed today, but the boundaries of Zionist aspirations are the concern of the Jewish people and no external factor will be able to limit them.
> (cited in *New Outlook*, April, 1977, via Chomsky, p. 161)

The above, and numerous other items of evidence, remove all doubt that dispossession and other aspects of the "Joshua method" were part of the Zionist plan from the "get go." "The violators of Deir Yassin and all those other towns didn't act on impulse. The leaders of the Haganah and politicians like Ben-Gurion – soon to be the first prime minister and minister of defense of Israel – were aware of everything and probably gave the orders.

Same old covenant. Same old moral dispensation. But there's a major difference between Joshua and Ben-Gurion. Joshua, we may surmise, really believed that a *really* existing (factual) entity, Yahweh, the God of Israel, ordained the war against the Canaanites and gave the Hebrews moral dispensation to kill women, children and old folk. But Ben-Gurion, according to Hertzberg, was not a believer: he was an agnostic and a thoroughly secular Jew. Where did his moral dispensation come from? If it was assumed just because the Jews considered themselves a nation, then any group that makes a similar claim can also claim moral dispensation – including the Palestinians and even the Germans of Nazi Germany.

I will leave the last words of this chapter to Israel's first prime-minister:

> We must use terror, assassination, land confiscation and the cutting of all social services to rid the Galilee of its Arab population."
> (David Ben-Gurion, May 1948, to the General Staff, as quoted in Michael Ben-Zohar, *Ben-Gurion, a Biography*, Delacorte Press, 1948.

One wonders who his mentors were!

Chapter XIX – The Occupation of Arab Land

Egypt, 4000 Years Later

Some 4,000 years after the Exodus led by Moses, the Israelis did the opposite: they invaded Egypt – twice. The first time, in 1956, was as allies of France and England. Gamel Nasser, president of Egypt, nationalized the Suez Canal. Fearful that Nasser might close the canal to them and cut off the movement of petroleum to Europe, England and France decided on military action. Israel, tired of Egyptian support to raiding Palestinians, was only too glad to join them. The IDF did most of the infantry work while the Europeans destroyed the Egyptian airforce and straffed Egyptian ground troops. The IDF killed several thousand Egyptians while suffering less than 200 casualties, but pressure from Russia, the US, the UN, and their own people forced England and France to abandon the project. Nasser was proclaimed a hero, the canal remained nationalized, the Europeans lost power and prestige in the region, and nothing much changed for Israel.

The Six-Day War

The second Egypt-Israel conflict had much more momentous consequences. This time it was Egypt, not Israel, that had allies: Syria and Jordan. After a decade of relative peace, the situation changed with the advent of the Palestine Liberation Organization (PLO) in 1964. In 1965, the military wing of the PLO, Al-Fattah, carried out its first operation, sabotaging a canal that brought water to central Israel. During the next two years, many raids were carried out by Fattah, mostly from Jordan and Lebanon. Israel mounted some reprisals. Syria got involved in a dispute over water from the Jordan River and shots were fired across the border by both sides.

Egyptian president Gamel Nasser ordered a military build-up in the Sinai Peninsula and this greatly displeased the Israeli leadership. Using this as pretext, Israel decided to attack. Israeli politicians and apologist have claimed that their aggression was really a defensive necessity – that, morally, the Egyptian divisions in the Sinai (part of the Egyptian territory) constituted a virtual act of war – thus legitimizing the seizure and occupation of Arab territory. But over the years the truth has come out:

> Top Israeli military commanders made it clear not long after that that Israel had faced no serious military threat and that a quick victory was anticipated with confidence – that the alleged threat was a "bluff."
> (Chomsky, p. 28, referring to "Abba Eban, Obstacles to Autonomy," *New Outlook*, Tel Aviv, 1982.

Menachem Begin himself concurred:

> In June 1967, we again had a choice. The Egyptian Army concentrations in the Sinai approaches do not prove that Nasser was really about to attack us. We must be honest with ourselves. We decided to attack him.
> (Menachem Begin, August 8 speech at the National Defense College, the *New York Time*, August 21, 1982, reprinted from the *Jerusalem Post*, via Chomsky)

The Israeli onslaught was swift, terribly effective, and not according to Hoyle:

> Much like the Japanese plan against the United States in 1941, the IDF battle plan hinged on an aerial master stroke – this one designed to incapacitate the opponents' air forces and, in consequence, render their ground forces vulnerable to a continuous pounding from the air. The plan … was to destroy the Egyptian air force on the ground.
> (Morris, p. 316)

Benny Morris, a Zionist and an honest historian, stopped short of mentioning the name with which the "Japanese plan" is associated: Pearl Harbor – the target of a sneak attack that in the words of President Roosevelt would live "in the annals of infamy." But with God on your side (especially of you *are* God, collectively) "all is fair in love and war." In other words, you have moral dispensation.

In two waves the IAF destroyed 304 out of the 419 Egyptian planes while losing less than a dozen. A third wave attacked Syria, Iraq and Jordan. Jordan lost its whole airforce (28 planes) and the other two countries' air services were rendered helpless. Arab ground soldiers were sitting ducks! According to Morris, the Israeli, not wanting to be slowed down by prisoners, let some go and mowed down the others.

The victory was quick and complete. It took just six days to rout the combined forces of the Arabs, hence the name: the *Six Day War*. The Israeli conquered the Sinai, the Gaza Strip, the West Bank and the Golan Heights – an area more than three times larger than Israel proper. (Morris, p.328). As a result one million Arabs passed under the control of Israel, a gain of dubious value, as the demographic problem was thereby aggravated. Approximately 10 to 15,000 Egyptians, 800 Jordanians, 500 Syrians, and 800 Israelis lost their lives.

Zionist Gratitude

One incident, to which I have already alluded, merits special scrutiny. The Security Council had imposed a cease-fire on June 10, but on June 12 the IDF broke it to attack the part of Syria known as the Golan Heights. Meanwhile a US spy ship, the US Liberty, was calmly cruising along in the Mediterranean near the Heights. Fearing that it might alert the US to the unlawful assault – speculation, but a reasonable one – or hoping to sink the ship and blame it on the Arabs, Israel attacked the defenseless vessel, killing 34 Americans and wounding 171. Apologists have asserted that it was all a regrettable mistake, but all the surviving American servicemen on the ship have been unanimous in insisting that the ship was clearly marked and that no mistake was possible.

(www.desert-voice.net_liberty.htm, also www.usliberty.org/)

What clinches it for me is the fact that President Lyndon Johnson threatened with court martial any sailor who talked about it. Also, in 2001, Hebrew language recordings of the attack were made public by the National Security Agency, removing all lingering doubt.

Two inferences can be drawn from the above:

1. Zionists have no concept of gratitude or loyalty outside their own group, since they do not hesitate to kill their staunchest allies.
2. Zionists have every reason to feel confident that the American government and the American press can be controlled and manipulated at will by their lobbyists.

Ethnic Cleansing and Jewish Settlements

Victory, so swift and complete, was heady stuff. The Zionists did not let opportunity slip through their fingers. Not satisfied with controlling territory, the IDF repeated some of the exploits of twenty years before:

> A number of IDF commanders, apparently without cabinet authorization, though probably with Dayan's approval, tried to repeat the experience of 1948 – to drive Palestinians into exile and demolish their homes. Altogether, some 200 - 300,000 Arabs fled or were driven from the West Bank and the Gaza Strip, most of them going to the East Bank of Jordan during the war and in the weeks immediately after. Another eighty to ninety thousand fled or were driven from the Golan Heights. (Morris, p. 327)

One quarter of the population of the West Bank became refugees, many of them for the second time.

In the first Arab-Israeli war, Orthodox Jews, who were generally not Zionists, had a minor role, but in 1967, a group of ultra-Orthodox rabbis, now hard-core Zionists, jumped at the chance to fill the vacuum and led their followers on settlement-building expeditions. Within one year of the cessation of fighting, there were already six Israeli settlements on the Golan Heights.

Religious nationalists considered the conquests the beginning of a divine redemption. Under Rabbi Zui Cook, son of one of the first "prophets" of Zionism, Rabbi Abraham Cook, pioneers marched out to establish settlements in the occupied territories. This, of course, was a way to eventually make these territories a permanent part of Israel. The government either acceded to the demands of the settlers or looked the other way. The strategy here was to create a situation that would render the very thought of granting real sovereignty to the Palestinians inconceivable. "What? Leave the Jews of the settlements at the mercy of vengeful Arabs? Unthinkable!"

In the process of establishing settlements many outrages were committed:

> After initial expropriations in 1969, military forces commanded by General Ariel Sharon, in January 1972, "drove off some ten thousand farmers and Bedouins, bulldozed or dynamited their houses, pulled down their tents, destroyed their crops, and filled their wells," to prepare the ground for the establishment of six Kibbutzim, nine villages and the city of Yamit. Subsequently Israel bulldozers uprooted orchards (what is called in technical terms "making the desert bloom"), Care aid from the US was withheld to force landowners to sell their lands, mosques and schools were destroyed and the one school to escape demolition was turned over to a new kibbutz.
> (Ammno Kapelink, *Le Monde*, May 15, via Chomsky, p. 106)

Ethical and Political Considerations

From the Universal Declaration of Human Rights of the Untied Nations (unanimously adopted with 8 abstentions on December 19, 1948):

> **Article 15.1**: Everyone has the right to a nationality.
> **Article 17.2**: No one shall be arbitrarily deprived of his property.
> **Article 29**: Nothing in this Declaration shall be interpreted as implying for any state, group or person any right to engage in any activity or to perform an act aimed at the destruction of any of the rights and freedom set forth herein.
> [Note that Israel was accepted within the Untied Nations in May 11, 1949.]

From the Hague Convention IV, 1907 (respecting the laws and customs of war on land):

> **Article 46 (excerpt)**: Private property cannot be confiscated.
> **Article 50**: No general penalty, pecuniary or otherwise, shall be inflicted upon a population on account of the acts of individuals for which they cannot be regarded as jointly and severally responsible.
> **Article 56 (excerpt)**: The property of municipalities … shall be treated as private property.

From the 4th Geneva Convention (August 12, 1949):

> **Article 33 (excerpt)**: No protected persons [non combatants] may be punished for an offence he or she has not committed. Collective penalties and likewise all measures of intimidation or of terrorism are prohibited ... Reprisals against protected persons and their property are prohibited.
> **Article 49 (excerpt)**: Individual or mass forcible transfers, as well as deportations of protected persons from occupied territory to the territory of the Occupying Power or to that of any other country, occupied or not, are prohibited, regardless of their motives.
> […]
> The Occupying Power shall not deport or transfer parts of its own civilian population into the territory it occupies.

There is little that Israel did during the Six-Day War and in the aftermath that was not a breech of the Declaration of Human Rights, of the Geneva Conventions, or of the principles of the Untied Nations. Moshe Dagan in his memoirs admits that in the villages houses were destroyed "not in battle but in punishment … and in order to chase away the inhabitants." (Morris, p. 328) Shooting fleeing (and presumably unarmed) soldiers rather than taking them prisoners is another egregious violation, not only of the Declaration and the Conventions, but also of common decency.

One would think that the cessation of fighting would bring a great diminution of war crimes and crimes against humanity, but the Gush Ermunim (Bloc of the Faithful, associated with the National Religious Party) used the war as a spring board for an illegal settlement movement active to this day. The United Nations unanimously passed Resolution

242, directing Israel to pull back its forces from occupied territories, but, as in almost every UN resolution regarding it, Israel simply disregarded the resolution.

[Israel did return the Sinai to Egypt in 1982, but that was purely a political move to eliminate a southern front in any subsequent conflict. The West Bank, East Jerusalem and the Golan Heights are still occupied – illegally.]

Apologists will advance that many of these settlements were the result of unsanctioned and almost spontaneous activity, but this argument does not hold water: spontaneous Palestinian uprisings never escaped the vigilance of the occupiers. Besides, what can be illegally erected can be legally taken down by the authorities, as was the case when Israel decided that protecting settlements in the Gaza Strip was not worth the trouble. Apologists also claim that whatever Israel did was ethically acceptable since the posting of military divisions on their own side of the border proved that Egyptians were planning for war, which made them the aggressors. I have already proffered evidence that Israeli military and political leaders did not think that an attack was in the cards, and that in the words of Menachem Begin, "We started it." Also, nothing in the Hague and Geneva conventions make any distinction, regarding the rights of civilians, between the aggressive side and the defending side: oppressing "protected persons" is equally forbidden to the attacking country and the defending one.

Promised Land and Promised Water

An important aspect of the occupation is the water distribution problem: Israel has used the Six-Day War not only to steal territory, but also to steal water:

> Before the 1967 War, Palestinians used 140 pumping units [of Jordan-River water] for irrigation. After the war, and from the very beginning of the occupation of the West Bank by Israel, the latter forbade to the Palestinians the use of the Jordan River's water [for irrigation].
> Rezeq Farej, *Palestine, Le refus de disparaître*, Pleine Lune, 2005, p. 127, my translation.)

On the next page, Faraj gives more specific information:

> According to data from the World Bank, Israel uses 90% of West Bank's water; the Palestinians have access to only the remaining 10%. The water resources of the Palestinians is among the most meager of the planet ... Irrigated cultivation in Israel represents about 50% of agricultural land, but constitutes less than 2% of the economy ... As for the Palestinian agricultural sector, it represents 15% of the gross national product and employs one fifth of the active population, but only 6% of arable land belonging to Palestinians can be irrigated.
> (Ibid, p. 128-129, my translation)

Faraj writes that the average annual water consumption of an Israelite is 357 cubic meters, that of a West Bank Palestinian is 84.6 cubic meters, and that the settlements irrigate 60% of their arable land, compared to 45% in Israel and only 6% in the Arab-owned West Bank.

To paraphrase Marie Antoinette's famous remark, "They have no water? Then let them drink beer."

A Masterpiece of Propaganda

Propagandists, apologists and lobbyists have performed an outstanding feat of linguistic and logical inversion in convincing most people that the Pearl-Harbor-like raids that destroyed Egypt's, Jordan's and half of Syria's air forces while parked on the ground were a purely defensive moves on the part of poor, outnumbered and outgunned Israel, facing the near certainty of deadly attacks by its powerful enemies. Egypt's moving of a few divisions of soldiers into the Sinai Peninsula – Egypt's territory, of course – was portrayed as an act of war against Israel. As we have seen above, in the 1980s both Abba Eban and Begin admitted that they had had no fear of these forces and had expected no attack from them. As for the claim that poor Israel was in deadly peril from these Arab hordes, the fact that they dispatched the combined Egyptian, Syrian and Jordanian armies in just five days exposes and destroys this Zionist misrepresentation.

But the propaganda worked, especially in America and especially among American Jews. Prior to 1967, the US had been a staunch supporter and supplier of Israel but had remained concerned about the ambitions and excesses of Zionism. In 1950, for example, the US had agreed with France and England on the need to balance the armaments of Israel and its Arab neighbors (a well-meaning but impotent understanding). Also, it was aware of the friendly relation between the USSR and the Arab states, especially Egypt, and had no desire to get into a serious conflict over Israel. During the Suez crisis, the US had pressured Israel's allies, France and England, to accept a UN demand for a cease-fire. As a result of the Six-Day War, the power of the Israel lobby increased by a quantum leap and "the tail started wagging the dog": the support of America became unquestioned – Israel could do no wrong.

One would think that since Israel proved much stronger than expected, US aid would be somewhat scaled down. In fact, aid was increased, probably because the country was now perceived as a powerful ally in the control of the oil-rich Middle East and in the struggle with communism.

[Note that even before the war, US aid was already massive and indispensable. The IDF killed Arabs with mostly American weapons and the IAF obliterated the enemy air forces with 192 American jet fighters.]

But the most dramatic and important change was in the American Jewish community. The Zionist propaganda machine, has always considered fellow Jews as the most important target. Previously, American Jews had generously supported Israel, but considered it as a separate entity and as a foreign, though favored, country. After the war they saw themselves as an integral part of world Jewry, the historical nation of victims, of which Israel was the spiritual capital.

Another consequence of this propaganda blitzkrieg was a sharp change in the political ethos of American Jews. Previously the majority of them had been liberal, slightly left-of-center supporters of the Democratic Party and of such causes as civil rights. After the Six-Day War they veered to the right, many of them becoming, eventually, the prime movers of the core of the neoconservative movement. The American left has not yet recovered from this defection.

The Yom Kipper War of 1973

The period between 1967 and 1972 was characterized by such an unremitting series of tit-for-tat raids that it was baptized *the War of Attrition*. At any time, either side could easily find a pretext for initiating an invasion. In the Yom Kipper war, for the first and only time the first punch was thrown by the Arab side, mostly Egypt and Syria. Both countries wanted to regain lost territory and lost pride. The move took a lot of courage. There was a new dimension to the conflict: both Sadat and Assad knew that Israel had "the bomb" and would not hesitate to launch a nuclear strike if they felt mortally threatened. On the other hand, Egypt had acquired large quantities of fairly sophisticated weapons, thanks to Russian generosity.

D-day was October 6, 1973 (hence another name for the event, the October War). Initially the Arabs enjoyed surprising success. Gradually Israel gained the upper hand, but by the time the Security Council Resolutions 339 and 340, dated October 23 and 25, ended the conflict, the Arabs had saved their honor by fighting valiantly, winning some battles and limiting Israeli gains. Their armies had not been routed. In Israel, normally the winning side, the war was seen as a defeat: accusations were directed against politicians and generals, and the political landscape was altered. Compared to other Arab-Israeli conflicts it was a relatively clean war: no ethnic cleansing, no outrages against civilians, no killing of prisoners. Israel lost some 2,300 dead, 5,500 wounded and 294 taken prisoners. Egypt lost 12,000; 35,000 and 8,400 in the above categories, and Syria 3,000; 5,600 and 411.

The war may have ended in October, 1973, but it took six years for the parties to arrive at a peace treaty. First, there was the Geneva Conference of 1973 where an attempt was made to negotiate an Israeli-Palestinian agreement based on UN Security Council Resolution 338, but where nothing was achieved except an understanding that the Sinai Peninsula would revert back to Egypt. In 1978, President Carter arranged a meeting between Begin and Sadat in Maryland.

Things got off to a rocky start, but Carter just would not give up. Finally, after 12 days of intense secret talks, two Camp David agreements were reached: *A Framework for Peace in the Middle East* and *A Framework for the Conclusion of a Peace Treaty between Egypt and Israel.* The latter led to the *Israel-Egypt Peace Treaty*, dated March 26, 1979. Israel gave up the Sinai but got a lot back in return. The normalization of relations between the two countries deprived the Arab World of its most populous, powerful and prestigious partner. In return for billions in aid and subsidies – from the US of course – Egypt signed the treaty without insisting on the rights of Palestinians to the lands occupied as a result of the Six-Day War, or on the dismantling of the illegal Zionist settlements. This last default was to prove the most pernicious obstacle to justice for the Arabs. Israel lost the Sinai but gained the fragmentation of the enemy camp and the elimination of the southern front in any future war with its Arab neighbor. (The Arab resentment toward Egypt brought about the assassination of Sadat in 1981.)

Before leaving, Israel spitefully bulldozed all the settlements it had established. The Egyptians offered $50 million for the town of Yamet and $56 million for a luxury hotel, but Israel preferred to let the bulldozers do their work.

The Lebanon War of 1982

The Palestine Liberation Organization (PLO) was born in 1959, in Kuwait. For five years it concentrated on fundraising and organizing under its leader, Yassar Arafat. Together with its military arm, al Fattah, it played an important role in the War of Attrition. The Six-Day War of 1967 brought more than a million Palestinian refugees under Israeli rule, and the PLO became their more-or-less official mouthpiece and management. Fattah and the PLO spread out into Israel's Arab neighbors and often became a state-within-a-state. This was particularly true in Lebanon where the PLO became the *de facto* government in the southern (Muslim) part of the country. Many Fattah fighters had taken refuge there during and after the Six-Day War, and Arafat eventually established his headquarters in Beirut.

Fattah mounted many raids against the northern part of Israel (Galilee) which, of course, were answered. Israel was chaffing at the bit in its desire to launch a full-fledged military campaign. On June 3, 1982, the Israeli ambassador in London, Slomo Argov, was wounded in an assassination attempt by a Palestinian splinter group opposed by the PLO (which, in fact, had condemned the group's leader, Abu Nidal, to death). Prime Minister Begin and his cabinet authorized air and artillery attacks on Beirut and on a number of PLO bases in Southern Lebanon. Israel committed "six to seven divisional task forces and an independent reinforced armored brigade, with more than fifteen hundred tanks, as well as the whole of the airforce and navy." (Morris, p. 517) Against this force the PLO had a semiprofessional army backed by 80 or so artillery pieces, about 100 obsolescent tanks and some antiaircraft guns and rockets without radar. Israel had stated that its ground forces would limit themselves to a 40-mile security zone north of its border, but this was quickly forgotten. The PLO was entirely alone in the fighting until the Israelis reached Beirut, at which point they confronted a Syrian infantry brigade.

On June 11 a cease-fire was declared, forced on Israel by he Americans who were worried that further fighting could force them into a confrontation with the Soviets. Nonetheless, many Israeli elements continued their advance. A few days later the IDF linked with the Phalange (Lebanese

Christian militia). A new-cease fire was agreed to with the Syrians, but fighting continued against PLO and Syrian troops in Beirut. The city was cruelly besieged for nine days: daily aerial and artillery attacks, sporadic ground assaults, cut-off of food, water and electricity. Civilians were the chief victims. The Christian director of intelligence for Lebanon's military complained to the Israelis that he couldn't carry on a massacre of Palestinian refugees because 70% of his soldiers were Muslims. (It seems that the idea of a massacre, when politically possible did not offend him, nor his Israeli overseers.)

Arafat realized that the PLO's situation was untenable and, on August 13, he agreed to leave Lebanon. For eleven days a multinational force of 23,000 Armenian, French, Italian and Lebanese soldiers guarded the evacuation. The PLO dispersed to Syria, Algeria, Yemen, Iraq, Jordan and Sudan, and moved its headquarters to Tunisia.

But some militiamen were still left in Muslim West Beirut. It was decided that the Phalange and the Lebanese army would take care of the clean-up, with some help from the ADF. Some 300,000 Palestinians still lived in Lebanon, many of them in refugee camps. Begin wanted them moved out of Southern Lebanon, especially out of the 40-mile security zone. Bashir Gemayel, a Christian who had already been picked to be the next president of Lebanon, was more aggressive: he wanted Palestinians exiled to Syria.

But on September 14, 1982, a Syrian agent exploded a bomb in a building housing the local headquarters of the Phalange while Bashir Gemayel was delivering a speech. The "next president" was killed. This incident threatened to destabilize the whole situation. Sharon decided that it was urgent to take care of West Beirut and the refugee camps. The plan was for the IDF to enter West Beirut and for the Phalange to take control and clear up the Palestinian refugee camps of Sabra and Shatilla. Benny Morris was quite clear on page 542: "Sharon knew what to expect. Christian Lebanese forces had already committed two outrages and, angered by the assassination of Bashir Gemayel, could be expected to exact massive revenge."

On September 15, the IDF entered Beirut unopposed, since both Syrians and the PLO had left weeks before. Next day the Phalange assaulted the two refugee camps. At the Phalange's request, "an IDF battery of 81 mortars began to send illumination rounds into the sky, to light the Phalangists' way. (Later IAF aircraft were to drop larger illumination flares.)" (Morris, p. 543) The Christian soldiers met with very little resistance. In short order they were able to settle down to a house-to-house search and murder operation that lasted thirty hours. According to Morris, news of the killing reached a number of Israeli headquarters that same night. Most of those reports came from Israeli soldiers stationed in observation posts. Nothing was done.

No one knows just how many victims were murdered in the massacre:

> The Lebanese army's chief prosecutor, Assad Germanos, who probed the affair on order from President Gemayel [Amin, brother of Bashir] found that a total of 460 persons had been killed, 15 of them women and 20 children. Most, 328, were Palestinian males; 109 Lebanese were among the dead, as were a handful of Iranians, Syrians, Algerians and Palestinians who had lived in Sabra and Shatilla. Israel intelligence reached a higher estimate: 700-800 dead.
> (Kahan Commission Report, p. 50, via Morris, p. 547)

As for the figures about the whole Lebanese campaign, estimates of death and injuries vary widely according to the source. According to Morris, "a Lebanese report from late 1982 speaks of 19,085 killed and 30,000 wounded, but this seems a vast exaggeration." (p. 558) Morris also gives other estimates without specifying the source: approximately 650 dead and 300 wounded for Israel; from 500 to 1,000 dead for Syria; and more than 1,000 dead for the PLO.

The Palestine Libration Organization survived and remained a potent factor in the Middle East, but it did have to leave Lebanon. The IDF withdrew from Beirut, at the request of the US, and took position in Southern Lebanon.

The First Intifada

One can expect such events after 20 years of harsh occupation. People have lost all hopes. They are completely frustrated. They don't know what to do. They have adopted a line of religious fundamentalism, which for them is the last resort. They have lost hope that Israel will ever give them rights. They feel that the PLO, which they regard as their representative, failed to achieve anything … What has happened is an expression of the frustration and pain over the continuing Israeli occupation.

These poignant comments by Rashad a-Shawa, ex-mayor of Gaza (reported by Morris, p. 562) convey the collective mood of Palestinian youths. The first Intifada was a manifestation of this desperation. On another occasion a-Shawa uttered this bleak phrase: "they have nothing to lose," which helps explain the many suicidal bomb attacks that started a few years later.

[Note: The dynamics that would explain the apparent ease with which al Qaeda and other non-Palestinian extremist Muslim groups find suicide bombers escapes me. Is the explanation an exaggerated emphasis on faith-for-the-sake-of-faith? Is it the seventy virgins in paradise? Is it the desire for fame and acceptance? Probably there exists a sophisticated scouting effort for identifying prospects at an early age, and an effective incubating system to bring them to readiness and early death. In the case of Palestinians, the answer is obvious: people have nothing to lose; they live in overcrowded and half-demolished buildings; they live in shit; they have few rights and get no respect; they have no prospect of any improvement in the foreseeable future.]

No one is sure what local incident (or incidents) was the flash point for the spontaneous uprising. (Some Israeli and some Palestinians have claimed that Arafat and the PLO instigated the whole thing, but there seems to be no evidence of this, although the PLO may well have used the uprising for its own end.) The beginning was probably an incident in the town of Jabulaya on December 6, 1987, when tires were burned and Israeli soldiers attacked. The rebellious movement spread to other refugee camps in both the West Bank and Gaza, including the Arab sector of Jerusalem. The main weapons of the rioters were stones, although there were periods when Molotov cocktails and even a few grenades were used. The uprising lasted for about six years, ending in September 1973, when the Oslo accord between Israel and the PLO was signed.

> According to Be'tselem [Israeli civil rights organization]: Israel's security forces killed 1,095 Palestinians during the period December 1987 – December 1993. Another 48 were killed by Israeli civilians – mostly settlers – between December 1987 and December 1991. Of those killed by security forces during the period December 1987 – 1992, 51 were twelve years old and younger, and 146 were thirteen to sixteen.
> [...]

> The number of Arabs injured by truncheons and bullets runs into the tens of thousands. One estimate is that between fifteen and twenty thousand were wounded in the first two years alone ... The number of IDF, police and GSS personnel killed from the start of the Intifada until the end of 1991 was twenty-two, with eighteen more in 1992 and twenty-five in 1993.
> (Morris, p. 596)

Morris notes that Palestinian figures are higher and IDF figures much lower. The later, however, are limited to victims of direct fire by the IDF, excluding victims of clubbing and, probably, deaths in hospitals.

Simple addition of the above figures gives the following results: 1,143 Arabs killed compared to 144 Israelis, a ratio of approximately 8 Arabs for each Israeli casualty. Wikipedia, the on-line encyclopedia, gives figures that are in the same ball park. Most statistics make no distinction between civilians and military casualties. This is understandable: there is a big difference between civilians throwing stones and civilians asleep in their beds. Still, I suspect that the ratio between Israeli soldiers killed by stones, and Palestinian stone throwers (mostly children and teenagers) killed by bullets must be obscene.

The Intifada proved costly to both sides. It shook institutions and organizations down to their roots, which resulted in many changes. It strengthened the cohesion and solidarity of Palestinians and further exposed some unseemly aspects of the Israeli state. If there is no evidence that the PLO planned it or started it, there is no doubt that Arafat's organization was the main beneficiary of the insurrection. In return for peace and recognition of its right to exist, Israel recognized the PLO as the official representative of the Palestinians and agreed to evacuate much of the West Bank and Gaza. Shortly, the US recognized the PLO and started engaging in dialogue with it. On the other hand, the Intifada also incubated two rivals to the PLO: Hamas and Islamic Jihad.

The Intifada gradually lost energy and virulence after 1991. Its last gasp coincided, more or less, with the signing of the Oslo Accord in September 1993. It had not really been defeated: rather, it dissolved because, having accomplished much, its usefulness was now questionable.

Ethical and Political Considerations

Nothing much changed. Same old recourse to Joshuan collective punishment:

> The IDF also resorted to collective punishment, such as sealing off a village from the outside world for weeks and cutting off its electricity. A major measure … was the demolition or sealing up of houses, which also rendered the imprisoned offender's family homeless.
> (Morris, p. 592)

Also,

> Retired General Schlomo Gazit, a former military intelligence chief, explains that "it's not enough do demolish the home of a terrorist [in practice, a person targeted for punishment on the flimsiest grounds]; this fails to act as a deterrent. We should demolish everything within a 300-400 meter radius of his house."
> (Chomsky, p. 482)

[Note that Israel does not permit the reconstruction of houses demolished as punishment.]

Same old recourse to ethnic cleansing:

> For years, West Bank residents have been subjected to rampaging settlers and violence by the Israeli Border Police and military, as extensively reported in the Hebrew press, rarely here. The purpose, Dov Yermiya wrote after a tour of the Deheisha refugee camp, is "to move the inhabitants away and clear the place for settlement plans."
> (Chomsky, p. 484, quoting from *Davar*, January 15, 1985.

Same old racist habits:

> A few days later Knesset Member Ran Cohen reported that the treatments of Arab workers by Border Guards in a Tel Aviv Hotel: "The Arab workers were cruelly beaten up, compelled to masturbate before the Border Guards,

> to lick the floor of their flat and to eat coffee mixed with sugar and toothpaste, and their money was stolen." They brought complaints to the authorities but after more than two months, there had been no investigation.
> (Chomsky, p. 489, referring to *Yediot Ahronot*, July 3; and *Hadashot*, July 7, 1987)

Also:

> The lesson taught to the Arabs is "that you should not raise your head," Israeli author Shulameth Hareven reports from Gaza, where the hallmark of the occupation for 20 years has been "degradation and constant harassment ... for its own sake, evil for its own sake."
> Chomsky, p. 487, referring to Shlamit Hareven, *Yediot Ahronot*, March 19, 1998.

It seems that the objects of racist attitudes are not limited to Arabs:

> ... they are dealing with "primitive people. Indians whom it is our duty to educate and discipline," teaching them that "they are children and we are parents who educate them," with the rod if necessary ... "if we had beaten them properly at the beginning, they would be properly tamed," so that it is necessary now to beat and humiliate them ...
> (Chomsky, p. 482, quoting from *Ha'aretz*, March 11, 1985)

Obviously these words belittle not only Arabs but also Indians. There are often references in both Morris and Chomsky to "red Indians" and to "Negroes, a backward race." (Later, we will touch on the cooperation and the arms trading of Israel with the apartheid government of South Africa.)

The Intifada, however, did bring something new to the Middle East: incarceration on an industrial scale.

> Before the uprising, military courts annually tried some 1,200 West Bank and Gaza Arabs for rioting. In its first three years, approximately 30,000 were tried on Intifada-related charges ... In addition, by December 1990

> about 14,000 West Bank and Gaza Arabs had been in administrative detention – in prison without trial – usually for periods of six months and more. [Quite reasonable, by Guantanamo standards.]
> (Morris, p. 592)

On page 597 Morris adds that "more than fifty thousand Palestinians served time during the Intifada."

There are many reports of horrible conditions in Israeli jails and IDF detention centers, including the use of forceful interrogation and various degrees of torture. These institutions crafted the template for Guantanamo Bay, Abu Ghraib and various secret prisons of the CIA.

Diplomacy in the Absence of Goodwill

The Geneva Conference of 1977; the Camp David Accords of 1978; the Egypt-Israel Peace Treaty of 1979; the Madrid Conference of 1991; the Road Map to Peace; the Oslo Accords of 1993; the Wye River Memorandum of 1999; the Camp David 2000 Summit; Crown Prince Abdullah's initiative of 2002 . . . . So many meetings, accords, conferences, initiatives going back to the 1919 Paris Peace Conference! The Middle East should be the most peaceful place on Earth, yet conflicts of all sorts persist: raids, rockets, killer robot planes, kidnappings, broken agreements, disregard of UN resolutions on an industrial scale, etc.

Except for the granting of very limited autonomy to the Palestinians and the recognition of the PLO as their official representative, as agreed to in the Camp David Accords, little was accomplished by all those initiatives. And even the Camp David Accord did little to improve the lot of the Arabs. Israel kept almost all the power, and merely transferred the burden of day-to-day administration to the Palestinians.

Almost all these initiatives were exercises in bad faith, mostly – but not wholly – on the part of Israel: hard-core Zionists have no intention of ever relinquishing its illegally occupied territories (with the exception of Gaza, which had become more a liability than an asset, and whose status has since changed from *illegally occupied territory* to *illegal mega prison).* Israel has purposely doted its occupied territories with illegal settlements populated by ultra conservative orthodox Jews, hard-core Zionists who do not hesitate to apply the methods and ethics of Joshua and an extreme interpretation of the principle of moral dispensation. These colonies were intended to be manifest symbols and physical claims (facts on the ground) of Israeli dominance and also stumbling blocks against any attempt to give the territories any kind of sovereignty. The fact that the settlers have done everything they could to humiliate and antagonize the Arabs falls in line with the Israeli program, which is to create a situation which makes coexistence between Palestinians and Jewish Israelis impossible without the compelling presence of Israeli power. This is why the many meetings, conferences and accords either make no mention of the settlements or defer the topic to a later meeting (which may or may not take place). This will become evident as we examine the Oslo Accords and the negotiations that led to them.

Oslo I

The full name of Oslo I was the "Declaration of Principles on Interim Self-Government Arrangements." It was signed by Arafat and Rabin during a Washington ceremony hosted by President Bill Clinton on September 13, 1993. Essentially it was just a Declaration of Principles setting the table for a further agreement, two years hence, laying down the rules of an interim arrangement. In the meantime the Israeli army was to redeploy out of the major population centers of the Arabs and establish bases elsewhere in the West Bank and Gaza. The IDF was to retain "responsibility for overall security of Israelis" and have complete access, along with Jewish settlers, to all roads and highways. The really important and difficult issues were to be deferred to later agreements (Oslo II in 1995, and the final treaty slated for no later than 1999).

Strangely, considering how complicated, serpentine, lengthy and arduous the bargaining had been, it was stipulated that the interim agreements would have no bearing on the final permanent status negotiations!

> Article V
> 4. The two parties agree that the outcome of the permanent status negotiations should not be prejudiced or preempted by agreements reached for the interim period.

While the politicians and diplomats were playing the chess game, the guns were not silent, especially in Lebanon, in and out of the 40-mile security border that had been established in southern Lebanon to protect Israel.

> Through 1991, the Israeli air force carried out 23 raids on Palestinians and Shiite Muslim bases in Lebanon, killing 31 people and wounding 108.
>
> Nineteen ninety-two opened with a January 10 attack by Israeli jets on an illegal guerrilla base near Beirut, killing 12 people (nine civilians) and wounding 14 … (Chomsky, p. 524, using Israeli newspaper sources.)

In 1993, the year Oslo I was signed, the UN Secretary General reported to the Security Council, on July 20m, that the level of hostilities had increased during the last six months, adding that "The practice of [Israeli] firing into populated areas continued, with resulting civilian casualties." (*NY Times* and *Boston Globe*, citing a UN Security Council press release, via Chomsky, p, 525)

[Note: The reader may feel that I am being unfair, reporting Israeli transgressions while neglecting to mention the Arab side of the tit-for-tat slapping. But the latter is reported and highlighted in the Western media (everybody hears about it) while Israeli violations are either unreported or buried somewhere in the back pages. There is more honest reporting of Israeli misdeeds in the Israeli press than in the American and Canadian media.]

The Role of the US

Paraphrasing an article by David Hoffman, "Israel's $10 billion Never mind," published in *WP Weekly* (June '93) Chomsky writes:

> Pursuing the project, Israel proceeds with the programs of expansion and integrating of territories, now helped by US loan guarantees, … demanded with much passion for Russian [Jewish] immigrants who were being forced to Israel by pressure on Germany, the US and others not to allow them a free choice, are now being used for infrastructure and business investment, it is frankly conceded – of course freeing funds for settlement in the territories.
> (Chomsky, p. 526)

Two paragraphs later he writes, "The Clinton Administration is regarded as even more extreme in rejection of Palestinian rights than the Government of Israel itself."

Oslo II

Oslo II got into the particulars much more than did Oslo I. It added much detail but carried no authority past the interim period. However, it did give the Palestinians an idea of which way the wind was blowing.

The West Bank was divided into three zones:

Zone A, covering 3% of the land, consisting of towns populated almost exclusively by Palestinians, to be controlled by the Palestinian Authority (PA).

Zone B, covering 30% of the land, consisting of a collection of scattered sectors, and in which the PA administers Palestinian villages under the final authority of Israel.

Zone C, covering 66% of the land, including all Israeli settlements and under complete control of Israel.

There is a fourth important and contentious zone; Jerusalem (including the Arab eastern part), the ancient holy city, which remains under complete Israeli control. Note that much land was grafted unto the Jerusalem municipal area so that it practically bisected the West Bank.

To understand the implications of the scheme, from the Palestinian point of view, one must realize that it necessitates a transportation system in which some roads would be open, but many would be for the exclusive use of Israelis. As a consequence, Palestinians would perforce live in semi-isolated areas ("Bantustans"), a situation that would seriously hinder personal, economic and political activity, and preclude the establishment of a sovereign state. (See the map in Chapter XIX).

> To summarize, as of September 1995, Israel controls Zone C (about 70% of the West Bank) unilaterally, and Zone B (close to 30%) effectively, while partially ceding Zone A (1-3%). Israel retains unilateral control over the whole West Bank to the extent that it (and its foreign protector) so decide and the legality of its essential claims is now placed beyond discussion. The principles extend to the Gaza Strip where Israel retains full control of the 30% that it considered of any value.
> (Chomsky, p. 541-2)

Another summary is offered by Ehud Barak (then Minister of the Interior) in an interview in *Ha'aretz*, October 12, 1995: Oslo II "insures Israel's absolute superiority in both the military and economic fields."

Things could hardly get worse for the Arabs, but they did: On May 29, 1996, Benjamin Netanyahu became prime minister of Israel. His party, the Likud was far-right and hard-core Zionist.

In 1996 there was an Israeli attack – Operation Grapes of Wrath – on a UN base at Qana, sheltering refugees. Over 100 of them were massacred. President Clinton called it "a tragic mistake during a legitimate defense move" (Chomsky, p. 529), figuring that Hezbollah had virtually attacked Israel by daring to place rockets near a civilian enclave.

To make his intentions even more clear, Netanyahu, according to Morris, declared in his party's Basic Guidelines:

> The government will oppose the establishment of an independent Palestinian state and will oppose the right of return of Arab populations to parts of the land of Israel west of the Jordan." Moreover the new government would "act to consolidate and develop the settlement enterprise." And "united Jerusalem, the capital of Israel ... will forever remain under [sole] Israeli sovereignty."
> (Morris, p. 641)

To Palestinian nostrils, the odors of fecal matter must have been overwhelming. Decades of meetings, declarations, initiatives, accords, conferences, understandings, sponsored by various intervening parties from different parts of the world – and this is what the Palestinians ended up with: substantial – but not complete – control over 3% of the land that by international law and common-sense justice should be theirs, and *that* only guaranteed for an interim period.

The *Israeli-Palestinian Interim Agreement* (Oslo II) was signed by Rabin, Perez and Arafat in Washington on September 28, 1995. Notwithstanding, terrorist attacks by Palestinians continued, as did the construction of illegal settlements by Israelis.

Morris masterfully summarizes the situation:

> Arafat's unwillingness or inability to control the terrorism, in part emanating from his self-rule enclave, clearly contravened the letter and spirit of the agreements. But

> Israel too violated a number of important provisions and certainly acted in a manner contrary to the spirit of the accord. It continued to expand settlements and increased construction in and around East Jerusalem in an effort to establish facts on the ground in advance of the permanent status negotiations, in which Jerusalem was expected to figure large. Israel also failed to activate "safe" corridors between the Strip and West Bank and failed to free all the prisoners it had agreed to release. Moreover, it repeatedly halted, in response to terrorist attacks, the talks on the further withdrawals from the West Bank cities to which it was committed.
> (Morris, p. 627)

In December, 1999, using the continuing expansion of Israeli settlements in the West Bank as justification, Arafat and the Palestinians suspended negotiations.

Ethical and Political Considerations

The Oslo process can be viewed as the archetype of all Israeli-US-Palestine interactions and negotiations. The complete sincerity of Arafat and his cohorts is questionable, but what becomes obvious upon close examination is the complete lack of good will and transparency on the part of the Israelis. As for the Americans, they were either compliant or willfully blind. No one in the small cabal of Israeli political and military leaders (the former usually culled from the ranks of the latter) has ever considered giving Palestinians true sovereignty, or relinquishing the West Bank settlements or stopping the expansion – in size or number – of these. Many of these leaders have said so unambiguously when addressing their own countrymen and maybe it's time to believe them. Their intentions are made obvious by their actions: building more and bigger settlements.

The settlements are the political land mines, scattered all along the "roadway to peace." They were not created to make room for Jews who had nowhere else to go, nor to populate buffer zones to protect the mother country; they were established to gradually infiltrate occupied Palestinian land and establish many points of Israeli presence – facts on the ground that would be very difficult to root out should the territories attain the final status of *sovereign country.* As already explained, the fact that the settlers were ultra orthodox and ultra Zionist, as well as racist, brutal and contemptuous, meshed in well with the plan of gradual colonization. The Arabs, once sovereign, could understandably turn the table on the settlers, which could lead to another pogrom: What better reason for Israel to deny the Palestinians full autonomy and the status of independent country!

What's the most probable outcome? Is it mutual destruction? – Not likely in the short or medium term: the Israelis have too much of an advantage in armaments and in technological infrastructure. Also, although the Palestinians have friends, none of the latter has both the means and the readiness to sacrifice and pay through the nose – and this includes Muslim friends.

Is it the continuation of the Palestinians' agony and their eventual disappearance as a nation? – Yes, unless the underwriter intervenes.

And the underwriter, of course, is the United States of America that keeps giving astronomical sums in aid, military aid, loans, loan guarantees, plus additional untraceable funds. And this assistance comes with the reliably of rainy season monsoons because, psychologically and politically, tiny Israel dominates the world's only superpower. The proof: Every time the US protests publicly against the establishment of an illegal settlement, Israel completely disregards the remonstrance and not one penny is deducted from its dole. It's like a parent who decries his child's drug consumption but gives him/her all the money needed to buy the drugs.

The settlements have to go! And the only way they'll go is if Uncle Sam turns the screws. Despite the perception that the tail wags the dog, in the last analysis the dog's wallet can exercise ultimate authority: it's up to the dog.

Post Oslo

Back to square one: tit-for-tat raids, incursions, rocket launchings, robot-terrorist attacks, border violations by planes and ships, etc. Either side could, at any time, point to a particular incident and use it as justification to attack the other side.

On June 24, 2006, the IDF kidnapped two Gaza civilians. Next day, June 25, Israeli Corporal Gilad Shalit was captured by Gaza terrorists at an IDF post near Gaza. There followed a severe escalation of Israeli artillery and airplane attacks against the Gaza population, taking many lives.

On July 12, Lebanese Hezbollah fighters kidnapped two Israeli soldiers and offered to exchange them for prisoners held in Israeli jails (many of them not charged with any crime). All hell broke loose! Swarms of Israeli planes armed with cluster bombs attacked not only the Hezbollah stronghold in southern Lebanon, but the entire civil infrastructure of the country. Hezbollah, of course, retaliated with rockets.

According to the web site of the *Arab Media Watch*, (an English, not an Arab organization), 1,301 Lebanese were killed, almost all of them civilians and 1/3 of them children. Only 63 of these casualties were Hezbollah fighters. The Israelis lost 160 dead of which 72% (117) were soldiers and 28% civilians, half of them Israeli Arabs. The ratio of Lebanese to Israeli civilian deaths was 30 to 1. A quarter of Lebanon's bridges and roads were destroyed or damaged. Approximately 1,000,000 were internally displaced or took refuge in Syria. Many of them had no house to return to since 130,000 were destroyed or damaged. 350,000 to 500,000 Israeli civilians were displaced to homes or shelters in the south, but most of them were later able to return to their homes. (These figures agree roughly with reports from Amnesty International and Human Rights Watch.)

On August 15, 2006, a cease-fire was declared, enforced by a UN force, and the IDF withdrew from Lebanon. As reported by the Israeli newspaper *Ha'aretz* on its web site (www. haaretz.com), a squadron of IAF warplanes flew over French peacekeepers in a dive-bomb formation on October 31, almost eliciting anti-aircraft fire. It seems that it was not a unique incident: French officials have regularly complained that Israel's overfights of Lebanon are "counter to UN Security Council resolution 1701, which included the cease-fire that brought an end to 34 days of fighting."

Note that air and sea incursions are border violations on par with troop incursions. The military superiority of Israel forces is particularly striking in aerial armaments. Israel can fly over the territory of its neighbors with impunity. For example, the UN reported that from August 1981 to May 1982, there were 2,125 violations of Lebanese airspace by the IDF.

Ethical and Political Considerations

The UN has practically made war illegal but, since it has affirmed the right of any country to defend itself, the moral onus is on the party that starts the war. As written above, the principle is hard to apply in the case of the Near East antagonists as both sides are regularly trading punches; border violations, extrajudicial assassinations, rocket attacks, etc. Israel – with the backing of its axis partner, the Untied States – claims that the kidnapping of an Israeli sergeant in Israel and the concomitant killing of Israeli soldiers by Lebanese Hezbollah fighters constituted an act of aggression justifying an all-out attack and collective punishment. But the kidnapping was no more egregious than many other violations by Israel, Palestinians and others. The Israeli response represented a quantum leap in violence, out of all proportion to recent activity by any side, resulting in hundreds of deaths, thousands of serious injuries, massive destruction of infrastructure and habitations, and a major oil spill in the Mediterranean. The case can be made that Israel was just waiting for an excuse for an attack and was therefore the real aggressor.

A similar argument can be advanced regarding the conflict between Israeli forces and the Gaza Palestinians, a contemporaneous clash, and one that has been overshadowed by the Lebanese war and neglected in the media. The ratio of Palestinian to Israeli casualties is even more lopsided in Gaza than in Lebanon. On November 21, 1996, CBC Newsworld reported that more than 300 Gaza civilians were killed in the previous 12 months, compared to one Israeli woman killed by a rocket fired from the Gaza Strip! The missiles used by the Arabs are very inaccurate. They can be compared to shotgun pellets fired at the sound of flying geese by a blind hunter. The main purpose of these firings is not so much to kill people as to make manifest the refusal of Palestinians to accept the violation of their collective rights. (Rights that are not defended are soon lost.)

The gross disproportion in casualties suggests an intriguing and disturbing question: Why is it that the side with the high-tech sophisticated weapons such as laser-guided "smart" bombs is the side that inflicts a high ratio of civilian to military casualties, while the side with comparatively primitive and inaccurate arms achieves a much lower ratio? Israel is constantly having to apologize for "regrettable mistakes" that cause death, injury and loss to non-combatants (including children) and to third-party military and humanitarian personnel. During the 2006 Lebanese war, clearly marked ambulances, convoys of humanitarian supplies, fleeing refugees and even a UN observer post have been hit, with tragic results. Anyone can make a mistake, but too many mistakes beg the question.

Israel and its American ventriloquist doll have often accused Arab fighters of using human shields because they fire their weapons from urban setting. Amnesty International and Human Rights Watch have found no evidence for this charge. Hezbollah insurgents are local Lebanese citizens; when they fire a rocket from a backyard, it's probably their own backyard. As for Gaza combatants, they live in, and fight from, the most densely populated territory on earth: there are no open civilian-free areas and if there were, anyone who would set up a rocket launcher there might as well paint a big red bull's eye and invite the IAF.

On April 26, 2007, CNN News showed a Palestinian woman apparently being used as a human shield by Israeli soldiers during a military search. In the same broadcast an eleven-year-old girl, Diane Abush, was shown climbing a stairway a few yards ahead of two soldiers. Subsequently interviewed, she was reported as having been forced and very scared. The difference between Arab and Israeli use of human shields is that the former are fighting in their own backyard and the shields happen to be there and do not seem to be coerced, while the latter are in enemy territory and have to force civilians to act as shields.

The US Role

Every Arab school-age child knows where the tanks that rumble, the planes that fly overhead, and the bombs that kill come form: from America – *made in the USA*. In the fifties American aid was comparable to that received from England and France, but after each Middle East war American aid to Israel increased very substantially: the stronger Israel got, the more aid it received. Of 507 planes used for the invasion of Lebanon 457 came from the US. When the Israelis urgently needed more aviation fuel, they got it. The New York Times of July 22, 1996, reported that "The Bush administration is rushing a delivery of precision-guided bombs to Israel, which requested the expedited shipment last week after beginning its air campaign.

In 1982, a former deputy mayor of Jerusalem, answering American criticism of some of Israel's actions, wrote:

> What's our army if not the product of American aid? Didn't Reagan proclaim Jewish settlements on the West Bank "not illegal"? Didn't Haig sanction the first phase of the Lebanese invasion? Everything that has happened in Israel until now has carried the stamp of American approval, or at least it was tolerated by your governments. If the genie is out of the bottle, it was Washington that helped to turn him loose.
> (Meron Benveniste, *Newsweek*, October 4, 1982, via Chomsky, p. 391.

The US has also used political and diplomatic means of being compliant with Israel. Secretary of State Condoleezza Rice and UN ambassador John Bolton have substantially helped Israel to kill more Hezbollah fighters and innocent civilians by using the American veto in the Security Council, as well as other delaying tactics, to defer the implementation of a cease-fire. Not a way to make friends and influence people in the Middle East!

Chapter XX – Numbers and Map

1. Basic Demographics

Total human population: about 6,083 M (million)
Total worldwide Jewish population: about 14 M
Jewish population before World War II: 17 M
Jewish population after World War II: 11 M
Percentage of Jews, world-wide: 0.23%
Percentage of Jews in US population: 2%
Percentage of Jews in Israeli population: 80%
40% of Jews live in the US
34.4% of Jews live in Israel
(Jewish Virtual Library)

West Bank:

Palestinian population: 2.46 M
Israeli-settler population: 187,000
Settlers represent: 7.6 % of the population
(CIA, The World Fact book)

Gaza Strip:

Palestinian population: 1.3 M
Israeli-settler population: 7,300 (September 2005)
Settlers represented: 0.56 % of the population
(BBC News)

2. The Conquest and Colonization of Palestine

After the First Arab-Palestinian War of 1948:

700,000 Arab refugees, half in Jordan (mostly West Bank)
200,000 in Gaza Strip
100,000 in Lebanon
60,000 in Syria
(Morris, p. 260-1)

During three post-war years Israeli population grew from 650,000 to 1,350,000 (with financial help from American Jews) while the Arab minority numbered 150,000
(Morris, p. 259-260)

"By May [1947] about 300,000 Arabs had fled, about 1/3 of them from territories assigned to the Palestinian State."
(Chomsky, p. 96)

According to the United Nation Relief and Works Agency (UNRWA), by 1950, some 997,000 Palestinian refugees had been displaced, 1/3 of them to the Gaza Strip, 1/3 to the West Bank, and the remainder to Jordan, Syria, Lebanon and other countries. Approximately 1/3 of them lived in refugee camps. Since Israel prevented their return, the situation only got worse: by 2004, out of a total population 8 million, 4,186,711 Palestinians were UNRWA-registered refugees, of which more than 1/4 of them were in camps. (Palestinian Research Net web site)

3. The Suez War of 1955-56

"Several thousand Egyptian soldiers were killed, 4,000 taken prisoners." Israelis suffered 190 killed, 800 injured and 20 captured.
(Morris, p. 296)

4. The Six-Day War of 1967

In the Sinai campaign:
Israel loses: 338 dead and 1,400 wounded
Egyptian losses: 10,000 to 15,000 dead and some 5,000 taken prisoner
In the Jordan sector:
Israel losses: about 300 dead
Jordanian loses: about 800 dead and 636 prisoners
Syrian loses: about 500 dead, 2,500 wounded, and 578 prisoners
(Morris, p. 327)
Ratio of Muslim to Israeli deaths: between 19 to 1 and 25 to 1.
Refugees:
200 to 250,000 Palestinians, about 1/4 of the Wet Bank population, were displaced to the East Bank (now Jordan), mostly due to heavy fighting in the Jericho area. Many of them were already refugees from previous conflicts. Up to 70,000 people fled from the Gaza Strip to Egypt and other countries.
(Morris, p. 328)

5. The Yom Kippur War of 1973 (aka the October War)

Israel lost some 2,300 dead; 5,500 wounded and 294 taken prisoner.
Egypt lost 12,000; 35,000 and 8,000 in the above categories.
Syria lost 3,000; 5,600 and 411.
(Morris, p. 431)
Ratio of Moslem to Israeli deaths: 6.5 to 1

6. The First Lebanon War of 1982

Body counts and estimates are all over the map, depending on the sources. Morris (whom I usually trust, but not this time) gives the following figures without specifying the source(s).

Israeli losses: 650 dead and 3,000 wounded

PLO losses: 500 to 1,000 dead
Syrian loses: 500 to 1,000 dead.

A Lebanese police report from late 1982 (characterized as "a vast exaggeration" by Morris) gives 19,085 Lebanese killed and 30,000 wounded. Other sources, from the internet, are in the same ballpark as the Lebanese police report. Some give higher figures. For example, William Eckardt, a known researcher in mass killings, as quoted by Wikipedia's *Twentieth Century Atlas*, estimates 40,000 civilian and 12,000 military deaths.

Other estimates include the Lebanese Civil War (1975-76), as well as numerous air raids by the IDF prior to the 1982 War:

The *LA Times*: 150,000 deaths (1975-2000)
The *Montréal Gazette*: 150,000 (1975-1985)

Finally, Israeli Minister of the Interior, Josef Burg, claimed that 10 Jews were killed by terrorists in 1980 and 8 in 1981 but that in 1982 Israel retaliated by killing a thousand terrorists and causing "the loss of life of thousands of the inhabitants of an enemy country." (Chomsky, p. 74).

It is impossible to come to a reliable ratio of Moslem to Israel's deaths from such divergent estimates, but it is obvious that it must be outrageously skewed in favor of Israelis.

7. The First Intifada (1987-93)

From 1987 to 1993, 1,143 Palestinians were killed by security forces or Israeli settlers.

51 were 12 years old or younger

146 were from 13 to 16

(reported by B'tselem, Israeli civil right organization, via Chomsky)

Tens of thousands of Palestinians were injured by truncheons and bullets (Morris, p. 596)

48 Israeli civilians were killed by Arabs inside Israel and 31 in the West Bank

and Gaza
65 security force personnel were killed
Ratio of Arab to Israeli deaths: 8 to 1
"More than fifty thousand Palestinians served time during the Intifada."
(Morris, p. 597)

8. The Second Intifada (aka the Al Aksa Intifada (2000-2005)

The BBC estimates that during 200-2004, 3,223 Palestinians and 980 Israeli were killed.
("Intifada Toll 200-2005," BBC, 08 February 2005, via Wikipedia.)
Ratio of Palestinian to Israeli deaths: 3 to 1

9. The Second Lebanon War (2006)

The historians have not written definitive books about this recent event, but fairly concordant body counts and estimates have come from such organizations as Amnesty International, Human Rights Watch, the Palestinian Center Transcript, Arab Media Watch (an English, not Arab organization) and more. Widipedia has summarized many of these findings. I can't vouch for the exactness of the following numbers and estimates, but they are all "in the ball park."

1,733 Lebanese deaths:	1,187	civilians
	500	Hezbollah
	46	Lebanese military
3,600 Lebanese wounded:	3,500	civilians
	100	military

1,000,000 Lebanese displaced or refugees

163 Israeli deaths:	44	civilians
	119	military
1,589 Israeli wounded:	1,489	civilians
	100	military

(Wikipedia)

1/3 of the Lebanese casualties were children
7 Jewish children were killed
350,000 to 500,000 Israelis fled south
(The Palestine Center transcript, October 4, 2006)

Ratio of Lebanese to Israeli military deaths:	10 to 1
Ration of Lebanese to Israeli civilian deaths:	27 to 1

10. US Military Aid to Israel

1949 to 1958:	0
1959 to 1973:	95.3 M per year (average)
1974	982.7 M loan + 1,000 M grant
1975 too 1984:	800 M loaned + 582 M grant per year (average)
1985 to 2005:	0 loans + 1,112.4 M grant per year (average)

(Clyde R. Mark, "Israel Foreign Assistance," congressional Research Service, July 12, 2004, via Jewish Central Library)

11. US Economic Aid to Israel

Loans:	1949 to 1980	47.4 M per year (average)
	1981 to 2005	0
Grants:	1949 to 1980	108.5 M per year (average)
	1981 to 2005	1,013 M per year (average)

Special Jewish Refugee grants for settlements in West Bank, Gaza and Golan Heights:

1949 to 1972	0
1978 to 2005	283.6 M per year (average)

Approximate total aid per settler, 1973 to 2000: 74,000
Total US aid to Israel, 1949 to 2995
(including Food for Peace and six other programs): 94,135.6 M
(Ibid)

Notes:

1. 7.9 billion in loan guaranties are not included.
2. "… the actual level of US aid may be as much as 60% higher than the publicly available figures," according to the General Accounting Office, *Philadelphia Enquirer*, August 25, 1982, via Chomsky, p. 10
3. There is no certainty that loans will be paid back.
4. Private donations by American Jews (and others) through Zionist organizations are not included.

12. Israel, the US, South Africa and the UN

From 1955 to 1992:
Number of UN resolutions critical of Israel: 65
Number of positive responses by Israel: 0
Note: Between 1955 and 1992, 698 resolutions were passed by the UN. 65 of them were directed at Israel, representing 9.3% of the total – out of all proportion for a country that represents a mere 0.1% of the world's population.

From 1972 to 2001:
Number of US vetoes of UN Security Council Resolutions critical of Israel: 33
Not vetoed by the US: 0
(US State Department, via www. action-for-un-renewal.org.uk)

Israel's voting record on UN resolutions condemning apartheid in South Africa, 1973-1979

Against:	2
Abstention:	4
Did not vote:	4
Absent:	0
For:	0

(Abdalaida Benalbdal, *L'Alliance Raciste Israëlo-Sud-Africaine*, 1979, Les Editions Canada-Monde-Arabe

13. Hard Water

Percent of West Bank water used by Israel:	90%
Percent of West Bank water used by Palestinians:	10%
Percent of arable land irrigated by settlements:	60%
Percent of arable land irrigated by Israel:	45%
Percent of arable land irrigated by West Bank:	6%
Average water consumption of an Israelite:	357 cubic meters/year
Average water consumption of a Palestinian:	84.6 cubic meters/year

(Rezek Faraj, *Palestine: Le Refus De Disparaître*, Pleine Lune, pp. 128-131).

14. Putting Numbers on Attitudes

Should Israel recognize Palestinians as a nation?
11% of Israeli public agree
35% agree under certain conditions
54% are entirely opposed
Should Israel accept a Palestine state in West Bank and Gaza?
5% of Israelis agree
18% agree under certain conditions
77% are completely opposed
(Survey by Haifa University and State University of New York, via Chomsky, p. 454)

15. God and Statistics

In the USA:
10% of nominal Protestants
21% of nominal Roman Catholics
52% of nominal Jews
Don't believe in God
47% of Protestants
35% of Catholics

15% of Jews
go to church or synagogue at least once a month
(Survey by Harris Interactive of 2,306 adults)

In Israel:
16% to 37% considered themselves atheist, agnostics or non-believers.
(Zuckerman, Phil, "Atheism: Contemporary Rates and Patterns," in *The Cambridge Companion to Atheism*, 2005.

Israel, 4th country (of 10 surveyed) with highest proportion of atheists: 25.6%
(International Social Survey Program study of religion, 1991, via www.adherants.com

Note:

B'Tselem, the Israeli civil rights organization has published in its web site a concise and well-organized compendium of important statistics. It can be found at:
www.btselem.org/english/statistics/index

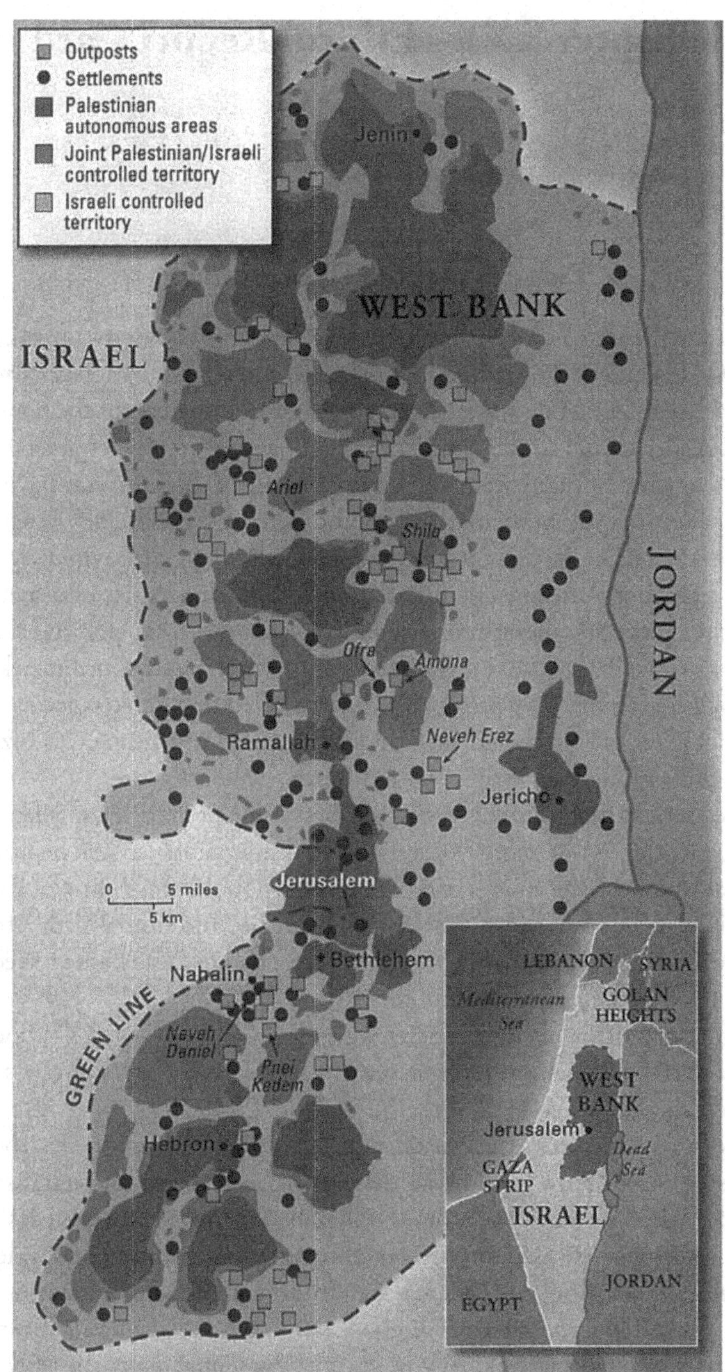
Outposts
Settlements
Palestinian autonomous areas
Joint Palestinian/Israeli controlled territory
Israeli controlled territory
WEST BANK
ISRAEL
JORDAN
Jenin
Ariel
Shilo
Ofra
Amona
Neveh Erez
Ramallah
Jericho
Jerusalem
0 5 miles
5 km
Bethlehem
Nahalin
GREEN LINE
Neveh Daniel
Pnei Kedem
Hebron
LEBANON
SYRIA
Mediterranean Sea
GOLAN HEIGHTS
WEST BANK
Jerusalem
Dead Sea
GAZA STRIP
ISRAEL
JORDAN
EGYPT

Postmodern Apartheid
© 2003 Baker Vail

Chapter XXI – Ethical Report Card

Zionism and the Old Testament

Zionism represents a stark return to the Old Testament – not to the beliefs of the Old Testament (how could non-believers and secular nationalists *really* believe the Bible) – but rather to the ethics, or lack thereof, of the book: to moral dispensation; to the "Joshua method" with its ethnic cleansing and crimes against humanity; to the appropriation of "houses you have not built, vineyards you have not planted, and cisterns you have not hewn."

Now, Israel, in its present state, is a more religious collectivity than was the motley (but somehow organized) group of Jewish socialists, Bolsheviks, agnostics, atheists and ultra-nationalist ideologues that got the whole project started. There are two reasons for this: First, the secular elite held an uneasy belief in piety-by-proxy and also perceived that a token acceptance of religious tradition would bring political dividends; hence this bizarre situation: a group of unbelievers founding a theocratic state.

Second, although Israel was established by Ashkenazi Jews, Sephardic Jews constituted the majority in subsequent immigration, so that Sephardic Jews are now a little more than 50% of the population. Many of them, especially those from other Middle East countries and from North Africa, are Orthodox Jews, and are particularly resentful of Arabs, due to recent experience in their country of origin.

In spite of this, formal adherents to ultra-Orthodox, neo-Orthodox, Conservative and Reform Judaism remain a minority of Jewish Israelis and an even smaller proportion of the ruling elite.

So, where does that leave *chosenness* and the *promised land*? In Hertzberg's words (p. 65), "How could one deny God and affirm chosenness?" – Because when a rationale becomes untenable, its object (the policies and actions it supported) may survive out of ingrained habit and out of a desire to maintain old privileges. We may call this phenomenon a *ghost rationale* (as in *ghost limb).* Underpinning ghost rationales are *ghost values*: values that a society doesn't hold anymore, but that continue to be effectual factors because – again – of the perseverance of habits and the preservation of advantages. Ghost rationales and ghost values are important dynamics in both religion and politics.

There are a number of occurrences where Israelis may consciously have been trying to reenact a scenario from the Old Testament. For example:

> One of the first relatively large-scale strikes was against the village of Sharalat, just south of Jerusalem on the night of February 6, 1951. Two houses, one of the them the village muktar's (headman's), were blown up to avenge a murder and rape at Manahat (al-Melike), south west of Jerusalem. About a dozen Arabs – mostly women and children – were killed.
> (Morris, p. 276)

Compare this to Genesis 34, where Jacob's sons killed all the males of a town and took all their wives and children as captives to avenge the rape of their sister.

There is a plethora of cases of collective punishment, ethic cleansing and killing of innocents in the Tanakh – and in the history of the state of Israel.

Zionism shares another point of similitude with the Old Testament: neither is truly monotheistic. As we have seen, the ancient Hebrews kept vacillating between henotheism (worshipping just one out of many existing gods) and outright polytheism, and didn't become truly monotheistic until shortly before the birth of Jesus. Zionists have rejected monotheism by elevating the collectivity (race, nation, etc.) to the rank of God. Remember from Chapter XVII:

> If is impossible to be a Jew in the religious sense without acknowledging our nationality, it is possible to be a Jew in the national sense without accepting many things in which religion requires belief.
> (Ahad Ha-am, via Hertzberg, p. 262)

This seems to place the collectivity above God. Samuel Landau, considered a Religious Zionist, did not hesitate to write that Jewish values are only significant "to the degree that they serve as instruments of the absolute – the nation." (Hertzberg, p. 434) Hertzberg, an ordained Conservative rabbi, wrote in page 21 of the introduction to *The Zionist Idea*:

> The ghetto and the concentration of Jewish life in the exile on the religious factor was merely an expression of the national will-to-live, which used religion, then as always, as one of its several instruments.

According to Hertzberg, another Zionist precursor, Horace Mayer Kallen, insisted that religion is not revealed but man-made, being "the expression of the highest values of the group." (p. 525)

Even an ordained cleric, Rabbi Samuel Schulman, in a paper presented at the 1935 convention of the CCAR, wrote:

> Not Reform Judaism but Jewish nationalism represented the crucial break in Jewish historical continuity, for in its secularism it enthroned Israel in the place of God. (Michael A. Mayer, *Response to Modernity: A history of the Reform Movement in Judaism*, p. 328, Oxford U. Press, 1988)

Zionism has two Gods, one essential, the Nation, and one optional, Yahweh. Like the ancient Hebrews, it is not monotheistic.

Zionism Is Anti-Talmudic

Not only is Zionism counter to the sprit of the Talmud, it directly contradicts a number of its basic laws.

One such is the principle proclaimed by Mar Samuel, one of the great sages of the Mishna, that "the law of the land is the law." This principle establishes that respect for, and compliance to, secular laws that do not contravene religious laws is a moral obligation for Jews. Reference to the law is found in tractate Baba Kama 113b, repeated in Baba Metzia 108a and Baba Batra 55a of Order Nazikin and also in tractate Gitten of Order Nashim.

Now, "the law of the land," in those days was local or national, as there did not exist any international body such as the United Nations, but in the contemporary world there *are* such laws. Israel, by contemptuously ignoring more than 60 UN resolutions has earned the unofficial title of *World's number one rogue nation* – by a wide margin. This is against the letter and spirit of the Talmud.

In Order Nezikin, Tractate Baba Batra, Chapter 3, the law of Chazakah, as it applies to real estate, is expounded in detail. The law stipulates that uncontested use of real estate, day and night for three years, establishes title. Simply put, if you have lived in a house and maintained it and the grounds attached to it for three years, without the previous owner or anyone else contesting your presence, you now own the property. As I have written in Chapter XIX, the Palestinians who were ejeted from their homes and displaced by the IDF in the 1948 war and the Six-Day War certainly had title to their property. Those crimes against humanity were not only against the Geneva Convention but also against the spirit and the letter of the Talmud.

In Tractate Kesuboth of Order Nashim on p. 11a, Rav Yehuda said that Jews were "bound by an oath not to ascend to Eretz Israel until the Final Redemption." Many rabbis have interpreted this to mean that contemporary Jews should not return to Palestine until the coming of the Messiah.

Rabbi Zeira, referring to some verses in the Song of Songs spoke of three oaths:

- (1) is that the Jewish people should not converge upon Erez Israel in a wall of force [as a sort of invasion]
- (2) and one is that the Holy One, Blessed is He, adjured the Jewish people not to rebel against the nations of the world;
- (3) and one is that the Holy One, Blessed is He, adjured the idolaters not to subjugate the Jewish people more than is sufficient. (Kesuboth, p. 111a, in the Shottenstein Edition)

Rabbi Zeira opines that these oaths permitted the return to Israel by individuals and families but not by large groups and not by force of arms. Thus, the return as condoned by Cyrus was proper.

Certainly the violent actions of Haganah and other Zionist military forces were nothing if not *en masse*, organized and forcible. Very anti-Talmudic! Note that the second oath is a command from God for the Israelites not to act negatively and aggressively toward the nations of the world – another divine command disregarded by Zionists, as evinced by all the UN resolutions they have flaunted.

Israel's Cardin Sin

Making a few small Semitic tribes pay for the grievous and murderous outrages committed against the Jews by the Nazis was indeed an egregious injustice, especially since this people was a very minor player in World War II. But we can't blame it all on the Jews: Britain, France and the US were complicit with the Zionists and share the moral onus. Besides, all parties had just gone through an exceptionally stressful experience, especially the Jews, and could therefore be given a little indulgence regarding their judgment on moral and political issues.

The cardinal sin of Israel was not its part in the First Arab-Israeli War in 1948, but the Six-Day War in 1967 and its aftermath.

Apologists pretend that because Egyptian troops had been posted on Egyptian soil – but near the Israeli border – Egypt had been the aggressor, and that this justified the occupation and *de facto* annexation of the West Bank, the Gaza Strip, and the Golan Heights – Arab land!

But, as we have seen in Chapter XIX, Menachem Begin admitted that Israel had been the attacker. The war started with a Pearl-Harbor-like sneak attack by the IAF that destroyed on the ground most of the Air Forces of Egypt, Jordan and Syria. This was followed by a savage six-day invasion in which prisoners were murdered, towns destroyed, and Arab populations driven off their land. The West Bank, the Gaza Strip, the Golan Heights and the Sinai Peninsula were appropriated despite universal objection (even the US, at first) and UN condemnation. (The Sinai was later restored to Egypt in return for a peace agreement.) Numerous Jewish settlements were established in the occupied Arab lands in order to consolidate the appropriation.

The moral onus for the Six-Day War rests squarely on the shoulders of Israel. It's actions violated the Universal Declaration of Human Rights, the Geneva Conventions, the Hague Conventions and the UN Resolutions 242, 338 and others. That is why any final resolution of the Middle East situation, if it is to have any semblance of justice, must undo to the greatest extent possible, the wrong done to the Palestinians by this war and its aftermath. This is often expressed as a "Return to the green line," that is, to the pre-war boundaries as advocated by Senator Fulbright, President Carter, King Abdullah and others.

Searching for a Rationale

Confronted by crimes against humanity, the human mind craves for a rationale. Certainly, there must be some reason – if not an excuse – for the deeds! Zionists have come up with a number of rationales, but have failed to substantiate any with convincing arguments. Let's analyze them:

1. *God chose the Jews and gave them the Promised Land:*

Rejoinder: It was not God, but *a* god, Yahweh, one of many Mesopotamian and Semitic deities. As a group they have a factuality index of zero. A god that doesn't exist cannot choose: The Hebrews did the choosing. As they became monotheist, they grafted those features of Yahweh that suited them unto God. The morphing was gradual and seamless: keeping the name of *Yahweh* made it almost automatic. The Arabs have as equal grounds for considering themselves descendants of Abraham as do the Jews – and therefore as entitled to the Holy Land. Besides, being in all probability the descendants of Edomites, Perizites, Amonites, Hittites, and other Canaanite tribes whose residency in Palestine both predated and postdated that of the Hebrews, Palestinians have the greater claim to historical ties to that land.

In Chapter II, I proved that the plagues of Egypt were a pure invention. This pulls the rug from under the claims to historicity and factuality of all three monotheistic religions. Regardless of whether the God of the three religions really does exist, since most of the Ashkenazi leaders have been unbelievers, this rationale is not available to them. How can an atheist or agnostic justify moral dispensation?

2. *Appeal to God is not necessary: the Nation is the absolute and is therefore sufficient reason for moral dispensation.*

Rejoinder: This argument rests on the premise that what is immoral for an individual may be moral for a collectivity. There is a strong tendency for people with a weak ethical sense to feel that way, especially if they are unbelievers. Mafia families have their own ethics and are probably as true to them as the rest of us are to ours. Teenagers also answer to a somewhat different set of moral imperatives than do adults. But there are policemen for Mafiosos, and parents, schools (and policemen) for teenagers, acting as agents and protectors of the other strata of society. But what has authority over nations? – Stronger nations (when they feel it's worth their while) and, during the Middle Ages, perhaps the Vatican. Now, of course, we have the United Nation, but unfortunately, Israel has nullified it in all matters involving the Middle East.

No one has ever proven logically or empirically that a nation – any nation – is God: the State Religion is a product of pure faith. Even if we accepted the arbitrary self-deification of Israel, that would not justify the recent history of Israel. Zionist philosophers and apologists would also have to prove that other nations cannot achieve such a status, and that proof has not been forthcoming. If Israel can claim moral dispensation because they are a nation, why not Germany or Russia? They too have ancient gods, heroic sagas, sacred myths, great national art (such as the beautiful operas of Wagner) and books of laws. If Israel can use nationhood to justify crimes against Arabs and Bedouins, why can't Germany use it to justify crimes against Jews?

3. *Jews are the direct descendants of the ancient Hebrews and therefore heirs to the promises and privileges bestowed upon the Hebrews.*

Rejoinder: No demographer or anthropologist considers the Jews a race. Except in Scandinavian countries, Jews have the physical features of the local population. Even in China, the small Jewish population looks Chinese. This is partly due to intermarriage and local conversions, but in the case of Ashkenazi Jews, it's due mostly to the conversion of a whole country, Khazaria, to Judaism, a unique event in history.

During the 8th century, the King of the Khazars (a people situated between the Black Sea and the Caspian Sea), wishing to remain independent of the advancing Muslims in the south and the powerful Christians of Europe, converted to Judaism. The ruling elite of the country followed suit, and gradually, so did most of the population. Some centuries later the Khazars started migrating, first to Hungary, then into Poland, Lithuania, the rest of Eastern Europe and Western Russia, eventually constituting the bulk of the Jewish population of those regions. It is from there that most of the Ashkenazis who formed the first wave of Israeli immigrants came from. There is little Semitic DNA in that population. (Arthur Koestler, *The Thirteenth Tribe*, Random House)

The argument from descendence doesn't survive analysis.

4. *Jews must have their own country, otherwise Judaism will disintegrate and eventually disappear.*

Rejoinder: Do Presbyterians or Baptists have heir own country? – No, yet they have survived without one for centuries. So have most religions. The best example of a religion maintaining unity and solidarity despite being spread out over most of the planet is Judaism itself. If the Talmudic rabbis could gather all the splintered remnants of the twelve tribes without recourse to modern communication and transportation, certainly contemporary rabbis, with the tools of radio, television and air travel, can sustain the integrity of the religion.

This argument is nothing more than an excuse.

5. *The Jews should be given greater license in ethical and political matters as compensation for the Holocaust.*

   Rejoinder: It is a commonplace that most child molesters have themselves been molested as children. But no one holds that this gives them the right to abuse children. *To have been a victim does not justify being an oppressor.* "Never again" is a beautiful slogan: it is most regrettable that Zionists have not seen it as a rallying cry for all oppressed humanity, including the Palestinians.

The Holocaust facilitated the activity of the Zionists in yet another way: by magnifying many fold the emotional charge of the word *anti-Semite.* Before the Holocaust it was a serious accusation, considering the duration and obstinacy of prejudice against Jews, but after the slaughter of 6 million Jews, it became priceless as a one-word demonization – a magical word which, unlike *abracadabra*, performs real magic. Zionists were quick to add the word to their arsenal by claiming that *anti-Zionist* meant the same as *anti-Semite*, thus putting anyone who disagreed with them in the same class as anyone who condoned the savage murder of millions – another instance of category mistake and fuzzy logic. This argument is not only weak: it is offensive.

The Hijacking of Judaism

Zionism is more than a return to the Old Treatment: it's a new religion, the third Jewish religion. As mentioned above, Zionism has invented a new God: *Israel* – although Zionists are free to also worship a secondary deity, Yahweh, also known as *The Lord*, *Adonai*, *Hashem*, etc. The distinction between Israel, as a country, and Israel, as the mystic body of all Jews – past, present and future – is smudged. In fact, it is simply not made, another instance of a useful category mistake. This new religion takes what it likes from the Tanakh and the Talmud and discards the rest. Two of its basic tenets are that Palestine is their possession for all time and that the Nation-God gives them moral dispensation in reclaiming that land. [Review the Ben Gurion citation in Chapter XVIII.]

It has been estimated that at the turn of the century no more than 10% of Jews were Zionists and that at the end of World War II a sizable number – perhaps a majority – of Jewish displaced persons (DPs) preferred the United States to Palestine as a settlement option. But most of them were not really given a choice. All the energy of the Palestine-or-bust gang was directed at the task of making sure that the large majority of

DPs would end up in Palestine. Ben Gurion stated that he would rather save half of them in Palestine than all of them somewhere else. (Shabtai Teveth, *Ben Gurion*, Wiseman Institute, Tel Aviv University) When the Anglo-American Committee of Inquiry was charged with determining the preferences of the DPs, Zionist organizations made sure that the latter were coached and that "the AAC met only Jews propounding the Zionists' solutions." (Morris, p. 177) The DPs were not so much coerced as corralled into going to Palestine.

In the US, Zionist organizations, figuring that the best way to get Jews into Palestine was to limit their access to other venues, showed no inclination to support any legislation to accept Jewish emigration to America. This strategy didn't end with the establishment of Israel. When Israel obtained the right of emigration for the Jews still in Russia and Eastern Europe, Zionists pressured Germany and other countries to refuse entrance to those Jews, thus forcing them to go to Israel.

The task of the Zionist apostles was made easier by the structure of the Jewish Diaspora. The rabbi is revered by his congregation, especially in the orthodox and conservative communities. His word is law and he is considered almost infallible; he is almost a mini-pope. The Zionist gained control by winning over most of the rabbis – a task facilitated by the fact that at the beginning of their careers they are concentrated in Yeshivas. The proselytizers masterfully used the hierarchical structure of Jewish authority. One of the most powerful weapons at their disposal was the word *traitor*, a charge as effective among Jews as *anti-Semite* is among Gentiles.

> Roosevelt's advisor, Morris Ernst, wrote in 1948 of his shock at the refusal of American Jewish leaders to consider the possibility of giving "these beaten people of Europe a choice" … the program he advanced "would free us from the hypocrisy of closing our own door while making sanctimonious demands on the Arabs," he wrote, adding that he "was amazed and even felt insulted when active Jewish leaders denied, sneered and then attacked me as if I were a traitor for suggesting that the survivors of the Holocaust be permitted the choice of emigrating to the United States.
> (Chomsky, p.93)

The Israeli courts have determined that Israel is the sovereign state of all Jewish people on Earth, implying that a Jew living in Akron, Ohio, who has never set foot in Israel, is as much an Israeli citizen as an Israeli-born Jew living in Tel Aviv. This is a slick move; any previously anti-Zionist Jew is now enjoined to support Israel because it's his country; any Jew can feel morally free to pass classified information from his county of residence to his moral country, Israel; American Jewish organizations can decide to place Israeli interests above US interests since Israel is equally their country; Israel can involve itself in any action of any government regarding any Jew since the latter is an Israeli citizen. This universal Israeli citizenship is a strong inducement for individual Jews to feel "national" regardless of their religious beliefs. Note that this leaves Arab-Israelis in a political no-man's land since neither birth nor residence in the country bestows citizenship – another example of fuzzy logic (when convenient) by Zionists. Governments and, perhaps, the UN should nullify this move by declaring that it has no legal significance outside Israel.

The hijacking of Rabbinical Judaism has been so successful that most Jews can be qualified as Zionists to some degree. Certainly many, perhaps most, are knee-jerk Zionists, simply "going with the flow," without bothering to look too closely at the situation, figuring that a Jew can't really disapprove of Israel. In 1986, Alfred A. Knopf published a book by Daniel Jonah Goldhaggen, *Hitler's Willing Executioners*, in which the author convincingly shows that most Germans and Austrians, far from being forced to oppress and kill Jews, willingly participated in the massacre. Part of the moral onus for the Holocaust was therefore borne by millions of ordinary people. By the same token, it would seem that part of the onus for the Palestinian "catastrophe" falls squarely on the shoulders of those Jews who support the actions, or just "go along with the flow." One is responsible for one's actions – and that includes voting, talking and writing as well as shooting and bombing.

What is needed is for rabbis who believe in the Talmud to take back their religion from the hijackers and for progressive secular Jews to support and assist them. This struggle would not set Orthodox, Conservative, Reform and secular Jews against each other: all sectors are a mixture of Zionists and anti-Zionists (although right now the former are in the majority).

Life and Property

Life was cheap in the Old Testament: men, women, old folk, children were dispatched without a second thought. At times Yahweh himself commanded the annihilation of all the inhabitants of certain cities. Sometimes this wasn't enough: domestic animals also had to be killed and buildings destroyed. To let a single person of a proscribed city keep his life was sin. Zionists, in their effort to emulate the ancient Hebrews, adopted a similar attitude toward life. In the old Testament, whoever infringed one of the written or oral laws was guilty, even if he did so unconsciously or out of ignorance: intent was not a factor. Hence the pharaoh, and later, King Abimelek were terrified because, not knowing that she was married, they had included Abrahm's (Abraham's) wife in their harems. King Josiah, on learning that the high priest had found long-lost scrolls that contained religious laws that the people had never heard of, expected the worst from an angry Yahweh. Likewise, Zionists consider anyone, including babies, guilty if they are in any way an obstacle or hindrance to the plans of the Nation-God:

> In South Lebanon we struck the civilian population because they deserved it ... the importance of [Chief of Staff] Gur's remarks is the admission that the Israeli army has always struck civilian populations purposely and consciously ... the army, he said, has never distinguished civilian [from military] targets, even when Israeli settlements had not been struck.
> (Military analyst Ze'ev Achiff summing up Chief of Staff Gu's remarks in Ha'Aretz, May 15, 1978, via Chomsky, p. 181)

In many cases the ratio of Arab to Israeli deaths is hard to establish, but in all cases it is very heavily skewed in favor of the Israeli side. From figures in Chapters XIX and XX, I estimate that the overall ratio may be somewhere between 6 to 1 and 9 to 1. In the cases of prisoners and wounded soldiers the ratio is also very heavily skewed to the advantage of the Israelis.

The above ratios do not take into account many raids and counter raids that happened in between wars and insurrections, such as those referred to in the following citation from the *Boston Globe*:

> Since the end of Israel's invasion of Lebanon in 1982, some 25,000 Lebanese and Palestinians have been killed

> according to Lebanese officials and international relief agencies, along with 900 Israeli soldiers.
> (Aliza Marcus, *Boston Globe*, March 1, 1999, via Chomsky, p. xx)

There is no evidence (or even indication) that Israel had made any effort to find a way of winning without inflicting so much damage. The only exception might be in the Intifadas, where the ratio in the first was 8 to 1, and in the second, 3 to 1. This is probably due to the fact that the IDF had almost no experience in crowd control prior to the first insurrection.

The statistics for the Second Lebanon War of 2006 confirms that casualty ratios are not improving for the Arabs. Approximately 10 Lebanese were killed for every Israeli. However, the ratio of Lebanese civilian deaths to Israeli civilian deaths was 27 to 1. Yet the Israelis are the ones with the American-made smart bombs and other accurate high-tech weapons, which should minimize civilian casualties. The Arabs, despite having comparatively primitive weapons, killed few civilians.

Another disquieting aspect of this war: Israel launched thousands of American cluster bombs, 90% of them during the last 72 hours before the agreed-upon cease-fire was to take effect (August 14, 2006). Why so much viciousness? And, to boot, that munitions was used in populated areas, which is in violation of international humanitarian laws.

To assess the value Zionists put on human life, we must not only look at their practices with their enemies, but also at their dealings with their friends. IN March 1947, the IZL (Irgun) killed twenty-some British soldiers in spite of the fact that Britain, the issuer of the Balfour Declaration, had been the Zionists' best friend for decades. (Morris, p. 181).

In July, 1954, a group of Israeli saboteurs were stopped before they could start a planned campaign of bombing British and American installations in Cairo and Alexandria, assuming that the Egyptians would be blamed (Morris, p. 282)

In June, 1967, as covered earlier, a clearly identified US ship, the Liberty, was attacked by Israeli ships and aircraft, killing 34 and wounding 75. (Chomsky, p. 31)

The evidence is clear: hard-core Zionists and their followers have no respect for, and attach no value to human life, except Jewish life.

Racism

In 1975, the UN General Assembly passed a resolution declaring that Zionism is a form of racism, and in 1991, it repealed it. The resolution was awkwardly worded: it should have said something like "Zionism is a racist ideology." But, this flaw aside, did the original proposition have merit? – Not if you are a believer in the literal word of the Bible: God, a really existing, factual entity, has chosen the Hebrews – arbitrarily, since Moses and Joshua have stated that they were not particularly meritorious – to be his chosen people, has promised them a land, and has given them moral dispensation. True believers are thus saved from the taint of racism, but at a price: by entailment God himself is represented as racist! But for the majority of Israelis, and the vast majority of humans, basic logic should conclude that for a non-believer, to use chosenness as an excuse for crimes against humanity is a racist stance. Many Zionists are not racists in their daily interactions – they accept and respect other races and other points of view – but to the extent that they support Zionist policies and actions, they are nonetheless racists (at least in the metaphysical sense).

Some Israelis are too busy with plain old, Klu-Klux-Klan-kind of racism to muse about metaphysical racism. In an article in the West Bank religious journal, *Nekudah*, Yedicha Segal, a scholar of the Gush Imunim, quotes Maimonides on how people conquered by Jews must be treated as degraded and low and must not "raise their heads" but must adopt an attitude of complete submission. (Chomsky, p. 124) Some border guards (and other soldiers and officials) have put such principles into practice. In Chapter XIX I quoted the Knesset member Ron Cohen reporting on the treatment of Arab workers by border guards in a Tel Aviv hotel. Let me repeat one sentence:

> The Arab workers were cruelly beaten up, and were compelled to masturbate before the Border Guards, to lick the floor of their flat and to eat coffee mixed with sugar and toothpaste, and their money was stolen.
> (Manachen Shifaf, *Hadaskot*, July 7, 1987, via Chomsky, p. 489)

Chomsky adds that the workers have brought complaints to the authorities, but that two months later they still had not received a response. This was – and is – par for the course.

The most blatantly racist statements have come mostly from some extremist Gush Emunim rabbis:

> – One million Arabs are not worth a Jewish fingernail. (Rabbi Yaacof Perrin, *N.Y. Times*, February 28, 1994, via Michael A. Hoffman II, *Judaism's Strange Gods.*)
> – If a Jew needs a liver, can he take the liver of an innocent non-Jew passing by to save him? The Torah would probably permit that. Jewish life has an infinite value. There is something infinitely more holy and unique about Jewish life than non-Jewish life.
> (Rabbi Yitzak Ginsburg, *Jewish Week*, April 26, 1996, via Hoffman)

Those rabbis have followers, not only among the Gush Emunim but also in government and in the military. In May 1990, seven unarmed Palestinians were murdered by an Israeli named Ami Popper. When Palestinians civilians protested the crimes, they were shot by the Israeli army. (*LA Times*, May 23, 1990, via Hoffman)

The *Wall Street Journal* of May 24, 1990, reported that a Rabbi Moshe Savenger received a sentence of only five months for the unprovoked murder of an unarmed Palestinian shopkeeper. Before his incarceration, the rabbi was the hero of a party attended by Israeli President Chaim Herzog and Israeli Army General Yitzak Mordechai. Another rabbi wrote a statement for the occasion in which he called on Jews to "shoot Arabs left and right without thinking without hesitating."

Many readers will recall the "exploit" of Baruch Goldstein, an officer of the Israeli Army (reserve), who, on February 25, 1994, entered a mosque and killed 40 Palestrina civilians, including children, and who was beaten to death by members of the congregation. This much was widely reported. What was not so widely broadcast was the fact that Goldstein was eulogized by many rabbis at his funeral, called a "holy martyr" and considered a saint by many.

The top leaders and ambassadors of Israel will not make declarations as blatantly and crudely racist as the rants of the Gush Emunim rabbis, but the Israeli government and courts put in practice the same moral stance. Chomsky refers to a number of court cases to prove the point:

> … 47 Arabs were murdered by Israeli Border guards in 1956. This was recognized to be a crime. The officer held responsible by the courts was fined one piaster (ten cents) for a "technical error." Gabriel Dahan, who was convicted

> of killing 43 Arabs in one hour, served just over a year, the longest sentence served, and was promptly engaged as officer for Arab affairs in Ramle.
> (Chomsky, p. 159)

Chomsky was not alone in noticing the rot that infects the Israeli judicial system:

> Sadistically inclined soldiers went on sprees of violence. Only a small minority of these malefactors were brought to book by the army's legal machinery – and were always let off with ludicrously light sentences. The civilian courts were just as slow to punish violence by the settlers; for example, a settler who shot and killed a pregnant woman in the West Bank village of al-Jib in December 1995 was sentenced by Jerusalem district court judge Eliahu Ben-Zimra to four months of community service.
> (Morris, p. 599)

Certainly, there must be honest judges in Israel doing their best to be fair, but it's clear that the judicial system has been corrupted and perverted by the principle of moral dispensation. When the courts are infected by such a bias, it can be asserted that the country practices institutional racism.

In Memoriam Rachel Corrie

One tragic incident stands out in this context. On March 16, 2003, Rachel Corrie, an American citizen and a member of the International Solidarity Movement (ISM) was deliberately killed by the operator of a Weaponized Caterpillar Bulldozer while trying to stop the destruction of Palestinian homes and farmland in the Gaza Strip. On the website of *The Electronic Intifada*, three affidavits by Corrie's co-protesters describe the incident. All three agree that Rachel was clearly visible from the point of view of the operator and that the incident was an act of cruel murder. To this date, as far as I know, the operator has not been arrested and no serious investigation has been made. This is not surprising: some fanatic rabbis have declared that the killing of a gentile is not a serious sin and not a capital crime. In fact the Israeli courts have consistently used the flimsiest of excuses to exonerate or to sentence to ridiculously light punishment Israeli murderers of Palestinians (as has been reported by Chomsky and others).

The last deed of Rachel Corrie's short life was an attempt to save Dr. Samir Masri's house from destruction. The reason for the bulldozing was to clear a number of structures that could shield potential snipers or rocket launchers. The reason for the protesters' actions was that Israel never offers a penny of compensation for the buildings and agricultural properties it so wantonly destroys. Note that security is not the only pretense for bulldozing: every illegal settlement necessitates the destruction of Palestinian property as land is cleared for the project and further expropriation for a safety zone and for road building. The security wall recently built around the West Bank has also resulted in massive destruction and land grab – again with no compensation. We shouldn't be surprised: if murder is covered by moral dispensation, why not thievery?

Genocide

Jews know about genocide. Could they, its most famous victims, have the stomach to perpetrate it themselves? Certainly they wouldn't march Palestinians by the hundreds to killing rooms and gas them. Certainly they wouldn't bury thousands upon thousands of bodies in common graves. Memory is too strong!

But is it possible not to go to the ultimate extreme and still stand accused of genocide? – Yes, because there are more than one kind of genocide. The Nazis performed physical genocide: extinguishing a people by killing as many of its individuals as possible. There is another way to eradicate a collectivity, to wit, by dissolving the cement that holds a group together. There are two ways of doing this: political genocide and cultural genocide. Israel has engaged in both.

> The Israeli invasion of Lebanon ... was designed to destroy once and for all any hope among the people of the West Bank and Gaza that the process of shaping the Palestinian people into a nation could succeed.
> (Harold Saunders [Ex-Assistant Secretary of State], "An Israeli-Palestinian Peace," *Foreign Affairs*, Fall 1982, via Chomsky, p. 340)

Also,

> [Israel's] strategy is to destroy the infrastructure of the universities as it is to destroy the infrastructure of Palestinian society ... Their ultimate aim is to destroy any Palestinian infrastructure in the homeland
> (*NY Times*, October 21, 1982, via Chomsky, p. 135)

One tactic has been to deny re-entry, wherever possible, to intellectuals and experts who have left the country (often as part of their work). Another has been to deny permits for cultural activities under the pretext that they might induce disruptive activities.

Israel has not limited its politico-cultural genocide to education and cultural activities; it has also prevented or limited economic activity, especially when it might represent serious competition to Israeli businesses. For example,

> One consequence of the Lebanon War was that Israel's national water company took over "total control of the scarce and disputed water resources in the West Bank," an important move toward further integration of the territories. Zvi Barel comments that the decision contradicts the Camp David principle that control over water should fall under the autonomy provisions, and that knowledgeable sources attributed the decision to practical factors, not technical considerations as was claimed.
> (Zvi Barel, *Ha'aretz*, September 9, 1982, via Chomsky, p. 47.

In a water-short land to restrict access to water is to seriously limit agricultural and industrial development – part of a strategy of political and cultural genocide.

The only argument that Israel can use to justify the attempted genocide is the Ben-Gurion-Golda Meir contention that Palestinians have no national rights because they have never been united and organized under a national flag: wasn't, that the situation of the Jews for 2,500 years? And don't they nonetheless claim national rights?

On Being Better Off

If Israel (the country) is necessary for the welfare of the Jews, for the survival of Judaism and for the redemption of the Human Race, after 60 years of sovereignty some of its benefits should be discernable. Someone, or rather, some group must be better off because Israel has existed for these 60 years. Who?

The Jewish citizens of Israel? – No. They are constantly wary of terrorist attacks. On average, their standard of living is inferior to that of Jews outside of Israel. Most of them would have more security, a better quality of life, and more peace of mind had they (or their parents) been allowed to emigrate to the United States, Canada, Australia, Argentina, or some other country where they could have settled without displacing another people. Many Jews have come to realize this, which explains why tens of thousands of Israeli citizens have returned to the US, Russia and other countries in a movement of reverse migrations.

The Arab citizens of Israel? – No. Being second-class citizens, they could hardly be expected to have a better quality of life than the rest of the population.

The Palestinians? – No. Living in a refugee camp or in half-demolished buildings, being mostly unemployed, having practically no civil rights, being constantly wary of state-terrorist attacks is better than hanging at the end of a rope – but not much.

The Jews of the Diaspora? – No. The end of World War II signaled the end of virulent anti-Semitism, but the oppression of the Palestinians, the instances of racist behavior, and the show of utter disrespect for the United Nations (that is, utter disrespect for the rest of humanity) may well rekindle the fire of anti-Semitism. And this time part of the onus would fall on the Jewish side.

The other people of the Middle East? – No. Just ask the Lebanese. Mostly because of Israel, the whole region is a tinderbox. All are scared of the 200 or so nuclear bombs in Israel's arsenal.

The American People? – No. Had Israel (as constituted) not been established, the 9-11 terrorist attack would probably not have happened. Because of its role in the Near East situation the US has suffered a loss of security, honor and respect. Also, Israel is a costly protégé: at least 3 billion a year, plus billions in aid to other Middle East countries just to keep the volatile situation under control.

The people of Planet Earth? – No. If the Middle East tinderbox ignites, the sparks could cover a large portion of the globe. And now we wouldn't be dealing with 200 nuclear bombs, but with thousands.

The only people who may be better off are the faithaholics who feel that they must fulfill some old prophesies of dubious contemporary relevance and who don't care how much it costs them – or the rest of us. These are a minority in Israel – and a minute minority on the planet.

To Be Fair

It would be unfair not to give credit to Israeli and Diaspora Jews who did not fall for the Ideological Zionists' siren song and who continued to resist the movement. Prominent among them is Noam Chomsky, whose name by now must be familiar to the reader. Another brave defender of human rights is Dr. Israel Shahak, who died in 2001, and was at some time president of the Israeli League for Human and Civil Rights. Even some political figures such as Teddy Kollek, ex-mayor of Jerusalem, deserve honorable mention. Among the more enlightened American Zionists is Arthur Ginsberg, the editor of *The Zionist Idea*, my main source for Chapter XVII, and the writer of a long and excellent introduction for that book. My choice of citations may give the impression that he was a hard-core, virulent Zionist. But in an op-ed article on the *NY Times*, August 27, 2003, he advocated that the US should cease funding the expansion of Jewish settlements, while also denying the Palestinians access to foreign funds used for violence. "The Untied States must act now to disarm both sides … We must end the threat of the settlements to a Palestinian state of the future. The Palestinian militants must be forced to stop threatening the lives of Israelis … (culled from Kevin McDonald, *Understanding Jewish Influence*, Washington Summit Press, 2004.) [He should have added, *and the Israelis must be forced to stop threatening the lives of Palestinians.*] There are a surprising number of individuals who resist the fascistic tendencies of Zionism and the State of Israel, working within a number of civil rights organizations. Unfortunately they have not yet coalesced into a movement. Considering the power that rabbis have – individually over their congregations and collectively over the government – it would seem that any progressive movement will not go very far without the involvement of some part of the clergy.

Some of the main Israeli Civil Rights organizations are:

- B'Tselem (The Israeli Information Center for Human Rights in the Occupied Territories)
- Machsom Watch – Women for Human Rights
- Gisha: Center for the Legal Protection of Freedom of Movement
- Massawa – the Advocacy center for Arab-Citizens of Israel
- Physicians for Human Rights – Israel
- The Public Committee Against Torture in Israel
- Rabbis for Human Rights
- The Association for Civil-Rights in Israel.
- Ha Moked: Center for the Defense of the Individual

The ethos of these groups and individuals is beautifully summarized by philosophy professor Judith Norman in an article posted at www.mysanantonio.com:

> I am sympathetic to the plight of the Palestinians living under military occupation because of my Jewish identity, not in spite of it. As victims of brutality and persecution, the Jewish people have a responsibly to oppose brutality and persecution wherever we find it.

There are brave reporters and honest newspapers in Israel. *Ha'Aretz*, one of the chief dailies is probably the most honest and fair; other newspapers such as *Yediot Ahronot* and *Hadashot* deserve honorable mention. [It's a sad commentary on the state of American media that an Israeli citizen is probably better informed of the political and military adventures of Israel than an American reader limited to the auto-censured media of his own country. (More on this later)]

Herzl and many other early militants thought that to ensure the security of the Jewish people it was essential that the latter have their own sovereign country. As it turned out, this was a mistake, but it was an understandable one. No one could have predicted how the 30s and 40s would change everything. For two thousand years, except during a few sunny periods, Jews had been, at worst, oppressed and, at best, tolerated. Not having a country meant not having a voice. It made sense therefore to mold the people into a nation and mobilize it to establish a country. But the Holocaust turned the world on its head. Humanity as a whole was so sickened and ashamed by the butchery and so guilt-ridden by the failure to do anything about it that classical anti-Semitism was finally defeated.

At the horrible cost of 6 million lives, the Jews had finally found salvation. Even the new anti-Semitism described by Herzl – the anti-Semitism of envy – was greatly reduced. But Herzl, Nordau and their associates couldn't possibly have foreseen this in the decades preceding the war.

The Palestinians, just because they are the most aggrieved party, must not be given a pass on matters of morality. The Israelis often protest that critics commit the error of moral equivalence by equating the reprisals of Israel with the terrorist aggressions of the Palestinians. This gambit deserves a second look. First, when the two parties are not engaging in a war they are exchanging tit-for-tat raids or rocket launchings, so that either side can qualify any of its military actions as retaliatory. Second, as can be verified in Chapter XX ("Numbers and Maps"), many more Palestinians are killed and injured than Israelis. Prior to the 1982 Lebanon War there were hundreds of IAF violations of the Lebanese border, and hundreds of Lebanese and PLO members killed. Therefore, taking a global perspective of the conflict, it is the Zionist side that is in moral deficit, not the Palestinian side. As Ben Gurion, Begin and others have candidly admitted, the Zionists "came and stole their country." It is probably the Arabs who should object to the concept of moral equivalence!

One problem is that Zionists seem to grant the same ethical grade to all sins, crimes or transgressions, as if stealing candy were equivalent to mugging old ladies, or kidnapping a soldier to bombing a city with fragmentation bombs. The moral universe is a continuum, which is why we have murder 1, murder 2 and manslaughter; and why the aggressor is usually judged more severely than the retaliator for the same injurious action.

The moral onus should be graded. Killing an Israeli soldier in the West Bank is on par with a French Resistance fighter killing a Nazi occupier during World War II, since the Israeli occupation is illegal according to the Geneva Convention, the UN Charter and almost all governments. Killing a Gush Emunim settler, however, presents us with a moral dilemma. Settlers are not soldiers (although they can carry guns almost anywhere they want) but are certainly occupiers. Occupation is their function and land grab is their purpose. The whole settlement program was designed to make it impossible for the Palestinians to achieve true independence and sovereignty. Not only is land confiscated without compensation, but a web of roads are constructed for the exclusive use of the settlers. These roads link the settlements but also divide the West Bank into a number of unconnected bantustans. The Israeli civil rights group B'Tselem has come to the conclusion that "while the built-up area of the settlements in the West Bank covers 1.7 percent of the West Bank, the settlements control 41.9% of the entire West Bank." (www.b'tselem.org/english) Can the Palestinians be blamed for not entertaining the greatest feelings of sympathy for the settlers? Is the onus of killing one on par with the onus of killing an occupying soldier?

The killing of Israelis in Israel proper, whether by rockets or suicide bombers, must be judged by other criteria. The victims here are innocent civilians, regardless of how they feel about Palestinians. The moral onus therefore falls heavier on these terrorists than in the former cases.

The most pitiful of the victims are the suicide bombers themselves. Often they are teenagers or young adults who have been selected, nurtured and prodded by political and religious leaders into committing holy suicide. As an atheist, I believe in neither Allah nor in life after death. And I can find no sympathy for this tactic.

The Israelis accuse the Palestinians of wanton disregard for human life because both rocket launchings and suicide bombings do not discriminate between military an civilian targets. The Arabs can counter with statistics that show that not only do the Israeli kill many more civilians than do the Arabs, but also that they have a much higher ratio of civilian to military victims (review statistics in Chapter XX). As I have written above, it begs the question that the side with the best technology, including laser-directed bombs, is also the side with the worst ratio, by far, of civilian to military casualties. The Palestinians do not discriminate between civilians and soldiers because they can't: the technological means at their disposal do not permit it.

[Note that until a recent drift toward radicalism – understandable, considering the constant provocation – the Palestinians had never been a part of the fundamentalist and extremist wing of Islam.]

It's difficult to come to any conclusion about moral equivalence between the actions of the two parties. As written above, the proactive side (Israel, if we take a historical perspective) must be judged more severely than the reactive side (the Palestinians). A more equitable comparison can be made between Israel and the Muslim government of Sudan. In the latter case, the proactive side is the government and the reactive side is represented by the Christian and Animist populations of the South and, more recently, the Black Muslim people of Darfur. The proactive sides in both conflicts show great similarity in ethos and tactics. Both have no respect for, and attach no value to, human life except their own. Both show little concern for human suffering. Both do not hesitate to resort to ethnic cleansing and other crimes against humanity. Both rely on powerful allies: the US, for Israel; and the Janjaweed, for the Sudan. Both have little respect for the truth. Both have no respect for the judgement of third parties, including the Untied Nations.

It seems that the Zionists have absorbed a few lessons from Nazi Germany and passed them on to the Sudan. Fascism is alive and well in the Middle East – and, unfortunately, in a few other places.

Other points of comparison can be found that suggest that Muslims should hesitate before pointing the finger at Zionists – the killing orgy between Sunnis and Chias in Iraq, for one (at least Jews don't kill each other) and the demented hatred of the Taliban for anything non-Taliban. There seems to be a kind of insanity in Iraq – as there has been in Cambodia under Pol Pot, for another example – that values death for its own sake, regardless of who the victims are (your side or theirs) as a token of victory and an offering to God: a modern form of human sacrifice, no less!

One principle must be stressed here: whatever crimes – including crimes against humanity – that non-Palestinian Muslims may have committed, that are not directly linked to the Israeli-Palestinian conflict, cannot excuse crimes by Israelis against Palestinians. Whatever terrorism the Taliban and al Quaeda are guilty of does not give moral dispensation to Zionists. Israelis cannot commit crimes against Palestinians and dismiss them by saying, "Look what the Taliban and al Quaeda are doing in Iraq."

Three Cheers for Humanism

A Gush Emunim rabbi, in an interview with a West Bank journal has said that, "There is no relation between the law of Israel [based on the Torah] and the atheistic modern humanism." (Yehuda Segal, *Nekudah*, September 3, 1982). Considering the rabbi's title and function in his community, we can assume that he considers "the law of Israel" greatly superior to the "atheistic modern humanism" and that he therefore considers a code that condones ethnic cleansing, arbitrary expropriation, collective punishment, and extrajudicial execution morally superior to a code that considers all humans metaphysically equal regardless of race, gender and age; that eschews reliance on violence and war unless defensive and absolutely necessary; values justice and happiness; and insures liberty of conscience and religion for all – surely the work of the Devil.

There is no incompatibility between religion and humanism. Among the very first humanists were Rabbi Hillel and Jesus Christ. Before them the prophets Amos and 2nd Isaiah also had humanist tendencies. In the 18th century in Europe and the 19th century in America, the Jewish Enlightenment movement championed humanism and instituted the branch of the religion known as Reform Judaism. For a few centuries humanism had slowly been making progress in most Christian churches, but in the 20th century it made a few giant strides with the papacy of John the 23rd.

In spite of recent retrogressive tendencies humanism is now an element of most religions. Religion devoid of humanism is bad religion.

Chapter XXII – The Axis of Injustice

Terrorism can be defined as the use of fear to achieve some end. This end can be political, territorial, religious, ideological, etc. Often there is no easily identifiable end: terrorism can be purely primitive and the perpetrator may just be very pissed off. Rightly or wrongly he may see himself as the victim and the object of his rage as his actual or symbolic oppressor.

There are uncountable acts of terrorism every day, all around us. The man who points a gun at someone and says, "Your money or your life" is a terrorist; so are the schoolyard bully, the violent husband the sadistic cop, the brutal pimp, and so on. Most acts of terrorism do not make the newspaper headlines: only the more egregious, spectacular and consequential ones are reported. Sometimes a certain amount of terrorism is understandable, even beneficial: the fear of imprisonment by a potential criminal is a good thing; so is the fear of punishment by a rebellious and undisciplined child.

A maxim of English common law is "the king can do no harm," which means that the state cannot be held accountable for injury it may inflict on a citizen. Fortunately this canon has by now lost most of its force: the king can, indeed, do harm, as can the court, the general, the pope, the imam, the rabbi – there is no end to this list.

There is no reason to call a suicide bomber a terrorist, but not so a pilot dumping fragmentation bombs or phosphorous bombs on a town. It makes no sense to call a bombing by an organization such as al Qaeda or Hamas an act of terrorism, but not the bombing or shelling of a hospital or a UN observation post by Israeli forces.

That state terrorism exists can easily be established:

Ben Gurion, Begin, Rabin, Shamir and others accepted terrorism as a legitimate tactic and strategy for the Zionist enterprise, and practiced it themselves as leaders of the Irgun and the LEHI (Stern Group).

It is commonly accepted by both Jewish and Gentile historians that the Haganah, the semi-official army of the Zionists, with the assistance of the Irgun, the LEHI and its own special rangers, the Palma, committed acts of terrorism in more than a dozen Arab towns, the most famous of which was Deir Yassin. Among the outrages committed during that campaign, people were lined up against walls and shot in cold blood. The intended consequence was that thousands of Arabs flew in panic and the areas around the massacred towns were taken over by the Israelis.

On May 14, 1948, Israel proclaimed itself a sovereign state and was almost immediately recognized by the US and Russia. On May 17, 1949, Israel was admitted into the United Nations, which implies that it accepted the institution's charter as binding.

The Haganah became the Israeli Defense Force (IDF) but the series of massacres and ethnic cleansings mentioned above continued.

If the actions of the Haganah constituted terrorism, then the similar actions of the IDF *after May 14, 1948* also constituted terrorism.

But now, since the IDF was the official armed force of the Sovereign State of Israel, the latter can be qualified as a terrorist state.

In 2001, after the World Trade Center bombing, President H.W. Bush declared that "Those who help terrorists are equally guilty of terrorism" – a self-incriminating statement, considering the role of the US in terrorist activities in Guatemala, Chile, Honduras, El Salvador and a few other places. This accusation has been paraphrased into such assertions as, "If you harbor a terrorist, you're a terrorist" and "If you finance a terrorist, you're a terrorist." The underlying proposition of all these we may call the *Bush Principle*, one of the very few Bush propositions I agree with completely.

Now, Britain, France and the US supported all the IDF actions mentioned above. Therefore, by the Bush principle, Britain, France and the US are terrorist states to the extent that Israel is a terrorist state.

In the first two decades of Israel's existence, Britain and France were the main enablers of Zionism, although money given by American (and other) Jews through Jewish organizations was also crucial. It was only during the Six-Day War (1967) and henceforth that the US became, by far, the principal enabler.

In a speech given in Haifa in 1944, Ben Gurion had said, "The meaning of the Jewish revolution is contained in one word – Independence!"

(Hertzberg, p. 609). But Israel would become the living proof that a country could be sovereign without being independent. At first it relied on the generosity of the diaspora (especially American) and of a few governments. After the Sinai war of 1953, the US started replacing Europe as the foremost sponsor of Israel. Since the Six-Day war of 1967, American help has become indispensable. If the US didn't exist, Israel would probably not exist today. What kind of independence is that?

Considering that from 1985 to 2005 the US gave, on average, $3.2 billion in outright grants to Israel, and considering that the US used its veto to annul more than 30 Security Council resolutions against Israel, it is reasonable to call the relationship between the two countries an axis. Since one of its main consequences is the unjust oppression of another people, the Palestinian Arabs, I suggest we call it the *axis of injustice.* The American end of this axis rests on a tripod, the three legs of which are the neo-conservatives, the Israeli lobby, and the right-wing Christian fundamentalists.

THE NEOCONSERVATIVES

The first leg of the tripod is more a movement than an organization. It doesn't have a president, nor a secretary, nor a treasurer, but it has solidarity and huge influence. It has changed the very profile of America.

To the extent that we can fix a timetable for its genesis, we can speculate that it started with the teaching of Professor Leo Strauss at the University of Chicago. Strauss' basic political philosophy is right out of Plato's *Republic*: admiration for military virtues (and vices); a strong inclination for military solutions; lip service to religious and political beliefs that are the "opium of the masses" but are not really believed by the ruling elite; and the use of manipulation and, when necessary, deception to achieve the elite's conception of the common good. In his monograph, *Understanding Jewish Influence* (Washington Summit Publishers), Kevin Mac Donald quotes Stephen Holmes:

> The good society, on this model, consists of the sedated masses, the promising puppies, and the philosophers who pursue knowledge, manipulate the gentlemen, anesthetize the people, and housebreak the most talented young. (Holmes, S., *The Anatomy of Anti-Liberation*, Harvard University Press, 1993, p. 74, via MacDonald)

Two of Strauss' students who were political animals, Richard Perle and Paul Wolfowitz, ended up as senior bureaucrats in the American government, Perle as Assistant Secretary of Defense for International Security Policy (under President Reagan) and Wolforitz as Deputy Secretary of Defense (under President W. H. Bush). It seems that when you hire a neocon, you end up hiring two or three more. For example, Perle hired Stephen Bryen as Deputy Assistant Secretary of Defense and Wolfowitz hired Douglas Feith as special counsel, and later as his deputy, in spite of the fact that the later had been fired from another government job because he was strongly suspected of having passed restricted documents to the Israeli embassy. Bryen was also suspected of spying. In *Understanding Jewish Influence*, Kevin McDonald writes:

> It is surprising that Perle was able to hire Bryen at all given that, beginning in 1978, Bryen was investigated for offering classified documents to the Mossad station chief of the Israeli embassy in the presence of an AIPAC [American-Israeli Public Affairs Committee] representative. Bryen's fingerprints were found on the documents in question despite his denials that he ever had the documents in his possession. (Bryen refused to take a polygraph test.) (p. 95)

It should surprise no one that Wolfowitz and Perle would be indulgent toward suspected spies: in 1978, Wolfowitz himself "was investigated for providing a classified document to the Israeli government through an AIPAC intermediary" (McDonald, p. 100) and Perle was recorded by the FBI in 1970, talking about classified information to the Israeli embassy. (p. 101)

Skimming through the political literature of (or about) the 70s, the same names keep showing up: Wohlstetter, Strauss, Perle, Wolfowitz, Podharetz, Kristol (father and sons) Dannhauser, Kagan, Himelfarb, Lidun, Lewis. The names sound Jewish and I believe the above are all Jewish: neo-conservatism is a Jewish invention. However, the neocons realized early that they would need to attract some prominent Gentiles in order to magnify their influence. Some early Gentile neocons were Jeanne Kirkpatrick, Daniel Patrick Moynihan and William Bennett.

Neocons come from a surprising variety of backgrounds: disaffected left wingers, ex-Trotskyites, social liberals, old-fashioned conservatives, Jews of all persuasions, Christian fundamentalists, agnostics, etc. The only things they have in common – the only coalescing forces – are a preference for the military option and devotion to a foreign country: Israel.

In the 80s neo-conservatism was rather dormant, but it slowly regained strength in the 90s, with the old cabal getting a second wind and new adherents, Jewish and Christian, joining the movement. Events in Bosnia, Somalia and the Balkans furnished the grist for the mill of neoconservative pronouncements and criticism.

The election of George W. Bush, however, signaled boom times for the movement. Vice President Cheney was already a neocon – and Bush practically so. Big jobs in the State Department and in Defense – key positions from which to promote the interests of Israel – went to Richard Armitage, as number-two at State, and Wolfowitz, as number-two at Defense. The latter, as is so common in the movement, managed to get two more neocons in top jobs: Douglas J. Feith and Dov Zakheim. This was not so difficult an accomplishment, however, since Bush had previously given the post of Secretary of Defense to a Gentile neocon, Donald Rumsfeld (one of the few neocons to have performed military service for his country).

In their book, *America Alone: The Neo-conservatives and the Global Order* (Cambridge), Stephen Halper and Jonathan Clarke (old style conservatives themselves) encapsulate the common themes that animate the movement:

Today's neo-conservatives unite around three common themes:

1. A belief deriving from religious conviction that the human condition is defined as a choice between good and evil and that the true measure of political character is to be found in the willingness by the former (themselves) to confront the latter.
2. An assertion that the fundamental determinant of the relation between states rests on military power and the willingness to use it.
3. A primary focus on the Middle East and global Islam as the principal theater for American overseas interests.
4. (Halper and Clarke, p.11)

Theme 3 deserves a second look. Neocons have little, if any, interest in the welfare of the Arabs, Bedouins or other Moslems who form the majority element of the Middle East population. *Focusing on the Middle East* is an euphemism for *focusing on the interests and demands of Israel.* This attitude can be epitomized by this paraphrase of a maxim by a past-CEO of General Motors: *what is good for Israel is good for America. Always!*

In light of those principles, neocons feel that America is, by definition, always "doing the right thing" in its dealings with the rest of the world, and that they, the neocons, are always in the right in any argument with other American individuals or groups. As a consequence they belittle the UN and any deliberative body or multilateral institution out of step with their music. One term expresses all these feelings and conditions: *global unilateralism*. As a result of this mindset, neocons are always ready to shoot first and ask questions later: in their view, military might and the readiness to use it are the hallmark of a great superpower.

This governance by reflex is clearly verbalized by the following statement by Vice President Cheney:

If there's a one percent chance that Pakistani scientists are helping al Qaeda build or develop a nuclear weapon, we have to treat it as a certainty in terms of our response ... It's not about our analysis or finding a preponderance of evidence ... it's about our response.

(Suskind, Ron, *the One Percent Doctrine*, Sinmon and Schuster, p. 62).

In other words: shoot first!

This paranoia imbues a September 2000 report of the Project for a New American Century, *Rebuilding America's Defenses* (available on line). Considering that in 2000 the US was by far the strongest military power on Earth, the very title of the paper signals its paranoid content. Some of the signatories were Paul Wolfowitz, Donald Kagan, Robert Kagan and Lewis Libby. Some of the points made by the paper are:

- the weaponization of space (with complete American domination)
- building underwater pods of missiles, ready to be fired
- the use of robotized weapons capable of inflicting heavy casualties and destruction without risking American lives
- the maintenance of numerous military bases capable of covering the entire planet
- the necessity to prevent any power, friend or foe, from being in a position to challenge American hegemony
- the ability to wage cyber warfare
- the preparation to wage biological warfare that can target specific groups [races] and "may transform biological warfare from the realm of terror to a politically useful tool" [Note the implication

that when a terrorist strategy is used by a state (US, in this case) it becomes a "politically useful tool."]

Tranquilizers Anyone?

The shadow of the covenant has not faded. Without displacing the Jews, neocons and their followers, like the Plymouth-Rock Pilgrims, see America as the new promised land and themselves as the chosen people. And, of course, they do not hesitate to serve themselves a generous helping of moral dispensation (can anything else justify considering a race-targeting weapon as "politically useful tool"?) Both the Israeli government and the neocons see the worlds through the same tinted lens.

THE ISRAELI LOBBY

The Israeli lobby, the Zionist lobby, the Jewish lobby, the American Jewish lobby, which should be the preferred moniker? Each has a slightly different extension, yet in many cases they are interchangeable. There are many Jewish organizations that are either outright lobbies or that can function as such when needed. The website of the United Jewish Communities lists more than 100 Jewish organizations active in the US. It's raining cats, dogs and Jewish organizations! Some of these may be apolitical, but most frequently make reference to Israel or Zionism. To this list must be added pro-Israel think tanks such as the Jewish Institute for National Security (JINSA) and the Washington Institute for Near East Policy (WINEP). How can two percent of the US population spawn more than a hundred such associations? A scenario may suggest an explanation:

Three good Jewish friends – let's call them Abe, David and Jacob – decide to work together to militate for Zionism. David, the brightest and most energetic of the group suggests that they should form, not one official association, but three; and the others agree. Within minutes three organizations are born: the Watchdog Committee for the Exposure of Anti-Semitism (WCEA) with David as president; the New York Jewish Protective League (NYSOL) presided by Abe; and the National Association for American-Israeli Cooperation (NdoubleAIC) presided by Jacob. All three organizations have the identical membership: David, Abe and Jacob.

Within a week each organization has its business cards and letterheads ready and has sent an application for tax-exempt status. Within a month four letter-to-the-editors have been published and one op-ed article: the words *anti-Semite* and *antisemitism* have been used five times in those writings.

The above is, of course, a mere fiction – and an exaggeration to boot – but it may help to understand the microstructure and some of the dynamics of organized American Jewry. The very abundance of organizations could easily lead to confusion and ineffectiveness, but two umbrella groups have been instrumental in controlling the troops: the Conference of Presidents of Major Jewish Organizations and the American-Israeli Public Affairs Committee, the famous AIPAC. Besides riding herd on other associations, both engage in a lot of lobbying activity, the Conference of Presidents specializing in influencing the executive branch, and AIPAC keeping close tabs on Congress.

AIPAC was founded in 1953, with the original name of the American Zionist Committee for Public Affairs. Renamed AIPAC, it is now active in fifty states and has over 100,000 members. In its website it gives this description of itself:

> As America's leading pro-Israel lobby, AIPAC works with both Democratic and Republican political leaders around the country to ensure that the U.S.-Israel relationship remains strong and vital. With the support of its members nationwide, AIPAC has worked with congress and the Executive Branch on numerous critical initiatives … (www.aipac.org)

The last phrase is worth repeating: "AIPAC has worked with congress and the Executive Branch on numerous critical initiatives." When a lobby works closely with a government in numerous initiatives, that lobby is virtually part of that government, and that government has ceded part of its sovereignty to that lobby. Note that AIPAC described itself as a "pro-Israel lobby", not as a Jewish lobby: it has shown little interest in the situation of American Jews. Conversely, some organizations, such as the Anti-Defamation League (that has done yeoman work defending the civil rights of Jews – and even Gentiles) have morphed into basically pro-Israel lobbies.

AIPAC's website is too modest. The organization's role went much farther, so that in 1987 the *New York Times* could describe it as "a major force in shaping United States policy in the Middle East, adding that:

> … the organization has gained power to influence a presidential candidate's choice of staff, to block practically any arms sale to an Arab country, and to serve as a catalyst for intimate military relations between the Pentagon and the Israeli army. Its officials are consulted by the State Department and White House policy makers, by senators and generals.
> (Skipler, D.K., "On Middle East Policy, a major Influence," *N.Y. Times*, 1987-07/06.)

It may come as a surprise to many that the White House has lobbyists whose job it is to influence Congress:

> The lobbyist knows that a roll call vote on aid to Israel will receive overwhelming support. In fact, administration lobbyists count on the support to carry the day for foreign aid worldwide. Working together the two groups of lobbyists perceive a common interest.
> (Paul Findlay, *They Dare to Speak Out: People and Institutions Confront Israel's Lobby,* Lawrence Hill Books, p. 53.)

In other words: in Findlay's analysis, the executive branch of government and an organization promoting the interest of a foreign government often work together to control the legislative branch of government. [Findlay should be taken seriously, as he was an Illinois congressman for 42 years and was a senior member of the House Middle East Committee.)

In the above *N.Y. Times* citation, Shipler wrote, "the organization [AIPAC] has gained power to influence a presidential candidate's choice of staff." Isn't that taking a rather big bite for a mere lobbyist? In one case the bite did prove to be too big. In 1992 the *Washington Times* received a tape in which the then president of AIPAC, David Steiner, claimed to have been "negotiating" with President Clinton over the appointment of the next secretary of state and national security advisor. At one point he said, "We have a dozen people in [Clinton's] campaign, in the headquarters … And they're all going to get big jobs." (Findley, p. 309). This caused a media *brouhaha* and Steiner resigned as president.

Often it seems that it's the legislators who solicit the services of the lobbyists:

> According to Douglas Bloomfield, a former AIPAC staff member, "It is common for members of Congress and their staffs to turn to AIPAC first when they need information, before calling the Library of Congress, the congressional Research Service, committee staff or administration experts." More importantly, he notes that AIPAC is "often called upon to draft speeches, work on legislation, advise on tactics, perform research, collect co-sponsors and marshal votes."
> (John J. Mearsheimer and Stephen M. Walt, "The Israel Lobby and US Foreign Policy," Kennedy School website, March 2009, originally reported by Camille Manager, *Beyond Alliance: Israel in US foreign Policy,* Columbia, 1994.)

With lobbyists like that, who needs a government?

To insinuate itself into the fabric of American government AIPAC (and its partners) need both a carrot and a stick, in fact, many carrots and many sticks. And it needs the strategy of propaganda in order to set the scene for the tactics of lobbying and political action. And it must aim that propaganda at fellow Jews as much as at Gentiles because it is what ensures that money and votes will be available when needed.

Note that AIPAC does not distribute money directly: under its supervision Political Action Committees (PACs) and other organizations do that. Also, AIPAC does not officially endorse any candidates: it leaves that to other groups under its umbrella.

THE CARROTS

As always, AIPAC did not forget American Jews in distributing the carrots. According to Findlay:

> Tours of Israel, which other Jewish groups arrange, help to establish a grassroots base for AIPAC's, program. For example, in April 1982, the Young Leadership Mission, an activity of United Jewish Appeal, arranged for 1,500 US Jews to take one-week tours. (Findley, p. 37)

But AIPAC's subsidiaries did not limit their dealings with travel agencies to a Jewish clientele. More than half of Congressmen and Senators have visited Israel with the cost shared between the US government (official business) and Jewish organizations and individuals. "AIPAC, as usual, didn't neglect high-level congressional staffers. Findley claims that AIPAC works with Israeli universities, who arrange expense-paid tours for staff members who occupy key positions." (p. 37)

> AIPAC spends as much energy in making sure that politicians *do not* visit Arab countries: only the Zionist story must be told! In 1983, when the National Association of Arab Americans invited all congressmen to a free trip to the Near East, AIPAC used its *Near East Report* to attack the project. Only three legislators went. In 1984, a similar offer was cancelled for lack of takers.
> (Findley, p. 37-38)

Money! Who doesn't like cash as a birthday or Christmas present? But AIPAC doesn't contribute cash to anyone. Rather, it suggests amounts to its various umbrella partners (especially PACs – Political Action Committees) and to rich Jews, and its suggestions are taken seriously. On the average, American Jews have a higher income than other ethnic groups, have higher turn-out rates in elections, and are more likely to follow the suggestions of their religious and political leaders. Also, they are concentrated in important states such as New York, Pennsylvania, Illinois, Florida and California. According to Mearsheimar and Walt, "The *Washington Post* once estimated that Democratic presidential candidates depend on Jewish supporters to supply as much as 60% of the money." (Mearsheimar and Walt, p. 18)

Note that this is not vulgar bribe money passed under the table to corrupt politicians or bureaucrats. When that happens, it's an exception. Generally, we are talking about money legally given to parties or individuals for election campaigns. Election money is the oil that lubricates and fuels the flawed political system we are currently vegetating under, *democratic lobbyism* (my term). AIPAC didn't invent it, but it brought it to a pinnacle of perfection, and became its teacher-by-example.

The expectation, of course, is that money will translate into votes. But the Lobby, through its many organizations, can also deliver votes by means other than financial, although these are more effective within the Jewish community. Telephone blitzes, rabbinical pronouncements, door-to-door solicitations and good old word-of-mouth are very effective despite the fact that Jews only represent about 2.5% of the population, because, as covered above, their numbers are concentrated in key states. In close races, 2.5% can make the difference.

Prestige is another carrot handed out by the lobby, but here the recipients are mostly Jews. The attainment of high office in any Jewish organization or think tank bestows honor, prestige and respect. There is never a lack of candidates.

THE STICKS

Votes that are a carrot for your opponent are a stick to you, but there are other sticks, some mean and personal.

First, there is the stick of political stalking: every member of congress and of the administration has a "guardian angel" who follows his every move, word and vote; who has been appraised of all the dirty laundry in his past; and who often has a make-or-break power over his political career. Can anyone accuse our politician of paranoia if he feels like a microbe under the lens of a microscope? And can anyone be surprised if his vote on issues pertinent to Israel is skewed by his paranoia? Even if every action in that scenario is legal – and it usually is – cannot an accusative forefinger be waved at the whole exercise? And who bears the preponderance of the guilt: the cagey lobbyist or the weak and morally corrupt politician?

The mean and relentless quality of the Lobby's political stalking is well-rendered in Findley's third chapter, "Stilling the Still, Small Voices." One of the examples he gives is the stalking of Republican Representative Paul McCloskey.

The congressman had returned from a 1979 trip to the Middle East convinced that the construction of illegal West Bank settlements and Israel's illegal use of US weapons were wrong and not in America's interest. He proposed that the 3 billion annual aid to Israel be reduced by 150 million, the sum Israel was spending on the settlements. He also said that AIPAC and other lobbies under its wings wielded too much power and that this was bad for peace in the Middle East.

In 1982 McCloskey sought the Republican nomination for a senatorial seat. He was viciously attacked in the Jewish press. The *B'nai B'rith Messenger* even printed lies that were later retracted. Other Jewish publications vilified him. His opponents all received Jewish financial support. He did not win the nomination.

He returned to private life, intending to rejoin a law firm he had helped establish years before. But the firm's biggest client threatened to take its business elsewhere. McCloskey withdrew his request to join the firm. He accepted a partnership with another firm, but again the firm was threatened because it had accepted a "known anti-Semite" as partner. However the firm did not yield.

But the Lobby doesn't quit easily. In Findley's words:

> A tracking system initiated by the Anti-Defamation League of B'nai B'Brith (ADL) assured that McCloskey would have no peace, even as a private citizen. The group distributed a memorandum containing details of his actions and speeches to its chapters around the country. According to the memo, it was designed to "assist" local ADL groups with "counteraction guidance" whenever McCloskey appeared in public.
> (Findley, p. 59)

McCloskey accepted an invitation by the student governing council of Stanford University to teach a course on Congress. The stalking continued: the baton was passed from the ADL to the Hillel Center, the Jewish students' club at Stanford. The invitation was characterized as "a slap in the face of the Jewish community," a Jewish student leader demanded the right to choose the guest lecturers (which was refused); the preparation of class material was delayed; guest lecturers were not paid on time; and McCloskey's own stipend was reduced from the agreed-upon $3,500 to $2,000. McCloskey eventually received an apology but before closing the whole matter, he claimed in an interview in the *Peninsula Times Tribune*, that AIPAC "has instructed college students all over the country to take [similar] actions." (Findley, p. 60)

McCloskey, however had the last word. In 1993, the district attorney of San Francisco released details of a vast spying conspiracy by the ADL against US citizens who were opposed to Israel's treatment of Palestinians and to the policy of apartheid of South Africa. The ADL was also accused of passing information to both countries. After much political pressure the charges were dropped but the victims filed a lawsuit and hired McCloskey as their attorney.

In Findley's own words:

> McCloskey and his clients, two of whom were Jews who had been subjected to spying after criticizing Israeli policy in the occupied territories, revealed an extensive operation

> headed by ADL undercover operative Roy Bullock, whose files contained the names of 10,000 individuals and 60 organizations, including thousands of Arab Americans and national civil rights groups such as the NAACP. Much of Bullock's information was gained illegally from confidential police records. In April 2002, after a nine-year legal battle, McCloskey won a landmark $150,000 court judgement.
> (Findley, p. 60-61).

Ah! Revenge is so sweet.

AIPAC and its cohorts do not hesitate to practice character assassination and career assassination. Again we will rely on Findley to furnish an exemplar of such an exercise, the political assassination of Adlai Stevenson III.

During two terms as Senator, Stevenson had built solid credentials with Jews and Jewish organizations, even though he didn't always follow the Lobby line one hundred percent. In 1980 he took a year-long vacation from politics and then announced that he would run for governor of Illinois in 1982. A segment of the Jewish Community decided they didn't like him. They obtained a document from AIPAC itemizing all the negative half-truths about the man (from a Zionist angle) and accused him of being anti-Semitic, anti-Israel, pro-Arab and very critical of US policy and aid. None of his many pro-Israel words and deeds were mentioned, nor the commendations and awards he had received from Jews.

What particularly galled Zionists was Stevenson's strong objection to the illegal settlements in the occupied territories and his sponsorship of an amendment to withhold aid to Israel by $150 million (out of 3,000 million) until the settlement program was ended.

> So, one of the staunchest defenders of civil right (in the tradition of his famous father) was subjected to charges of anti-Semitism; the "coalition for the re-election of Jim Thomson" (the Republican incumbent) was organized; and a telephone and leaflet-distributing campaign was set up in Jewish neighborhoods and synagogues. In the end Stevenson lost the election by a close margin and that marked the end of his political career. (Findley, p. 82-9).

A postal blitz is another effective stick, usually directed at the administration or at members of congress. For example, in 1975 President Gerald Ford, finding Israel's behavior towards Palestinians and other Middle East neighbors objectionable, threatened to reassess the role of the US in the Middle East. Israel didn't bother to respond to the White House. Instead it went to the senate through AIPAC. Three-fourths of the senators signed a letter backing Israel's position:

The letter was a demonstration of impressive clout. Created and circulated by AIPAC it had been endorsed, overnight, by a majority of the Senate membership. Several senators who at first had said no quickly changed their position. Senator John Calver admitted candidly, "The pressure was too great. I caved." So did President Ford. He backed down and never again challenged the lobby. (Findley, p. 101).

And neither has anyone else! Note that when Senator Culver said, I caved," he was virtually admitting that he did something that was against his better judgement, or even his conscience, because he feared the consequences on his career of resisting the political stalking of the Lobby.

Multiply this moral scenario a thousand fold and you get an idea of the power of the lobby and of its distortion of democracy. But who are more to blame, the relentless lobbyists or the gutless and venal politicians?

When letters are not enough, AIPAC and its cohorts resort to demonstrations. They can quickly muster an almost unbelievable number of militants. According to Findley, when, in 1981, President George H.W. Bush refused to immediately approve a $10 billion loan guarantee because its purpose was to build illegal settlements in the occupied territories, "almost one thousand pro-Israel lobbyists swamped Capitol Hill." In Bush's own words:

> I heard today there were something like a thousand lobbyists on the Hill working the other side of the question. We've got only one little guy [Bush himself] doing it. ("Bush vs. Sharon: the Sequel," www.antiwar.com, April 9, 2002, via Findley, p. 145)

At first, Congress backed Bush and he held fast in spite of being called an anti-Semite. But the pressure never abated and, in 1982, Bush approved the loan guarantee, although the settlement program had never slowed.

We have already broached the topic of the Lobby's surveillance of academia in the story of ex-congressman Paul McCloskey's misadventures at

Stanford University. AIPAC, *et al*, find it more difficult to hound academics than any other group because "independent research" is sacrosanct in most universities, and many professors have tenure, which makes them almost immune to dismissal. As in the Stanford case, the job is often assigned to Hillel clubs or other on-campus Jewish organizations. Many philanthropists who give to universities are Jewish, and that represents another avenue for AIPAC to apply pressure.

The Lobby has an easier time with the press since the Jewish presence is very strong in the media. Many newspapers such as the *New York Times* are Jewish owned. Others are owned by companies with Jewish CEOs or high officials. In *The Israeli Lobby and US Foreign Policy*, Meirsheimer and Welt claim that most American newspaper commentators are pro-Israel, signaling out the *Wall Street Journal*, the *Chicago Sun-Times*, the *Washington Times,* and even the *New York Times* (although the latter is somewhat less biased). Noam Chomsky has made the point that Israeli reporters and commentators enjoy much greater freedom of the press than their American counterparts. Newspapers such as *Ha'Haretz, Yediot Aranov,* the *Jewish Post, Hadashot* do not hesitate to be critical of Israeli politicians, military leaders and policies, whereas American newspapers are so terrified of possibly being called anti-Semitic that they exercise auto censorship: any item that may cast a negative image of Israel is either unprinted or buried in an inconspicuous corner of, say, page 12.

Some periodicals have an open Zionist and pro-Israel policy – which, of course, is their right. The extent to which some of them can approach outright extremism, fanaticism and military adventurism can be judged by this excerpt from *Commentary*:

> The regimes that rightly deserve to be overthrown and replaced are not confined to the three singled-out members of the axis of evil [Iraq, Iran and North Korea]. At a minimum, the axis should extend to Syria, Lebanon, and Libya, as well as "friends of America" like the Saudi royal family and Egypt's Hasni Mubarak, along with the Palestinian Authority whether headed by Arafat or one of his henchmen.
> (Norman Podhoretz, "In praise of the Bush Doctrine," *Commentary*, September 2002).

Of course, the paying, fighting and dying would be borne by the US, the super vassal state. If Podhoretz wrote this under the influence of a psychoactive substance, it's a problem. If not, it's an even bigger problem.

Sometimes an unruly publication prints something that rankles the Lobby, which then swings into action:

To discourage unfavorable reporting on Israel, the Lobby organizes letter-writing campaigns, demonstrations and boycotts against news outlets whose content it considers anti-Israel. One CNN executive has said that he sometimes gets 6,000 e-mail messages in a single day complaining that a story is anti-Israel. (Felicity Barringer, "Some U.S. Backers of Israel Boycott Dailies over Mideast Coverage that They Deplore," *NY Times*, May 23, 2002, via Mearsheimer and Walt, p. 21.)

Scary stuff for a media executive: letter-writing and e-mail-sending campaigns, boycotts, demonstrations. But these tactics depend on the strategic use of the Zionists' weapon of mass intimidation: one word, "anti-Semite," and its variants, "anti-Semitic" and "anti-Semitism." There's a lot of history behind that word, and one recent horrendous experience. It brings back not only historical memories, but also the guilt that not enough was done to save the Jews. The world's democracies, and especially the US, were left with a bad case of *logophobia*, the pathological fear of a word, and the neocons and lobbyists have jumped on the weakness. But they have used the weapon abusively and indiscriminately, using it to demonize anyone who disagrees with them and anyone who refuses to discriminate against whoever they consider an enemy.

Of course neocons in the media – most notably David Frum, Max Boot, Lawrence F. Kaplan, Jonah Goldberg, and Alan Wald – have been busy labeling their opponents "anti-Semites." (Kevin McDonald, *Understanding Jewish Influence: A study in Ethnic Activism*, Washington Summit Publishing, p. 74)

To call someone an anti-Semite just because he disagrees with you is to place that person in the same category as people who enslaved Jews, then marched them into killing rooms and finally murdered them with poison gas – a blatant category mistake and an egregious case of word abuse!

THE CHRISTIAN RIGHT

President Carter described himself as a *born-again Christian*, but he was not part of the Christian Right. In my extended family I know a husband-and-wife couple who are committed and fundamentalist (or almost) Christians. They are as humanist as they are Christian; they are unprejudiced and as open-minded as their faith will permit; they respect everyone: they are not part of the Christian Right. In South America, many Evangelical Christian congregations are openly left-wing: obviously, they are not part of the Christian Right.

Who is? – In the American context, the religious right is composed of people who combine a fundamentalist (Evangelical) approach to religion and a neoconservative approach to politics, and consider the fusion as righteous in the eyes of God.

There is no need for a discursive exposition of the Christian Right's doctrine. The Bible has all the answers and faith in Jesus is as good as papal infallibility. The Evangelicals have interpreted some esoteric apocalyptic scripture and some prophetic verses to come to the conclusion that Jews must first return to Palestine before the Second Coming of Christ can be expected. Of course, any act by anyone that promotes this great return is part of God's plan, and benefits from moral dispensation.

The emergence of the Christian Right was a piece of good luck for the Zionists. Little effort was needed to haul in the Evangelicals as useful allies and generous contributors.

> As Middle East tensions rose, after the failure of the Camp David initiative, Ralph Reed joined together with Rabbi Yechiel Eckstein to found the Stand for Israel, designed to mobilize political support among the grassroots Christian community for the state of Israel and later the war on terror. The group was created out of the International Fellowship of Christians and Jews (IFCF), which has been a central forum for promoting the relationship between evangelical Christians and American Jews since 1983. (Halper and Clarke, *America Alone*, p. 199)

Sometimes, Jewish organizations make a point of having some prominent Evangelicals in their membership:

> The [Jewish] Lobby also includes prominent Christian evangelicals like Gary Bauer, Jerry Falwell, Ralph Reed, and Pat Roberston, as well as Dick Armey and Tom DeLay, former majority leaders in the House of Representatives. They believe Israel's rebirth is a part of Biblical prophecy, support its expansionist agenda, and think pressing

> Israel is contrary to God's will. In addition, the Lobby's membership includes neoconservative gentiles ... (Mearsheimer and Walt, p. 1)

THE DEFORMATION OF REFORM

The Enlightenment was a movement that strove to break the stifling hold of the establishment in matters religious and political – especially the former. It secured a place for the human element and for human values alongside theological and doctrinal considerations. It was centered in France, but also very influential in England and Germany. It started in the 1600s and is usually considered to have ended in the late 1700s, but the latter is a misleading date. It did not significantly alter European and American society until the 19th century. In a way, it is still with us, as the antithesis of the religious right and of authoritarian politics. Some of its early intellectual leaders were Hume, Descartes, Kant, Voltaire, Rousseau and most of the scientific community.

A parallel movement emerged later in the Jewish world, the Haskalah, also known as the Jewish Enlightenment. Its beginning and ending dates are usually given as the 1770s to the 1980s, but like the European enlightenment its influence continued to the present. The Haskalah had a definite Jewish character. It promoted the learning and use of the Hebrew language and spawned a Jewish press; it encouraged the entry of Jews into previously forbidden occupations and activities; it participated in the religious evolution of the Talmudists; it had a profound influence on Zionism and Reform Judaism. By the 1880s, the pogroms in Eastern Europe and Russia, as well as the lack of acceptance generally, convinced most Jews that their enlightenment was in vain and the Haskalah petered out as a more-or-less organized movement.

The spirit of Haskalah crossed the Atlantic with a group of German rabbis who emigrated to the US. In November 1869 thirteen of them met in Philadelphia and deliberated – in German – for four days before adopting seven basic principles. The two most important ones stressed the universality of Reform Judaism (the name by which American Haskalah is known), just by stating that the messianic goal of Israel – the mystical body of all Jews – was the union of all humanity, and then by asserting that chosenness, though not repudiated, must not stand in the way of the universal aim of the movement, but must affirm the "equal love of God for all his children." (Michael A. Mayer, *Response to Modernity: A History of the Reform Movement in Judaism*, Oxford, p. 256.)

In November 1885, a group of 19 Reform rabbis met in Pittsburgh and forged the Pittsburg Platform that formally established the basic principles of American Reform Judaism. Some of these were immediately attacked by some rabbis or some groups, yet the platform remained the guide of the Reform movement for half a century, earning the title of *Classical Reform.* (Over the years four Platforms have been issued by the movement. The first three are included as an Appendix to Mayer's *Response to Modernity* and all four can be Googled under *Platforms of Reform Judaism.*)

As with the Philadelphia statement of principles, the overriding idea in Pittsburgh was universalism:

> We recognize in every religion an attempt to grasp the Infinite and in every mode, source or book of Revelations, held sacred in any religious system , the consciousness of the indwelling of God in man. We acknowledge that the spirit of broad humanity in our age is our ally in the fulfillment of our mission, and, therefore, we extend the hand of fellowship to all who cooperate with us in the establishment of the reign of truth and righteousness among men.

The Platform grants recognition to, and shows respect for the Mosaic and Talmudic laws, but refuses to grant them absolute authority for all times and all places. It dismisses those that regulate diet, priestly purity and dress, and insists that all laws must make sense and be relevant in changing times.

Regarding Zionism, the platform is quite explicit:

> We recognize in the modern era of universal culture of heart and intellect the approaching of the realization of Israel's great Messianic hope for the establishment of the kingdom of truth, justice and peace among all men. We consider ourselves no longer a nation, but a religious community, and, therefore expect neither a return to Palestine nor a sacrificial worship under the sons of Aaron, nor the restoration of any of the laws concerning the Jewish state.

In the final article the Platform asserts that it is reform's duty "to participate in the great task of modern times, to solve, on the basis of justice and righteousness, the problem presented by contrasts and evils of the present organization of society."

The Pittsburgh Platform is an eloquent synopsis of the principles of humanism and of the Jewish Enlightenment. Unfortunately, it represents the acme of Classical Reform Judaism: like a tire with a slow leak it has been losing air ever since.

In 1937, the Central Conference of American Rabbis (CCAR), the leading Reform institution, held a gathering in Columbus and issued another declaration of principles. In part, it reiterated the content of the Pittsburgh Platform, but there was one major point of disagreement. The ideologues and propagandists of ideological Zionism had, it seems, established a beach-head in Reform: whereas the Pittsburgh Platform had refused to militate for a return to Palestine, the Columbus Platform adopted a strong Zionist position:

> In the rehabilitation to Palestine, the land hallowed by memories and hopes, we behold the promise of renewed life for many of our brethren. We affirm the obligation of all Jewry to aid in its upbuilding as a Jewish homeland by endeavoring to make it not only a haven of refuge for the oppressed but also a center of Jewish culture and spiritual life.

The words, "We affirm the obligation of all Jewry to aid in its upbuilding as a Jewish homeland" establishes as a moral imperative for all Jews the support of, and the cooperation with the Zionist enterprise.

Note that there's no hint of recourse to violence here. The Platform espouses pacifism:

> Judaism from the days of the prophet has proclaimed to mankind the ideal of universal peace. The spiritual and physical disarmament of all nations has been one of its essential teachings. It abhors all violence and relies upon moral education, love and sympathy to secure human progress. It regards justice as the foundation of the well-being of nations and the condition of enduring peace. It urges organized international action for disarmament, collective

> security and world peace. [Do the authors have in mind such institutions as the League of Nations and, later, the UN when mentioning "organized international action"?]

[Personal note: I can't resist a little sarcasm here, but where did the authors acquire their knowledge of the "days of the prophets"? (Review Chapters 1 and 2). And if those sentences are intended as a prophecy of the ethics and actions of the future state of Israel, the writers should have their prophet's licenses revoked!]

In 1976, the CCAR, which by then had become the brain and the voice of Reform, used the centenaries of the Union of American Hebrew Congregations (UAHC) and the Hebrew Union College (HUC) to issue another state-of-the-movement message, the San Francisco Platform.

The overall tenor of the document is conservative and Zionist. It is more God-conscious than the previous platforms and more concerned with religious practice such as:

> ... creating a Jewish home centered on family devotion, life-long study; private prayer and public worship; daily religious observance; keeping the Sabbath and the holy days; celebrating the major events of life; involvement with the synagogue and community; and other activities ...

The term *chosen people* is not used but the specialness of Isreal-the-people's relation to God is strongly implied by such phrases as "the people of Isreal is unique because of its involvement with God." The universalism of the Reform movement is reaffirmed, but now it is stressed that Judaism is both the (chosen?) model and guide for the redemption of humanity, and is charged with "working toward the fulfillment of its messianic expectations." (Note how the messiah is not a person or a heavenly envoy, but Israel itself – another instance of entangling words and categories.)

But it is in regard to the state of Israel that the San Francisco Platform most directly clashed with Classical Reform. Whereas the Philadelphia statement of principles and the Pittsburgh Platform had avoided any hint of militancy for a future state of Israel, the San Francisco conference practically made it a religious duty for all Jews to actively contribute to the furtherance of the Zionist enterprise.

Of course, the Columbia Platform had been almost equally enthusiastic about the project, but that was in 1937, eleven years before the birth of the

State of Israel: all dreams and aspirations were possible. But the San Francisco meeting was held in 1976, twenty-eight years after the establishment of Isreal – twenty-eight years of massacres, ethnic cleansing, land theft, nullification of UN resolutions. The rabbis had to know! Anyone who bothered to look listen and read with an open mind knew; all the more must clerics in touch with the ruling elite of Judaism and Isreal have known!

The Reform Rabbis had fallen under the spell of the Palestine-or-bust gang and their successors. The inheritors of a noble blend of Judaism and Humanism had lost their moral fiber and muffled their critical faculties. They, who should have been the first to hold the feet of Israel to the fire had caved in and dropped the ball. Not only had they failed to resist the hijacking of Judaism: they had actively participated in the exercise. Reform had become a mere refuge for Jews too lazy to deal with the strictures of the Torah and the Talmud.

In 1997 the CCAR issued yet another platform, the Miami Platform, dealing exclusively with the relationship between Reform and Zionism. It contains little that was not already covered in the Columbus and San Francisco documents. It leaves no doubt that the CCAR is firmly in the camp of the ideological Zionists, pledging that Reform Judaism will "help promote the security of *Medinat Yisrael* [the country of Israel] and ensure the welfare of its citizens"; promising "continued political support and financial assistance," and resolving to "implement educational programs and religious practices that reflect and reinforce the bond between Reform Judaism and Zionism." It also recommends to its adherents frequent trips to Israel and encourages emigration to that country. Ben Gurion himself could not have written a more pro-Zionist program (or a more anti-Classical Reform one).

Of course, universalism, the hallmark quality of Reform receives the required salute. The existence of Isreal is deemed "a necessary condition for the physical and spiritual redemption of the Jewish people and of all humanity," and for "the fulfillment of our messianic dream of universal peace under the sovereignty of God." Unfortunately, this is feel-good stuff only, without any substance, since the Platform makes no reference to any of Israel's many violations of the principle of universalism. How can a Jewish organization preach universalism and the redemption of the whole human race, and not hold Israel's feet to the fire?

In March 2007 the CCAR was slated to visit the Carter Center during its 2007 convention in Atlanta. But in 2006 Jimmy Carter's latest book, *Palestine: Peace not Apartheid* was published and the CCAR was not amused. It issued a statement cancelling the visit and attacking the book. (www.ccarnet.org, or search: carter center)

The rabbis claimed that "it contains numerous distortions of history and interpretation, and apparently outright fabrications as well," but it doesn't single out any inaccuracy nor offer any evidence. Besides, what does "and apparently, outright fabrication" mean, if not that the writers don't know if the "fabrications" are really fabrications. Now, Jimmy Carter's book is not a scholarly treatise: it is, at least partly, a memoir of the author's intimate and extensive relations with all parties in the Middle East conflict, as President of the US, as sponsor and participant in the Camp David meetings, and later, as a private citizen and head of the Carter Center. This, together with his Nobel Prize and his well-deserved reputation for integrity and humanism, should suffice to ensure careful and respectful reading.

While the book has almost no citations and no footnotes or endnotes, it does have nine maps clearly showing territories, settlement locations, and the Israeli-only roads that divide the West Bank into unconnected "Bantustans." It also has seven appendices quoting part or all of UN resolutions 242, 338, 465; the Camp David Accord; the Framework for the Egypt-Isreal Peace Treaty; the 2002 Arab Peace Proposal; and Israel's 2003 response to the Roadmap.

The Rabbis particularly objected to the use of the word *Apartheid*, especially in the title, claiming that it demonizes Israel – this from people who call anyone who disagrees with them an anti-Semite. Case in point: in the same paragraph we read that "These [Carter's] statements are not only false; they make public use of classic anti-Semitic themes … ."

The fact is that each settlement in the West Bank is surrounded by a buffer and connected to other settlements by roads that Arabs are forbidden to use, thus making it very difficult for them to travel in their own land. Isn't this a form of Apartheid? Note that Israel has never voted to support any UN resolution condemning Apartheid in South Africa and has cooperated in nuclear weapon-research with the latter. (Review Chapter 20)

The Rabbis' letter confirms it:

- The Central Committee of American Rabbis speaks for Reform and calls the shots.
- The hijackers of Judaism have driven Classical Reforms out of the picture.

- Because of their demographic edge (more rabbis, synagogues and adherents) Reform is now the dominant Zionist element of observant Jews.

One characteristic of Ideological Zionism is made manifest by the document:

The idea of an honest broker or of a level playing field is anathema. Anyone who refuses to adopt a racist attitude toward Palestinians (and other Muslims) stands in danger of being called an anti-Semite. In Chapter 17, I quoted Ben Gurion who believed that a Zionist should "adhere without any moral, ideological or political qualifications to the demands of the Jewish Revolution."

Zionist organizations have a similar expectation from "good Gentiles" who should be ready to put aside the principles of their religion, culture or personal conscience wherever and whenever Zionists deem them a hindrance to the ambitions and doings of Israel.

TO BE FAIR

Not all Reform Jews are Zionists. The American Council for Judaism (ACJ) keeps the flame alive for Classical Reform and the principles of the Pittsburgh Platform. However, anti-Zionist Reform is now a marginalized dissident minority and the ACJ controls no more than a half-dozen or so synagogues.

In 1945, the ACJ proposed a plan for a unified country called Palestine that would be neither Moslem, Christian nor Jewish; that, in partnership with international commissions, would control migration; and that, also with international guidance, would institute home rule. The problem of Jewish displaced persons in Europe would also be solved cooperatively, with the DPs choosing the destination of their choice from a number of practical possibilities, including, but not limited to, Palestine. (This noble document is included in Appendix IV, and can be found on line at www.zionism-Isreal.com/hdoc/ACJ_plan_for_palestine_1945.htm).

Such a proposal would have no chance of implementation today. There is too much bad blood; there are too many "facts on the ground," such as settlements and Israeli-only roads. But in 1945 this plan was in the realm of the possible. It was, in the words of Robert Frost, "the path not taken," and we know where the path that *was* taken has led us.

Chapter XXIII – Epilogue

The Hebrews of the Old Testament worshipped a cruel and vindictive god: anyone could do anything to anyone, Hebrew or Gentile, as long as he could claim that he was doing it for Yahweh, especially if he asserted that he was merely obeying Yahweh's command. Without completely revoking the metaphysical racism that still persists in the religion, the rabbis of the Talmud considerably humanized the Torah and acknowledged the validity of secular authority.

But Rabbinic Judaism nonetheless remained an inbred, particular entity within humanity, and that was due partly to Gentile persecution and partly to Jewish ethnocentricity. It was the Haskalah (Jewish Enlightenment) that brought a universalistic scope to Judaism: respect for all honorable members of the human family, for their beliefs, and for their rights; and the acceptance of the obligation to participate in the unending task of improving the human condition for everyone.

In America, where close to 50% of Jews live, the spirit of Haskalah dwelt within the Reform movement as expounded in the Pittsburgh Platform of 1885. But the rabbis dropped the ball! The succession of platforms from 1885 to 1997 delineates the progressive surrender of Reform to the atavistic program of the Palestinian-or-bust gang and their successors. Certainly, lyrical phrases were spouted about the salvation of the whole human race, about Israel being a light to the world, about protecting the weak of the world (Ben Gurion, had already invented and used many of those nice formulas) but what the Reform rabbis and leaders (the AJC excepted) did and what real positions they took belied their rhetoric and pointed in the opposite direction: It was back to chosenness and moral dispensation – with or without Yahweh.

Considering that, in the US, Reform has more adherents than the other branches of Judaism, one can hardly overestimate the political importance of this shift in position. As I have written in Chapter XVII, before the Zionist propagandists and lobbyists could influence Gentiles they had to corral the majority of their coreligionists. This they achieved with great success in the case of American Reform. Now, without the backing of Reform, AIPAC could have little impact and neoconservatives would be a much weaker force. The US government's policy toward Israel would probably be much less supportive. Without America's unquestioned support for Israel, the Middle East would not exist in its present state, and Palestinians might have their own country.

The Rabbis' defection from classical reform has had far-reaching and negative consequences in both the domestic and international situations. One of these is the virtual disappearance of the Jewish left, which deprived the left wing of American politics of perhaps its most vital element. The irony is that many of the defecting Jews have not changed their basic outlook on civil society, but feel that as Jews they have a duty to follow the rabbis and support Israel with their votes and their money.

The ethical and political profile of AIPAC and its subsidiary brood is quite different from that of the Reform rabbinate, in spite of the close relation between them. The latter, together with influential lay leaders, work on American Jewry, while the former deal with the legislative and executive branches of government. As I have written in the previous chapter, AIPAC has been implicated in a number of questionable affairs that call for ethical and political examination:

1. **Spying allegations**: The courts have already determined that spying by Jewish-American citizens for the benefit of Israel has occurred. What is not so definitely ascertained is whether AIPAC was the go-between in passing the information and documents. On the basis of solid evidence there's a strong probability that this is the case, and that therefore AIPAC should be made to register as an agent of a foreign country. AIPAC's own definition of itself on its own web site should be enough to require this, which brings up the question of divided loyalty.
   Now, the US is a democracy and, as such, cannot demand exclusive loyalty. One is free to value loyalty to family above loyalty to country, or loyalty to one's religion above loyalty to country. But the State of Isreal is a country, not a religion. Even a liberal democracy can demand that its citizens pledge undivided loyalty to it, over loyalty to any other

state (which does not preclude having a soft spot for your country of origin or for the country of your ancestors). Israel is a foreign country: therefore spying for Israel against the US is treason!

2. **Stalking congressmen and senators**: With the probable exception of the spying allegations, AIPAC stays within the bounds of legality: there are no laws to prevent one from noting and making public the words, votes and deeds of legislators (as long as one stays clear of such things as illegal wiretapping). Likewise, there are no laws (depending on the methods used) against investigating the background of a public official for the purpose of building a dossier that might be used, should the occasion arise, to threaten and to control said official in the performance of his official duties. It's not illegal, but it's not right. AIPAC, in stalking congress 24/7 is behaving in an unethical and un-American way.
3. **Besmirching the good name and subverting the integrity of individuals**: AIPAC is ruthless and heartless in killing the reputations and the careers of those whom it considers to be a hindrance to the ambitions of Israel. Both the stalking and the personal attacks are reminiscent of the tactics of Senators Joe McCarthy and of the House Un-American Activities Committee (separate entities, but traveling along parallel paths in the 50s and confusedly melded in public consciousness under the rubric of McCarthyism). Whereas McCarthyism abused the word "communist" to demonize individuals and institutions, AIPAC (and its ducklings) use "anti-Semite" for the same purpose. Whereas McCarthyism focused on individuals in show business, AIPAC specializes in politicians, high-level bureaucrats and media honchos. Whereas McCarthyism tormented many and ended many careers, AIPAC morally terrorizes many – and also ends many careers. McCarthyism ended when the American people realized that the movement was anti-democratic, anti-American and mean-spirited. Perhaps AIPAC, and the negative elements of the Jewish Lobby, will start to fade away when Americans, including Jewish Americans, come to realize that those organizations are likewise anti-democratic, anti-American and mean-spirited.
4. **Infiltrating government**: In the previous chapter we have seen how AIPAC has infiltrated government like a virus slipping into a computer. But the computer is not complicit in its own vitiation, whereas the US government practically invites, and cooperates with the intrusion of the Lobby. When a senator solicits the help of AIPAC in formulating

> a proposal helpful to Israel, he is opening a door that should not be opened. When a congressman allows AIPAC to check out a speech before he delivers it, he is allowing an intrusion into the sanctum of the legislative body. When the White House accepts the assistance of AIPAC in lobbying congress for the passing of desired legislation, it is giving AIPAC's hand a spot on the steering wheel of government. To the extent that such moves are harmful to US interests (and to those of the planet) the preponderance of the moral onus rests squarely on the shoulders of American politicians and bureaucrats. Without the wink-wink-nod-nod attitude of the US government the harmful aspect of the Lobby's activities would be very much diminished.

The most distressing aspect of this situation is the loss of sovereignty suffered by the United States of America. When the top leader of the executive branch tolerates being pressured in the selection of department heads and high-level staffers, he is handing a chunk of American sovereignty on a silver platter to the Lobby and to a foreign country. When Andrew Young was forced to resign as UN ambassador for having met with a PLO official, another self-inflicted blow was struck against American sovereignty. (The US had promised Israel that it would not communicate with the PLO, and it was the Israeli spy agency, the Mossad, that reported the incident.) Does Israel seek US permission before talking to its neighbors? It's time the US remind Israel that, "Me dog, you tail." It's, time that the American people – Gentile and Jewish – realize the similarity between the tactics of AIPAC and those typical of McCarthyism. It's time that US politicians stop handing over chunks of American sovereignty to a small group of individuals who have appointed themselves leaders of 2.5% of the country's population.

A real change in attitude on the part of both American leadership and the populace (Gentile and Jewish) is crucial. Israel will do nothing to bring justice to the Palestinians. It has demonstrated no respect for the value of human life (except Jewish life); it has shown utter contempt for the United Nations (that is, for the rest of humanity); it has demonstrated a complete lack of good will in the Camp David and Oslo deliberations. European powers have limited interest and no leverage in the Middle East. Russia and China are not ready to incur risk – financial and other – to defend ethical principles in foreign lands.

The ball falls, by the force of political gravity, squarely in the hands of America – which happens to be the lone superpower. That would be true even if the US were not joined at the hip with the State of Israel and with the wider Zionist movement. But it is! And the ramifications of this fact are world-wide. The etiology of most contemporary global problems leads directly back to Israel-Palestine, and, more specifically, the foundation of Israel; to the recognition of that state by most powers; and to the consequent ethnic cleansing. Without this historical sequence there would have been no 9/11 and no "clash of civilizations." (This, of course does not shift all the blame from the Muslims to the Jews and Christians. As the biblical Moses said, "each one bears his guilt.")This line of thinking deserves more attention. History has shown that persecution often strengthens rather than vitiates religion: Roman persecution led to the establishment of Christianity as the state religion of Rome; institutional anti-Semitism, pogroms and the Holocaust all failed to destroy Judaism. When a religious or ideological group is persecuted, its adherents usually gird their loins, strengthen their resolve and, one way or another, fight back. This usually empowers the more fundamentalist and aggressive elements. In my opinion, one of the more unfortunate consequences of the oppression of the Palestinians is that it has prevented a struggle to take place what should – that must – take place between the frozen-in-time Muslim fundamentalists and the more liberal and humanistic elements in Islam – and it did that by giving a shot of steroids to the former.

It is amazing that such a tiny portion of the Earth's surface, inhabited by such a tiny portion of humanity should weigh so heavily on the planet and its peoples. The Israel-Palestine imbroglio is like a small cancer that has metastasized and is sending toxic particles throughout the body. At least part of the explanation has become obvious: the most powerful country has become the great enabler of one of the parties involved. One would think that the powerful country would control the tiny country and use it for its own purposes, but the opposite is closer to the truth.

It's all about the use of power. For many years the US has misapplied its great power and has consequently lost much of the respect and good will it once held. Yet, if the Palestinians are to find justice and if the "clash of civilizations" is to be avoided, the US must engage in another exercise of power.

But first it must reclaim that portion of its sovereignty it has yielded to the Israeli/Zionist lobby. Since the principal tool used by the Lobby is contributions to political campaigns, this can easily be nullified by giving our elected representatives the benefit of an instrument that ordinary citizens have and that is essential to real democracy: the secret ballot. Roll call voting should be abolished! Thus, political stalking, as currently employed by AIPAC and its brood, would loose much of its political terrorism and effectiveness.

[This would also free democracies from the corrosive effects of other big lobbies, such as the oil lobby, the armament lobby, and various chief executive lobbies. Everyone and every group has the right to advocate its position and should have access to the wheels of power. What no one should have is the right to subvert democracy with money, perks, or threats.]

Another possibility would be to nationalize the election business, by having the federal government fund the elections – a complicated exercise, the details of which are beyond the scope of this book.

A giant step would be for some political and media honchos to fight back against logophobia: no one who is terrified of ever being called an anti-Semite can be an honest broker, analyst or reporter regarding Zionists, Jews, Arabs, the Middle East, etc.

Another simple and amply justified move would be to have AIPAC register as an agent of a foreign country. In its own description of itself it claims to be "America's leading pro-Israel lobby." That, together with the spying allegations referred to in Chapter XXI, should be more than enough to justify that measure. The US doesn't need recourse to its military power to establish the dog-tail relationship with Israel: the threat of reduction or elimination of the three billion plus annual aid and of the automatic vetoes at the security council should suffice. The power ratio between the two members of the US-Israel axis having been understood, the US would be in position to call the shots by redefining the roadway to peace, and giving the Palestinians guarantees that would spare them another futile and humiliating charade. To use a football analogy, the US must be both quarterback and coach.

In most deliberations, including Oslo, the Israelis have insisted that Palestinians must disarm before any substantive items are tackled. In such a confrontational situation who would be crazy enough to disarm unilaterally? The axis is promising the Palestinians a pot of gold at the end of the rainbow, if they disarm, but without giving any guarantees! If, upon reaching the end of the rainbow, they discover that the pot is full of fecal matter instead of gold, what can the Palestinians do, having disarmed themselves? Disarmament, especially if unilateral, must be done with iron-clad guarantees from a third party, in this case the US, preferably with the backing of the UN or other center of power.

On the other hand, Israel is right when it balks at negotiating with any party that refuses to recognize its existence as a legitimate country. How can you deal with me if I insist you don't exist? (This is exactly what Golda Meir did when she declared that the Palestinians didn't exist). The issues of recognition and disarmament must be de-linked. Now, the PLO and a number of Middle East countries have formally stated that they recognize Israel's right to exist. Other parties have hinted that they would do likewise under some conditions. But Israel has lobbied strongly against the US entering into any bilateral talks with any party that Israel considers an enemy. This makes it easier for Zionists to paint the latter as potential genocidal killers of Israelis. The problem of recognition is probably not as thorny as it has been painted by Zionists.

This is an example of the use by Israel and its lobby of its second most powerful weapon (after the exploitation of the word anti-Semite): ignorance. The Israelis have managed to control the flow of information about the Middle-East and about their enemies that reaches America, thus influencing public perception and opinion. When a legislator, on his own initiative, has a meeting with an Arab that is considered a *persona non grata* by Israel, he risks having his career terminated at the next election, if not sooner. When, in 1983, the National Association of Arab Americans invited all congressmen and their spouses to a free tour of Jordan and the East Bank, only three had the guts to take the offer. When a similar offer was made a year later, it found no takers. (Findley, p. 37) When real ignorance doesn't rise to the challenge, conditioned ignorance will do the trick. During the political debates over the possibility of Iran achieving nuclear capabilities almost never was it mentioned that Israel has some 200 atomic bombs, a fact well-known to political and military analysts.

Recognition is a yes-or-no matter, but disarmament is more complicated. Suppose that Russia and America decided on total mutual nuclear disarmament. How could either side be sure that the other would not hide just a few bombs, thus giving itself a huge advantage? Worse, how could the US, for example, be sure that China, knowing the Americans have nothing in their holster, wouldn't strike a deadly blow? Disarmament in the Middle East must be a gradual process. All parties must show signs of good will, and the US, again, must act as guarantor. Perhaps the way to start would be for the US and Israel to sit opposite the other parties, one by one, as terrorist to terrorist, and find ways to reduce – and eventually end – violence and terror.

What assurances must the Palestinians receive before venturing, once again, on the roadway to peace? -- The US, and its partners in the project, must vouch for the contents, *grosso modo*, of the pot at the end of the rainbow: the deliberations must, in a sense, start with the end. How can we right the wrong that the Americans, the British, the French and the Zionists did to the Palestinians? It is impossible to completely reverse the flow of history (America cannot "give the country back to the Indians") yet major corrections are possible. In Chapter XXI I opined that the Six-day War, not the First Arab-Israeli war, was Israel's cardinal sin. (There were mitigating factors and three accomplices in the latter, but the moral onus for starting the former rests squarely and exclusively on Israel's shoulders.) But that sin can be redeemed. Senator Fulbright was probably the first to propose, in 1970, that Israel withdraw to the pre-1967 borders. In return the US would guarantee its border and support its sovereignty politically and, if need be, militarily. He also had the guts to advocate withholding all military and development aid until Israel complied. (Of course, President Ford chose not to venture into these waters.) Others have since advocated the back-to-1967 solution, most notably President Carter and Prince (now King) Faisal of Saudi Arabia.

None of these suggestions or proposals, however, tackles the most basic and untreatable problem: the illegal settlements. (The Jewish movement, Naturai Karta, and Rabi Lerner's Tikkun magazine are notably among the very few voices that have openly and honestly addressed this problem.) As previously expounded in Chapter XX, those settlements not only steal land from the Palestinians of the West Bank, but also make a normal life impossible for them: in order to get from A to B, they have to play hopscotch around Israeli–only roads and stand in line at check-points; they are constantly in danger of having their house and land confiscated without compensation for a number of reasons of, at best, dubious validity; they are residents of the West Bank, but citizens of no country; and so on. The settlements have to go! They were purposely placed there to be stumbling blocks in the way of Palestinian statehood. The settlers were chosen among the most Anti-Arab segment of the population. Too much bad blood has been spilt: leaving the settlers there without a dominant Israeli military presence would be unconceivable. Both the military and the settlers have to leave (The former would have to be temporally replaced by UN or Arab League soldiers.)

Israel would argue that:

1. The settlers would fight the move to their last breath.
   Rejoinder: Israel has already removed all the settlers from the Gaza strip without loss of life.
2. There is not enough room in their small country to accommodate the settlers.

Rejoinder: Most of the latter were already settled in Israel before moving to the West Bank. Also, Israel is constantly inviting Jewish immigration.

3. God gave Israel all the land between the Euphrates River and the Mediterranean Sea (including the Sinai Peninsula?) and North to the Litani River in Lebanon.
   Rejoinder: That god was not the unique God as defined by Philo of Alexandria and understood by the three main monotheistic religions. The Yahweh of the Torah was just one of many Semitic and Mesopotamian gods. The whole lot of them, including that Yahweh, have a score of Zero (or incrementally close to zero) on the factuality index. The promise is meaningless.
4. The new Palestine state would be a military threat to Israel.
   Rejoinder: The new country would not significantly alter the balance of power. The US, as guarantor, would use its army, navy and air force to deter any military move against Israel. Also, the West Bank wall, so far quite successful in thwarting infiltration and terrorist attacks, would act as a protector for both sides. (Of course, those sections of the wall that stole more land from the Arabs should be torn down and rebuilt on Israeli land).
5. The cost of the move would be prohibitive.
   Rejoinder: No doubt, the cost would be very high, but the benefits, peace and justice, would be priceless. There would be no question of simply loading the settlers on buses and dumping them in Israel (although that kind of treatment was inflicted on Palestinians on a number of occasions). Israel has found the money to pay compensation to the ousted settlers of Gaza (200 to 300 thousand dollars, if memory serves me). The country receives more than three billion dollars in aid from the US, much of which is harmful to the Palestinians and to Israel's Muslim neighbors. This money has resulted in egregious military imbalance . The idea that Israel is a small, weak and vulnerable nation surrounded by populous, powerful and menacing neighbors has been shown, time and again, to be fiction and propaganda. This imbalance, in the long run, might turn out to be a destabilizing factor, harmful to everyone, including Israel. American aid, especially military, should be significantly reduced and the subtrahend spent on relocating the settlers. Also, instead of bulldozing the houses (as Israel has done in the Sinai and Gaza) these could be sold to the

> Palestinians and the proceeds used for resettlement of the settlers. The Palestinians probably don't have the money, but rich Arab countries like Saudi Arabia and Kuwait could help with loans or grants. Money should be no object.

As a last recourse, it might be possible to redraw the green line so as to include within Israel a few settlements that are very close to the border, provided a fair exchange in land is given the Palestinians. Perhaps East Jerusalem?

BEYOND THE MIDDLE EAST

Some Israelis have not hesitated to remind the US that self-interest shouldn't be used as a reason to deny Israel the aid and support it demands: the US, through public and private channels, has made promises and established precedents, and Israel expects Americans to fulfill them even when doing so would be against their self-interest.

I fully agree that national self-interest, though a necessary responsibility of a government, is not sufficient for the fulfillment of its mandate. But substituting the self-interest of another country (such as Israel) is a giant step backward, not an improvement. It's a basic article of most ethical systems that the self is one of the ethical objects that each person must take into account. As Rabbi Hillel has said: "If I am not for myself, who is for me?" But immediately he added, "And if I am for myself alone, then what am I?" The ethics of collectivities such as nations and countries are not a straightforward projection of the ethical world of individuals – things are not so simple – yet the basic principles apply to both domains. Two thousand years after Hillel, another Jewish sage clearly understood the parallel:

> But no nation in the world has this as its only task, for just as an individual who wishes merely to preserve and assert himself leads an unjustified and meaningless existence, so a nation with no other claim deserves to pass away.
> (Martin Buber, Hebrew Humanism, repeated from Chapter XVII)

So, what is it that will complement self-interest to provide a basic ethical profile of a righteous country? Martin Buber hit the nail on the head when he decried those of us who "act justly in man-to-man relationships but [believe that they] can and even should practice injustice in national relationships." (ibid)

The inference is that a government should not only pursue its collective self-interest, but should also champion justice and be ready to forego its interest when pursuing it would inflict injustice to other countries or peoples. It follows that the US should limit its promotion of Israel's self-interest in the many cases where that exercise would inflict egregious injustice to other parties.

Justice is for everyone. Even your worst enemy is due justice for the same reason that a boxer is given the protection of the Queensberry rules by the boxer who is trying to knock him out. If you give justice to A, B, and C, but deny it to D, you are not a just person. Israelis, Palestinians, Christians, Moslems, Blacks, Whites, Asians, young, old, males, females, gays, straights are all equally due justice.

(Note that being a champion of justice doesn't infer being soft on crime, or being an easy mark, and doesn't preclude being a hard bargainer.)

There is a direct connection between the notions of justice and respect. How can you inflict egregious injustice on a people you respect? How can you claim to respect people whose rights you trample on? Extreme disrespect kills – not only the spirit, but also the body. Conquistadors had so little respect for Amerindians that they had no qualms about hunting them for sport, as though they were worth no more than rabbits, ducks or deer.

If everyone is due justice, then serial killers, torturers and ethnic cleansers are also due justice. But justice can be retributive and even punitive. A Hitler or a Stalin fully deserves permanent imprisonment or even the death penalty (though not torture). In cases where an individual found guilty of crimes against humanity could continue to be a serious threat from behind prison walls – either as a living symbol or by exercising authority surreptitiously – the death penalty might be justified. What is never justified is counter repression that would end up replacing repression of collectivity A by repression of collectivity B. However, when there is a regime change (whether by revolution, negotiation or otherwise) the member of the previously oppressive collectivity must be ready to forego advantages unjustly held in the old days. But, even here, there are limitations: history can be redirected and compensation can be made, but history cannot be rewritten – for example, Americans cannot "Give it back to the Indians" (although much more should be done in the name of justice)

It is well known that in the case of twins there is competition in the womb for nutriments so that one baby is often born bigger and stronger than the other. Of course, there is no moral onus on the bigger one: there can be no notions of justice without intelligence, experience and judgment – and without good will, without which nothing works. This chronological priority of self-interest doesn't bestow moral dispensation. Although the notion of justice is beyond the understanding of infants, by the time the latter reach the age of reason – approximately 7 years – they have a clear intuitive understanding of the notion of justice, as evinced by their favorite complaint, "It's not fair." The fact that the crafty little rascals often use the accusation dishonestly to gain advantage – a habit some will carry into adulthood – doesn't change the reality: they don't need any formal definition to know the meaning of " It's not fair" and to understand the notion of justice. When Assyrian children, millenniums ago, said, "It's not fair," they probably meant the same thing as when our kids utter the same words.

Apologists of untrammeled national self-interest will claim such an order of priorities could spell the decline or demise of a country or institution. Not so, as long as the principle is followed that the subject (whether a person, collectivity or institution) of an ethical judgment can, itself, be an object of said judgment. In other words, being fair to one's self is as important as being fair to others. It's a responsibility and a moral imperative. One of the most sacred duties of a government is to defend the country against any injustice perpetrated against it by any party, while giving the latter the same consideration. (Isn't this the golden rule?) In the medium to long run, by placing justice ahead of self-interest, a government enhances its security, its influence, and the welfare of its people, much like the laws it imposes on its citizens – based on a national conception of justice – protect the very citizens that are curbed by these laws. (Note that self-interest is not synonymous to self-defense, nor to self-preservation).

Naysayers will hold that the political ethos here extolled is a pipe dream, that governments have put national self-interest ahead of moral considerations for millenniums and that this is the way it is and will be, period. But no government has ever operated with such a policy within its borders. Imagine that you find a lost wallet containing $500.00 and enough personal information (address, phone number, etc.) to find the owner. If there are no witnesses, it is in your self-interest to take the $500 and leave the wallet. But in most countries this would be a criminal act. If there was a witness and you were reported you could be arrested and prosecuted. Governments have always put the conception of justice prevalent in their society ahead of the self-interest of their citizens – at least officially – and this has afforded protection to all citizens. Why should the state (and sometimes other collectivities) give itself the unquestioned right to kill, steal and oppress, when it forcibly denies these acts to its citizens? With or without God, this is moral dispensation!

It's baffling that the moral consensus that has evolved within countries, societies and other collectivities has not crossed physical and mental boundaries and spread into the international arena. And yet, almost no one has preached or written to argue the case for this moral insularism! It has not been necessary because almost no one has vetted critically the gratuitous assumptions of this moral stance. It's as if a great block has been missing from the structure of history and no one has noticed. The whole issue has been relegated to the huge limbo in the mind of the average go-along-with-the-flow human and, consequently, in the collective mind of the species. (Perhaps logophobia might furnish a partial explanation: No one wants to be called unpatriotic, or a traitor to the group, or soft on the enemy.)

Few have asked these critical questions:

- Why do most countries base their laws on some conception of justice, but refuse to consider justice as a foundational principle of international affairs? (note that, if we substitute the more general word *rules* for *laws*, the word *countries* could be replaced by *governments, nations, tribes, families, corporations,*or other collectivities).
- Why are individuals, acting on behalf of such collectivities, afforded the same moral dispensations as is given to the latter?
- What proof is there that basing its foreign policy on the notion of justice is harmful to a country?

The principle of justice has a long history, but it still has a long way to go. Its history can be analyzed as a progressive sequence of three stages, of which the last has hardly been established:

Stage1: The state (or tribe, or other collectivity) imposes the justice-first principle upon the citizens; the principle is reciprocal between any two citizens, but not in the relation between the state and the citizen, the former not considering itself bound by it.

Stage 2: The state now considers itself bound by the principle: government places justice toward individual citizens (or groups of citizens) above its collective self-interest. In dealing with other countries, however, the state considers its self-interest to be its primary value and responsibility.

Stage 3: The state now recognizes that the principle also applies to relations between countries and is reciprocal.

Note that dictatorships and fascist regimes are, at best, stuck in Stage 1; that democracies have reached Stage 2; and that no state has reached Stage 3. The missing block must be grafted unto the structure of history. A sea-change in collective attitudes is needed. A new and different globalism must emerge!

THE JUSTICE NATION

Early Zionist thinkers, such as Ahad Ha-am, and Leo Pinkster, maintained that a people must emancipate itself ("auto-emancipation") and that a nation must create itself. They considered the Jewish disapora as the citizenship of their nation and most Zionists continued to hold this view after the establishment of the State of Israel. Nationhood can transcend geography, race, religion, political identity, etc. An Auto-created nation may pick and choose the criteria by which it can be identified, but it must end up with a finite number of them.

I propose the creation of a new nation that would be defined and identified by two criteria: adherence to one principle and to one corollary.

Basic Principle
JUSTICE TRUMPS SELF-INTEREST

Corollary
THE SELF IS AN ETHICAL OBJECT

Note that the Basic Principle is universal: it applies to relations between individuals, between individuals and the state, and between states. Other entities such as religious organizations, political parties, non-governmental organizations, etc. are also covered. In the relations between humans and other species the Principle is not so absolute. Nonetheless it exerts considerable influence: many countries give some rights to animals. They generally give protection to pets and wild animals but, except for Sweden, almost none to farm animals.

The corollary insures that the Basic Principle not be interpreted so as to put a party at mortal risk for having followed it. The Justice-Nation would probably start as a virtual nation on the Internet. It would establish links with many human rights and peace-promoting NGOs, such as Amnesty International, Human Rights Watch, the Canadian Center for Policy Alternatives, Global Rights, Unitarian Universalist Service Committee, Human Rights Resource Center, Trans Africa Forum, International Peace Bureau, Jewish Voice for Peace, The Millennium People's Assembly Network, and many others. Even organizations more focused on aid than on politics, such as Oxfam and Care would be natural allies. Eventually, the Justice-Nation might have an office in the UN headquarters and even a chair as a UN observer.

The Justice-Nations would have two objectives:

1. To advertise, broadcast, herald, promote and propagandize the Basic Principle, Justice Trumps Self-Interest, focusing on the sphere of international politics.
2. To gather all the various organizations and individuals that accept the Basic Principle into one moral entity and to be its eyes, ears and voice in the four corners of the world.

The promotions of the Basic Principle should be aggressive and pervasive, using the Internet, all forms of media, peaceful demonstrations, pins, flags, printed T-shirts, etc. Once established the movement should periodically hold world-wide convocations. The ingathering of kindred people and organizations should be accomplished with all due respect for the autonomy of all groups. The activity of the Justice-Nation should be seen as an addition to the work of individuals and organizations, not as an appropriation. It should result in a confederation rather than a federation. The Justice-Nation might end up as an umbrella body, but not in the sense that AIPAC is – not with the latter's dominating character. The leadership of the movement should come from the affiliated groups.

Moral persuasion should start with the pre-existing network of kindred souls (see Appendix I) and then proceed to the general population. Amnesty International has demonstrated the effectiveness of the active witness in influencing even the most entrenched and intransigent governments.

EPILOGUE OF THE EPILOGUE: WITHOUT GOOD WILL NOTHING WORKS!

Chapter XXIV-Apologia Pro Liber Meus

Some who have had an advance look at the manuscript have opined that the work is bottom-heavy, that too many pages are devoted to recent history, especially the Middle-East situation. They have a point: the book is bottom-heavy. But for cause: the Middle East is where the dark force of the covenantal mindset is most consequential.

Nothing can be done for the victims of Joshua's hordes. Nothing can be done for the enslaved or massacred Hindu victims of the Delhi sultans. Nothing can be done for the millions of Amerindian victims of the Conquistadors and their English successors. But the casket of history has not yet closed on the Palestinians. Salvation – real, in-this-world salvation – is still possible.

This is why my book is bottom-heavy.

And this is why I am particularly sympathetic to the plight of the Palestinian people, the collective scapegoat ironically suffering at the hands of the collective scapegoat of a previous era.

(Personal note: After reading a description of the human sacrifices that the Aztecs felt obligated to perform in order to satisfy the Sun-god's constant hunger for human blood, I imagined the following Parable: The world is ruled by a cruel and demonic god who can only be assuaged by the suffering and cries of tortured humans. The priests of this god have built a temple with an open-sky altar on which one human being after another must be tortured for the amusement of the god. Every victim must be chosen at random, but must be blameless: the chosen must be neither a criminal nor a moral degenerate. The torture is to be prolonged as much as possible, but upon the death of a victim another person must immediately take his or her place, so that the spectacle may continue without interruption – so that the world may continue to exist.) I have come to the realization that I would not want to live in such a world, and that I could not worship such a god.

But if we replace our victims by collectivities and dispense with the temple, we can find many analogs to this scenario. Throughout history there have been groups that have suffered oppression for centuries without the rest of the world taking much notice. The Jews, the Hindus of Northern India and the Amerindians are some examples. Since 1948, the Palestinians have filled this role. With the advent of modern means of communication it has become difficult to dismiss such situations. Our collective comfort is becoming rather uncomfortable.

Not all Muslim groups, however, are the recipients of so much sympathy on my part. Bin Laden and the al Qaeda group are religious automatons rendered soulless by their relationship with their faith. Death and destruction are all they know. It is regrettable that bin Laden managed to escape with his life when he was cornered at Tora Bora. He should have been found and he should have left his hiding place in handcuffs or a casket, preferably the latter. Yet, credit must be given where credit is due: in blaming the US as much as Israel for the Palestinians' catastrophe, Bin Laden is right!

The Taliban are another story. Their natural enemy should be the majority of Muslims who do not approve of the cutting off of hands and feet for minor crimes, the imprisonment of women inside the burka tent or behind the face-erasing full veil (isn't your face your public signature?), the condemnation of all females to ignorance, the brainwashing of children, the human sacrifices of suicidal bombings – and the list goes on. But as long as Jewish and Christian Zionists maintain their animosity against Islam, the Taliban will maintain their hold on the Muslim psyche.

The sins of the ideological Zionists have mostly been surveyed in the last chapters of the book, but there is one aspect of the Zionist strategy that I would like to expose before I sign off on this project: the manipulation of truth. A simple lie, such as "The dog ate my homework" or "I was in the office working on a contract," or "I was at my girlfriend's house all night," is a sin, but this pales as an assault on truth compared to the corruption or the very notion of truth exemplified by propaganda issued by the State of Israel, reinforced by American Zionist organizations such as AIPAC and ADL, and swallowed whole by the US government. We are asked to accept as "bible truth" any apology that emanates from Israel: "It was an unfortunate mistake and we offer our sincere condolences to all aggrieved parties," or "The settlements are legal because Egypt attacked us," etc.

It's easy for Israel to lie to the US: the latter is committed to backing Israel at the UN, no matter what. It must therefore "believe" anything that Israel offers as explanation for any transgression to the UN charter. It must accept any official lie with the self-imposed credulity of a resigned wife who is grateful that her philandering husband has enough respect for her to lie about his adventures. Israel has succeeded in creating a political "reality show" in which it is a small helpless country surrounded by hostile and powerful neighbors. (So, if it takes liberties with the rules of engagement, it is understandable and pardonable.) But it has gone one masterful step beyond that. In America there are a number truths about the Middle East that are widely known but that, by common consent, are never mentioned. I have personally observed an example of this Zionist Omerta: since February 1993, I have followed the Iraq war – the war fought over the nuclear bomb that Iraq doesn't have – and only once, one time, did I hear any mention of the 200 or so nuclear weapons (including hydrogen and neutron bombs) that Israel is known to have. Living a lie is worse than telling a lie; but to distort, corrupt or bury truth is worse than the most shameless lie.

It is unavoidable that the Middle East situation would have a strong influence on the perception of Jews felt by Gentiles and vice versa. There has long existed a belief that Jews, 2.5 percent of the US population, form a tightly knit ethnic group that wields economic and political power out of proportion of its numbers. This is a demonstrable fact. So? As long as Jews prosper because they work hard, work together and value education – good for them! (Especially since some sectors of Gentile society reap benefit from Jewish solidarity.) But when Jewish solidarity is used abusively to inflict injustice to another collectivity, Gentiles have a moral obligation to protest, and to protect the aggrieved party. And when this solidarity is used to undermine and enfeeble American sovereignty for the benefit of a foreign state, Americans and their government have a moral and political obligation to resist.

Justice trumps self-interest!

When all is said and done, morally and politically it boils down to the answer to one question: WHAT DO WE OWE THE JEWS ?

We owe them, individually and collectively, what we owe any individual or collectivity: JUSTICE – no less and no more. (The harsh corners and asperities of justice, rigidly interpreted, can be rounded and softened, but never at the expense of the principle. Also, more can be given than what is owed, but there is no obligation to do so, and it must never be at the cost of injustice to other parties.)

Many Jews and Gentiles feel that the former have suffered so much abuse for so long that they deserve something more than mere justice, even if this overflow is at other peoples' expense, and that they should be awarded moral dispensation when they turn the table and abuse other folk. No! Having been a victim doesn't justify being an oppressor!

There's a common notion that the Jews have suffered more oppression than any other group. Solid historical evidence contradicts this misconception. Anthropologist Henry Dobbins has estimated that, at the time of initial contact with Europeans, there were some 18 million Amerindians in North America, including 10 million in what is now US territory. (Note that it is a commonplace that pre-Columbian Mexico City was one of the largest cities in the world.) According to David E. Stannard, of Hawaii University," It is a firmly established fact that a mere 250,000 Native Americans were still alive in the territory of the United States at the end of the 19th century."

Although it is difficult to determine which part of the Amerindian Holocaust was due to smallpox and other old-world diseases and which to genocidal acts, it seems clear that the harm done to the Amerindians greatly exceeds that inflicted on the Jews.

There is a great holocaust that cannot be even partly attributed to disease: the ravage of the Hindus of northern India by the Moslem sultans of Delhi, some of whom considered torture as an art form. Historian Will Durant, who estimated Hindu deaths at 80 million, suggested that, "The Mohammedan conquest of India is probably the bloodiest story in history." (*Our Oriental Heritage,* p.459) It is elucidating to compare the present living conditions of the descendents of the above groups to the living conditions of contemporary Jews.

But do we give these oppressed people, individually and collectively, the moral dispensation that would allow them to abuse, dispossess and assassinate people; and to practice collective punishment and ethnic cleansing? – No we don't! So why should the Jews, notwithstanding their long history of discrimination and injustice, be given such a dispensation?

The Jews should be reminded that, despite the persistence of prejudice, they were also the recipients of a number of generous humanitarian endeavors on the part of some Gentiles. The greatest example of these was the right of voluntary return to their homeland munificently granted to the Babylonian Jews by the Syrian kings Cyrus and Darius, together with the necessary political and material support. Also notable was the offer of refuge and protection to the Iberian Jews from the Ottoman Sultan Beyazit.

Having been a victim doesn't justify being an oppressor!

To summarize:

We owe the Jews, individually and collectively, what we owe any individual or collectivity: JUSTICE –no less and no more.

Protecting the Jews does not imply enabling them in any act of injustice to others.

PROTECT—YES! ENABLE—NO!

Appendix I – A Historical Pattern

The structure and dynamics of the US-Israel axis are complex and confusing. In my efforts to understand it I tried to conjure some allegories and graphic representations, but most did not prove helpful.

One of them was the old elephant-and-mouse metaphor. It failed because we are dealing with two mice, not one: the Israeli mouse and the American-Zionist mouse. This conceit, however, did illuminate two aspects of the axis:

1. Israel and its lobbyists sometimes try to describe the military aspect of the relationship as some sort of mutual-defense pact – a "you watch my back, I'll watch yours" quid-pro-quo – but a mutual defense pact between an elephant and a mouse is as unidirectional as any mutuality can be.
2. The axis can work to Israel's benefit (as in fact it does) only if the American and Israeli mice work together to control the American elephant. No one can read the minds of Perle, Frum, Wofowitz, Lieberman, *et al.*, but it is clear that, collectively, they must focus first and foremost on the welfare of the Israeli state in order to fulfill their self-appointed role.

The US, being a democracy, cannot demand 100% loyalty from its citizens. One is free to place the allegiance to his religion, family, philosophy ahead of allegiance to his country. One is free to consider himself a Catholic first and an American second. But even in a liberal democracy, to place loyalty to a foreign state above loyalty to country of citizenship is considered, at least, unpatriotic and, at worst, treasonable.

The expression *divided loyalty* is often used to describe the state of mind of one hovering between allegiance and betrayal.

Such metaphors and models could take me no further until I realized that there had been at least one historical analog to the axis. Its locus, as luck would have it, was the Middle East, or that part of it then known as the Holy Land. Its chronology spanned the era from, roughly, 1000 CE to 1350. It consisted of nine expeditions collectively known as the Crusades.

At that time the popes were not only spiritual leaders but also sovereigns of a political entity known as the Papal States, a realm that had all the trappings of an ordinary country, including a standing army. But compared to the main European countries – France, England, Germany, etc. – the pope's country was militarily weak and paltry. Yet, the Crusades were primarily a papal enterprise. How was that possible? – Because the Roman Church had roots and tendrils penetrating all levels of European society, including the secular power structure. Priests and prelates (bishops and cardinals) were part of government; priests and prelates were confessors to the most powerful feudal potentates, holding their souls hostage; the Roman Church controlled a "fifth column" that permeated European society.

We can already discern a parallel with contemporary Zionism. Although Israel has a strong and competent army and air force, compared to the big boys – the US, Russia and China – it is still puny. What it lacks in power it makes up in the efficacy and dedication of its agents, lobbyists and organizations. Where Rome used a network of clerics and dedicated laymen, Zionists use AIPAC (and other) lobbyists who manage to virtually become part of the US government. Where the church used the absolution of sins and the opportunity for loot and conquest to attract fighters, the Lobby uses political campaign contributions and trips to Israel to rope in politicians and staffers. Where Rome used the threat of excommunication (and the consequent damnation) to control medieval knights and peasants, the Lobby uses the word "anti-Semite" to demonize its perceived enemies, and political stalking to ruin their careers.

History repeats itself: theme and variations. It is possible to outline roughly a basic structure common to many religions and political movements. First, a germinal nucleus coalesces, which is usually numerically small – often less than a dozen individuals – with or without a dominant leader. Then a network of militants is gradually established. Finally, a population of nominal and passive supporters is gathered in, many of whom many not agree with much of the platform of the movement (if they bother to learn it) but who are willing to "go along with the flow."

Priests, prelates, rabbis and imams represent ready-made networks, if they can be roped in. (With enough intelligence and diligence an organizational core – whether religious, secular, cultural, political or other – can usually find the embryo of a network already existing somewhere in society.) The Catholic Church has institutionalized the above structure with the pope and the holy office as the nucleus, the priests and bishops as the network, and the parishioners and secular semi-observant "catholics" as the *hoi polloi*.

Appendix II – The Limits of Faith

You are walking east on 17th Street. You reach the corner of Avenue 13 and, since the traffic light is red, you stop. In a few seconds the light turns green. Out of the corner of your eye you see a truck and in the next lane, a car rolling toward the intersection. You know they are going to stop, so you boldly cross the street.

You have just performed an act of faith: faith in the drivers of those vehicles; faith in the efficacy of traffic laws; faith in the engineering of brakes, which is a particular article of your faith in technology. Every day of your life you perform a large number of such acts of confidence (*faith* is just a sublimation of *confidence*). Without faith it would be almost impossible to get through the day. Even common habits are dependant upon faith, that is, upon the confidence that similar actions under similar circumstances will have similar consequences.

Even very rational people – scientists, philosophers, jurists – need faith. Physicists don't understand the dual nature of the electron (they can't decide if an electron is a wave or a particle like an incredibly small billiard ball) but they are wise enough to keep working on their theories and to use electrons in electric and electronic devices. Psychologists can't solve the mind/body problem (how the physical activity in the brain can cause the existence of perceptions, which are not physical things). Nonetheless, psychologists do not wring their hands in despair and stop trying to understand the workings of the mind.

In both these cases there is a gap in a cognitive system, but the injury isn't mortal and it's possible to jump over the crevasse and keep on soldiering. We can think of it this way: each cognitive system – of a person, of collectivity, of the whole species – can be represented by a wall on which all pertinent knowledge is inscribed. But in this fine plaster-of-Paris wall there are cracks and holes, the ravages of ignorance. However, we can spackle over those cracks and holes and keep navigating on the cognitive wall. The spackle represents faith. As long as the wall maintains its fundamental integrity, the spackle is a good thing.

But if we end up with more spackling than solid plaster – more faith than rational constructs and empirical evidence – our cognitive wall will fall apart. Faith must remain in a supporting role to reason and experience.

[Note: So far we have used *faith* in the sense of *confidence* – confidence in one's own faculties, and/or confidence in the truthfulness of some external entity: person, book, institution, etc. But the word, especially when capitalized, can have another meaning: Faith can mean the aggregate of the essential beliefs in a religion, ideology, political movement, or other institution. Thus, we speak of the Catholic Faith, the Buddhist Faith, and so on. The notion of confidence is, of course, still essential.]

Faith can be involved when and where we would not, at first blush, suspect that it is a factor:

Imagine that you are a judge in criminal court. Lately you have been reading David Hume and other empiricists and have found their arguments against free will quite convincing. Oh sure, at some superficial level, and depending on the definition we use, its existence can be assumed: you have free will if you can do what you want to do. But are you free to want what you want, or are there internal and external factors (your genetic makeup, your upbringing, etc.) that compels you to desire what you desire? As we dig deeper and deeper into the hierarchy of causes and effects (*a* causes *b*, *b* causes *c*, and so on) we come to a point where freewill has evaporated. Yet, without doing violence to the meanings of words, we can assert that John, who has committed a crime without external coercion, has more freedom of the will than Harry, who has committed a similar crime while coerced at gunpoint. And you, as a judge, have pondered: Is such a truncated and diluted conception of free will sufficient to justify your function in court?

In desperation, you have read Immanuel Kant, one of the toughest defenders of freewill, and you have, to your horror, found that he admitted that freewill can neither be clearly defined nor explained. Your belief in freewill now shattered, you have come to the realization that, logically, there are two opposite corollaries that are germane to your work as a judge: either criminals are to be deemed not guilty, since they have no choice but to follow the path of strict determinism; or they should be permanently incarcerated or executed as soon as there are sufficient signs, from their behavioral history, or from some psychological test, or from a brain scan that they are and always have been born criminals.

Flabbergasted, you almost decide to resign and quit the profession when another train of thought enters your mind: would society be better off if either of the two above corollaries were followed in practice, or would it be better off if the current ethos and practices were maintained, in spite of the weakness of their basic premises. After all, jurisprudence has done a fairly good job of protecting society and individuals, including even those accused of crimes. And it is constantly being tweaked, emended and, we hope, improved. And wouldn't pre-emptive incarceration or execution set us all on the slippery slope, which could lead to redefinitions of criteria and, possibly, to new pogroms against new "undesirables."

So, despite the severe injury to the philosophical grounding of our legal system, you decide to go with the tradition and with the books. Henceforth you will enter the courtroom and sit at the bench with a feeling of quiet confidence, in spite of being aware that you condemn people, not for what they did, but for what they are, *as evinced by what they did*. Without being aware of it, you have performed an act of faith.

[Personal note: In my effort to be fair and thorough I wracked my brain, looking for an instance where, in my own judgement, faith would take precedence over rationality or experience. I found the above, and it bothered me –it still does. But note that though faith, here, trumps the rational, it still defers to empiricism, since it is based on experience. Also, the principle of necessity comes into play, as the application of either of the two corollaries would cause the destruction of the fabric of all liberal societies.]

It is especially in the domain of religion and ideology that the limits of faith must be understood and respected. Let us look at two scenarios of which there are innumerable examples in history:

1. Jack believes in article of faith *a* while Jill believes in article of faith *b*, which is incompatible with, and adversarial to *a*. Jack's faith in *a* is extremely strong and uncompromising: he would stake his life (and other people's) on the truth of *a* and is unable to countenance the possibility that any competing article of faith could hold an iota of truth. Jill, on the other hand, has faith in *b* but is aware that she is not infallible and that there are cogent arguments against *b*. Knowing nothing more about Jack, Jill, and

the articles of faith *a* and *b*, can we surmise that Jack's belief has more chance of being true (has a higher factuality index) than Jill's, considering that his faith is stronger? – History and common experience suffice to establish that the strength of one's faith has no bearing on its truth-value. We all know someone who believes fervently in something that the overwhelming majority of rational people think is simply crazy. We also all know someone who, at some point, believed strongly in some article of faith, but who later rejected that belief.

2. Article of faith *c* is held by hundreds of millions of people while incompatible and adversarial item *d* is held by a small minority of believers. Should we assume that *c* is more likely to be true since it has many more adherents? – Just think of the Greek and Roman religions and of the small number of dissident martyrs. What is the factuality index of all those gods, now? And just think of the millions of Aztecs, who were convinced that the Sun god had to be constantly nourished with the flowing blood of human sacrifices! Obviously the number of adherents to any item of faith has no bearing on factuality of same. FAITH HAS NO PROBATIVE VALUE. It's about how one feels about one's beliefs, not about the factuality of these.

Faith may have a positive, as well as negative, effect on the faithful. The medical profession acknowledges the effectiveness of the placebo effect, which is based on faith. The more you think that your pill is good medicine, and the more you believe in the competence of your doctor, the more you are likely to receive benefit from your treatment. Your prayers may also have a positive effect on your recovery, but whether you pray to Jesus or to the great God Ehroch has no influence on the results – although, in this case, the strength of your faith may well be a factor. FAITH HAS ITS PLACE IN THE HUMAN PSYCHE, BUT CANNOT PROVE THE FACTUALITY OF ANYTHING.

Prophets and theologians have interesting, surprising and even radical things to say about freewill and faith. The Bible, and especially the Koran, are very inconsistent, trying to be thoroughly deterministic while defending free will. The writer/editors of the New Testament, and the Prophet Muhammad, were so awestruck by the infinite power of their deity that they couldn't leave room for chance or accident (ditto for the prophets of the Tanakh, once true monotheism had been established).

Jeremiah wrote, "I know, O Lord, that man's road is not his [to choose], That man, as he walks, cannot direct his own steps." (Jeremiah 10:23). Third Isaiah asked, "Why, Lord, do you make us stray from your way?" (Isaiah 63:17).

Jesus, in the verses that are repeated as *The Lord's Prayer*, beseeches God to "not lead us into temptation."

But it is Muhammad (or the Angel Jibril) who comes closest to outright rejection of the notion of freewill: one of the most frequently repeated sentences in the Koran is "Allah saves whom he wills."

Whatever was left of the freewill idea was obliterated by Calvin's dogma of *predestination* which claims that every thing and every event in the universe was established in its minutest details in God's mind at the moment of creation (or from eternity) and that nothing can be changed, not even the DNA structure, the environment and the history of a single human being.

How can one be held accountable and incur guilt if the will is not free? Yet all these prophets and theologians are constantly blaming sinners for their transgressions, and forecasting punishment in this life and in the hereafter. But if God creates and manages everything, does he not also create sin? The Bible and the Koran have no answer.

Many Christians, however, have devised a way of avoiding the whole problem: St. Paul has decreed that faith in Jesus Christ is all that is needed to assure salvation. Don't worry about freewill, guilt or any other element of that discourse: faith will get you into Heaven. You don't have to bother with works or the law: faith in Jesus justifies salvation.

No one expressed this view more bluntly than Martin Luther. In a letter to his friend Philip Melanchthon, dated August 1, 1521, he wrote:

> It is sufficient [for salvation] that we recognize through the wealth of God's glory that the lamb [Jesus] bears the sins of the world; from this, sin does not sever us [from salvation] even if thousands, thousands of times we should fornicate or murder.
> (cited in Walter Kaufman, *Religion in Four Dimensions*, McGraw Hill, p. 156)

The *ne plus ultra* of faith is infallibility, the absolute refusal to consider even the possibly of error. The Catholic Church, considering itself a continuation of Christ's mission has always assumed that it is infallible because Christ is infallible. In 1870, at the first Vatican council, the church made it a dogma that the pope, as head of the institution, is infallible when speaking officially on matters of faith and morals.

But in the final analysis it becomes a personal matter. If a person tells you that the pope (or a prophet or an imam) is infallible, ask her if *she* is infallible. If she answers yes, then suggest that she has no need for papal infallibility, being error-free herself; but if she answers no, then tell her that her judgment that the pope can't possibly be wrong could be erroneous, in which case the pope *can* be wrong. In short, x cannot claim that y is infallible unless x is, herself, infallible. And, of course, the pope cannot say that he *knows* he's infallible because he *is* infallible! That argument is as circular as $2\pi r$.

Therefore, everyone should be an agnostic. There are many levels of doubt. There is a baseline agnosticism that is simply the recognition that one is not infallible. One can be a baseline agnostic and still be a sincere religionist – even a priest, rabbi or imam. One can be confident and enthusiastic in his beliefs and still be a baseline agnostic.

At the other end of the scale is the true believer, the fanatic, the faithaholic, who simply cannot conceive that he could possibly be wrong – at least not in his most cherished beliefs. This is a dangerous person, potentially an oppressor of non-believers, a killer of men, women and children, a fomenter of wars. Only belief in one's infallibility can turn a normal person – not a criminal or psychopath – into a torturer or a mass killer.

In the contemporary world, the champions of faithaholism are found among those devotees of Islamic fundamentalism who practice justification by death – their adversaries, their coreligionists, even their own personal death. So absolutely certain are they of the heavenly rewards (including the 30 virgins) that are promised to martyrs that they willingly blow themselves up in the process of blowing up other people. The most scholarly syllogisms are helpless against such unbreakable faith … unfortunately.

Appendix III – The Anatomy of Nonsense

Nonsense is all around us. Most nonsense is due either to an inadequacy of reason or to a curtailment of reason by passion, negligence or prejudice. But there is a kind of nonsense that is due to an overreaching of reason. Those who are prone to this kind of nonsense are usually very intelligent and very educated. They just don't know where and when to stop! They don't pay due diligence to the notion of limits.

But before we can discuss the where and when, we must study the topography of the domain in question. It's a huge domain: let's call it all-there-be. It includes the whole cosmos, the worlds of ideas, emotions and feelings; the world of mathematical objects; possibly other worlds that are not made up of space, time and stuff; possibly immaterial persons such as angels, djins, gods, devils; and, possibly God, that than which there is non greater.

Note that all-there-be includes all-that-was, since not even God can uncreate what has existed. All-that-will-be is another matter. From the point of view of some God-conceptions, all-that-will-be is predestined and therefore already existing in God's mind, since God is beyond time. From the point of view of us poor run-of-the-mill humans, all-that-will-be is a matter of probability, at best.

Between all-that-was and all-that-will-be is the present, all-that-is, not to be confused with all-there-be. Logically and mathematically the present is an infinitesimal point on the time line, separating the past and the future. Since human perception cannot seize the infinitesimal, the best we can do is to graft some of the past and even a little of the expected future to that evanescent instant. This is the "present as experienced by man," sometimes called the *specious present.* How much of the past and future is grafted to all-that-is depends on the context and the situation. From the point of view of this exposition, all-that-is is a comparatively uninteresting part of all-there-be.

Theologians agree that God is unknowable and ineffable. That is what they say in the first chapters of their books, after which they write many chapters telling us about God. A priori, God may be transcendent (outside and above the world), immanent (inside and involved with the world), or a combination of both (as in the God of Philo, the deity of Judaism, Christianity and Islam). He may be the creator of the world, or the latter may be as eternal as Him. Plato conceived him as indivisible, but this doctrine was muddled, if not negated, by the doctrines of emanations (of the neo-Platonists) and of the Trinity (of the Christians). There is, a priori, no logical reason to prefer one or another of the above positions.

There is, however, a way of eliminating most of them by bypassing logic and resorting to empiricism. For at least 4,000 years, the believers in a partly imminent God have waged philosophical (and sometimes physical and violent) war against each other without a clear victor. Perhaps the war has been unwinable because no victor has emerged that can sustain its occupation of philosophical space. Whatever God has been proposed cannot survive the clear, logical scrutiny of the critical mind.

If my God is all-powerful, then his failure to deliver his message after 4000 years of trying is puzzling. If he has a managerial function in our world, then his competency can surely be questioned. Certainly any claim to perfection is unsustainable. When humans look for divine guidance in earthly matters, wars, pogroms and crimes against humanity are the usual consequences.

We have a fulsome world. There is no end of things to do without leaving the boundaries of our world. We can engage in arts and crafts, in science, in philosophy (as long as we stay in our world), in politics, in sports. We can devote our energy to the care of our families, to the betterment of mankind, to the husbandry of our planet. The list is endless.

When we try to reach beyond that list, we plunge into the sea of ignorance (the ignorance is ours, not the sea's), where we have no senses to capture any data, no mental faculties to understand, no system of categories to sort things.

Let me propose a thought experiment:

I have mentioned above the possibility of that other worlds not made up of spiritual stuff like God, gods and angels, and not constituted of space, time and matter, but just as real in their own way as our world is.

Now try to invent such a world (whether it really exists is irrelevant), just try to imagine it and describe it roughly.

You are incapable! What would replace space and time? What kind of substance would sustain it? We lack the senses, the mental faculties and the categories to even apprehend such a world, even as fiction. How then, could we pretend to understand the God or gods – if any – that would create and/or sustain such a world?

He who sallies forth to discover the unknown is a hero; he who embarks on a mission to discover the unknowable is attempting a foolish and futile endeavor. If Albert Einstein had devoted his whole life to penetrating the sea of ignorance he would have gotten no further than would the village idiot. Take a healthy horse and a sickly one and drop them both in the middle of the Pacific ocean: neither has more chance of survival than the other. Ditto for healthy and sickly fish left in the Sahara desert.

A theologian, brilliant as he may be, is a fish out of water. One of the main reasons for this bad career choice may be a misunderstanding of the nature of infinity. Any line segment represents a set of an infinite number of points: a line segment of one centimeter therefore represents an infinity. George Cantor, the great mathematician and philosopher, proved that some infinities are greater than others. For example, since we can make a one-to-one match between thee series of even numbers and the series of counting numbers (2 with 1, 4 with 2, 6 with 3, etc.) we can say, according to Cantor, that both infinite sets contain the same number of elements. However, since we cannot do this with the sets of real numbers and of counting numbers, we conclude that one set (real numbers) is greater than the other, although both are infinite.

Because we can handle all those infinities of our world, some of us think that we can extrapolate and handle the infinities of any world. But all-there-be is an infinity of its own unique order. One cannot ride the puny little infinities of our world to penetrate into the sea of ignorance.

This is how theologians – men of great brilliance, learning, integrity and dedication – speak nonsense of the most fundamental type.

Appendix IV – American Council for Judaism

1945 ACJ Proposal on Palestine

The future of the displaced Jews in Europe continues in uncertainty. Their plight - with the rigors of winter ahead - remains desperately tragic. Meanwhile, conditions in Palestine have reached a stage alarming to the peace of the world. We have had saber rattling, boycott, recriminations, rioting, bloodshed and threats of still more bloodshed.

This situation is not eased by the issuance of belligerent notes by sovereign states of the Near East, or by demonstrations and nationalist propaganda on the part of Zionists in and out of Palestine.

It is high time to call a halt to this dangerous course.

So-called promises made or implied decades ago, ambiguous and mutually contradictory, and variously interpreted by various parties, must no longer be determinant in the face of a new and grave situation. There is no reason why realistic conditions today should not lead to a complete reconsideration of the Palestine problem as there has been of other world problems.

The necessity of reaching a workable and peaceful solution outweighs all other considerations. The peace of the world demands it. A solution of the Palestine problem can become a token of our earnest resolve to deal with broad world problems before they reach the crisis stage.

We urge the following as a basis for fair and peaceful settlement:

1. There shall be a United Nations Declaration that Palestine shall not be a Moslem, Christian or Jewish state but shall be a country in which people of all faiths can play their full and equal part, sharing fully in the rights and responsibilities of citizenship.
2. All official declarations on Palestine in any way discriminating for or against a segment of the population shall be formally repudiated; in their place shall be a renewed pledge of full freedom of religious expression and equality for all in Palestine.
3. Palestine, as a ward of the civilized world, shall receive financial help for the expansion of its economy, and the enlargement of its immigration opportunities.
4. Immigration into Palestine shall be maintained on the basis of absorptive capacity and without privilege or discrimination.
5. Immigration procedures shall be controlled by representative bodies of all the inhabitants of Palestine, in association with properly instituted international commissions.
6. Institutions of home rule for Palestine shall be progressively and rapidly instituted under the aegis of an international commission.
7. The problem of the displaced Jews in Europe shall be treated separately, in the following way:

   (a) The above policy on Palestine shall be made known to them.
   (b) On the basis of such knowledge a poll shall be taken in which the displaced persons would list, in order of preference, the lands of their choice for their individual resettlement.
   (c) Based on these findings, an International Displaced Persons Committee shall, with the cooperation of the United Nations bring about the resettlement of the displaced on a basis corresponding as nearly as possible to their preferences, with countries of the United Nations co-operating to take in a fair number of the displaced. Action by the United States Government to make available unused and current immigrant quotas, and the necessary consular and visa machinery for the immigration of displaced persons of all faiths, would set a high moral example to the rest of the world of our determination to contribute to the solution of world problems and would, in fact, bring about the rapid solution of the refugee problem.

THE AMERICAN COUNCIL FOR JUDAISM IS PLEDGED TO ADVANCE THIS PROGRAM AS A CONTRIBUTION TO PEACE IN PALESTINE, HUMANITARIAN AID FOR THOSE IN DISTRESS AND FOR THE INTEGRATION OF THOSE OF JEWISH FAITH AS FREE AND EQUAL CITIZENS EVERYWHERE.

Lessing J. Rosenwald

http:// zionism-israel.com/hdoc/ACJ_Plan_For_Palestine_1945.htm

Appendix V – Self-Defense and the *Rodef*

Every individual and every collectivity has the right of self-defense. This basic principle is acknowledged by both the right and the left. It is a fundamental principle of the United Nations.

Animals and even plants resist aggression: it's a law of nature. Animal fights between members of the same species seldom end in death. Whichever combatant started it, the fight ends when one of the adversaries establishes his superiority and the other retreats.

It's not so simple with humans. Although the right of self defense is axiomatic, it is rife with ethical problems, especially when we're dealing with two collectivities or two sovereign states.

In the old days it was relatively uncomplicated: country A invades country B, country B pushes country A's forces across its borders; perhaps country B decides to teach A a lesson and occupy *its* land. Already we have an ethical problem but it's nothing compared to the problems that a modern military assault would present.

Now we can attack and even destroy a country without a single soldier stepping across its borders, simply by sending rockets armed with high-explosive or even nuclear payloads. If country A obliterates a town in country B with a rocket attack, killing thousands of innocent civilians, what is country B supposed to do? Neither the UN charter nor the Hague and Geneva conventions are of any help.

The ethical problems may be intractable, but though there is no clear prescription in the offing, there is an axiomatic principle to guide us: *there is no moral dispensation.* No matter how cruel the aggression may have been, and how justified a severe retaliation may be, the injured party cannot claim emancipation from all moral considerations. In other words, the right of self-defense does not eliminate all limits in the response.

Although moral judgement in such an intractable matter must ultimately – and by default – be intuitive, some notions can be helpful.

Who Started It? Not always as easy to answer as one would expect. On a personal level, imagine that Harry has, for years, slandered Robert, insulted his wife and family, and has engaged in fraudulent practices that have cost Robert money. If the latter attacks Harry physically and a fierce fight ensues, who "started it"? In criminal court, certainly, Robert would be charged with assault but, transposing this to the area of international politics and replacing Harry by country A, and Robert by country B, the situation is not so clear. There is an International Court of Criminal Justice that has had some success prosecuting individuals, but this court has never summoned a country to bar, let alone prosecuted and sentenced one.

Are there cases where the party who did *not* throw the first punch (that is, aggress violently) may nonetheless be judged to have "started it"? Let's go back to our friends Harry and Robert: isn't it conceivable that Harry might have intentionally – and without provocation – harmed Robert so egregiously as to be considered the one who "started it"? Harry may have committed what may be called *nonviolent aggression*.

Can countries be guilty of non-violent aggression? Let me answer this with a scenario:

For centuries, country B has depended on the Great River for household, industrial and agricultural water to the extent that the river has been, and is, its lifeblood. The Great River's source, however, is situated in country A. If the latter diverted the stream so as to maximize its benefit to itself and, in so doing, deprived country B of its lifeblood, wouldn't this be sufficient cause to judge country A guilty of nonviolent aggression?

What if country A used its power and influence over third parties so as to violate and ruin country B (by the use of embargoes, blockades, etc.)? Would this not be a case of nonviolent aggression?

Proportionality: Even though B is the aggressed party, there must be a limit to the harm inflicted upon A, the aggressor, by the retaliation. (We have touched upon this in Chapter XIX.) Even in a kill-or-be-killed situation, there is a limit: an aggressed person may kill his attacker to save his own life, but he may not torture him, nor kill his family. The basic principle is that the retaliation must be in some way proportional to the harm done by the oppressor.

Many religious traditions are adverse to the concept of proportionality: a sin is a sin is a sin. The Catholic Church considers both masturbation and murder as mortal sins, which infers that both are equally punishable by eternal damnation. Both Muhammad and Martin Luther preached that unbelief in their teachings was a greater sin that murder. During the Intifada youths were shot for throwing stones in the direction of Israeli troops. The kidnapping of two IDF soldiers by Lebanon-based Hezbollah fighters, and the concomitant killing of two Israeli soldiers (Chapter XII) was certainly an egregious violation (although no more so than other transgressions by both sides) but did it justify the all-out invasion and the savage destruction of infrastructure?

THE RODEF

In Hebrew a *rodef* is anyone who represents a potentially mortal threat to you. Rabbis permit preemptive measures, including killing, to the potential victim, but stipulate that non-lethal steps should be taken before resorting to homicide.

A *rodef* need not be a person: it could be a criminal gang, or a nation – or your neighbor's pitbull. In 1967 the Israeli government followed the *rodef* principle to launch a "pre-emptive strike" (neocon English) against Egypt because Nasser had the temerity to move some divisions well within his country, but too close to Israel for the latter's comfort. The Six-Day War ensued (chapter XVIX). Israel attacked and easily defeated Egypt and its allies, Syria, Jordan, and Iraq. This was followed by a vast, illegal and still continuing settlement progam. (Chapter XVIX)

The Six-Day War represents the application of the *rodef* principle at its worst. As Eban and Begin would later admit, Egypt didn't present a credible threat to Israel, in spite of the deployment of troops on its own territory. Only an aberrant interpretation could see a *rodef* there. Also, Israel made no attempt to assuage its concerns peacefully. The main problem with the principle is that it invites political paranoia an/or political dishonesty. Note that a *rodef* can be absolutely innocent of any evil intention or may not even be aware of his role in the situation: it doesn't matter. A person with tuberculosis who coughs near you is a *rodef.*

The *rodef* principle found natural adherents in America. The neocons adopted it enthusiastically, especially after the shock wave of 9/11. As we saw in Chapter XXII, Vice President Cheney advocated that a one per cent chance that a regime may have weapons of mass destruction should elicit the same response as a certainly. Even before 9/11, the Project for a New American Century – a neocon think tank – issued a Classic of paranoid politics, Rebuilding America's Defenses (Chapter XXII).

One problem with extreme '*rodefism*' is that a '*rodefist*' will soon be seen as a *rofer* himself by his neighbors since the former is always looking for a reason to launch a preemptive attack against the latter. "*Rodefism*" doesn't bring security, but rather invites danger.

Another problem is that *rodef* thinking makes a person or collectivity too risk-adverse to accept the democratic risk. Any politically liberal society must accept this risk. Without this acceptance the secret police will quickly make its appearance and such things as privacy, the right of association, freedom of conscience, free speech and liberty of the press will start to erode.

Appendix VI – Birth Control and Abortion

All the criticism and reproach addressed herein at monotheism were directed at certain consequences of the convenantal mindset. I would now like to take up a contentious topic that is not directly related to the covenant but that is of paramount importance: birth control.

Judaism, which has always accepted sex as natural and concordant with God's laws, has accepted contraception although some fundamentalist rabbis have militated for certain restrictions and for outright rejection of *some* methods. Islam has been surprisingly liberal on this as well as on abortion, although some imams and schools have been far from enthusiastic. Until fairly recently, most Christian denominations considered contraception sinful. Since the 1930s, however, almost all protestant churches have reversed that position. The Catholic Church is now, by far, the most active and militant force against birth control.

What's the rationale for this position? The biblical basis for it is very weak at best:

One of Judah's sons, Er, was killed by Yahweh for being evil. Jacob told another son, Onan, to copulate with Er's wife, Shaah, so that Er might have an heir. Onan, not wanting to be a sexual proxy for his brother, pulled out and spilled his semen on the floor. Yahweh was angry and killed him. (Genesis 38:6-10).

It seems evident that Onan was punished for disobeying Yahweh's command, as delivered through Jacob, and that *coitus interuptus*, was just the method of his refusal. The Church chose to fixate on the detail and use the verse to condemn contraception, abortion and masturbation as mortal sins. Slim pickings, as biblical passages go!

There are two explanations for this excessive stance. First, the Catholic aversion to sex, which started with St. Paul's unnatural hatred for that aspect of human experience; and, second, the entrenched belief that there is strength in numbers – that the religion with the most adherents is the winner.

This last point deserves scrutiny:

In Western countries the demographic weight of most Christian churches is constantly falling and the strength of this flock is diminishing as many adherents stay in the fold out of habit, without taking their faith seriously. The Catholic Church is counting on Africa and, especially, Latin America to maintain its position in both religion and politics. The last thing it wants is for the birth rate of Catholics in those two continents to decrease. In a way somewhat analogous to the strategy of AIPAC, the Church has persuaded the world's lone superpower to support its agenda, even though Catholics represent only about 24% of the US population. (This move was facilitated by the fact that the White House was inhabited by intellectually challenged neocons.) The US accepted to impose conditions on its foreign aid that bolstered the Church's natalist policy. Birth control programs and abortion clinics were sacrificed on the altar of foreign aid.

[Strange, that a country where contraception and abortion are legal and largely accepted, and whose constitution mandates the separation of church and state, would put its power and wealth at the service of the Roman Church!]

The Church has linked the moral aspects of birth control and abortion. This is a logical and legitimate move, since some contraceptives can sometimes kill the zygote (fertilized egg).

There are two classes of contraceptives:

1. Barrier contraceptives, such as condoms, diaphragms, cervical caps and sponges, that prevent fertilization by simply blocking entry of the sperm into the fallopian tubes. This in no way constitutes abortion. Sometimes a spermicidal compound is used in conjunction with the barriers for greater effectiveness, but killing sperm also doesn't constitute abortion.
2. Hormonal contraceptives, such as the pill, Depo-Provera, Norplant, and the morning-after pill that have multiple mechanisms of action. They suppress ovulation by preventing the production of the egg or the release of the egg into the reproductive track. But in a minority of cases where the egg *is* produced, does enter the

fallopian tube, and does unite with a spermatozoon, a secondary effect of the drug will prevent the implantation of the fertilized egg into the lining of the uterus, thus acting as an abortifacient (a non-surgical cause of abortion). Without going into details, we add the "morning after pill" (such as RU-486) to the list of abortifacients, almost by definition. As for the Intrauterine Device (IUD), it is primarily a spermicide and an ovicide. Killing an ovum or a spermatozoon is not abortion! (There are some 40 million spermatozoa in the average male ejaculation.)

To make ethical and political sense of this, we must clarify three problems.

1. The Definitional Problem:
   What does the term *human being* mean? Right-to-life people give it the widest possible extension so as to include the zygote – the union of one ovum and one spermatozoon – within the definition. But that is not what is meant by ordinary people using the expression. Of course we can deconstruction the term: *being* can mean anything that exits as a physical or spiritual substance, and *human* can mean anything of or related to our species. Thus a zygote, embryo or fetus of our species would qualify as a "human being," but so would a human cadaver or skeleton. But no ordinary person would call a heap of bones a "human being." Calling an embryo a human being or a child is a category mistake.
2. The Identity Problem:
   Catholics and other opponents of birth control sometimes accuse those who practice it of killing the person who would possibly be born if a contraceptive had not been used (and, of cause, all his descendants). But an average ejaculation contains some 40 million spermatozoa. Which one is killed by the use of a contraceptive? How can one kill someone who doesn't exist and can't even be identified in the sense that a person can be identified as, say, the 50th (future) president of the US? (In the case of an abortion, of course, there is no identity problem: from the moment of fertilization, identity is firmly established.)
3. The Metaphysical Problem.
   Sensation is the *sine qua non* – the primal basis – for any mental activity. Without sensation there can be no mentation (another

> word for *mental activity*) and without mentation there can be no animal life: it is the distinguishing criterion between vegetal and animal organisms. A worm that can feel pain or tactile pressure is, in a sense, higher on the scale of being than a human embryo incapable of sensation.

There is something magical about a sensation. Something physical in the brain – chemicals, neurons, electrical circuits, etc. – causes the creation of something that is not physical: sensation. It is, in a sense, a "quantum leap" from one category to another. There is no process involved that science can study or intellect understand: it just happens. Given sensations, the brains of higher animals can store and process them to achieve perceptions. These in turn can be stored in memory. Starting with sensations it's possible to build a cognitive network all the way to consciousness (which may be a sort of super perception).

It's essential to differentiate the vegetal from the animal stage of development of the unborn. For this, it's necessary to determine as closely as possible the earliest evidence of sensation. Not all senses mature at the same time: the sense of touch seems to be the first. Not even scientists sympathetic to the pro-life side have claimed that the first signs of sensation appear any sooner than the 7th week of gestation.

Metaphysically, an organism without sensation cannot be a human being; it cannot even be categorized as an animal. However, as soon as one sensation is experienced, the unborn leaves the vegetal and enters the animal category. Only then can it be considered a metaphysically integral human entity. It is at this point that the embryo becomes a fetus.

Laws should take this categorical change into account. It suggests that no laws should restrict the abortion of a vegetal entity, but that a sentient human entity should be considered a person and accorded protection of life and limb. Abortion would then become a civil right issue! (However, in cases where the fetus threatens the mother's life, because her physical and psychological suffering would be much greater than for the fetus, abortion would be permitted after a vetting by medical authorities.)

Since contraceptives such as the "morning-after" pill, that are often alleged to be abortifacients, are used during the earliest part of pregnancy, whether they kill the embryo or not is irrelevant to any moral or legal judgment regarding birth control.

To come to an overall ethical judgment on birth control we must look beyond the rights of the embryo or fetus. We must also consider the rights of the mother, of the family, of society, of our species, and even of other species.

There are too many of us – way too many! Medical science and modern sanitation have brought us death control, but failure to balance it with birth control may change the boon to a disaster. Not only are we too numerous, but we keep adding to our numbers at an ever increasing rate. According to the United Nations Population Division, in 1804 there were 1 billion of us; it took 123 years to double that number to 2 billion (1929); the next increase of 1 billion took 14 years; then 13 year; until, 12 years later (1999), the total was 6 billion. This cannot continue. Humans exact a very high price from the planet, especially those enjoying the lifestyle common in developed countries. We have poisoned the atmosphere, polluted the seas and even degraded our topsoil on which we depend for most of our food. We have partially emptied our forests and plains of wildlife and our seas of fish. And now emerging countries with huge populations – especially China and India – feel that they deserve our lifestyle as much as we do.

Experiments with laboratory mice and rats have shown that when a colony of these rodents is allowed to grow unchecked, the animals eventually start aggressing and killing each other. There is no proof that humans would behave thusly but common sense leads us to think that when the means of survival are wanting, wars will ensue, crime and treachery will be rampant, and mores and cultures will be degraded. The milk of human kindness will dry up and nations will no longer feel a responsibly for the species.

Birth control is not a sin: it is a moral imperative!

Bibliography

Ahmad al-Bastani, Abbas, *Recueil de Hadiths du Prophet (P)*, Montreal, La Cité du Savoir, 2000.

Ahmad al-Bastani, Abbas, *Les sources de la noble sunna*, Montreal, La Cité du Savoir, 2002.

Akenson, Donald Harman, *Surpassing Wonder: The Invention of the Bible and the Talmuds*, Montreal, Mc-Gill-Queen's University Press, 1998.

Blair, Edward P., Abingdon Bible Handbook, Nashville, Abingdon Press, 1983.

Braudel, Fernand, *A History of Civilization*, Richard Maynes, translator, London, Penguin, 1995.

Carter, Jimmy, *Palestine: Peace not Apartheid*, New York, Simon and Schuster, 2006.

Crepon, Pierre, *Les Religions et la guerre*, Paris, Edition Albin Michel, 1991.

Dawkins, Richard, *The God Delusion*, Boston, Houghton Mifflin, 2006.

Chavel, Rabbi Charles B, Translator and commentator. *The Book of Divine Commandments* [by Maimonides] Soncino Press, 1940. Chomsky, Noam, *Fateful Triangle: The United States, Israel and the Palestinians,* Cambridge, South End Press, 1983.

Faraj, Rezeg, *Palestine: Le refus de disparaître*, Lachine, Éditions de la Plume Lune, 2005.

Findlay, Paul, *They Dare to Speak Out: People and Institutions Confront Israel's Lobby,* Chicago, Lawrence Hill Books, 1997.

Finkelstein, Norman G., *The Holocaust Industry: Reflections on the Exploitation of Jewish Suffering*, Verso, 2003.

Goldhagen, Daniel Johah, *Hitler's Willing Executioners: Ordinary Germans and the Holocaust*, New York, Vintage, 1997.
Halper, Stephen and Clarke, Jonathan, *America Alone: The Neo-Conservatives and the Global Order*, Cambridge University Press, 2005.
Hertzbert, Arthur, ed. *The Zionist Idea: A Historical Analysis and Reader*, Philadelphia, The Jewish Publication Society, 1997.
Hitchens, Christopher, *god is not Great:; How Religion Poisons Everything*, New York, Twelve Hachete Book Group USA, 2007.
Ingersoll, Robert. *Some Mistakes of Moses*, Amherst, Prometheus Books, 1986.
Koester, Arthur, *The Thirteenth Tribe: The Khazar Empire and Its Heritage*, New York, Random House, 1976.
Luther, Martin, *Table Talk*, Orlando, Bridge-Logos, 2004 (trans. By William Hezlitt, the Lutheran Publication Society).
MacDonald, Kevin, *Understanding Jewish Influence: A Study in Ethnic Activism*, Augusta, Washington Summit Publishers, 2004.
McCabe, Joseph, *The Forgery of the Old Testament and Other Essays*, Buffalo, Prometheus Books, 1993.
Merk, Frederick, *Manifest Destiny and Mission in American History*, Cambridge, Harvard University Press, 1995.
Meyer, Michal A., *Response to Modernity: A History of the Reform Movement in Judaism*, New York, Oxford, 1988.
Milloy, John, *A National Crime: The Residential School System, 1979 to 1986, Winnipeg, The University of Manitoba Press, 2006.*
Morris, Benny, *Righteous Victims: A History of the Zionist-Arab Conflict, 1881-2001*, New York, Viking, 2001.
Philbrick, Nathaniel, *Mayflower: A Story of Courage, Community and War*, New York, Viking, 2006.
Pickthall, Marmaduke, *The Meaning of the Glorious Koran: An Exploratory Translation*, New York, Dorset Press.
Robinson, Maxime, *Israel A Colonial-Settler State?*, (trans. By David Thorstad), New York, Monad Press, 1980.
Stannard, David E., *American Holocaust: The Conquest of the New World*, Oxford University Press, 1993.
Suskind, Ron. *The One Percent Doctrine: Deep Inside America's Pursuit of its Enemies Since 9|11*, New York, Simon and Schuster, 2006.
Telushkin, Rabbi Joseph,Biblical Literacy: The Most Important People, Events, and Ideas of the Bible, New York, Harper Collins Publishers, 1997.

Index

J

K

L

M

N

O

P

R

S

T

U

V

W

Y

Z